Young Hickory

Designed by Barbara Werden

Published by Taylor Publishing Company
1550 West Mockingbird Lane
Dallas, Texas 75235

Library of Congress Cataloging-in-Publication Data

Booraem, Hendrik, 1939–
   Young Hickory : the making of Andrew Jackson / Hendrik Booraem.
     p. cm.
   Includes bibliographical references and index.
   ISBN0-87833-263-4
     1. Jackson, Andrew, 1767–1845. 2. Jackson, Andrew, 1767–1845—
Childhood and youth. 3. Presidents—United States—Biography.
4. Jackson family. I. Title.

E382 .B67 2001
973.5'6'092—dc21
[B]   00-048820

10 9 8 7 6 5 4 3 2 1

Printed in the United States of America

. . . .

FOR NANCY CROCKETT AND LOUISE PETTUS

two outstanding local historians

What is required in the sixth commandment?
    The sixth commandment requireth all lawful endeavors to
    preserve our own life and the life of others.

What is forbidden in the sixth commandment?
    The sixth commandment forbiddeth the taking away of our
    own life, or the life of our neighbor unjustly, or whatsoever
    tendeth thereunto.

SHORTER CATECHISM OF THE
PRESBYTERIAN CHURCH

prearrangement, both fired into the air instead of at each other. A compromise had been worked out, and Jackson's honor was satisfied.[1]

The main player in this episode is instantly recognizable as the Andrew Jackson of history. His conduct had all the hallmarks of his later military-political career (including bad spelling): a willingness to challenge older and more powerful people, regardless of the proprieties; an immense self-confidence in spite of a deficient education; a touchy concern about his personal image and public perceptions of his "charector"; an unhesitating resort to a quick, simple, and in this case violent method of handling a problem; and in the end, a levelheaded perception of reality. In other words, Jackson at twenty-one was essentially the same person he would be for the rest of his life. Tennessee would be the theater of his exploits, but it did nothing to shape his personality. His character had been shaped before he crossed the mountains.

This book is about the early development of Jackson's character. I have tried to examine all the factors—in his society, his family, and his personal history—that made him the man he was. In earlier biographies I attempted to do the same for two other presidents, James A. Garfield and Calvin Coolidge, but Jackson's colorful, decisive personality and his importance in early American history have made writing this book especially absorbing. The story of his early life, which unfolded during the American Revolution in the Carolinas, is highly dramatic. He nearly died of smallpox after being wounded and imprisoned at the age of fourteen. The war destroyed his home and his immediate family. He constructed an entirely new identity to replace the one he had lost. After becoming a successful lawyer, he turned his attention toward the land west of the mountains.

This story has already been told, in its basic outlines, by several first-class biographers, including, in the twentieth century, Marquis James and Robert V. Remini. They devoted two or three chapters, and then went on, as they had to, to deal with the crises and conflicts of his adulthood. By focusing strictly on Jackson's early years, this book adds some context and depth to the standard version and enriches it with some new material. I have tried to give a full picture of Jackson's early environment—by recreating the life of the Carolina backcountry in general and in particular the Waxhaws, that little-known but important region on the North Carolina–South Carolina border where he grew up. Later, when the story moves to Charleston, South Carolina, and

. . . .

Preface

then to the farms and courthouses of central North Carolina, I have done the same for those settings. Throughout, the aim was to understand Jackson better by understanding the society that produced him.

A secondary aim of this book is corrective. Writings about Jackson's youth have been plagued for the past century by a mass of false material, stories invented by an uncommonly gifted pseudohistorian named Augustus C. Buell. Robert V. Remini, in his biography published some years ago, clearly indicated the fraudulent nature of Buell's account, but bits of it continue to appear in the Jackson literature. In an effort to lay Buell's fabrications to rest, this book includes an appendix identifying and correcting all of them for the period of Jackson's early life.

archives of the two Carolinas, the South Carolina Department of Archives and History in Columbia and the North Carolina State Archives in Raleigh, where most of the arduous work was done.

Individuals shared their specialized knowledge with me at every step of the process. I can never thank them all, but I must mention the most outstanding. In South Carolina I owe a special word of thanks to Jack Weaver of Winthrop College for his encouragement and vital information at the beginning of the project; Bobby G. Moss for the benefit of his incomparable knowledge of Revolutionary South Carolina; Agnes Corbett for help at the Camden Archives; Ruth Reddick for access to the collections of Historic Camden; Dr. Dave Crass for putting me in touch with the current studies of archaeologists in the backcountry; and above all to the two historians of the Waxhaws named in the dedication, Nancy Crockett and Louise Pettus.

On a quick visit to Ulster, I received generous and important help from Dr. Alan Gailey of the Ulster Folk and Transport Museum and Philip Robinson and Linda Ballard, scholars on the museum staff; Helen Rankin of Carrickfergus; and Robert H. Bonar of the Presbyterian Historical Society in Belfast.

Several other individuals deserve special mention. James G. Barber of the Smithsonian Institution helped me with his knowledge of Jackson portraiture. Mary Jane Fowler of Salisbury, North Carolina, uncovered Archibald Henderson's long-lost articles on Jackson's North Carolina years and other choice bits of Salisbury history. Sharon McPherson of the Hermitage gave me vital information from her extensive knowledge of Jackson and his life. William Perry of the Greensboro Historical Museum answered my questions about log-house construction. Todd Gillespie and Jerry Gambrell helped me understand what young Jackson's personality must have been like. To each of them I am indebted for any merits this book may have.

To earlier Jackson biographers James Parton, Marquis James, Archibald Henderson, and Robert V. Remini, I express thanks for awakening my interest in this remarkable American and for setting a high standard for writing about him.

Finally, and most important, thanks to Richard, for everything.

With all this high-quality assistance, this book ought to be well-nigh perfect. To the extent that it falls short, the flaws are my responsibility.

Young Hickory

The influx of hundreds of Irish to South Carolina was only a small part of a migration that had been going on for nearly fifty years. Irish Protestants (practically all of whom were Presbyterian), a footloose, adaptable people, had begun leaving for America in large numbers around 1720. They had no roots in Ireland and were accustomed to moving around; the parents or grandparents of most of them had come over from Scotland or the north of England during the troubles of the seventeenth century. Many were desperately poor, but even those who had some money and a middling place in society were restless and receptive to the idea of moving when they saw a chance to better their lot.[3]

A small amount of information about the woman standing on deck, Betty Hutchinson Jackson, and her family has survived. She was an energetic, talkative, physically tough young woman, probably in her middle twenties. An expert spinner, she came from a family that labored in the linen trade, like many, perhaps most Irish Presbyterians. The Irish linen industry, in fact, was almost a barometer of emigration to America: whenever the linen trade was in trouble for any reason, the number of emigrants increased. The fairly prosperous Hutchinson family was settled in county Antrim, near the old town of Carrickfergus.[4]

On the other hand, no truly reliable information about her husband, Andrew Jackson, exists. Nothing solid is known about what he looked like, what he did for a living, what his family was like or where they lived in Ireland. One early account has it that his father was a soldier in the garrison of Carrickfergus Castle. His "condition in life," according to his son Andrew, late in life, was "independent"—in other words, he and Betty had enough money to pay for comfortable passage to Carolina. And unlike many of their shipmates, they intended to buy land, not to apply for the bounty.[5]

The featureless blur where the image of the elder Andrew Jackson should be is less important than it might have been, for by going to Carolina, Andrew and Betty Jackson were moving into a settlement where he had no connections, and she had many. Betty was the youngest of six sisters, five of whom had married; and in the early 1760s, all six Hutchinson sisters, with their husbands and children, converged on the region of Carolina called the Waxhaws, a community of less than a thousand people located on the border between North and South Carolina.

There is no accepted explanation why they did so. It may be that they and other settlers, all from the same neighborhood in Antrim, were attempting to recreate a portion of it in America by settling together. Another explanation, not incompatible with the first, is that they were invited or encouraged by a settler named Robert Crawford, a brother of one of the Hutchinson sisters' husbands. Crawford, who came from a prosperous linen-manufacturing family, had emigrated a few years earlier with some money of his own and was on his way to becoming an important man in the Waxhaws. The Hutchinson connection may have thought of his presence as a guarantee of help if they ran into problems getting established. In any event, it was typical for settlers from Ulster to emigrate to America in large, clan-like units. By 1766, besides the Jacksons, the families of Margaret Hutchinson McCamie, Sarah Hutchinson Leslie, Mary Hutchinson Leslie, Jane Hutchinson Crawford, and perhaps a Hutchinson brother, would have settled in the Waxhaws, three sisters in North Carolina and two in South Carolina.[6]

The last son of Andrew and Betty Jackson, Andrew the younger, grew up entirely among his mother's people, the Hutchinsons and Crawfords. There were no other Jacksons there, and after the members of his immediate family died, he was the only Jackson left in that part of America, with no connection to his family in Ireland. Writers who generalize about the social status or personality traits of the Jacksons or the Jackson family in America seriously exaggerate. In terms of environmental influences, Andrew Jackson was a Crawford, a member of his mother's brother-in-law's family. His father contributed only half his genes and his surname.[7]

So, Andrew and Betty Jackson had no feeling of venturing alone into the unknown as they sailed away from Ireland. They knew what they would find when they arrived, who would meet them, whom they could count on for help. This security was part of migration by clans, and many Irish immigrants experienced the voyage to America as part of a long, variegated family history. Even in the literal sense, moreover, they may not have been alone on the ship. There is good reason for supposing that Betty's sister Jane, her husband, James Crawford, and their children traveled with them. Jane, the sister to whom Betty was closest, perhaps had health problems; at a slightly later period she would be described as an invalid. James, a quiet, steady, hardworking man, was less assertive than his brother Robert. They had four boys ranging in age from ten to four.[8]

As their ship sailed west, the emigrants reviewed in their minds what they

fewer swamps and no Spanish moss, only rank upon rank of tall hardwood trees with immense trunks whose foliage shut out the sunlight and created a parklike appearance, almost free of underbrush, on the forest floor. From time to time there were clearings, some patches of bare rock, some of sparse grass and luxuriant vines. The soil changed from gray sand to a reddish clay. They were now on the Catawba Path, which connected to the Great Wagon Road, the long, heavily traveled dirt track that ran north to Virginia and even Pennsylvania and provided the main thoroughfare for any kind of travel in the backcountry.[15]

One more day of travel, and they arrived at the Waxhaws. They saw for the first time the big, barnlike Waxhaw Meeting House at the center of the settlement. Around it, in a radius of ten or fifteen miles on the east side of the wide, deep Catawba River, were scattered the houses and farms of the settlers. The houses were not grouped as in an Irish village; almost all were out of sight of each other, separated by fields and forests. Probably they stayed the first few nights at Robert Crawford's house on the Wagon Road near the point where it forded Waxhaw Creek.

The houses were familiar in many ways. "Log cabins," the term for them, sounded natural to Irish ears—Irish houses, too, were called "cabins," although they were made of stone or mud, with thatched roofs. (The word "cabin" in British usage, applied to a residence, meant a small, rude, primitive dwelling.) The Carolinian cabins were about sixteen feet deep and twenty-two or twenty-four feet wide, with doors in front and back, a chimney at one end, and very few windows. All this was like Ulster. Only the material was different—logs with clay or mud filling between them. (Sometimes there was so much clay filling that the cabin resembled a half-timbered Tudor building.) Overlapping pieces split from logs shingled the roof, as in county Armagh, and there was usually a loft where the children slept and household goods were stored. Often there were two rooms, a kitchen at one end and a small room at the opposite end for sleeping, but just as often the whole family slept naked on blankets in front of the fire, as poorer people did in Ireland. Sometimes there was an earthen floor, as in many Irish cabins; sometimes it was of puncheons, rough slabs split from tree trunks and dressed so that they were almost level.[16]

Cabins like these, however, were starter houses for the Waxhaw settlers,

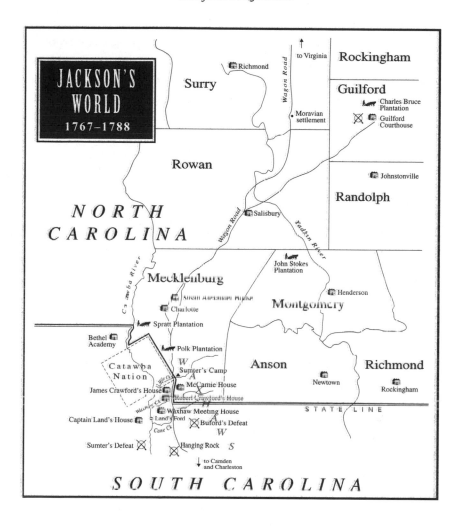

JACKSON'S
WORLD
1767–1788

Surry

Richmond

to Virginia

Rockingham

Guilford

Charles Bruce
Plantation

Guilford
Courthouse

Wagon Road

Moravian
settlement

Rowan

Johnstonville

Randolph

NORTH
CAROLINA

Salisbury

Wagon Road

Yadkin River

Catawba River

John Stokes
Plantation

Mecklenburg

Susan Alexander House

Charlotte

Henderson

Montgomery

Spratt Plantation

Bethel
Academy

Polk Plantation

Catawba
Nation

W

Sumter's Camp

James Crawford's House

McCamie House

Robert Crawford's House

Waxhaw Meeting House

Captain Land's House

Land's Ford

Cane Ck.

Buford's Defeat

Sumter's Defeat

Hanging Rock

Anson

Newtown

Richmond

Rockingham

STATE LINE

A

W

S

to Camden
and Charleston

SOUTH CAROLINA

built typically by a family that had just arrived. A family that had been there longer and had had any luck in farming or trade lived in a more elaborate home, perhaps a log house of two full stories, covered on the outside with clapboards to present a more civilized appearance, with shutters on the windows. William Richardson, minister of Waxhaw Presbyterian, was living in a two-story house when he died in 1771. John Barnett, who lived north of the Waxhaws on Little Sugar Creek near Charlotte, had a three-story log house.

Dirt-floored log cabins like this reconstructed example in York County, South Carolina, were the first houses put up by new settlers. Andrew Jackson's father may have erected one like it on his land near Twelve Mile Creek, in Mecklenburg County, North Carolina.

HISTORIC BRATTONSVILLE, BRATTONSVILLE, S.C.

exists to explain what caused his death. Surely, his death could not have come at a worse time for his family. It was midwinter, and Betty was pregnant. Neighbors helped convey the body to the Waxhaw Presbyterian meeting house. A persistent tradition holds that it slid out of the wagon en route and that the bearers, fortified with whiskey against the cold, failed to notice its absence until they arrived at the meeting house; then they had to go back and retrieve it.[22]

In her condition, it was impossible for Betty to return to the farm alone; she would have to stay with one of her sisters until the baby came. Since she ultimately ended up staying with her sister Jane Crawford for fourteen years, it seems reasonable to assume that the baby was born at the Crawford place, and this assumption was the one held by her son in later years; but there is a persistent strand of oral tradition, said to be based on eyewitness testimony, that she gave birth at the house of her sister Peggy McCamie. The two houses, Crawford's and McCamie's, were only a mile apart, and the whole

These two granite markers, about one mile apart in the Waxhaws but on different roads, tell their own story: Jackson was born in one of two log cabins, one in North Carolina and one in South Carolina. The image of the McCamie cabin on the North Carolina marker is from a nineteenth-century engraving and may or may not be accurate.

PHOTOGRAPHS BY LINDSAY PETTUS

question would be unimportant except for two things. The son she bore on March 15, 1767, named Andrew for his dead father, was to become a towering figure in early American history, the Hero of New Orleans, and seventh president of the United States; and against all odds, when the state line was finally drawn, the two houses ended up in different states, the Crawford house in South Carolina and the McCamie house in North Carolina.

A Jackson biographer is supposed, for no very good reason, to have an opinion on this controversy, which has become basically one of state institutional pride. It is difficult to form one, because the two cases are fundamentally dissimilar. The Crawford–South Carolina case rests entirely on Andrew Jackson's own belief, repeated often in his later life but never supported by any other person or any documentary evidence, that he was born in the Crawford house. The McCamie–North Carolina case rests on the testimony of Jackson's first cousin Sarah Leslie, who claimed she was present at the birth and passed her version down to her children. In the Irish culture of the Wax-

Middling families like the Crawfords in the Carolina backcountry lived in houses like this one-story-and-a-half log structure covered with clapboard. Only a few windows admitted light, but the doors stood open all day.

HISTORIC BRATTONSVILLE, BRATTONSVILLE, S.C.

their bearings and write down the directions. At the end of the day they had made four miles.[1]

There was every reason for little Andy Jackson, slender, agile, and energetic, to be in the crowd that followed the surveyors up the road. Exciting events like this were rare in the Waxhaws; besides, the surveyors' route ran past the lane that led to his house, that is, to his uncle James Crawford's house. Like many farmhouses in the area, it was about three-quarters of a mile off the road, among its own fields and woods.[2]

Betty Jackson had moved in with her sister and brother-in-law shortly after Andy's birth. It made sense for her to do so; Jane was often too ill to work, and Betty could handle all the jobs that fell to the woman of the house. She still owned her late husband's land in North Carolina but had neither the money nor the strength to farm it on her own. The Crawford cabin was not large, but all the boys could sleep upstairs in the loft. (There were four Crawford boys, Tommy, Jim, Joey, and Will, ranging from ages twelve to six.) The

*Backcountry cooking and dining both took place around the hearth, which was more often
stone than brick and was usually larger than the one pictured here. Chairs, stools, and
benches were arranged around the hearth for meals, with or without a table.*

HISTORIC BRATTONSVILLE, BRATTONSVILLE, S.C.

three adults worked out an arrangement downstairs. The cabin may have
been divided, like many Irish and Irish-American dwellings, into two rooms,
allowing the possibility of privacy.[3]

Not enough is known about the composition of households in the area to
determine if such a joint arrangement was unusual; but Betty Jackson and her
sons stayed in the Crawford house fourteen years without any adverse comment that has survived. To be sure, she was thought of as distinct from the
Crawfords—a poor woman, a widow "of not much property" as one of her
neighbors put it. There was even a tradition in later years, possibly current at
the time, that Andy had been born in the McCamie house but that his mother
had then moved in with the Crawfords because they had more money, a report that carried the fairly clear implication that the Jacksons were sponging.[4]

The community seems to have generally agreed, however, that "Aunt
Betty" was upright and pious, and that she showed her reluctance to be a burden on her brother-in-law by sending her oldest son Hugh to live with George

The single room in most backcountry log houses (sometimes partitioned in two) served for sleeping as well as food preparation. Commonly, the parents and small children slept downstairs while older children, especially boys, slept in the loft.

HISTORIC BRATTONSVILLE, BRATTONSVILLE, S.C.

and Peggy McCamie when he was old enough, six or seven, perhaps. The McCamies had no children of their own, and Huey could be useful doing small chores around the McCamie house. The widow Jackson and her two younger sons stayed at the Crawford home.[5]

It was a moderately prosperous home by the standards of the Waxhaws. Crawford owned several hundred acres around the house, most of them still forested. In scattered fields he grew corn, oats, flax, and barley, augmenting his income by the seasonal trade of distilling, making whiskey and brandy from his neighbors' grain and fruit. He was less prominent and affluent than his brother Robert, who was captain of the local militia by the 1770s; James Crawford served in the rank and file. Robert seems to have owned several slaves; there is no evidence that James owned any. Instead of the imposing (for the area) two-story dwelling of Robert Crawford, his brother probably lived in a conventional log house.[6]

Robin and Andy Jackson were too young to be aware of the nuances of social status and property-owning in the community. To them the Crawford house was home and the Crawford boys were brothers. They accepted the naturalness of walking down the road to see Huey at the McCamies', often on their way to Walkup's mill, a short distance farther on. In the other direction was the home of their "uncle" Robert Crawford. As they roamed the area near their home, they became familiar with its landscape and the way their neighbors lived.

The first and biggest thing in the Jackson boys' experience was the forest. Beyond the small cultivated fields clustered around cabins, woodland was pervasive in the Waxhaws. According to one estimate, at the time of the Revolution nine-tenths of the land was forested, including the land between the Crawford house and the road. It was almost primeval Southeastern forest, large oaks and hickories with occasional stands of pine or blackjack oak where the soil was poor. But it was not frontier. Under the pressure of European settlement, the big animals and game animals had begun moving west; bear and buffalo were gone, the beaver were going. The most dangerous beasts in the woods, apart from an occasional wildcat or wolf, were the hogs and cattle that settlers left there to roam around and forage.[7]

Deer and small game were still plentiful, however, and a man in the Waxhaws could feed his family by hunting. Most households in the area had guns. (Michael A. Bellesiles has recently argued the contrary for the northern United States in this era, but probate records show that gun ownership was common in the Carolina backcountry.) Luigi Castiglioni, traveling through the backcountry just after the Revolution, spent an afternoon talking with a settler who bragged "about his prowess as a hunter, never inserting anything that had to do with farming, which showed all the signs of being neglected, since just a few acres around the house were planted to corn."[8]

Boys began learning about guns at an early age. Andy Jackson cannot have been more than eight years old when a group of older boys gave him a shotgun to fire, loaded to the muzzle with a heavy charge of powder. He fired it, but the recoil knocked him down and sent him sprawling. Small as he was, Andy knew how an Irish lad was supposed to react, competitive and feisty. He got to his feet and said, "By God, if any of you laughs, I'll kill him."[9]

Beyond the trees lay the Camden Road, another focus of experience for the young Jacksons. It was the link that connected their settlement with Charles Town on one end and Virginia and Pennsylvania (the Waxhaw settlers called them Virginny and Pensilvaney) on the other. Traffic on it was not thick, but it was steady—men on horseback, sometimes well-dressed men from the coast, merchants or lawyers; droves of lowing cattle, herded by men on horseback and their dogs, headed for the beef market at Charles Town. Occasionally there would be a wagon carrying a family bound for its new settlement or goods bound for Camden.[10]

Some of the goods were local. Flour ground at Andrew Foster's mill from locally grown wheat (William Moultrie, head of the South Carolina survey party, noticed "a great many large wheat fields" in the Waxhaws) was shipped to the merchant Joseph Kershaw in Camden. Herds of cattle from the east side of the Waxhaws, where an immigrant from Antrim named John Walker ran a country store, were among those that made the long trek to Charles Town. (John Walker's son Andy, an expert horseman who drove many of them, in a few years would be involved with Andy Jackson in a painful and tragic wartime incident.)[11]

The first place Robin and Andy Jackson became acquainted with beyond their immediate neighborhood was doubtless the meeting house, four miles away. They went every Sunday, down the Camden Road, fording Waxhaw Creek, and then off through the woods to the meeting house. Possibly they walked, but riding horseback was much more prestigious in the settlement, even for women and children. The meeting house was in a clearing, the area around it worn to bare red earth by the worshippers and their horses. Other log buildings stood nearby—a spring house, a shed, a schoolhouse—and there were the beginnings of a graveyard with a few markers, mostly primitive with one or two startling exceptions.[12]

The meeting house did not survive the Revolution, and nothing is known of its design except that it had two doors. It must have been large; people attended from all the country around, sometimes as many as a thousand according to one source. Occasionally the worshippers overflowed the building and services were held outside. If it was like other backcountry meeting houses from Pennsylvania to Carolina, it had no paint and no steeple; the severe Presbyterian taste placed little value on external ornaments. Its doors were "batten" doors, wide boards nailed together, without paneling. Open windows, fitted with shutters, let light and air inside, which had a floor and ceiling of rough plank. Rows of crude, uncomfortable wooden benches faced the raised clapboard pulpit, with a special bench under the pulpit for the pre-

The first Waxhaw Meeting House was similar in construction to this Presbyterian church,
built around 1795 in central North Carolina—just a large log structure covered with
clapboard. There would have been no glass in the windows at Waxhaw.
COURTESY OF HISTORIC BRATTONSVILLE, BRATTONSVILLE, S.C.

sentor, who "lined out" the psalms for the worshippers, that is, called out the lines which were to be sung. The elders, who oversaw the congregation, had a bench of their own.[13]

Beside their mother, who always carried her Bible covered with checked cloth, the Jackson boys sat as still as they could through the two-hour service, as the minister preached and the congregation sang, loudly and unmusically, one of the Twelve Tunes used in Presbyterian worship. Some Sundays there was communion, which meant the congregation attended two days of services, Saturday and Sunday. The Waxhaw minister, William Richardson, would invite another from a neighboring congregation, and the visitor would preach on Saturday. Richardson handed out small lead tokens to those present. Only those who had heard the Saturday sermon and handed in their tokens could take communion on Sunday, when Richardson preached.[14]

The Jackson boys were well-acquainted with William Richardson, an energetic, learned man in his forties who ministered to the Waxhaw congregation

*Betty Jackson is said to have covered her Bible in cloth, like many backcountry Presbyterians.
This Bible, similarly covered, belonged to the Caldwell family of
Rowan County, North Carolina.*

THE ROWAN MUSEUM; PHOTOGRAPH BY WAYNE HINSHAW

until his sudden death in 1771. His two-story log home near the meeting house
had more comforts than most Waxhaw dwellings; for instance, at the time of
his death he had received glass panes for the windows, though they were not
yet put in. His study held dozens of books, many in Greek, Hebrew, and
Latin, and he owned four slaves, far more than most white residents. His wife,
Nancy, was a good friend of Betty Jackson.[15]

Mr. Richardson stopped often at the Crawford home on his periodic visits
around the congregation. It was his duty to lead the families in prayer and to
check on the education of the children. Every Presbyterian child in the Waxhaws had to memorize the Westminster Catechism, a series of 107 questions
and answers that summarized Christian doctrine. Parents taught it to them,
and elders and the minister had the Question Book recited for them when

they called. It seems a prodigious amount of memory work, but was less so in an oral culture where memorization was highly developed. To Andy and his contemporaries, the spoken words of the catechism were a constant presence in the mind defining right and wrong, the visible and the invisible:

1. *What is the chief end of man?*
   Man's chief end is to glorify God and to enjoy Him forever.
2. *What rule hath God given to direct us how we may glorify and enjoy Him?*
   The word of God, which is contained in the Scriptures of the Old and New Testaments, is the only rule to direct us how we may glorify and enjoy Him.
3. *What do the Scriptures principally teach?*
   The Scriptures principally teach what man is to believe concerning God, and what duty God requires of man.[16]

Parson Richardson was found dead in his study, a bridle wrapped around his neck, in July 1771. The evidence suggested murder, but the church elders preferred to call it suicide and pointed out that the minister had seemed overworked and depressed in the months before his death. Mrs. Richardson had a splendid gravestone carved in Charles Town, listing her dead husband's virtues and achievements. Then she married George Dunlap, a member of one of the old Pennsylvania Irish, or "Cohees," who dominated Waxhaw society, unlike "Bounty Irish" latecomers like the Crawfords. Her doing so stirred up ugly talk about her husband's death, and some time in 1772, in the presence of the whole congregation—certainly including the Jacksons and Crawfords she was forced to touch her finger to the skull of Richardson's disinterred corpse in the meeting house graveyard. If the finger bled, according to Scottish tradition, she was the murderer. Andy must have seen an expression of relief on his mother's face when Nancy Richardson's finger did not bleed.[17]

For years after 1771, the Waxhaw church was without a minister, and the elders had to supervise the congregation, helped by occasional sermons from visiting ministers. It was understood that qualified ministers were hard to get, but the congregation had hope: Richardson had left most of his library to his nephew, a bright fifteen-year-old named William Richardson Davie, who was already at an academy in Charlotte learning Latin and Greek, the languages of an educated man. Davie, the congregation hoped, would come back in time to take his uncle's place. (Davie actually had a more exciting destiny before him, one that would make him Andy Jackson's heroic ideal.)[18]

Only a few years after the boundary survey, the Jackson boys had the opportunity to begin their own education. It was at what was called a "common" or "English" school, beyond the McCamies' cabin, in the area that was now officially North Carolina. Israel Walkup, of the Walkup's mill family, was a schoolmate, and so were a couple of boys named Massey whose family had recently moved down from Virginia. This kind of school was a fairly common institution in communities like the Waxhaws—a little cabin in the woods where a young master in his teens or twenties received a small fee to teach boys and girls their letters and the rules of arithmetic during part of the year. Literacy was generally high in Ulster Irish communities, around seventy or eighty percent; Irish Presbyterians wanted their children to be able to read the Bible and avoid being hoodwinked in business deals. Instruction in reading often began at home, and it may have done so in Jackson's case. At school, scholars brought Bibles or religious books from home, and the young master helped them puzzle out the words, while holding a switch to punish the wiggly, country-smart children for any "pinching or picking at one a nother or lafing," or "Scribling on one a nother's Books." Andy must have been six or seven then, eight at most; by the time he was nine or ten he was attending a more advanced school.[19]

Before and after the six or eight hours of study, and during recesses, the boys raced and fought. Andy was a real competitor, young as he was. George McWhorter often wrestled him and usually won, because he was five years older and heavier; but Andy always wanted a rematch. One of the Huey boys put it vividly: "He was dead game. I could throw him, but he wouldn't stay throwed." Skinny and lithe, the youngest Jackson was good at wrestling, foot races, and jumping, and always wanted to be first, despite his age. He was also good in school. By the time it closed, his mother was convinced that Andy deserved a better education, perhaps one as good as young Davie's.[20]

Around the time Andy was learning his letters, in 1774, Tommy, the oldest Crawford boy, took a wife and set up his own household. He was then in his early twenties; his bride, Elizabeth Stephenson, was twenty-one. Both were

23

. . . .

The Carolina Irish

older than average for a Waxhaws couple. It was, nevertheless, the first wedding for them both and was celebrated with all the revelry and joy reserved
for such occasions in an Irish community.[21]

The ceremony no doubt took place at the Stephenson house in the valley
of Cane Creek; and since John Stephenson, the bride's father, was an elder of
the Waxhaw congregation, there was most likely a minister from one of the
neighboring congregations there to unite the pair. But the vows themselves
were not central to a backcountry wedding; the main events were the feasting, the dancing, and especially the drinking. Whiskey, a beverage unique to
Irish settlements, which visitors often found repulsive, was the drink. The
precise character of the celebration varied, naturally, according to the families
involved, and it is possible that the Stephensons were a bit more straitlaced
than their neighbors; but the general outlines of a wedding in the Waxhaws
are clear.

The morning of the wedding, the groom and all his family, with their
friends and neighbors, formed a cavalcade, and riding two by two, with a
great deal of random firing of guns and passing around of the communal
whiskey bottle, proceeded laughing and hollering to the bride's plantation (as
a farm, even a small one, was called), where they treated the bride's party to
their whiskey as well. Bride and groom both wore their best clothes. Without
attendants, the couple stood before the minister, who, in true Presbyterian
fashion, began with a sermon on "the institution, use, and ends of marriage"
as defined in Scripture. The couple joined hands, and the minister closed with
a quick blessing. A huge feed had been set out for them on long tables in the
yard; there was no question of going inside a cabin in large numbers. There
was venison and turkey, ham and sausage, cornbread, "light bread" (wheat
bread), and lots of butter, seasonal vegetables and fruits, cold buttermilk fresh
from the spring, and plenty of whiskey, cider, and peach brandy.

After the feast there was a "frolic"—shooting matches and athletic contests for the young men, jigs to the music of a fiddle for the young of both
sexes. The dancing was spontaneous and free form; an amused guest at a
dance in the Waxhaws noted that his fellow dancers "were above minding the
Tune, but continued on Just as it happen'd." The elders danced a while, then
sat a while and told tales. The younger boys found a place at a distance from
the house, kindled up a fire of their own, and began running, jumping, and

wrestling contests refereed by the older boys; after these, they were paired off in boxing matches, from which any boy who backed out was called a coward. Andy stood out in these contests.

Almost everyone for miles around was there. The feasting and drinking and dancing (and occasional fighting) went on until late in the night. At some point the celebrants put the newlyweds to bed in an upstairs room or in the loft. The Stephensons were affluent enough to have a feather bed and a bedstead to put it in; Tommy and Betty would have been snuggled in, given joking advice and a few swigs of whiskey, and left to their own devices while the merriment went on outside.

It all began again the next day. The young couple was to live on the Stephenson place, and if Tommy had already erected a cabin, as he probably had, this was the day of the "infare"; merrymakers escorted the newlyweds to their new home with more hilarity and drinking. Nor was this the end; the Sunday after the wedding Tommy and Betty would attend church in their wedding clothes; this was called "making their appearance." Indeed, the feasting and frolicking could go on for days; few of the people of the community had urgent responsibilities. The corn would grow, the hogs fatten, the mash ferment, while they were busy celebrating. A good wedding was an occasion to enjoy.[22]

Some time after Tommy's wedding—the exact time is not known, but it happened while Andy was still a boy—there was a different kind of community ceremony at the Crawford house. Aunt Jane Crawford had died, and the people of the Waxhaws gathered for the wake. In this case as with a wedding, forms were standard in Ireland or in Carolina. The body was set on a table in the middle of the main room of the "big house," as the cabin was called whether it was big or not. Coins were placed on the eyes, a plate of salt on the chest. The sparse furniture of the room was moved around, and all the stools, chests, and benches in the place were brought in so that visitors would have room to sit around the corpse. If there was a looking glass, it was covered. Jackson's mother had surely prepared food for the visitors. In Ulster it might have been bread and cheese; the settlers in Carolina made little cheese, and here it was probably a light supper of Indian bread and ham or turkey. There was plenty of whiskey to pass around. The dead woman's other sisters, Sally and Mary Leslie and Peggy McCamie, helped with the food, and the sons,

Tommy and Jimmy, Joey and Will, and their father, were all there as they prepared to watch through the night.

The atmosphere was subdued but not sad or even particularly religious. Neighbors came in, took a drink of whiskey, and sat around the fire and the corpse, talking not of consolation and eternity but of more mundane topics. Men might talk quietly of the crops or business deals. Far from the firelight, young unmarried men like Joey or Will Crawford might try "discoursing" with an unattached neighborhood girl and make a little progress toward a more intimate acquaintance. Women shared community news. The older people remembered things the dead woman had said or done, and these shaded into other stories of Waxhaw people and their experiences. The main object was not to praise the deceased or worry about her soul; it was simply to be together and keep the family company.

As the night went on the gathering became quieter. Huey, Robin, and Andy went to sleep upstairs. Some adults got quietly drunk; others got up and went outside to talk or urinate, or went home; others came in. Toward daybreak a hushed conversation probably arose of ghosts and haunts. People related strange experiences they had in the woods and omens of impending death. (The Irish backcountry people were deeply superstitious. One settler near the Catawba in this era kept a manual of charms and magical cures.) Then the sun rose, and it was over. Some men went to dig the grave. James Crawford's family did not bury its dead at the meeting house, apparently, and Jane was probably buried on the place. Without a minister, no divine service was possible, but everyone knew the customary prayers for the occasion.[23]

This was the kind of community where the young Andrew Jackson grew up—tightly knit with bonds of kinship and tradition, religion and neighborliness, a settlement where hunting and song, whiskey and doctrine, fighting and feasting were all important. Its people, by their manners and their brogue, as the accent was called, were demonstrably Irish; strangers recognized them instantly. As the settlement matured and people moved into it from other parts of the South, its character would change; but in the years of Jackson's boyhood, just before the War of Independence, it was becoming more Irish every year, as new families from Antrim, Down, and Tyrone continued moving in.[24]

Later generations would prefer the term "Scotch-Irish" for the people of the Waxhaws and elsewhere in the Southern backcountry, adding "Scotch" in an effort to stress a distinct set of characteristics—determination, logic, love of gain. But to judge from travelers' accounts and other surviving evidence, the simple label they gave themselves, "Irish," is more accurately evocative for the settlers in the Waxhaws before the Revolution. They were feisty and verbal, easygoing and fun loving. They were also combative and capable of enormous sacrifice. Andrew Jackson, as he matured, was to display a personality that forcefully echoed all these traits.[25]

. . . .

CHAPTER THREE

Andy
1776–1780

—⁓⊙⊙⁓—

AROUND 1776, Andy moved in with his uncle Captain Robert
Crawford at the big log house near Waxhaw Creek. The occasion
was his entering another school, an academy where Latin and
Greek, the passports to serious learning; reading; and mathemat-
ics were offered. It was at the Waxhaw meeting house, three
miles from Captain Crawford's. He attended with his cousin Will Crawford;
the two of them, and probably a third boy, stayed at the Crawford home while
school was in session. Neither of his brothers went.[1]

Presbyterian churches and schools went together. Presbyterian ministers,
by definition educated men with a knowledge of the classical languages,
often taught the boys of their congregation, for a fee, during the week, and
sometimes taught the girls as well. Since the death of William Richardson,
the log schoolhouse next to the meeting house had been vacant; but in 1776 a
"dominie"—a schoolmaster capable of teaching Latin and Greek—named
William Humphries arrived and, no doubt with the permission of the elders,
reopened the school.[2]

It soon attracted many boys (no girls are mentioned in connection with
it), including some from beyond the settlement who boarded with families
near the meeting house. Some were almost grown; the fact suggests just how
long it had been since classical schooling was available in the neighborhood.
John Adair, son of a Scottish immigrant from across the river, was eighteen or

A log schoolhouse built in 1785 at a Presbyterian meeting house in North Carolina
suggests what the Waxhaw Academy building looked like—minus the
window glass and brick chimney, of course.

PRESBYTERIAN HISTORICAL SOCIETY, MONTREAT, N.C., PHOTOGRAPH BY BOB PLYLER

nineteen; and James White Stephenson, who lived near the meeting house, was twenty. Will Crawford, Billy Smith, and John Douglass were in their middle teens, as was Ulster-born Johnny Brown from across the river. Andy Jackson, true to the pattern that held throughout his youth, was among the youngest but held his own because he looked and acted older than his years. All of them attended because they or their parents envisioned their having careers as educated men in the ministry, medicine, or law. Andy's mother wanted her son to be a minister.[3]

He must have enjoyed living at Major Crawford's, where he was no longer the youngest child; rather, he was nearly the eldest. Robert and Jean Crawford's two oldest children were girls, both near Andy's age. Andy liked and respected Sarah, slightly older than he, a well-bred girl whom a Pennsylvania traveler through the Waxhaws later described as the only genteel girl he had met south of Harrisburg. All the boys were younger; he could ride herd on them without challenge. There were house slaves to do some of the menial work. One, a girl named Phyllis, who was then in her teens, recalled as an old woman how she tended Andy when he had the "big itch."[4]

The big itch, as distinguished in the Carolina settlers' folklore from the "toe itch" or "ground itch," which was athlete's foot, was their term for the skin disease called scabies. It was an infestation of microscopic insects picked up from another person, associated with what its main chronicler politely calls "defective personal hygiene." It seems an apt disease for the Ulster Irish, who were noted in both Ireland and America for dirtiness. They seldom bathed, perhaps once a year. An observer in County Down called them "neither neat nor clean in their habitations," an observation echoed by many American travelers. Scabies was fairly common among them, especially among children who slept in the same bed or loft and exchanged the parasites.[5]

The symptoms are subtle at first—random itches, little red welts and lines on the inner wrists and the webs between the fingers—but as it progresses it attacks the hidden, warm places of the body, the armpits, the buttocks, and in boys, the penis, and causes violent itching at night. Eventually it took over the whole body; it "frighten[ed] a body powerful," as one witness said. Apothecaries in seaports like Charles Town and Philadelphia sold a moderately effective sulfur-mercury ointment treatment that was unavailable in the Waxhaws. Probably Phyllis used the standard Southern folk treatment—boiling the roots of pokeweed, the big fleshy weed with purple berries that were used for dyeing, and then applying the water, sometimes called a "strong ooze of pokeweed"—to the itching parts. (It "will make you think hell ain't a mile away, but it sure does cure the eetch," one informant said.) Andy and most likely his roommates, Will Crawford and the other boy, who doubtless all slept together, endured the cure; it was just an incident of backcountry living.[6]

Andy doubtless enjoyed the variety of company at his uncle's house. The house, at a convenient halting place right on the Camden Road, attracted a variety of travelers—drovers, professional men and, after the war began, Continental army officers as well. Robert Crawford may have kept a tavern as his fellow militia officer John Barkley did; in any case, he surely had travelers who spent the night, as was customary at any big house on a main road. They were welcome because they brought news—and the news in those years was

Hezekiah Alexander's stone house in Mecklenburg County, N.C., built in 1774, gives an impression of the lifestyle of a prosperous, established Carolina Irish family. Jackson, who grew up thirty miles away, was doubtless familiar with the house from boyhood.
HISTORIC BRATTONSVILLE, BRATTONSVILLE, S.C.

often momentous, about the Congress in Philadelphia, the Declaration, the bloodshed in Boston, and the arrival of the British fleet off New York.

To a nine- or ten-year-old, even a bright one, this war talk was remote and abstract, but the manners and clothes of the visitors were interesting. Charles Town men often dressed in a way that men in the Waxhaws reserved for church or feasts, wearing greatcoats with long rows of elaborately worked buttons, knee breeches of fine, elegant, colored cloth; ruffled shirts; and silver buckled shoes. Some were more careful about their personal appearance than Waxhaw people; they smelled better, or at least smelled less. Many had a fine, pleasant courtesy in their manners that suggested they were used to associating with a different kind of society. They were, in a word, gentlemen.[7]

Whether there were gentlemen in the Waxhaws was debatable. Robert Crawford, John Barkley, the justice of the peace John Gaston, and other such men held honorable positions and received respect from their neighbors, and some of them, Crawford and Gaston for instance, had had a fair education.

Andy

With the plaster, paneling, and substantial furniture of their home, the Alexanders clearly
lived better than the Crawfords and most people in the backcountry.
HESEKIAH ALEXANDER HOUSE, CHARLOTTE, N.C.

They had knee breeches and elegant coats and may have worn them fairly regularly, even at work, as was the case on the Tennessee frontier. But their manners were not polished by contact with the genteel world, and their personal appearance often left something to be desired—one genteel traveler called Barkley "our greasy landlord." It was certainly possible, however, to leave the Waxhaws and become a gentleman. Parson Richardson's nephew, William Richardson Davie, was proof of that. His uncle had intended him for the ministry, sent him to the College of New Jersey in Princeton, and left him all his Greek and Hebrew books. He now lived in Salisbury, North Carolina, and returned from time to time to see his father, Archy Davie, a weaver who lived near the meeting house. William was tall, well-dressed, well-spoken, and genteel in every way.[8]

Schoolmaster Humphries surely wore the gentleman's outfit to underline his superior status—at least the buckled shoes, stockings, knee breeches, shirt, stock (the ruffled collar that went around the neck), dark broadcloth coat, and three-cornered hat. Andy and his schoolmates probably did not. Growing boys in the Waxhaws could not afford a fine outfit that would be too small in a year, and what fine clothes they had, if any, they reserved, like their elders, for Sunday. Their everyday attire consisted of light homespun linen shirts, homespun linen or buckskin breeches like those of grown men, shoes, and wide-brimmed, floppy black hats like their elders'. (All men in the Waxhaws wore hats; they kept the sun and rain off a man's head and were a necessity for people who lived mostly outdoors.) Surely, however, they scrubbed their faces and tried to comb their hair before setting out for class; this was an academy, after all.[9]

In a time when the only sources of light after dark were the hearth, a flaming piece of fat pine wood ("lightwood"), a cattail soaked in grease—or, if one lived on a well-run plantation, a candle—daylight was at a premium, and school probably began shortly after dawn. That was the case at Mount Zion Academy, a Presbyterian school in another part of the backcountry, where Humphries taught a few years later. There someone blew a horn at daybreak; the boys got up, washed, and dressed. At sunrise another blast "summoned them to roll-call and prayers, after which they went to their studies. At eight o'clock they were dismissed for breakfast; from nine to twelve they were brought together for study. After an intermission, study hours began again at two and continued until five, when they were again dismissed after roll-call and prayers." Chances are, thus, that Andy and his friends got up at daybreak, walked down the dusty road to the meeting house in the morning freshness before dawn, and were on their log benches in the log schoolhouse at sunrise, ready to look into old Latin and Greek books, sharpen their pens, mix their ink, and write compositions and translations on rough brown paper. They spent most of the daylight hours there studying, with the periodic whippings from Humphries and bare-chested fights with each other that were part of backwoods schooling. For lunch they carried cornbread in their pockets.[10]

Humphries's school lasted until 1779. A change in the military situation led indirectly to its closure. After several years of fighting in the remote northern colonies, the British decided to attack the South, and in the spring of 1779, Charles Town was threatened for the first time by a siege. Charles Town Presbyterians, eager to find a safe haven for themselves and their children, pressed forward with their idea of funding an academy in the backcountry.

Humphries took a position at the new Mount Zion Academy in the tiny settlement of Winnsboro, fifty miles away. Many of his older students at Waxhaw congregation quit school altogether to join militia units that were
marching to the relief of Charles Town.[11]

Andy Jackson and the younger boys would have been left without a
school except that the parents of James White Stephenson, Tommy Crawford's brother-in-law and one of Humphries's older students, were reluctant
to let him join the militia and arranged for James to continue in the master's
place, teaching the younger students reading, writing, and perhaps some classics in the cabin at the meeting house. He had a school of twelve or fifteen
students for part of that year. Andy was in it, as were the younger Stephenson
boys, Tommy and Nat, who were near him in age, and at least one of the
Montgomery boys from down on Camp Creek. (Years later Montgomery reminded Jackson of their going to school under "old Mr. Stephenson";
Stephenson, though heavy set and forceful, was at most twenty-three at the
time.[12]

There are some indications, without firm evidence, that after Stephenson's school closed Andy was sent for a short time to Liberty Hall Academy,
formerly Queen's Academy, the Presbyterian school in Charlotte, where
Davie had begun his education. Fifty or sixty boys attended there. A man who
claimed he was Andy's fellow student there remarked on his fondness for ath-
letics (i.e., schoolboy games after class, not organized sports) and "his ardent
and rather quick temperament." If he did indeed go to Liberty Hall, the fact
is another illustration of Betty Jackson's faith in the talent and intelligence of
her youngest son, and her willingness to spend money for his education. But
if he attended, his stay was very brief, for Liberty Hall shut down in February
1780 when the British invasion began.[13]

This period—a year or two studying Greek and Latin under Humphries,
followed by a term under Stephenson and possibly a term at Liberty Hall—
was the longest sustained schooling of Andrew Jackson's life, and one would
like to be able to assess its influence on him. In Jackson's case, to do so is unusually hard. For him and his contemporaries, the normal processes of growing and learning were interrupted by the Revolution, which destroyed their
childhood world and, very likely, some of the values and habits they had
begun to acquire from it. The only statement one can confidently make about
his early schooling is negative: the classics did not stimulate Andy as they did

34

Young Hickory

some students, and he did not remember any Latin or Greek he may have learned. More broadly, one can say that though Andy "learned his letters," as the saying went, the idea of reading for knowledge or entertainment never really took hold in his mind. In mature life he read a great deal as part of his business—law books, letters, documents, newspapers, and the like—but not literature, and certainly not the classics.

Yet the sparse anecdotal evidence about Jackson's early years suggests that he had considerable talent with words. There is, for instance, Betty Jackson's decision to educate her youngest son for the ministry, which biographers have chuckled about for generations. But a minister is, first of all, a preacher; fluent speech is a job requirement. Andy evidently spoke well and forcefully, even as a youngster, and better than his oldest brother Hugh, of whom Mrs. Jackson was very fond. When time came to educate the boys—perhaps there was only enough money to educate one—Andy and not Huey or Robin was the one she sent to the academy.[14]

Some of the anecdotes about young Jackson that the biographer Parton collected in the Waxhaws in the 1800s stress verbal fluency. One schoolmate remembered Andy for a glib nonsense routine that he was fond of rattling off, probably as he grabbed and manhandled another boy. It went "Set the case, now; you are Shauney Kerr's mare, and me Billy Buck; and I should mount you, and you should kick, fall, fling and break your neck; should I be to blame for that?"—a line of bullying patter neatly anticipating Jackson's life as a young adult, with its content of horses, law, and aggression. Someone else recalled his debating one of his Crawford uncles at length about what makes a gentleman—good breeding, as his uncle said, or education, according to Andy. Who won the debate is not recorded and is unimportant in this context; the point of the story was that Andy was a confident talker, unafraid to take on an adult in conversation, in a community where ready, entertaining speech was highly valued.[15]

One cannot infer too much, then, from young Jackson's failure to engage with classic texts at Humphries's school. He may or may not have been a poor scholar—there is simply no evidence—but he was not a dull boy. His interests lay elsewhere. By his middle teens he was a superb horseman, a good shot, and a competent gambler, and these presumably were the skills he was perfecting, under the tutelage of older Waxhaw men, at the same time he studied under Humphries and Stephenson; there are, unfortunately, no details.

. . . .

Andy

Using the scant evidence that exists, it is barely possible to draw a sketch of Andy Jackson as he was when he finished Stephenson's school, before the disorder of the Revolution destroyed his world. To the neighbors he would have been "one of the Crawford boys," even though Jackson was his surname, and would have shared in the identity of the Crawford clan. They were, according to a later resident, a family "of great liberality, but strong in their prejudices, either of friendship or hatred." But the personalities varied among these earnest, generous Crawford men; Tommy, James Crawford's eldest son, was quiet, steady, and unassuming. Captain Robert Crawford, the middle son, was a much stronger personality, stiff and severe in manner but an articulate talker and shrewd politician with his neighbors. Will Crawford, James's third son, was perhaps more like the captain, verbal and ambitious; James Crawford himself, to judge from his relative obscurity in the community, may have been retiring like his son Thomas.[16]

Approval of quiet and reliable men like Tommy Crawford and (perhaps) his father tended to shade into pity or even contempt, as in this thumbnail sketch of a man born in the Waxhaws around this time: ". . . a very quiet say nothing kind of a man, had but little energy, troubled nobody, honest as the day was long, and could be led around by the nose, by anyone mean enough to do so." More admired were the bold ones, "chatty," "entertainin," and "full of sport," as people in a modern Ulster community put it, who might bring trouble along with fun and competition. From the available evidence, Andy Jackson, like his older brother Hugh, his foster brother Will Crawford, and the major, was one of the bold ones.[17]

He was thin as a rail and tall for his age. He may have had sandy hair, as an early biographer was told, although his earliest adult portraits show it as dark brown. His eyes were blue, large, and expressive. Though lean, he was agile and athletic; he enjoyed running and jumping, and got excited at the thought of physical competition. He was "mischievous," "always up to his pranks," according to Phyllis, and a bit of a bully. A ready talker, articulate, with a good memory, he was smooth and well-mannered in the Ulster Irish fashion, except when he lost his temper. Phyllis recalled that once he "slobbered" (salivated excessively) and was touchy when teased about it. It had something to do with an ailment she called the "water-rush." Like most boys in an Irish community, he enjoyed being a daredevil and having fun, and on the threshold of his teens was about to move up to the big adventures and scrapes of the

Young Hickory

This statue, Boy of the Waxhaws, *by famed sculptor Anna Hyatt Huntington, stands in Andrew Jackson State Park, outside Lancaster, South Carolina, on the site of the James Crawford farm where Jackson grew up. The likeness is probably inaccurate, but the statue catches the spirit of growing up in the backcountry.*
PHOTOGRAPH BY LINDSAY PETTUS

older boys. Undoubtedly many details are missing from this picture, but it is as far as one can go consistent with the available evidence.[18]

Using what is known about life in the Waxhaws and Jackson's personality, one can sketch an outline of his daily routine in the early summer of 1780, just before the fighting that was to destroy his world broke out:

Andy woke around daybreak. He, Will, Joey, and Robin had slept sprawled in one or two beds in the stuffy, dusty, cramped upstairs. The prickly straw-stuffed mattresses were full of chinches, like every bed in the backcountry. They had bitten him, off and on, all night. Fresh spots of blood were on the mattress ticking.[19]

His skinny thirteen-year-old body, the bones easily visible in the hips and shoulders, showed white in the semidarkness of the upstairs (there were no windows) as he took yesterday's clothes from the pegs on the wall and put them on. The older boys did the same. They wore no undergarments, just rough shirts of homespun, pulled on over their heads, that hung to their thighs. Over them they wore trousers or overalls, work pants of homespun linen in which the legs hung loose all the way to the ankles, unlike gentlemen's breeches, which buttoned at the knee. Their shoes, shapeless leather creations made by a local cobbler, were stuffed with moss or deer hair to fit tighter.[20]

The boys clattered down the steep, winding steps in the corner of the house, in a hurry for breakfast—in fact, it had probably been Betty Jackson's call that woke them in the first place. She had been up early, bringing in water in wooden buckets and cooking over the big open fire where pots of different sizes hung on hooks or nestled in the ashes. The main dish at breakfast was boiled corn meal, or "mush." It was cooked in a big iron pot and may well have been served in one or in a big bowl from which James Crawford and the boys ate, each with his own pewter spoon. So well-connected a settler as General Matthew Locke and his family, in Mecklenburg County, were still eating mush in this fashion, mixed with milk, when they entertained a traveler in 1782. Some backcountry homes had earthenware or china dishes for daily use, but pewter or wood were more common.[21]

If not mush, the main dish was hot cornbread baked on the coals, johnnycake or hoecake as it was called, probably with a side dish of fried bacon. Eggs were a possibility in summer, but unlikely—few settlers seem to have kept fowls. The beverage, as at most Irish meals, was "sweet milk" or buttermilk, in a gourd or mug. Coffee for breakfast was not an Irish custom, although the Virginians who had begun settling in the Waxhaws drank it every morning, from dishlike saucers. A number of settlers started the day with peach brandy or whiskey.[22]

In many Presbyterian homes, the head of the house led prayer and psalm singing after breakfast. The family would sing psalms they knew from church without accompaniment. It was probably more noise than music; Scottish and Irish Presbyterian psalmody was proverbially awful. For most of the family, too, the custom was more formal than devotional; it was not a matter of deep communion with God, but simply something one did in the morning. Uncle Crawford would lead the prayers. Afterward, the family scattered to their daily tasks.[23]

Betty Jackson's tasks were certainly the most varied. She had to milk the cows—exclusively women's work in the Carolina backcountry—and carry the milk down to the spring house to cool and separate. She kept the fire going and collected the wood ashes for making household products like hominy and soap. Perhaps she cleaned the pots, though the Ulster Irish were known for their indifference in that department. She carried bones and refuse to a trash pit away from the house. She weeded and hoed the red-clay soil and took care of the vegetable garden nearby, where the beans were beginning to climb and the new potatoes to swell. She had dinner to plan—whether to dress the carcass of a recently killed animal, or take a piece of smoked meat from the storehouse and set it to boil, perhaps to bake some cornbread or light bread in front of the fire. In addition, she had charge of all the clothing. If it was washday, she would be boiling the family's clothes, her own and the men's. Some days she dyed cloth with pokeweed, oak bark, or onion peelings. When she had none of these tasks before her, she was busy with some phase of making cloth from flax.[24]

Flax processing and linen making occupied every member of the family at some time in the year. This year's crop, with its pale blue flowers, was still in the field; it had been sown around the first of April (on Good Friday, traditionally) and would be harvested in July, not cut, but pulled up carefully so as not to damage the fiber. Last year's crop was all around the Crawford house in various stages of processing. During the fall or winter, the bundles of flax had been retted, soaked in water or left out in the weather until the outer covering of the stalk was weakened; then the boys had spread them out to dry and the men had swingled them—beaten them with heavy wooden blades until the outer covering fell off and only the grayish-blond fiber was left. Then Betty had heckled them—drawn them through metal teeth mounted on a board, to straighten them and comb out any defective fiber. Hanks of this heckled flax hung in the loft, ready for spinning when Betty had the time. She was an expert spinner; her family in Carrickfergus had been in the business. Now and then she still received parcels of linen from the old country. On the walls hung bundles of her yarn. In odd corners of the house there were heaps of tow, the frizzy fibers heckled from the rest of the flax, light, highly flammable stuff that she would spin eventually into cheap, lightweight yarn.[25]

Meanwhile, James Crawford and the boys left the house for the fields and the growing heat of a summer morning, the prelude to the kind of day evoked by South Carolina writer W. J. Cash, who later grew up in nearly the same area, where "pale blue fogs [hung] above the valleys in the morning, the atmosphere smoke[d] faintly at midday, and through the long, slow afternoon, cloud-stacks tower[ed] from the horizon and the earth-heat quaver[ed] upward through the iridescent air, blurring every outline and rendering every object vague and problematical." The fields, at this season, were beautiful, often covered with flowers; a traveler in the middle country of South Carolina that June wrote of camping next to a field covered with the purple-and-white passion flower and the pink-tufted sensitive plant. The corn was a couple of feet high now and needed constant hoeing to keep down the invading grass; since the family had no slaves, this was boys' work, and Andy and Robin might spend a few sweaty hours before noon in the corn patch. Or they might be assigned to carry water from the spring for their mother's washing and cooking.[26]

The lush coolness of the woods near the spring was agreeable. To Andy, who had grown up in the woods, the snakes, chiggers, and seed ticks that inhabited the forests and bothered travelers were no problem; he accepted them as part of life. One location near the spring was especially familiar to him: the still house. He and his brothers had spent much time there helping out, since childhood. The still was a largely masculine province, a theater of male skill, just as Betty Jackson's spinning was a demonstration of female prowess. Andy had learned distilling as a part of growing up.[27]

A still did not run all year. John Osborne, a whiskey maker who lived in the Waxhaws in the generation after the Revolution, "sot [his] stills arun[n]ing" at two different seasons, briefly in midsummer, to make hard cider and peach or plum brandy, and for several months in midwinter, to distill whiskey. There could be no fixed schedule because distilling depended on the rainfall and the crops. But both operations, brandy and whiskey, were similar. The still was near a branch of Waxhaw Creek because it needed a lot of water to sprout the barley so that it could ferment into beer, then to condense the distilled vapor as it ran through the worm, the spiral copper coil, at the end of the process.[28]

A working still required frequent attention. First, the barley had to be cooked over a steady fire to make the mash. (Crawford, like Osborne, made a barley-based whiskey, essentially Irish whiskey; corn whiskey had not yet been developed.) After fermenting for a week or so, the mash was run through the still. The first distillation was then run through again. Especially during distillation, the distiller tested the liquid coming from the worm periodically. If the fire burned low, distillation stopped; if it burned hot, it would scorch the mash, blow the cap off, or make the still "puke" mash into the worm.

John Osborne often watched his still late into the night, and so, no doubt, did Crawford, with help from his sons and nephews. The boys, even the young ones, were no strangers to the product, either as it came dripping from the worm or in the jugs and square "case" bottles in which it was passed around among men and women. A man who grew up in that part of South Carolina a generation later recalled that he and his brothers, as children, "were given a small quantity of whiskey before breakfast every morning" for health's sake. Potter Collins, a seventeen-year-old who lived west of the Catawba, was allowed about a dram of whiskey a week by his father and usually managed to sneak more. Andy Jackson, at thirteen, had doubtless had his share, perhaps not enough at one time to get "groggy" yet.[29]

Sooner or later, on a typical day, Andy's errands led him to his favorite place on the Crawford farm, the stable. James Crawford, like any Waxhaw settler, had several horses for work and for riding, including one for each son or nephew. They were kept in the stable with all the tack—saddles, saddlecloths, bridles, and so forth. Occasionally, they were turned loose to graze. In the society of the Waxhaws, horses were absolutely central; they did the work of plowing and hauling, and provided the only practical means of traveling long distances. Necessary possessions, they were also marks of status. A man was judged by the horse he rode. It was natural that boys, who began riding as young as ten or eleven, were fascinated by the big, imposing animals, more than by the dogs and cats that formed part of every backcountry home.

Andy Jackson, who had to take care of the family's horses and take them out to pasture, shared this fascination, but he did more. By his early teens, he was not only a good rider but an initiate in the horse lore some men shared among themselves—how to judge a horse's age by its teeth, its physical condition by a variety of signs; what feed different kinds of horses required; equine illnesses and how to treat them; and particularly the training of race horses. He was intimately familiar with what was probably the finest horse in the Waxhaws—his uncle Robert Crawford's "three quarters Blooded gelding fifteen hands high," a large animal of pedigreed stock, known throughout the area. Perhaps this horse stimulated his ambition. At any rate, by his late adolescence, he was thought of as a youth who was more at home in the stable than in the law office. He had earned a place in the tight, intense group of adepts who spent their time in the potentially lucrative business of training and racing horses. An early biographer described him at twenty as "one of those who must own a horse, if they do not a house, an acre, or a coat."[30]

Andy rode out sometime during the day, alone or with Robin or a cousin, to his uncle's just down the road, to get corn ground at Walkup's mill, or to Andrew Foster's store, beyond the meeting house, to make purchases for the family. A clever, confident boy, he was able to take care of himself even in the unsettled times that prevailed then, with roving British and Tories, and sometimes large groups of refugees from Georgia or other parts of South Carolina, passing through and living off the country. He chatted affably with the neighbors he met, sometimes staying on his horse, sometimes stopping in for a gourdful of water or buttermilk.

At various places where he went he saw a slave or two working, in the castoff or "negro" clothing their owners furnished them. They were faintly pitiable creatures to him, not only for their servile status but also because of their alienness—they could barely speak English—and the odor which so many whites found "rank" and "disagreeable." If Andy thought about the rightness of their treatment at all, he probably connected it somehow, as most Americans did, with their black skin. Moreover, slavery was mentioned, and apparently authorized, in the Bible.[31]

(One can only infer Jackson's impressions of slavery as a child from his later conduct, which was thoroughly typical of a Southern white man of his generation. As soon as he had sufficient money, he began buying slaves; by the time he reached the presidency, he owned 150. As a master, he was neither unusually lenient nor unusually severe. He had no hesitation in using the whip and chains when he deemed them necessary.)[32]

Often he timed his errands, whether on the farm or at the neighbors', to be back home by midafternoon, time for the big meal of the day—some sort of meat, generally bacon or smoked ham, but sometimes beef or wild game, with beans or greens, hot cornbread, and perhaps potatoes. (The meat and potatoes were cooked swimming in deep fat.) If he was at someone else's house, he would be expected to stay and eat with the family. Virtually all families in the community were fellow worshipers at the Waxhaw meeting house; most were also kin by blood or marriage. Food was abundant and hospitality was standard.[33]

This was the routine on weekday mornings. Sundays, of course, were different. Even without a regular minister, Presbyterians kept the Sabbath in the Waxhaws. There was no work done, and very little visiting. Breakfast was served cold. When there was a visiting minister—Joseph Alexander of Bullock's Creek, John Simpson of Fishing Creek, or William Martin of Rocky Creek—people dressed in their best clothes, saddled up, and rode to the meeting house for a morning and afternoon of sermons and psalms.[34]

In a society where God's commandments reverberated in people's minds from childhood, one would expect generally godly behavior, and broadly speaking the Waxhaw community met this expectation. The people kept most of the Commandments: they observed the Sabbath, they refrained from murder and theft. On the Third Commandment, however—not taking the Lord's name in vain—some of them stumbled. A number of males in the community, Andy Jackson among them, sprinkled their conversation with "by God," "in the name of God," and "God damn." The function of such swearing was, as it always is, to underline the speaker's own bravery by deliberately defying authority. Not all men in the community swore, and it is not clear what factors divided those who did from those who did not; one cannot conjecture, then, where Andy picked up the habit—whether in his own family or elsewhere. But it may be significant that he picked it up so early. Profanity was a tool a man used in social situations to assert control, to proclaim himself "a slashing hell of a fellow," in the often-quoted phrase of W. J. Cash. Along with other pieces of evidence from his boyhood, this one suggests that control was important to Andy. From an early age, he liked to dominate situations.[35]

In the late afternoons, that June, almost every day the towering cloud masses would darken and come together and a furious thunderstorm would break out, with slashing rain and swirling wind and terrifying crashes of lightning. Sometimes the creeks would flood briefly and make the fords impassable. But the storm was of short duration. Toward sunset the sun came out and people emerged from their houses. The workday was over and there was time to visit with the neighbors. Sometimes a few men would gather at someone's house for a frolic of some sort, a shooting match, or a cockfight. Plenty of liquor was available, and many got drunk, some quietly, some more aggressively. The pattern of behavior is clear from sources such as the Osborne diary, and seems to have involved older as well as younger men. Some later descendants of James Crawford had serious drinking problems, and one is tempted to conjecture that one reason why James was less prominent than his brother Robert is that he indulged too freely in his own product. But there is no direct evidence either to confirm or to deny this.[36]

Whether the Crawford men fought cocks is another interesting question. One piece of evidence suggests that they did: the earliest document in Andrew Jackson's papers is a set of instructions, dated March 1779, for feeding a gamecock before a match. ("Take and give him some Pickle Beaf Cut fine 3 times a Day and give him sweet Milk Instead of water to Drink.") It is not in Andy's writing, and there is no way of knowing precisely when it came into his hands; but it does suggest an intense practical interest from an early age. Perhaps, then, James Crawford or one of his sons was the proud owner of one of those "[s]ymbols of strength and vitality . . . with impressive, glossy feathers," as the sport's historian B. W. C. Roberts described them, that contributed such excitement to backcountry life. Certainly many prosperous men of good social standing devoted themselves to this sport; both in Carolina and in Ireland it was considered honorable for a man to know, as the Ulster poet James Orr put it, "the way to heel, an' han', a guid game bird." Owners spent many absorbing hours training the birds, trimming their combs and feathers before a match, and attaching the gaffs, the artificial metal claws that did their deadly work on the opponent. A single cockfight was brief, perhaps two minutes, and always ended with at least one bird an inert mess of blood and feathers; for that reason, they were usually staged in a group of eleven or more, a "main." The possessor of a prize fighting cock could make significant money betting on this blood sport.[37]

Eventually the evening diversions ended. Crawfords and Jacksons made their way home in the soft warmth of a Carolina night, tired and ready for sleep. There were fewer of them now than there had been only a couple of months earlier. Jim had followed Tommy's lead that spring and married Christiana White, a niece of Mrs. Robert Crawford. James Crawford deeded them a piece of the farm, and now Jim and Christiana were set up under their own roof. It would not be long before others left—Joey and Will were both in their late teens or early twenties and of marriageable age. Soon there would be only the Jackson boys, their mother, and Uncle Crawford. Then it might be time to reconfigure the household; Uncle Crawford might invite a son and daughter-in-law into the home, while Betty Jackson moved in with another sister until one of the boys was ready to begin farming his father's land and give her a home. Life went on—or would go on if one could remove the looming threat of the British and Tories. But that was not to happen. The steady rumble of war was about to overpower the music of everyday life.[38]

CHAPTER FOUR

War Comes to the Waxhaws
1778–1780

AT FIRST, people in the Waxhaws learned about the sequence of events modern historians call the American Revolution through newspapers and word of mouth. Several people in Camden subscribed to a newspaper in Charles Town, the *South Carolina Gazette*. Old John Gaston, justice of the peace, sent one of his sons across the river to Camden every week to pick up his copy. Other Waxhaw people like the miller and storekeeper Andrew Foster visited Camden regularly on business and heard the gossip there. Through such channels they learned of the disturbances in Boston, the punitive British reaction, the meeting of the Continental Congress in 1774, the first bloodshed at Lexington and Concord in 1775, and the Declaration of Independence in 1776.[1]

In the forests of the backcountry, these quarrels might have seemed remote, but some Waxhaw settlers felt strongly about the issues involved. The Hutchinsons and the Crawfords were almost unanimously Whigs—partisans who opposed British interference and favored American freedom. Betty Jackson, who told her sons stories about the English landlords in Ulster and their "oppressions on the laboring poor," may have been typical of settlers who had brought their resentments from Ireland. Many of her neighbors felt the same way. Few in the Waxhaws took the British side, but some—young Daniel Harper, for instance, an immigrant from Antrim who was the only physician on that side of the river—dared to speak out for the king.[2]

Young Hickory

*"Liberty or Death" on this iron fireback, made in the South Carolina
backcountry, expresses the strong Whig feelings of some Carolina Irish
in 1778. William (Billy) Hill, the ironmaster who made it, became a
militia leader at the Battle of Hanging Rock.*
MUSEUM OF EARLY SOUTHERN DECORATIVE ARTS,
WINSTON-SALEM, N.C.

Occasionally, the Whigs had a chance to back up their views with action.
In 1775 and 1776, the new anti-British state authorities, rich Charles Town men
who favored separating from the mother country, asked for volunteer soldiers
for military campaigns. Both times they got a strong response from the Waxhaws. The men mounted their horses and loaded their guns in 1775 to subdue
Cherokees and Loyalists in the western part of the state, and again in 1776 to
repel a British attack on Charles Town. Both campaigns were successful,
short, and marred by only a little bloodshed. A Whig could come home, hang
up his weapon, and feel the satisfaction of having done his duty.[3]

In 1779 this comfortable state of affairs began to change. That spring there was again word of a British attack on Charles Town, and this one seemed more serious; the enemy had taken much of Georgia and was now expected to advance on South Carolina by land and sea. Some backcountry residents prudently moved to North Carolina. Several militia companies set out from the Waxhaws to help defend the capital—on horseback, of course, as they were reluctant to march, like most backcountry men. Captain Crawford led one company, and Robert Montgomery and George Dunlap commanded others. Most of the Crawford men went. Around the same time, William Richardson Davie, who had been studying law in North Carolina, reappeared in the Waxhaws, riding a fine horse. He was now a lieutenant, in command of a North Carolina cavalry company sent to defend Charles Town. Hugh Jackson, sixteen or seventeen years old and eager to fight, had not joined the militia, but now got his mother's permission to join Davie's company. On a horse he had bought or borrowed, he rode down the road to Charles Town with the other cavalrymen, no doubt swaggering a little as he left.[4]

For the next several weeks, through April and May, Waxhaw people with husbands, brothers, or sons in the militia anxiously asked travelers on the Camden Road for news of the campaign. They heard first that General Benjamin Lincoln had marched to recapture Georgia from the British; next, that he had turned around and hastened back because the British were at the gates of Charles Town, and then, that there had almost been a battle, but that the British retreated at the last minute and camped at a distance from the city. In the middle of June, Dunlap's company rode back with the news that there would be no fight, that the British were camped on an island near the coast and would probably retreat to Georgia.[5]

Toward the end of the month, Crawford's and Montgomery's companies returned with a different story. General Lincoln had attacked the British on their island; there had been a battle at a place called Stono, and the Americans had fought badly and lost. Silas Barr from Gill's Creek was dead, Lieutenant Davie was wounded, and Huey Jackson was dying. He had been sick, and Davie had ordered him to stay out of the engagement, but he had gone into battle anyway and had collapsed from exhaustion after it was over. He barely made it home, died almost at once, and was buried quickly in the churchyard.[6]

The recollections many years later of an old woman, Susan Alexander, are the only evidence of the family's reaction. According to her, the mother was distraught at the death of her eldest son and still lamented his loss a year later. Hugh may have been a remarkable lad. The circumstances of his death suggest a determination and boldness like that of his famous youngest brother. Otherwise, beyond the fact that he was no scholar, nothing is known about him. His death darkened the year 1779 for the Jacksons and the Crawfords, but he had given his life for a cause he believed in, not entirely in vain; although the British overcame the Continentals at Stono, they continued their retreat to Georgia, and the invasion was over.[7]

But not for long. In the spring of the following year, 1780, a massive British force descended on Charles Town by land and sea. The call for volunteers went out again, and again the men of the Waxhaws responded, as always including the Crawfords. Robin and Andy Jackson may have wanted to ride with them, but their mother was adamantly opposed. Besides, they were too young: Andy had just turned thirteen, and Robin was no older than sixteen.

It was well for them that they stayed. This time the enemy was too much for the Carolinians. British soldiers and ships besieged the town on all sides, and the defenders, including a large force of Continental troops led by General Lincoln, surrendered. They were released on parole—that is, officers like Robert Crawford (who had been promoted to major) had to give their word not to take up arms again against His Majesty George III. Savoring their victory, the British under Lord Charles Cornwallis began extending their control over the whole province of South Carolina while the defeated Waxhaw men made their way home.[8]

Charles Town capitulated on May 12. On Sunday night, May 28, word reached the Waxhaws that a British cavalry force of several hundred men was moving rapidly toward the area, apparently in pursuit of a Continental army unit that was retreating to North Carolina. To James Crawford and his fellow Whigs, this was disturbing news; they were already marked as enemies of the British, and they could not be sure what these armed men intended. To be on the safe side, they took up their rifles and slipped into the fresh green of the spring woods. Andy and Robin Jackson went with them. There were rumors sweeping the backcountry that the British kidnapped boys and forced them to serve in the army, and Betty Jackson was scared enough to let her sons go with their uncle and cousins.[9]

On May 30, Andy and a Crawford cousin, hidden with their rifles near the edge of the forest along the Camden Road, heard the sound of massed hoof-beats on the road and then saw the troop of green-jacketed cavalrymen riding north on their fine horses. The British dragoons were coming from a battle; they had caught up with the Continental unit and defeated it the day before and were now riding to the Nation to enlist the support of the Catawbas. Andy noticed especially the commander, a lieutenant colonel whose name, Banastre Tarleton, was soon to become a byword for cruelty in the back-country. "Tarleton passed within a hundred yards of where I was," he recalled years later. "I could have shot him," he added, perhaps implying that he and his cousin had their guns loaded and at the ready.[10]

Their business done, Tarleton and his men rode back south the next day toward Camden, and the Whigs were free to come out of hiding. The women of the Waxhaws, doubtless including Betty Jackson, had already hitched up their wagons and headed for the site of the battle, some eleven or twelve miles to the east on what was called the Salisbury Road, to see if they could help the wounded Americans. Terrified survivors, fleeing through the forest, brought word of a slaughter, and that was what the women found. Mass graves held the bodies of over one hundred dead; another hundred and fifty men lay on the field, too badly wounded to move. Tarleton had surveyed the severely wounded and left them on the ground to die; he had taken fifty-five American prisoners to Camden. Their wounds were almost all sword cuts, numerous and deep; arms were chopped off, and at least one American's head was almost severed. ("I have cut 170 Off'rs and Men to pieces" was the way Tarleton described the engagement in his official report.) The survivors in-sisted that Tarleton's force had overpowered them and that the American commander, Colonel Buford, had asked for quarter. The cavalry then at-tacked them again under a flag of truce, killing many more. "Tarleton's quar-ter" and "Bloody Tarleton" became familiar phrases that summer, filling Americans with fear and hatred.[11]

They brought the survivors to the meeting house, which was turned into a hospital: the benches had been moved, and straw had been spread on the floor. Local women, both old and young, took care of the men, changing their bandages, applying poultices, giving them food and water or whiskey. Women came not only from the vicinity but from the settlements across the river as well. The older ones wore long skirts and bonnets; the younger women wore bonnets and the short, tight-fitting shifts and petticoats common in the backcountry.[12]

Andy vividly recalled seeing the wounded there and getting his first impression of what war meant. The men were from Virginia. Most were in their early twenties, same as the older Crawford boys. Some had one arm cut off, some both, but all were covered with gaping wounds. He counted them. "None of the men had less than three or four, and some as many as thirteen gashes on them," he remembered as an old man.[13]

A few days later Colonel Tarleton returned to the neighborhood with a detachment of infantry. He camped at Robert Crockett's farm, or plantation, as it was called. His mission was to have every adult male in the Waxhaws swear an oath of allegiance to King George and promise in writing not to fight against His Majesty. In return, he would guarantee every man who took the oath all the rights of a British subject, including protection from "disorderly people." He sent out a notice for the people to assemble and began giving oaths.[14]

None of the Crawford men intended to take the oath; therefore, they had to avoid Tarleton and his soldiers. ("All true Whiggs kept out of their way," Jackson recalled.) Fortunately, the state line offered them a way. On the North Carolina side, a hastily summoned militia prepared to oppose British entry into their state; they were probably numerous enough to stop Tarleton. The enemy, therefore, would stay out of North Carolina for now. James Crawford, with his sons and nephews, crossed the road into Mecklenburg County and rode through the forest to hide out with the Whigs they knew. Mecklenburg County was full of them, like Colonel Thomas Polk, a good friend, farmer, and militia leader with four wild, daredevil sons involved in the American cause.[15]

They received word of what was happening ten or fifteen miles away at home. They heard that quite a few men had "taken protection," but also that minor frictions were developing with the settlers. It is hard to reconstruct now what these were. The British may have been a little careless about taking settlers' cattle, wheat, and so forth; they were supposed to give receipts but often did not. A British party under the command of one Leonard was attacked and fired on. In any case, Lord Cornwallis recalled Tarleton and replaced him with Francis Lord Rawdon, commander of the Volunteers of Ireland. It was clearly a bridge-building effort, though a clumsy one. Rawdon was the Irish-born, twenty-six-year-old son of the Earl of Moira. The hope was that he would develop a rapport with the Carolina Irish, even though he was a landlord and an Anglican, not a tenant and Presbyterian.[16]

On Saturday, June 10, Rawdon and his soldiers, Ulstermen who had deserted from the American army and enlisted with the British, marched up to the Waxhaws. They made their headquarters on Camp Creek, at the farm of Betty Jackson's brother-in-law John Leslie, and the commander sent for community leaders to talk with him. Several showed up, he reported, who "professed the warmest desire to live under the British Government." One can imagine these Fosters, Dunlaps, or Stephensons—whoever they were—colorfully dressed in their best breeches and coats for the occasion. Mostly Whigs at heart, they took the oath from a mixture of motives, described by a young settler who lived not far away: "some through fear, some through willingness, and others, perhaps, through a hope that all things would settle down and the war cease." Some may have known his lordship from County Down and identified themselves. For his part, the tall, dark, homely young nobleman with the genteel speech and military bearing felt satisfied they were honest, if not entirely cooperative.[17]

He proposed that they form a militia to fight for the king; they temporized, and he did not insist. As for supplying grain for the king's forces, the Waxhaws, they said, was a poor country; but they would provide some cattle, "tho' even in that article," Rawdon reported, "they plead poverty." The attack on the British party, they explained, had been a mistake. They had taken them for "a set of thieves who have long lived in a loose manner," preying on isolated cabins. "They wish much that evidence should be heard upon it," Rawdon told his commander Cornwallis.[18]

A newcomer to the area, Rawdon was ill-equipped to detect that he was being lied to. The Waxhaws was far from poor—there was abundance of grain and cattle. But Waxhaw people, like any small Scottish and Irish farmers, would say whatever they had to say to ward off outsiders. The Anglican missionary Charles Woodmason had learned the same thing fifteen years earlier, when Waxhaw residents coolly told him they had no food or drink in the house in order to get rid of an unwelcome traveler whom they saw as a representative of "priestcraft" and "idolatry." To Woodmason, Waxhaw Presbyterians were crafty double-dealers who traded in horses they knew had been stolen (from Anglicans) and blandly pretended to know nothing about it.[19]

In one claim, though, they were quite sincere. They feared thieves. For ten years or more, parts of the backcountry had been troubled by gangs of outlaws. There was no court nearer than Camden, forty miles away, and no way to catch and punish criminals. Shadowy bands of unknown men—small farmers, hunters, escaped slaves—attacked farms, robbing and sometimes killing their inhabitants. These bands, many of whom would shortly take British protection and become known as "Tories," struck fear into backcountry people. One of the few surviving letters from the Waxhaws, from Jennet Linn to her husband John, who had marched with the militia to Charles Town in 1779, contains a revealing sentence: "No person hath molested me to rob me as yet, though I am many times in great fear when dogs bark at night."[20]

On 12 June, the day after his conference, Rawdon directed a unit of Irish troops to camp at Hanging Rock, on the Camden Road not far from the southern end of the Waxhaws, and rode back to Camden satisfied. It was the last time any British officer would visit the Waxhaws in peace.[21]

And Andy, the youngest of the Crawford men, slipped back into South Carolina with his uncles and cousins and listened as they debated what to do next.

CHAPTER FIVE

Uprising
June–July 1780

F OR THE REST of the summer of 1780, thirteen-year-old Andrew Jackson and his family were like chips of debris on a surging river, powerless to control events, witnesses to violent and important happenings, in danger of going under at any moment. Young Jackson is almost invisible in the historical record, which is hardly surprising; he was far too young to take a leadership role. The few stories about his activities in this stage of the Revolution are either fictitious or confused transpositions of later events. Although he was not making the decisions, he was keenly aware of the issues and keenly observant of the men around him; for instance, that summer he witnessed the beginning of the career of the man he would later describe as the best commander he had ever known, William R. Davie. It is important to try to follow him through the tumult of this summer, and the best way of doing so is to track the actions of his kinsmen, the Crawfords.[1]

James Crawford, his sons, and the Jackson brothers crossed the border to their homes as soon as Rawdon left. The older Crawfords found themselves in a frustrating situation. Committed Whigs, they wanted to oppose the British, but there was no instrument they could use. The patriot South Carolina government had collapsed; there was no state support for their militia. Robert Crawford, George Dunlap, and Robert Montgomery, nominal leaders of the Waxhaw men, could muster only two or three hundred, hardly enough to confront Rawdon or Tarleton without help from outside. And they could not count on all their neighbors. Some had taken the oath; others had talked peace with Rawdon.

The alternative was to leave their homes, go into North Carolina, and join a military unit there, and a few may actually have done that—there is evidence that Will Crawford, for instance, joined a North Carolina company around this time. But by doing so they would leave their farms and their families at the mercy of the enemy and the roving bands of outlaws. It was nearly impossible for men like James and Robert Crawford, who possessed large families and substantial property.[2]

Fortunately, events moved swiftly and soon made their course clear. On 14 June, three days after Lord Rawdon rode back to Camden, alarming news arrived from across the river. British Colonel George Turnbull, Rawdon's counterpart west of the Catawba, had sent one of his captains on Sunday, 11 June, on a raid into the Irish settlements there. The captain was a Loyalist from one of the Northern states, New York or Pennsylvania (backcountry Whigs soon called them all "York Tories"), named Christian Huyck or Huck. His orders were to arrest two Presbyterian ministers, William Martin and John Simpson, who had been advising their congregations not to take the oath. (Waxhaw congregation still had no minister; if it had, he probably would have been in similar trouble.) Huyck had missed Simpson, who was preaching elsewhere that day, but arrested Martin. His men burned Simpson's house and library, stole his possessions, and raided other homes, where they shot a young man dead for resisting their theft of a bridle. All Rawdon's assurances about peace and security under British protection were suddenly revealed as so much empty talk.[3]

The Waxhaws and the communities to the west were, in effect, one big Irish Presbyterian settlement. Word of Huyck's threats and exploits flew across the Catawba and became more vivid as it spread. His attacks on ministers touched a fear constant in Presbyterians' minds: that British Anglicans, covert allies of the Pope, were trying once again to wipe out the true church. The stories about Huyck emphasized his enmity to religion. He was said to have cursed all Presbyterians, burned Bibles, and blasphemed against God. Some settlers had the impression that he was an English nobleman, and called him "Lord Hook." At the Strongs' house, it was alleged, he cut off the head of a tame pigeon in the yard and told Mrs. Strong, "Madam, I have cut off the head of the Holy Ghost." His men killed young William Strong, who was reading his Bible, and then hacked him with their swords. Reports like this galvanized the Carolina Irish in a way that nothing else could have done; it seemed that an incarnate devil was loose in the backcountry, brought by the British to persecute the faithful.[4]

Beginning on June 11, a steady stream of young men from both sides of the river left their homes and crossed into North Carolina looking to join a unit. A few days later, an ill-advised decision by British high commander Sir Henry Clinton turned the stream into a flood. The settlers had been granted protection up to now on condition that they not fight against the British; but beginning June 20, they would have to take a new oath and promise to fight for the British when called upon. If not, they would be treated as enemies.[5]

At this point, the Crawfords gained support from their more moderate neighbors. There was no way that community leaders like Robert and James Crawford, Andrew Foster, and George Dunlap could take that oath and pledge themselves to fire on fellow American Whigs. They had to resist, but the problems of organizing a resistance were huge. Who would be their leader? Where would they get supplies? Could they expect any help from the Congress in Philadelphia or from the North Carolina state troops? The Crawford household seems to have been a rather verbal one, and Andy Jackson probably heard these questions debated frequently between James Crawford and his neighbors.

As they debated, the picture continued to change. The hundreds of South Carolinians in North Carolina, who had at first enlisted in that state's units, organized their own company. On June 15 they selected a commander, Thomas Sumter, an immigrant from Virginia who lived below Camden. Tarleton had burned the dark-haired, pugnacious militia colonel's home in May.[6]

At first his men fought under North Carolina command. On June 20, they were at the scene of the Battle of Ramseur's Mill (they took no part owing to a mix-up), in which a force of Loyalists was defeated, but a few days later Sumter decided to fight the British regulars in South Carolina. He moved the camp to a branch of Sugar Creek on the state line, at the edge of the thick-forested, primeval, fifteen-mile-square tract belonging to the Catawbas, and called for more recruits. This was the opportunity the Waxhaw men had been waiting for. Whether or not they had sworn allegiance to the king, they saddled their horses, grabbed their rifles and shot bags, and poured in.[7]

*Virginia-born Thomas Sumter was forty-five years old when he became the
military leader of South Carolina's Whigs. His fighting spirit and his
eloquence almost made up for his casual generalship.*
SOUTH CAROLINIANA LIBRARY, UNIVERSITY OF
SOUTH CAROLINA, COLUMBIA, S.C.

The Crawfords were among the first to arrive. Will Crawford signed up as
Sumter's adjutant on June 21. Tommy joined June 23, and Jim two days later.
Indeed, on June 25 the men of the Waxhaws enlisted en masse. Several militia
captains—George Dunlap, Robert Montgomery, Robert Crawford—went
over to Sumter that day with their entire companies, and took an oath to drive
the British from South Carolina. (By doing so, they violated their paroles and
laid themselves open to summary hanging if captured.) Chief New River and
several of his Catawbas arrived to swell the force. Andrew Foster, with his
storekeeping experience, joined a few days later as Sumter's quartermaster.
Until the fighting got rough, these men drilled with Sumter's troops on
Clem's Branch by day and rode home to their farms at night.[8]

William R. Davie, the nephew of the minister at Waxhaw Meeting House
and eleven years older than Jackson, achieved everything that Jackson
aspired to: he became a daring cavalry leader in the Revolution, a successful
lawyer, and a prosperous slaveholder. They knew each other
but were not close friends.

NORTH CAROLINA DEPARTMENT OF ARCHIVES AND HISTORY

Robin and Andy Jackson were at the camp frequently, but not as soldiers. At their mother's orders, they could drill but not fight. They helped with the supply wagons; many Waxhaw farmers sent flour or meat to feed the Whig soldiers camped at the edge of the Catawba Nation's land. (Lord Rawdon, in Camden, fumed that the Waxhaw people whom he had trusted were playing "a double game," and that unless he did something "all the wheat of the country [would] be carried off to the Enemy.") These goods were paid for in indents—I.O.U.s—drawn on the South Carolina state government; if the Whigs won the war, the farmers would be repaid.[9]

Andy and Robin watched, and probably joined in, as the men went through their exercises, races, and wrestling and jumping contests in the deep woods, just like the boys' sports in the Waxhaws. This was the only kind of drill Sumter could afford; his men had precious little powder and shot to waste on practice. Waxhaw housewives contributed pewter dishes and utensils for them to melt for bullets, but still they had hardly enough for a battle. Indeed, they had none of the equipment of an eighteenth-century army—no medical supplies, no cannon, no cooking equipment, no uniforms—and none of the discipline; according to an observer, the guard they mounted around their camp was "careless and slovenly." All they had was what they brought, mostly horses and guns. Sumter and a few other officers had their militia uniforms; the rest—"poor hunting-shirt fellows," as a partisan that summer described himself and his mates—wore work clothes, hunting shirts, wool hats, and tow trousers or overalls. What they did have, though, was numbers—several hundred by the beginning of July. Some observers estimated a thousand.[10]

At that time, a familiar face showed up in the Waxhaws. William R. Davie arrived on the northern side of the Waxhaws in late June with a corps of cavalry. His official mission was "to prevent the Enemy from foraging on the borders of the State adjacent to the Waxhaws and check the depredations of the Loyalists who infested that part of the Country." He interpreted these orders liberally enough to send detachments into South Carolina against British foraging parties; skirmishes happened every day for some time, he recalled, until the British became "more cautious and respectful." Davie, now promoted to major in the North Carolina militia, was learning the military trade well; methodical and cautious, he was also persistently aggressive, even with his small force. A number of men from Robert Crawford's company began serving under his command.[11]

Davie was frequently at Major Crawford's house planning operations and discussing strategy; Andy Jackson had ample opportunity to observe close-up the man he would later call the finest soldier he had ever known. Twenty-four-year-old Davie was, like the adult Jackson, tall and lean, with dark hair and a long nose in a long face ("face not so good tho' handsome enough," as a North Carolina lady described it), a good horseman, poised, genteel, incisive in speech, and had the loud voice a commander needed.[12]

Early in July, Davie and Sumter mounted a joint operation only a mile from Andy's home, at the Waxhaw Creek ford. They planned to ambush two units of regulars sent by Rawdon to the Waxhaws to confiscate the rest of the wheat and prevent its falling into Whig hands. Davie's horsemen and one hundred "gunmen" hid in the open woods overlooking the ford from the north side, while five hundred of Sumter's riflemen concealed themselves in a thick wood west of the road, too thick for cavalry to act. Clearly, memories of the wounded from Buford's defeat were still vivid. The British would be checked by the fire from across the creek, and Sumter's men would close the trap behind them. But the British heard through informers that several hundred armed men were waiting for them and turned back to Camden. The men waited all night and saw no enemy.[13]

Doubtless, many Waxhaw men, including the young Jacksons, were frustrated and disappointed at not coming to grips with the enemy. Sumter, however, thinking it over, was probably glad. His men simply were not well enough equipped. They might have used up all their ammunition in that one encounter. Around 9 or 10 July, he disbanded his troops, sent them all home for a week or more to harvest their wheat and to recruit new fighters, while he traveled the backcountry in search of powder and bullets. Davie's cavalry watched the Waxhaws in his absence.[14]

Three or four days after Sumter's departure, electrifying news reached the Waxhaws from across the river: Captain Huyck was dead, shot down in an ambush by some of Sumter's men acting under their own commanders. The backcountry Whigs, when they heard the news, were joyful and full of fight. As Billy Hill, one of Sumter's officers, put it, the affair "had the tendency to inspire the Americans with courage & fortitude & to teach them that the enemy was not invincible."[15]

At the same time, the Whigs learned that an army of Continentals was on its way south to defend the Carolinas. Commanded by the Baron de Kalb, it was already in North Carolina and would probably come through the Waxhaws soon. Its approach offered local Whigs, emboldened by Huyck's death, a good chance to strike at the British and weaken them. Davie decided to try an attack. The British post at Hanging Rock had exhausted all the food available from nearby farms in that rather barren area and was getting its food and supplies by wagon from the headquarters in Camden. He and his men would ambush a provision wagon. The evening of 20 July, they left camp and marched all night through the woods, bypassing the Hanging Rock post and coming out on the Camden Road at the Flat Rock, four and a half miles farther south. Some volunteers from the Waxhaws went with them, led by Will

Polk, Thomas Polk's son, a fearless, experienced fighter. Some of the Crawfords were probably among them. They hid by the road until afternoon, when the wagon showed up. They stopped it, overpowered the wagoners and guards, destroyed the provisions, and galloped back to the Waxhaws with a few prisoners, evading a Tory ambush on the way. Davie's action showed that it was possible for the Whigs to hit the enemy, rather than waiting for the enemy to strike them.[16]

When Sumter returned around July 22 with the promise of more powder and ball, he and Davie planned a coordinated attack. Several of his captains had been scouting the British post at Rocky Mount, west of the river, and were convinced that with enough numbers they could seize it. Hanging Rock was on the east. The general (Sumter's men had elected him general) and the major planned to attack both posts at the same time and keep them from reinforcing each other. It was a bold, really a foolhardy plan, with Sumter's untrained, ill-supplied troops and Davie's small numbers, but they conferred and agreed to try it.[17]

Late in the afternoon of Saturday, July 29, the two groups of Whig soldiers moved out on horseback, Sumter's infantry as well as Davie's cavalry. Sumter's hundreds of men, west of the crossing at Land's Ford, headed for Rocky Mount south through the woods. Davie's eighty horsemen, east of the ford, headed for Hanging Rock. The Crawford men rode with Sumter. Though the day was sultry and brooding with thunderstorms, the families of the Waxhaw men watched them go with enthusiasm. Surely, they thought, God would use them to punish the wicked British oppressor.[18]

Two days later Davie's troops were back. They had arrived at Hanging Rock in the afternoon and spotted a group of North Carolina Tories camped some distance from the British tents. They attacked and took them completely off guard. They forced them into the corner of a fenced yard, where they hacked many of them to death with homemade swords. Davie took no prisoners; he did not want to be slowed down by captives if the British regulars pursued him. His raid netted "sixty valuable Horses with their furniture together with one hundred muskets and rifles" and the beginnings of a reputation comparable to Tarleton's. The British called his men "the bloody corps." He had not lost a single man.[19]

Word from Sumter was slower in coming, but on the third or fourth of August people in the Waxhaws heard that his attack failed and he lost a few men. The enemy fort had been too strong. But he was still full of fight. People in the Waxhaws began calling him "the Gamecock" that summer, and for good reason: like a champion fighting cock, he would absorb a blow, a bloody gash, a loss, and come right back. While still near Rocky Mount, his scouts observed a reinforcement of several hundred men march in from Hanging Rock. To Sumter, that meant one thing: Hanging Rock was weak and undermanned, ripe for an attack. If his and Davie's men joined forces and hit the depleted garrison at Hanging Rock, they would likely win a major victory.[20]

Davie was agreeable, if Sumter could get his men across the river. The Catawba was high, almost flooded. The Direction Rock at Land's Ford, the Catawbas' gauge of whether it was safe to cross, was underwater. Sumter ordered a crossing that nearly ended in disaster. For the militia, it was "deep wading" through a rapid current. Horses lost their footing and were swept downstream, packs of supplies fell off and were lost, and men nearly drowned. Not long before dark on the afternoon of 5 August, they all had crossed the river. Sumter let his wet and exhausted men rest a couple of hours before the march.[21]

Everyone was keyed up that afternoon. Young Captain James White Stephenson, Andy's old teacher, joined the attacking army with his local company. A company of two Mecklenburg County militia had joined. There was a sense of great events impending; Sumter's men were full of "great spirit & cheerfulness." They were going to capture Hanging Rock and needed every man who could take part. Amazingly, the Crawford men prevailed on Betty Jackson to let Andy and Robin go with them, not to fight, just to help out. They promised to take good care of them.[22]

At dusk, the troops mustered at the ford. Jackson as a grown man made no attempt to describe what his feelings were then, as a thirteen-year old. Perhaps he did not need to—one can supply a description from the standard eve-of-battle repertory: exhilaration, doubt, worry, joy, fear. And in Jackson's case, probably keen, fierce anticipation.

CHAPTER SIX

Hanging Rock
August 1780

—⚬⚬⚬—

I N THE DARK, under the dim light of a setting moon, the Jackson boys rode south toward Hanging Rock amid Sumter's five hundred men and the North Carolinians. The night was warm and damp; the scent of summer vegetation surrounded them. The men stank of horses, sweat, and tobacco. They acted easy and casual, as men in that culture tended to do before battle, but Andy soon learned they had cause to be nervous. Many were nearly out of ammunition, having only two or three bullets. So, they had to surprise the British. It was like still-hunting for deer. Every shot had to count.[1]

Those who had no gun at all would stay with the horses as the action began. When an enemy soldier fell or ran away, they would grab his musket and go into the fight. Their strategy underscored what, for most of Sumter's men, the engagement was all about. It was less a battle than a raid. These backcountrymen aimed to frighten the enemy, run them off, killing as many or as few as necessary, and then plunder their property—horses, guns, and stores. That would be a victory.[2]

Long after midnight, the raiders stopped at a place only a couple of miles from the British camp and waited for all the men to catch up. They were expecting two spies to come back from the enemy camp and report. Meanwhile, they halted stragglers on the dark road and put them under guard so that the British would get no hint of their presence.[3]

Hanging Rock

Hanging Rock, a well-known landmark on the Camden Road (seen here in a photo from the 1970s), was in a creek valley south of the Waxhaws. The rock's overhang was large enough to shelter several men. The battle of Hanging Rock was fought on a hilltop above the creek valley.

LANCASTER COUNTY HISTORICAL SOCIETY

Andy and Robin no doubt stayed with their cousins, as the custom was in the backcountry. Kinsmen provided a support system to defend or avenge each other. Lieutenant Jim Crawford probably sat in on the strategy councils with his Uncle Robert. Close to Major Crawford, then, or to Major Davie, Andy and Robin may have heard some of the discussions and plans for attack, carried on in the soft accents of County Antrim and County Tyrone.[4]

The British, according to Davie, were camped in a clearing on the Camden Road, an old fallow field next to the big house of the Ingram family. Woods bordered it on two sides. Some Tories, the same ones Davie had mauled, were camped in the woods along the road some distance away. The whole site was on the top of a hill, above Hanging Rock Creek. The giant rock outcropping near the creek was a landmark for miles around. They would ford the creek, come up the slope, and find tents, horses, wagons, and all. The only British fortifications were some earthworks facing the road. But if the Whigs attempted a frontal attack from the road, they would be exposed to the full fire of the British regulars, and that of the Tories on their flank.[5]

Sumter's idea was to leave the road for the woods, with the help of a local guide, and use the ravine of Hanging Rock Creek to get to the foot of the hill. He had hoped to position his men during the night for a daybreak attack, but the delay at Land's Ford had slowed things down. Nevertheless, in a council of war with Davie and the other senior officers, they decided to stick with the plan: Before sunrise, they would ride off the road and approach the hill as silently as possible. Most of Sumter's men and the Mecklenburg militia would go left to engage the British; Davie and Colonel Winn would turn right to surprise the Tories. Meanwhile, they caught a little sleep.[6]

Just before setting out at daybreak, they captured two Tories who had unwelcome news: The three hundred men sent to Rocky Mount had returned to camp in the middle of the night, so the enemy was at full strength, with over a thousand men counting Bryan's Tories. The Whigs had fewer than five hundred men with guns, but they had the advantage of surprise. As the sun rose on the morning of August 6, the council of war reconvened to consider the bad tidings, with everyone a little shaken; but as Richard Winn remembered it, "no officer was willing to be outdone by the others in bravery," so "the action immediately commenced."[7]

Sumter's band rode down the forested morning freshness of the ravine and got to the foot of the hill, eluding the British picket guards on the road. The smell of the campfires and the sound of horses' bells told them they were close. They dismounted, leaving their horses in the charge of the unarmed Africans and youngsters like Andy, and silently crossed the creek. Some stuck green leaves in their hats so that their fellow Whigs could identify them in the heat of battle, since neither they nor the Tories wore uniforms. (Whig officers apparently wore coats in token of their rank. Sumter wore one, and so did Jim Crawford.) With weapons loaded, powder in their pockets, and musket balls in their mouths for ready availability, the men moved quietly up the steep slope. A number of them had homemade bayonets mounted on their firearms.[8]

Whether Robin Jackson went with them is unknown. Certainly, boys his age, fifteen or sixteen, were among the attackers; on the other hand, so many men stayed with the horses that it would have been no disgrace for him to do so.

Andy, in any case, certainly stayed behind. The historians and other writers who have portrayed him as participating overlook not only Betty Jackson's fierce determination to keep her youngest out of the fight, but also the fact that Jackson himself as an old man, reviewing his Revolutionary War experience, declared himself unable to give an account of the battle. Not only had he not participated in the fighting, he had not even seen it. He was down in the wooded ravine from six to ten in the morning, while the sun rose higher, the day grew hotter, and the battle raged on the heights above him.[9]

The men and boys down below must have experienced the Battle of Hanging Rock primarily as a series of noises. No doubt, from time to time, somebody scurried up the hill to have a look at what was going on, but the smoke, confusion, and danger made it difficult and unrewarding. Increasingly, wounded men stumbled down the slope, some with minor wounds, others with ghastly ones. Others came down with items of plunder they stashed near their horses and told how the battle was progressing. But mainly there were noises. First, they heard the crack of muskets and an outbreak of Native American-style war whoops (the "Indian hollo," Colonel Winn called it, a high-pitched howl similar to the later Rebel yell) as the Whigs attacked from ambush. There was answering fire; bullets whistled overhead, flicked through the leaves, and occasionally landed near them. The gunfire slackened; then, about half an hour later, there was a much more substantial burst of fire, slightly farther away, which went on fiercely for a long time. Then there were distant sounds of fife and drum, the war whoops again, men yelling, horses neighing, and the heavy thump of cannon firing. It continued for perhaps an hour, then died down to an occasional pop of a musket. For a time there was quiet, interrupted by a couple of distant exchanges of fire and then, oddly enough, the sound of three cheers, several times repeated. Soon after, survivors of the battle began coming down the hill, leading horses laden with saddles and guns, carrying boxes and pieces of gear, many of them with faces black with gunpowder.

What happened, as Andy later pieced it together, was this. The guide led the attackers too far to the right; instead of Sumter attacking the British and Davie the Tories, the whole Whig force fell on the unfortunate North Carolina Tories, firing one shot and then rushing the enemy with their weapons reversed to use as clubs. The Tories, being almost as poorly armed as Sumter's men, put up only brief resistance and then ran away. The Whigs took over their camp and proceeded to attack the Prince of Wales regiment in the center of the camp. Many of the men in this regiment were, like their attackers, Irish born; it was Ireland confronting Ireland in the forests of Carolina. This was where the bloody fighting took place. At one point, some of the British staged a regular charge with fife, drum, and bayonet, but their officers were cut down by American sharpshooters firing from behind or up in the trees. The Americans also took heavy losses before the remaining British finally surrendered to Davie.

Then there was a lull. The British on the far left, gathered near the Ingram house, formed a hollow square to resist a Whig attack, while the backcountrymen busied themselves looting the camp in the center of all the clothing, valuables, and guns. Foaming with sweat and thirsty from the hot blast of gunpowder, they concentrated on the British rum. Both Sumter and Davie tried to muster an attack to finish the battle, but the men, hot, tired, and disorganized or drunk or both, were in no mood for more fighting. The arrival of a small British reinforcement squelched any plans for an attack, and the Americans gradually retreated under the eyes of the enemy, who let them go unmolested and gave three cheers for King George. The Carolinians answered, with Irish combativeness, with three cheers for General Washington as they gathered up their wounded and their plunder.[10]

That was the course of the battle. As they rode back, Andy heard many stories of the fighting. Exactly what he heard is impossible to know two centuries later, but the tales about Hanging Rock—the blood, the fear, the slaughter—that were handed down the generations and picked up by nineteenth-century collectors give the flavor:

Two backcountry Whigs, Alex Walker and John McFadden, were pursuing the Tories when they cut and ran, but since everyone was wearing the hat, hunting shirt, and overalls of the backcountry, it was hard to tell friend from foe as the pursuit went on. Walker raised his musket to fire, and a man caught his arm. "Those are on our side!" he shouted. Then he looked at Walker. "What is that green leaf in your hat for?" All at once it occurred to Walker that he and McFadden had run in among a group of armed Tories without knowing it. Realizing who they were, the Tories pointed their guns at Walker.

Hanging Rock

One lunged at him with a bayonet. Walker ran as someone fired. He raced back downhill toward the creek. Nothing was hurting, but he could hear something dripping on the leaves as he ran through them. He assumed it was blood. He would die of exhaustion and loss of blood as he had seen men die at Rocky Mount. When he reached the creek he flung himself down for a last drink of water, and found he was not hurt, but that his powder horn had been punctured by a rifle ball and had been leaking its contents all during his flight. He also realized McFadden was not with him. McFadden, in fact, was back on top of the hill, dead.[11]

Four sons of John Gaston, Robert, David, Ebenezer, and Joseph—Robert in his thirties, Joseph only seventeen, the others in between—rushed into the attack on the British camp together, as brothers did in battle. It was an unfortunate move. Two of the older brothers were killed instantly; the third, wounded, died on top of their bodies. Joseph, the youngest, raised his gun to fire at a British soldier who was aiming straight at him. A ball grazed his nose and tore through the side of his cheek. Spitting blood and broken teeth, he got to the edge of the battleground and dropped flat. A little later, after the fife-and-drum charge, he managed to ask another Carolinian with a better view how the battle was going. "We are killing them like wild turkeys," he was told. He hoped so.[12]

Dick Wright cornered a British officer who offered him his gold watch to spare his life. Perhaps with "Tarleton's quarter" in mind, Dick ran the man through the guts with his bayonet, then took the watch and other gold from his pockets.[13]

Officers were not immune to injuries. Whig officers, one veteran recalled, "fought like common soldiers and animated their men by their example, and they suffered severely." Sumter was shot in the thigh but concealed the wound until the battle was over. Colonel Winn took a hit from a ball that penetrated one arm, grazed his chest, and went through the other arm. Colonel Billy Hill "was shot under the shoulder blade and the blood spirted [sic] out— seeing which, the surgeon said—'let me take you to the field—you cannot long survive—& had better be where you will not be run over.' 'If I die, I'll die upon Flim Nap [his horse],' said the wounded Colonel, & putting spurs to his horse, dashed off." Colonel Hill survived.[14]

As the victors descended the hill with their loot and their wounded, young Jackson watched for Robin and the Crawfords. He finally spotted them, their faces blackened like the rest, carrying Jim Crawford, who had taken a bullet through the body and was evidently dying. It had gone straight through; someone had drawn a pocket handkerchief through the wound to clean it out. Jim was faint and unable to ride. Tommy, Uncle Crawford, and Will debated what to do and finally laid him at the edge of the creek, put his coat underneath his head for a pillow, said their goodbyes, and rode away north. In a day or two the women would come and recover his body.[15]

Riding back exhausted under the blazing sun of an August noon, Hanging Rock felt like a victory to most of Sumter's men. It had been a successful raid: they had badly bloodied the British and brought away a lot of plunder—"about one hundred horses, two hundred & fifty stand of arms, with other articles of Considerable Value," Sumter wrote proudly in a letter intended for the eyes of General Horatio Gates, who had taken command of the Continental force marching to confront the British. But Sumter knew, as did Davie and anyone who could see the larger picture, that it was a half-victory at best. They had failed to smash or capture the British units. They had abandoned the field and left the enemy in possession. Sumter, in his report, blamed the failure on "want of led"; his men could not defeat an army while they were desperately scavenging the fallen enemy for ammunition. Davie saw a fundamental cause: in a local militia like Sumter's, the men obeyed only their company commanders, who were their neighbors or kinsmen. Once a battle began, it was impossible for a general commander to order them to take advantage of a new situation. Only a disciplined army, like Gates and his Continentals, would be able to coordinate its action well enough to beat the British.[16]

To families like the Crawfords and Jacksons, the battle brought mingled satisfaction and sorrow. They had struck a blow for freedom and against popery; they had perhaps shared in the spoils; but they had paid a price. Will Crawford had lost a horse, and Christiana Crawford had lost her husband of four months.[17]

Andy and Robin reached the Crawford house with their sad news late in the afternoon. The next morning, Betty Jackson and Christiana Crawford put on their bonnets, hitched up the wagon, and set out to recover Jim's body. They were not alone. Many women—wives, sisters, and mothers, some with children in tow—headed for the battlefield to find their missing men. Meantime, the survivors of the battle went their separate ways. Davie and his troops rode to Charlotte to set up a hospital. Sumter, after distributing the plunder, had his wound dressed and sent his men to gallop home for a quick visit with their families. The dozen or so Catawbas who had fought on the Whig side went home to their land. The Waxhaw meeting house was again full of the wounded.

Driving a wagon down the dusty, rutted road was slower going than on horseback, and the two women did not reach the area until nightfall. To their joy and complete surprise, they found Jim alive. The exact circumstances are not quite clear. By one account, he had been moved to a nearby cabin by a compassionate Irish soldier who came from the same part of County Antrim. A Tory had stolen his coat and may have wounded him further. In any event, he was alive, but very weak. They brought him home the next day. He recovered surprisingly fast. By fall, he was out fighting again.[18]

With Sumter's men encamped on Cane Creek, the settlement was abuzz with rumors, news, and questions. When were Gates and the Continental troops coming? Would Lord Rawdon attack the Waxhaws? At the same time, it was the height of harvest season, and there was work to do. Boys Andy Jackson's age were out in the orchards picking peaches and taking them to the still house to ferment and be run off into peach brandy. Others were in the wheat fields harvesting the grain and then taking it to the mill. They'd lounge around the big bare interior talking war news with the miller as the noisy stones ground the wheat into flour. The corn was not ready for full harvest, but some of the golden, tender ears known as roasting ears—similar to corn on the cob, but rather smaller— could be picked and cooked over the fire. As often as they could, however, the boys slipped off to Sumter's camp to examine the plundered British horses and guns, hear battle tales and techniques, and listen to the songs men were making, as they fitted their commander's deeds into the Irish ballad tradition:

> When we were first in banishment bold Sumter took command
> And on the borders of our state there we did make a stand
> For to subdue the English and keep down Popery
> Huzza for General Sumter! Huzza for Liberty![19]

Abruptly, on August 12, the situation changed. Captain Fred Kimball, whom Sumter had sent with his letter to Gates, came galloping back. Gates and three thousand Continentals were only a day's ride away, he said. They had come not by the Wagon Road but by way of the Cheraws and were approaching Camden from the east. A major battle was clearly going to take place at Camden, and Sumter could help by getting out and harassing British supply routes.[20]

No more welcome assignment could have been given to Sumter and his hungry men. Joined by dozens of new recruits from west of the river, they struck camp and rode out confidently that day, across Land's Ford and then southward. With the wounding of two senior colonels at Hanging Rock, Robert Crawford was now a field commander in Sumter's army; his nephews, Tommy, Joey, and Will, rode with him, along with his captains, Henry Coffey, Hugh White, Moses Stephenson, and George Dunlap, and a host of assorted Whites, Crocketts, Dunlaps, Fosters, and Montgomerys. The men of the Waxhaws were out en masse, and not merely the younger men. With the success of Sumter's army at Hanging Rock, his efforts to drive back the enemy had attracted the support of community leaders, fathers, and grandfathers of families, "grey headed men," in Davie's words, who "turned out to encourage & animate" their juniors.[21]

Andy Jackson definitely did not ride with them, but there is some reason to suppose that Robin did. He was, for one thing, just old enough to fight; more importantly, his name vanishes from the records of the Jackson family for the next few months. There is little enough data about any of the Jacksons in late 1780 and early 1781, but Robin is missing from what little there is. He may well have been with his Crawford cousins, separated from his mother and brother by the cataclysm that was about to sweep over the Waxhaws.[22]

Under the deadly August heat, the settlement was strangely quiet in the days after August 12, when Sumter's men rode away. The women and children, boys, old men, and African laborers left on the farms went about their work with an ear cocked for the sound of hoofbeats, gunfire, the boom of a distant cannon, any clue about what was happening to the armies. Early on August 15, Major Davie and his North Carolinians passed through, on their way to reinforce Gates.[23]

The following day, around midmorning, there was a sudden surge of traffic on the Camden Road: men on sweaty horses galloping northward or driving wagons furiously in the same direction. Gates had been defeated, they said; his army had been smashed by Lord Cornwallis north of Camden. Waxhaw settlers who were on the road at precisely the right time saw Gates him-

Hanging Rock

self, a portly man in a sky-blue coat and velvet breeches, stop to change horses as he galloped hell-for-leather toward Charlotte.

This unexpected defeat was among the most severe losses suffered by the American army during the war. In the late afternoon, exhausted, hungry foot soldiers began appearing on the road and in the woods, stopping at the Crawford houses for water and food. Their retreat had been an ordeal; the butcher Tarleton and his cavalry had pursued the fleeing Americans with their sabers, killing and taking prisoners. But he had turned back after twenty miles. Bands of Tory raiders and plunderers were also after them, but Davie and a few others had mounted a rear-guard action and kept them off.[24]

Sumter and his troops had not been in the battle. Presumably they were safe, but no one could tell where they were. Through the sweltering heat of August 17 and 18, the Waxhaw people tried to cope with the flood of hungry, wounded Virginians, Marylanders, and North Carolinians passing through their homes while wondering about the fate of their own fathers and brothers.[25]

It was probably late in the afternoon of 18 August when one or two frantic men on horseback rode into the settlement. Tarleton had struck again, they said. In a separate attack, he crossed the river and surprised Sumter's men while they were resting, exhausted by the heat, on the bank of Fishing Creek. Sumter himself escaped, but many local men were dead or taken prisoner. The news had implications of deadly fear. The women, children, and older people of the settlement were now open to the malice of enemies who wanted their property and cared nothing for their lives; and there was no one left to defend them.[26]

CHAPTER SEVEN

Refugees
August 1780–January 1781

VOLUBLE, BUSY BETTY JACKSON was a decisive woman. From the moment the news came, she knew what to do, although it was the hardest decision she had faced since her husband's death. She, Andy, and Robin would have to abandon all the property, the comfort she and her sister's family had wrung out of the wilderness—linen, still house, pigs, peach trees, spinning wheels—and take to the road to save their lives. Moreover, they would have to act fast and perhaps separately. The British and Tories might descend on the settlement at any moment.

She crossed the road to Peggy and George McCamie's cabin. They too had heard the news and were preparing to flee with their movable property, some horses, and a slave girl named Charlotte. George had cousins in Mecklenburg who could give them shelter as long as necessary. Betty Jackson decided she and Andy would go with them, joining the throngs of refugees fleeing the Waxhaws.[1]

It was not an easy choice. The recollections, years later, of a woman who helped to shelter the Jacksons on their flight state positively that Robin Jackson was not with them. There were only five in the party: two Jacksons, two McCamies, and Charlotte. Robin must have been with his male Crawford relatives—safe, but wholly out of touch. Nor did Betty's foster son Jim Crawford, sick at home, go with them; his wound probably prevented him from traveling. Perhaps he found shelter with his wife's family, the Whites. The sudden breakup of family ties suggests the pressure under which they were all acting.[2]

One would like to know how much reliable information Betty was able to sift from all the reports flying around about Sumter's defeat, as the engagement came to be called. For instance, did she know that Tommy and his father were safe, but that Will and Joey were captives of the British? Did she hear that Major Crawford, who was safe but lost his horse and his silver mounted sword, was being blamed for the defeat? As officer of the day, he was responsible for posting guards while the army rested; but he found a bottle of whiskey, drank freely, and passed out. It was not entirely his fault; the day was stiflingly hot, and he, like all of Sumter's men, was exhausted from a day of hard riding, trying to get out of range of the British. Sumter himself thought they were safe. They camped on a neck of land between Fishing Creek and the river, protected on two sides. A number of the men were bathing in the river when Tarleton's horsemen burst on them without warning. Wakened by the attack, Crawford ran to the river and swam across. On the far side of the broad river, out of range of enemy guns and still drunk, he turned and slapped his buttocks contemptuously at the British before running for cover.[3]

The main impact of Sumter's Defeat, though, lay not in individual stories but in the community trauma. Every single grown man in the Waxhaws, apart from a few Tories, had been fighting with Sumter. Now all the men, the protectors of the community, were dead, wounded, prisoners, or at best fugitives. In the cool, detached language of eighteenth-century prose, William R. Davie summarized his neighbors' tragedy: "Sumpters [sic] defeat was marked with the capture and slaughter of a large part of the inhabitants of this populous settlement." As in Liberia or the Balkans of the late twentieth century, the whole human structure of the Waxhaw settlement was destroyed. The whites were dead or refugees; most of the Africans had fled to the British lines, where they understood (incorrectly) that they would be freed—except for those, like Charlotte, who were forced to accompany their white owners.[4]

Probably the Jacksons and Crawfords, like many Ulster Irish families, had a treasure or two—gold coins, silver, perhaps a piece of jewelry—hoarded away in a box under the house or in the well or in the fireplace. Just before they left, Andy and his mother buried these items somewhere on the family's land, to be unearthed if they returned safely. Then they loaded their little horses with saddlebags full of foodstuffs and went to join their kinsmen.[5]

The Jacksons and McCamies spent the next day in a throng of fleeing neighbors with their possessions, wagons, and livestock, pouring north, full of rumors and fragments of news about Sumter and his men. As usual with refugees, the company was all old men, women, boys, and slaves. They crossed Twelve Mile Creek and the empty lands of the Catawba Nation. They forded McAlpin's Creek and sweated up the steep bank on the far side. Actually, they were lucky that the weather was hot and dry. A strong thundershower could have converted either creek into a raging torrent and shut off all traffic on the road. South of Charlotte, the dusty road divided, with the left-hand fork going into the town and the right-hand one off toward Sugar Creek Church and Salisbury. A militia officer on horseback stood at the fork, urging the refugees to the right, toward Salisbury and beyond the reach of immediate enemy attack. He asked people what they knew about Sumter's fate and the movements of the British. Betty Jackson and her party followed the crowd to the right.[6]

Toward the end of the day, their homespun stained with sweat, they arrived at the log house of a kinswoman of McCamie's northeast of Charlotte. As in the Waxhaws, the men were out fighting. This was a household of women and children. Mrs. Smart was pregnant, and her married daughter Susan Alexander was nursing a child and perhaps a couple of younger children. "They told us they just come in to stay under our roof," Susan Alexander recalled years later. Hiding their horses in the woods to escape the notice of Tories and other raiders, they moved in uneasily, prepared to pack up and flee at any moment.[7]

Their stay at the Smarts' turned out to be longer than they expected. There had been a general assumption that Lord Cornwallis, having wiped out Gates and Sumter, would move north from Camden at once, spreading fire and slaughter; but the British stayed in Camden for three weeks. (Although the Americans had no idea of the fact, Cornwallis was worried about his supplies and the health of his men in the Carolina summer heat.) It was certainly not safe to return to the Waxhaws, though Betty Jackson missed her home very much. She sighed for the Conococheague peach trees brought from

Pennsylvania, whose fruit was ripening behind the Crawford house. She longed for them as the Israelites had longed for the leeks and onions of Egypt, Susan Alexander recalled years later, using the language of Presbyterianism that both women shared. But there was no reason to flee farther, so they stayed.[8]

Andy adapted. Only thirteen, he could not appreciate fully the tragedy of what his family was undergoing; to him the flight into Mecklenburg was in most ways an adventure. Moreover, men in his culture were supposed to be nonchalant in the face of danger. So, even if he missed his brothers, his home, and its surroundings, he would not have said so. With an easy smile, he fitted into the work of the farm. He brought in wood and took corn to the mill for grinding. He pulled fodder for the cattle and picked beans for the family's meals. (Another kinswoman, Margaret Wilson, remembered that he was fond of beans, which she cooked with corn for supper.) He and Susan Alexander harvested pumpkins and broke them up for the cow to eat. Together, they spread out and watered the pulled flax stalks and maintained the split-rail fences around the cornfields, which were apt to get knocked over by Whig horsemen galloping across country on wartime errands. Occasionally, she let him hold her baby.[9]

Polite and accommodating with women (a pattern that held throughout his youth), he was domineering with other males. Eleven-year-old John Wilson found him hard to get along with. To him, Andy was self willed, bossy, and aggressive. He also swore a lot. John, who had grown up in a pious home, was shocked. Andy had brought no gun with him when they left—perhaps he had never had one of his own—but he wanted a weapon. He made a bow and arrows and shot birds for the table. When he took Widow Wilson's household utensils to the blacksmith for repair, he always managed to find a spare piece of metal, have it made into something like a bayonet or sword, and use it for his work in the garden, wishing aloud that he was a grown man and could use it on the British. It was more than play; he wanted to fight, if necessary to kill. "Mother, Andy will fight his way in the world," John reported to his mother. "He had a great idea of some military business," Susan Alexander recalled.[10]

Betty Jackson was less keen on war. Day after day, she sat at the spinning wheel turning out quantities of fine flaxen yarn for weaving ("the best you ever saw," according to Susan), lamenting to the other women the death of

Hugh and voicing her fears of the British and other foreign enemies, like the Cherokees and the "heathen" Hessians, who kidnapped boys and took them back to Germany, so the settlers heard.[11]

On his visits to the blacksmith in Charlotte, Andy listened for news of the fighting. A smithy was a great place for men to gather and swap news as they hung around the stone forge with its giant bellows and little mound of glowing coals, waiting to have their horses shod. The little village was full of refugees from the Waxhaws, grim men on horseback carrying rifles and waiting for the British advance.

It was September before the British did anything. Word reached Charlotte the second week in that month that the whole enemy army was marching north on the Camden Road, and then that it arrived at the Waxhaw settlement and stopped. Lord Cornwallis set up his headquarters at Robert Crawford's house, and the British were grinding their wheat at Blair's mill. Enemy soldiers were all over the settlement, slaughtering the Crawfords' animals, harvesting their crops, ransacking their houses. They stayed there for nearly two weeks, again oddly slow in their advance. Part of the reason this time, which the Americans may not have known, was that Tarleton, on whom Cornwallis relied heavily, was dangerously ill.[12]

While they were there, Davie and his North Carolina cavalry struck them again. It was not a big engagement, but it cheered Waxhaw people, because Davie was the only defender they had left after the smashing of Gates's and Sumter's forces. (The Congress in Philadelphia was hurrying more troops southward for a stand against Cornwallis somewhere in North Carolina, but they were still few and unorganized.) It also cheered them because, like all Davie's operations, it was sudden, precise, and successful.

Davie did not strike the British directly; instead, he went after a band of Tories, horse thieves and renegades, who had been shadowing Cornwallis's army and using its advance as a cover to rob and terrorize Whig families. They were after treasure in particular: at Baron Adair's, for instance, Huck's party had stripped the rings from Mrs. Adair's hands, the lace handkerchief from her neck, and the silver buckles from her shoes. These Tories hung old Hugh McCain, who was reputed to have considerable money cached somewhere, by the neck from a walnut tree to make him reveal its hiding place and would have killed him if his slaves had not run them off. At James Walkup's plantation, they strung up his young son by the thumbs to make him tell where his father's pot of gold coins was hidden. Margaret Walkup and her children were being held hostage in the cabin, along with two other sets of women and children.[13]

Davie decided to attack while the Tories were at Walkup's. Captain Walkup himself led half the attack. The house, like many Waxhaw cabins, was off the main road, on a lane surrounded by cornfields. At dawn on 21 September, Davie led a group of cavalry down the lane, Walkup another group through the corn, to attack the sleeping Tories in and around the cabin. They achieved complete surprise, killing fifteen or twenty Tories and wounding forty others. Captain Walkup kissed his wife and children, and left with the Whigs, ninety horses, and a hundred and twenty stand of arms before Tarleton's legion, which was camped nearby with its just-recovered commander, could get to the scene. All Tarleton could do was burn down the cabin, which he did. Only a single Whig was wounded. It was a superb example of careful planning. Andy Jackson, when he heard about it, was thrilled not only by the boldness but by the thought behind it. Davie, the genteel, college-trained fighter, became his ideal commander.[14]

But this was, after all, only the smallest of victories. Only a couple of days later, the main British army was on the march again, heading for Charlotte. As rumor of their movement spread, McCamie's kinswomen once again had to consider what to do. Mrs. Smart, Margaret Wilson, and their children decided to stay and try to cope with British occupation; the McCamies, to protect their human property, needed to leave and flee further. Betty Jackson and her son went with the McCamies.

For four or five months after the day of their departure, September 25, 1780, Andy Jackson and his kinfolk almost disappear from the historical record. There is only the slightest indication of where they went when they left Sugar Creek. Susan Alexander thought they were going home to the Waxhaws, but that decision would have been both unwise and unlikely. Jackson himself recalled that they passed Charlotte—presumably heading north—a few hours before the British advance guard entered it on September 26. According to Amos Kendall's early biography, prepared with Jackson's cooperation, their destination was Guilford County, North Carolina, two or three days' journey to the north.[15]

Kendall gives no reason why they headed for Guilford, saying merely that it was to visit a Mr. McCulloch. No likely individual of that name appears in the surviving records. Susan Alexander, confronted as an old woman with the report that they went that way, offered an educated guess: "They may have taken the turn along with other company they met going to Guilford, if they considered it unsafe to go home. A power of people went to Guilford, where our army was to be stationed and where the whole country crowded to."[16]

But there are in fact convincing reasons, unmentioned by either source, why they might have chosen it for a refuge. Some Waxhaw people had already taken refuge there. The wife of the Presbyterian minister in Guilford, Rachel Caldwell, had sisters who lived in the Waxhaws, and they and their families had fled to her home for safety. One was a good friend of Betty Jackson—Nancy, the widow of Parson Richardson, who had since married George Dunlap. Moreover, Robert McCamie, Margaret Wilson's brother, a prosperous farmer and a justice of the peace, lived only a few miles from the courthouse. That the Jacksons and McCamies sought shelter with him is nowhere stated, but it would fit exactly with the Irish pattern of seeking help from kinsmen, and it dovetails with the vague report in one source that Jackson spent a part of his youth in Guilford County.[17]

Suppose, then, that Andy and Betty Jackson took refuge at Robert McCamie's home in late September of 1780 and stayed there until January or February of 1781, when Cornwallis's army bore down on central North Carolina and put them in harm's way again. What might their experience have been like?

In the frigid predawn hours of September 26, the Jackson-McCamie party, one unit among a host of country people, rode frantically north toward Charlotte. They had given up any thoughts of returning home, with Cornwallis's entire army advancing behind them. They rode into the town itself. The little cluster of cabins, with its awkward log courthouse on ten-foot-tall brick pillars in the center, was nearly deserted in the chilly light of dawn. Major Davie and a few of his men were organizing an ambush, to fire on the enemy as they entered town and then ride for their lives. The refugees passed quickly through.[18]

The Wagon Road north of town was crowded with fleeing people, some distraught, some starving, some maimed veterans of the summer's battles. The whole countryside seemed in motion. General Jethro Sumner and his Continentals were moving the public supply of arms, ammunition, and clothing from Charlotte out of the British reach; their train of creaking wagons oc-

79

. . . .
Refugees

cupied miles of the road. Private families, in their Conestoga wagons, the covered wagons of the later westward migration, were moving too. Continental officers and militiamen galloped back and forth with intelligence of what the British were doing. Fortunately, the road was good and level, and it was possible to travel fast if one could find food for the horses. The weather was clear but unusually cold for that time of year; frost had killed much of the standing corn. When night fell, the refugees sought shelter in the cabins and outbuildings of the families who lived along the Wagon Road.[19]

A day's ride brought them to Salisbury, a large town for that part of the country, bigger than Charlotte, with numerous cabins and a couple of large, pretentious houses. A company of North Carolina militia was here, not enough to resist Cornwallis, and the officers were following British movements with increasing nervousness. Just beyond Salisbury their road crossed the Yadkin, a broad, swift river like the Catawba, reddish-yellow from the clay of the country. There was a ferry at the crossing, which the Jacksons and Mc-Camies probably used. General Sumner, the same day, crossed his troops and stores at a ford farther north. The "river was arising," he was told, and he wanted to put its high water between him and the enemy.[20]

At Salisbury, the Wagon Road proper veered off to the left, toward the German settlements at Salem and the Virginia backcountry; the Jacksons and McCamies followed a "very bad" road, full of mudholes and rough spots, thirty miles farther to Guilford Courthouse, a tiny hamlet in a rolling, forested country interspersed with small fields of wheat and corn.

Regardless of what Susan Alexander and the Charlotte people had heard, the main Continental encampment was not there, but at Hillsborough, further east. There was only a quantity of guns and ammunition deposited in William Dent's big, windowless store building next to the courthouse, and a large, disorderly company of Virginia militia stationed there to guard it. The courthouse itself, at the crest of a hill, was nothing special—a frame building thirty-six feet long and twenty-six feet wide, with a porch, unglazed windows, and a chimney "of indiferent bricks and Indiferent workmanship." A two-story log jail stood at one side. There were a few log houses around the courthouse. Most were "ordinaries," taverns to refresh thirsty lawyers, clients, and spectators on the days the court met. The rest of the time they were homes.[21]

The pathetic state of the Virginians camped around the courthouse let Andy glimpse the unheroic side of military life. Most of the men, according

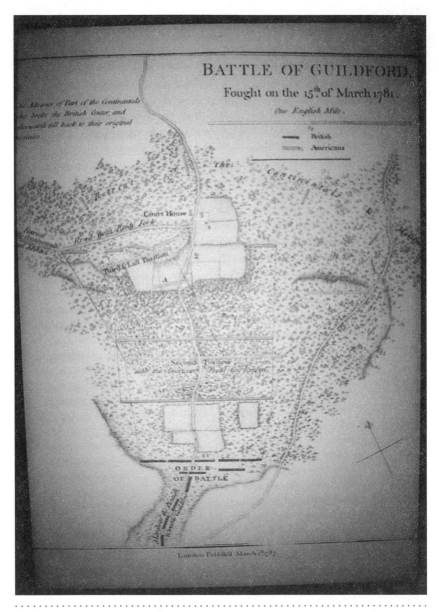

This British-drawn map depicts the site of the Battle of Guilford Courthouse, which was fought only weeks after Jackson and his mother left the area in 1781. It shows the extensive forests, the small fields, and scattered houses of a typical backcountry Irish community.

GUILFORD COURTHOUSE NATIONAL MILITARY PARK

to their commander, had neither shoes, blankets, or guns. Some had "hardly rags sufficient to cover their nakedness"—in other words, shirts and breeches, but no coats and possibly no stockings. Materially, they were worse off than Sumter's guerrillas had been in June. They had few officers, and their discipline was inferior to that of Davie's men.[22]

The Guilford community itself was much like home—in fact, it was known as the "Irish settlement." The inhabitants were from Pennsylvania or Ulster, and there were two Presbyterian churches of slightly different persuasions not far from the courthouse. A traveling Continental officer who spent a night in the settlement described a family worship service in the Presbyterian fashion, in the household of the local militia colonel, whose members spoke with a "very broad" accent. It consisted of the standard parts: scripture reading, loud, tuneless psalm singing ("a burlesque on singing or rather on religion"), and lengthy prayers, during which the African "wench" nearly fell asleep and received from her mistress "a stroke on the side of her head that laid her sprawling." As in the Waxhaws, a few families owned an African or two, and they disciplined them severely. The following year, a Continental soldier saw stuck on two saplings between the courthouse and the taverns the head and hand of a slave who had been hanged and quartered for killing his master.[23]

The people were stubborn and tough. The records of the Buffalo Church session, which dealt repeatedly with difficulties between members, document that fact. The flavor of local life probably resembled that in most Carolina Irish communities. It was a place where people told time by the sun ("the sun was an hour and a half high") and dressed up for court days; many men carried pistols, and almost every man was now and then seen "quicken'd with Liquor," if not actually drunk. Gossip about neighbors seems to have been the chief pastime—who had borrowed tools and not returned them, or what young man and young woman were seen by the fence "in an unbecoming position," or what young man was actually seen "a gouging" a young woman.[24]

In some ways Guilford was different from the Waxhaws. Being fairly close to the German settlement at Salem, it was better supplied with some goods, like tobacco pipes and local crockery, than much of the South Carolina backcountry. There was a fair amount of brick made. Some houses, like that of the minister David Caldwell, had cellars and bake ovens. Just down the road was a large settlement of Quakers, busy, prosperous people whose plantations were generally neater and more productive than those of the Presbyterian Irish. They were taking no part in the war—it was against their religion—and owned few African slaves. They kept to themselves and were consequently the objects of much suspicion and some hostility from their Presbyterian neighbors.[25]

Robert McCamie, George's kinsman, probably owned a slave. He had a fair amount of land and several sons older than Andy. He was generally esteemed in the area, unlike feckless old George. Some records of the time refer to him as "esquire," in North Carolina a term often used for lawyers; but there is no record of his practicing in the county. He was certainly in a position to give his destitute relations a home for a few months.[26]

A boy as self-confident and competitive as Andy Jackson would have had little difficulty making acquaintances in Guilford. There were foot races and wrestling matches with the other youngsters of the neighborhood, and cockfights and impromptu horse races, as in the Waxhaws. In November, during the session of court, the grand theater of legal proceedings, the local gentry, like Robert McCamie, issued orders for collection of debt, assigned orphans to be apprenticed and roads to be repaired, and generally reaffirmed their dominance over the county. The county court sessions of North Carolina, visible symbols of the social order, had no counterpart in the South Carolina part of the Waxhaws, where the nearest court was at Camden, a day's journey away. In most of the South Carolina backcountry, society was less structured, held together more by interpersonal influences and less by institutional rules. Evidently, the drama and ceremony of the law as it was practiced in North Carolina appealed to Andy, since this was the profession he eventually chose.[27]

During the last months of 1780, he met for the first time some people who re-entered his life a few years later, when he returned as a young law student. Francis McNairy, a quarrelsome farmer who lived close to the courthouse, had several sons, among them John, five years young Jackson's senior, who was sometimes at home, sometimes in the militia chasing Tories. Seven years later he would be Jackson's best friend. Edinburgh-born Charles Bruce, a well-to-do farmer who lived not far from Robert McCamie, raised fine horses and had a reputation for hospitality, both of which would have attracted young Jackson to him. Moreover, he had an actual "race path" on his farm, a flat course dedicated to racing, probably the first Andy saw in his life, and definitely not the last.[28]

Meantime, Sumter had reorganized his forces and was harassing the enemy again, but now he was away from the Waxhaws, in the western part of South Carolina. These tidings they heard from travelers and soldiers on the move between Charlotte and Hillsborough with letters and rumors. The courthouse was not on the main route, but it was close enough to receive a lot of visitors. Andy, his mother, and the other refugees (there were doubtless many others) asked everyone coming from the south for news of their home and their loved ones. Little by little, they found answers. It would not be surprising if by Christmas the Jacksons had learned where the Crawfords had taken shelter and how they were faring. News of the war was almost as important as food and drink; it kept the refugees in touch with their past lives and encouraged them to hope that soon they could return home.

The fighting that fall went differently than people had expected. At the end of September, when Andy and his mother came to Guilford, Cornwallis had taken Charlotte and was expected to advance on Salisbury at any moment. There were hardly enough Americans to oppose him. Instead, he stayed in Charlotte two weeks. Early in October, a detachment of Tories under one of his officers was surrounded by Whig riflemen and wiped out on Kings Mountain, thirty miles west of Charlotte. The British commander, despondent and coming down with fever, decided to retreat to South Carolina through the heavy October rains. He ended up in winter quarters at Winnsboro, west of the Catawba. Now the Americans became bold. In November, the Continental army advanced from Hillsborough and took up positions outside Charlotte. Scouts were sent down toward Camden. They reported that the Waxhaws were devastated and almost deserted. In December, Nathaniel Greene, a Yankee from Rhode Island selected by General Washington, arrived to command the Continentals.[29]

The Jacksons and McCamies wore away the fall in a house that was not their own, objects of pity and charity, helping as they could with the farm work, flax scutching, hog slaughtering, cider making, corn husking, and cotton picking. Betty spun fine yarn for the McCamies and Andy helped care for their horses, as they shared in the life of an Ulster Irish family, the prayers, the sips of whiskey, the breakfasts of ham and corn meal mush and eggs, the long evenings of talk and singing.

After the new year, things began to change. General Greene sent General Morgan with his troops marching west into upper South Carolina. In mid-January the refugees heard with excitement that Morgan battled with Tarleton at a place called the Cowpens and defeated him soundly. Lord Cornwallis, although it was midwinter, put the whole British army in motion to catch Morgan, who retreated into North Carolina to join Greene. Suddenly, at the end of January, the situation was back where it had been in September: the British were moving into North Carolina in force. This time the Continentals were a little better prepared to confront them. There would be major fighting, it was certain, at Charlotte, or Salisbury, or conceivably even right there at Guilford Courthouse.[30]

As soon as the British began to move, word went out among the scattered "South refugees"—it was time to go home and reclaim their farms, even in the cold rains of January. But who knew what they would find?

CHAPTER EIGHT

The Death of Captain Land
February–April 1781

———— ✧❁✧ ————

ANDY AWAKENED SUDDENLY and reached for the musket propped against the log wall. It was after midnight. The fire had burned low. Out the open door he could see only dim starlight and the bare earth of the yard. The man who had roused him said something about people moving outside. He grabbed his gun, wakened the British deserter next to him, and moved quietly toward the door.

He was not in his own house. He, Robin, Uncle Crawford, and four or five other men were west of the river, in the cabin of John Land, a captain in Sumter's forces. Captain Land was home for a night, risking his life to visit his family. The Tories in the area, too weak to attack Sumter's army, eagerly awaited the times when an officer was back home, relatively off guard and relatively defenseless. It gave them a chance to surprise and kill him. Land knew his danger. He kept the time of his visit secret and, just in case it leaked out, asked some neighborhood Whigs, including the Crawfords and Jacksons, to come along as his bodyguards. Andy was among them; almost fourteen, he counted now as a fighting man.[1]

He and the deserter stepped out cautiously into the cold March night, releasing the catches on their muskets and pulling them back to full cock. Far away to the right, next to the corn crib, there were shadows that could be men. Andy rested his musket in the fork of an apple tree; he was not going to be caught by the recoil the way he had as a boy. "Who goes there?" he shouted.

Nobody answered, and he pulled the trigger.

Flashes of fire burst at the edge of the yard, and bullets whistled next to him. The deserter at his side fell dead. The yard filled with acrid smoke. Andy grasped his gun and scooted for the cabin door.

By the time he reached safety, he had seen a dozen, perhaps a score of Tories coming toward the house from the other end of the yard. Land's home, like many backcountry houses, was in the center of a yard that was fenced to keep the livestock out. The attackers were climbing through the fence rails. Like many other Waxhaw cabins, too, it had two outside doors, one at each end. Shouting to his uncle and Robin, Andy ran toward the far door, the one at the west end. Frantically he reloaded: first priming the pan, then the powder poured into the barrel, then the ball and its wadding, rammed down deep. They opened the west door and fired together on the advancing Tories. Silhouetted against the dim firelight inside, they were better targets for the Tories than the Tories were for them. Uncle Crawford and the man on the other side of Andy were both hit.

It was hard to tell just how many attackers were out there. To the desperate defenders it looked like a hundred. That was standard Tory practice, to attack from ambush with a heavy advantage in numbers. (Of course, the Whigs did it too, when they had the chance.) Land and his friends were badly outnumbered; of the nine men in the cabin, one was already dead and at least two were wounded. Mrs. Land and the children could not help. But the defenders did what they could. They extinguished the hearth fire and began shooting through crevices between the logs, trying to keep the Tories away from the building, which they might try to set ablaze. Andy stuffed a couple of bullets into his mouth, as men did in a firefight, for convenient reloading.

Then, as suddenly as it had begun, the attack ceased, and in a moment they began hearing the sound of horses galloping away. No one was sure what had spared their lives; Jackson, as an old man, recalled that two groups of Tories had fired on each other by accident and that the resulting confusion had made them give up the attempt. He did not know, or did not remember, that one of the defenders' shots had brought down Lewis Yarborough, the Tories' second in command. He did recall, however, that just at the time the Tories were hesitating, they heard the sound of a cavalry bugle nearby in the

The Death of Captain Land

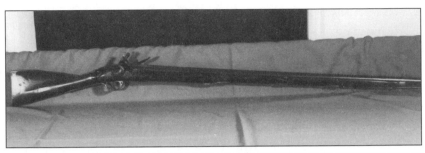

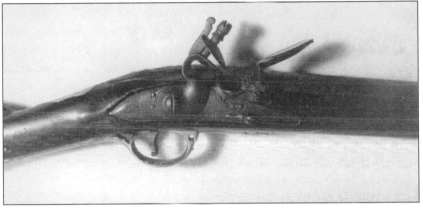

*Brown Bess muskets, the standard issue of the British army, were the most common firearms
in America in the Revolutionary era. The gun Jackson used in defending Land's cabin was
probably very much like this Tower of London model (above), made in 1765.
The photo below shows a detail of the firing mechanism.*

OLD BARRACKS MUSEUM, TRENTON, N.J.

woods and decided to leave before Whig reinforcements arrived. Later that
night, Land and his comrades learned that the bugler had been Land's neighbor Littleton Isbell, a wild, reckless Virginian who fought on the Whig side
and was trying to see if he could trick the Tories into leaving by simulating a
Whig charge.[2]

It was a modest victory. Land could return safely to Sumter's camp the
next day. But it came at a dreadful price for Andrew Jackson and the Crawford
family. They brought James Crawford home mortally wounded. Evidently, he
hung on for some weeks; his signature is on a deed conveying some land to
his son Jim on April 2. But he "afterward died of that wound," according to
Jackson, and it certainly happened before May, when young Andrew himself

was on the brink of death from smallpox. The obscure farmer-distiller was the closest thing to a father the Jackson boys ever had. He was also a pillar of the Waxhaw settlement and the Presbyterian church, and the breadwinner for Betty Jackson and her sons. Who in the family would now shelter them was quite uncertain. For the moment, under the pressure of the Tory attack, the only problem for them all was sheer survival.[3]

The war had passed into a strange shadowy phase after the main British army left Camden in January. About a thousand British forces remained in Camden, commanded by Lord Rawdon. They sent patrols occasionally into the surrounding country. But there was little to attract them there. The area was exhausted by four months of active fighting and British occupation. The crops had been taken by the armies, and the settlers were virtually starving. Jane Brown, the sister of Andy's schoolmate Johnny Brown, remembered her family's having to eat cornmeal swept from the floor. In January, Major Crawford bought sixty-six bushels of corn "for the Use of the Destressed Inhabitants." Many settlers did not return; their burned or abandoned cabins symbolized the ravages of the war.[4]

The main threat to the returning settlers came not from hunger or the British, but from their Loyalist neighbors. In the months after Gates's defeat, they had things their own way in the Waxhaws. The backcountry Loyalists were of two sorts, according to a contemporary: some supported the king on principle, while others, confident that the Whigs would finally lose, aimed to become rich from the war—"they resorted to murdering and plunder, and every means to get hold of property." While the Whigs were in exile, Tories of the first kind lived in ease under British protection, and those of the second kind systematically plundered whatever the Whigs left behind and consolidated whatever they had taken during the British advance in the fall—horses, livestock, treasures, goods of every description. To both groups, the return of the Whig settlers represented a threat. The first group feared harassment; the second group, revenge attacks from their Whig victims. They collaborated in trying to keep a Whig resistance from forming, which meant killing Whig leaders and potential leaders or intimidating them so that they would leave the area.[5]

There were definitely Loyalists in the Waxhaws, although they have left comparatively little mark on the historical record. The best known is Dr. Daniel Harper, who was probably a Loyalist on principle. He had suffered property losses from Whig attacks in the summer of 1780. He probably dreaded the Whigs' return and joined forces with the Tory plunderers to kill and intimidate Whig leaders. (Whatever he did, it was enough to incur lasting hatred from his Whig neighbors; he was forced to go back to Ulster after the war, and when he tried to return to South Carolina in the 1790s, he was shot dead by an unforgiving Whig.)

Other Loyalists are known only by their names, or even more tenuous references. John Hutchinson was threatened by local Whigs in September 1780 and given protection by Cornwallis; a man named Johnson served as a guide for the British in April 1781; a Tory woman named Sally Featherston had a bastard child by Littleton Isbell; unnamed Loyalists were members of John Simpson's congregation. Exactly where in the Waxhaws these people lived is unknown, but probably the same pattern obtained as elsewhere in the backcountry, where there were Tory neighborhoods and Whig neighborhoods. Most Loyalists lived close to each other. Loyalist men who lived among Whig neighbors found it unsafe to spend much time at their homes; typically, they hid out in the woods or creek bottoms, joining their cohorts when needed for a raid on a Whig target.[6]

As the Whig settlers returned to their farms in late January or early February (Betty Jackson, her sons, and the Crawford men probably came back at this time), they found that they were being stalked—that, in the words of one, "the friends of American liberty were [being] hunted like deer." Not all Whigs were equally threatened, it seems. Major Robert Crawford, John Barkley, and Andrew Foster moved back to their big houses and were relatively unmolested, either because they had ceased to take an active part in the fighting and were merely providing the Whigs with food and supplies or because their places were so well-guarded and fortified. But young, vigorous men who took an active role in combat were especially at risk. Naturally, they organized themselves and their friends into bands for protection and, when possible, surprise attacks on Tory strongholds. Any man able to carry a rifle was encouraged to join, from men as old as James Crawford, well into his fifties, to half-grown boys as young as Andy Jackson.[7]

From January on, the war in the Waxhaws was like a conflict out of a Western film. Bands of mounted men wearing broad-brimmed hats and carrying guns—sometimes a dozen, sometimes a hundred—trotted ten or fifteen miles down the stiff, half-frozen red clay roads, especially after dark, on their way to attack a cabin or ambush a leader of the opposing party. The results were frequently bloody, sometimes brutal. Military men from outside, whether British or American, found this kind of warfare unfamiliar and appalling. A Continental officer from Pennsylvania deplored in 1782 the "cruel, savage manner" in which the war had been waged. "'Tis almost impossible to believe," he added, "without being an eye witness to the destruction. . . . While this Country was in possession of the enemy the Whig and Tory inhabitants shot at each other, wherever they happened to meet, as all parties rode with their rifles, and numbers of Whigs were murdered in their beds, and their houses destroyed." General Nathaniel Greene confirmed this picture in January 1781: "The Whigs and Tories persecute each other, with little less than savage fury. There is nothing but murders and destructions in every quarter." He observed again in April, "The whole country is one continued scene of blood and slaughter."[8]

British judgments were no less severe. "Every misery which the bloodiest cruel War produces, we have constantly before us," wrote Colonel Charles O'Hara from Camden in January 1781. "[E]very house exhibits dreadfull, wanton Mischiefs, Murders, and Violences of every kind, unheard of before.— [W]e find the Country in great measure abandoned, and the few, who venture to remain at home in hourly expectation of being murdered, or striped of all their property." Months later he delivered his final judgment on what he was seeing: "Quelle chienne de guerre. (What a bitch of a war.)"[9]

Actually, the conflict was not one of unrestrained savagery. There were rules of engagement, and they were strictly observed. Women were never raped or killed, though they might be verbally abused. Children and older people were not bothered. On either side, there were two clear aims: to kill fighting men from the other side and to plunder or destroy enemy property down to the least item of value. They were carried out with some precision; for instance, a Tory fighter was shot dead from ambush while sitting at home with his wife, and she was left unharmed. Hugh Coffey of the Waxhaws recalled that he "was robed [sic] by the British and Tories of every thing he was possessed of even to his very knives and forks." Tories were thorough in destroying household property they did not intend to plunder; they cut open feather beds and scattered the contents, and burned books or ripped them apart. In retaliation, Whigs in one area of the backcountry, late in the war, meticulously took Tories' cabins apart, log by log. This kind of punitive property destruction had roots in Irish tradition, in which people who wished to hurt an enemy did so by damaging his livestock or his house. Typically, the combatants avoided spending much time at their houses, in order not to make themselves targets for the enemy, as John Land had; Whigs and Tories alike hid in the woods, alone or in bands.[10]

Many of the Whig fighters, including Tommy and Jim Crawford, left the Waxhaws at times to ride with Sumter when he had an operation underway. The Gamecock's fame had lost some of its luster since 1780. He had been surprised again by the British in the fall and then wounded in battle. Laid up all winter, he had missed the decisive battle at Cowpens. Now some officers were complaining that he had become selfish and money hungry, but most Carolina Whigs still revered him for his deeds in the early part of the war. His lieutenants from the Waxhaws were young men who had made names for themselves during the fighting—Tommy Thomson, a blacksmith from Cane Creek; Billy and Johnny Nisbet, who lived nearby (Johnny had escaped from the Fishing Creek disaster by swimming the Catawba "without one stitch of clothing," Billy by cutting a horse loose from a wagon and riding away); Andy Walker, the cowboy; and Fred Kimball, remembered by later residents as "a terror to the British." When these men were not fighting for Sumter, they led the local Whig partisans.[11]

Robin and Andy rode with one of these bands. Betty Jackson had gotten over her fear of letting Andy fight. It was no longer a matter of sending boys off to war, as it had been with Hugh; now it was a question of protecting their homes. They had their own rifles, their own horses, and their own swords, as Andy had hoped for the previous summer. The horse and equipment, of course, belonged to the Crawford family, for like Sumter's men the year before, the Waxhaw Whigs outfitted themselves. "[W]e furnished our own clothes," recalled a man who had ridden with a Whig band in that part of the backcountry as an adolescent, "composed of coarse materials, and all home spun; our over dress was a hunting shirt, of what was called linsey woolsey, well belted around us. We furnished our own horses, saddles, bridles, guns, swords, butcher knives, and our own spurs; we got our powder and lead as we could, and had often to apply to the old women of the country, for their old pewter dishes and guns, to supply the place of lead."[12]

Jackson in maturity said just enough about his activities as a Whig partisan to make it certain that he was part of such a group. There is no reason to doubt that he participated fully in riding to attack Tory targets, sharing in the plunder, hiding out in the leafless woods, in creek bottoms and dense stands of pine, for days at a time. "We carried no camp equipage, no cooking utensils, nothing to encumber us," recalled the same backcountry Whig; "we depended upon what chance or kind providence might cast in our way, and were always ready to decamp in a short time, so that we were what might be called the harum-scarum-ramstan boys—the ranting squad." To elude Tory pursuers, they sometimes rode as far as thirty miles away, if the memory of Susan Spratt in Mecklenburg County is accurate. Her father had a slaughter pen seven miles southwest of Charlotte at "a place of general resort for the Whigs who came there to consult and transact their business." She recalled, as a girl of eleven, noticing a boy named Andrew Jackson, who was hiding out with his friends from their enemies in the Waxhaws.[13]

There was the excitement of close shaves. One isolated reminiscence from this time concerns Will Polk, Colonel Thomas Polk's son, a large man and a hardened warrior who had already been wounded twice. Polk, who thrived on fighting, was back in the Waxhaws that spring preparing to enlist under Sumter. He and Andy, for some reason, were pursued by enemy cavalry down a long lane bordered by high rail fences, and they got away by riding madly.[14]

Most of the time it was fun—lots of physical exertion and rough joking. Food was no harder to come by than at home; often sympathizers fed Whig fighters, camped out in the woods, on makeshift tables, with guards posted around. An observant boy like Andy could learn a lot about spotting the signs of enemy movement, or improving his accuracy with a rifle (some of the Whig gunmen were incredibly accurate), or organizing a dawn attack. He learned also that the bravest deeds, the most heroic sacrifices, could be in vain. John Land, whose life they had saved, was "butchered in cold blood" about three weeks later as he rendezvoused with his men. A party of British dragoons had been sent to surprise him. Informers had passed word of the rendezvous to the British, who, like the Tories, were interested in eliminating all of Sumter's lieutenants.[15]

After his uncle's death, Andy had another powerful stimulant to focus his attention: the thirst for revenge. Fierce, implacable hatred had deep roots in the Celtic culture of the backcountry, going back to the blood feuds of Scotland and the Irish peasants' long struggle against English landlords. It involved a set of roles that everyone knew how to play. That April of 1781, he experienced the same crystallization of hatred that came at other moments during the war to other young Whigs. Fifteen-year-old Thomas Young, for instance, who lived west of Broad River, heard in 1780 of his brother's death in a Tory ambush. "I do not believe," he remembered, "I had ever used an oath before that day, but then I tore open my bosom, and swore that I would never rest until I had avenged his death." Nineteen-year-old James Gaston's moment came in October of 1780. He had been taken prisoner at Hanging Rock. Paroled after two months, he made his way back to his father's farm near the battlefield and found it "and everything thereon destroyed. He threw his parole in the fire and turned volunteer" in a company that fought local Tories. Andy himself knew a man from the Waxhaws who had found a friend murdered and horribly mutilated by Tory plunderers. From then on he "made it his business to hunt and kill" Tories.[16]

Personal revenge was a fuel that fed many Whigs' actions. Whig women, unable to revenge themselves by killing, vented their hatred symbolically. One group of women, asked to give some Tories a decent burial, interred them face down—"Let them go down to Hell," was the message. Male Whigs, too, found satisfaction in indignities against Tory corpses. After the battle of Kings Mountain, for instance, the victors carefully buried their own dead, then casually disposed of their enemies in mass graves— "covered with old logs, the bark of old trees, and rocks," one Whig recalled, "yet not so as to secure them from becoming a prey to the beasts of the forest, or the birds of the air." At John Barnett's house near Charlotte a young Whig brought a Tory prisoner in. "After eating, he drank freely," and began "recurring to the scenes of the battle" in which his brother had been killed by the British. He "became violently excited, and struck his prisoner on the head. The blood spouted from the wound."[17]

Later, after the fighting was over, most backcountry people were uncomfortable remembering the ferocity of their hatred during the war, and expressed their uneasiness in tales about the final fate of those who had been too eager to shed Tory blood. Too much hatred, these stories taught, unhinged a man. The Whig who shot and killed the Tory in his wife's lap later "became nervous & cowardly—he was especially afraid of thunder storms," it was said. The militiaman who tried to pay a young soldier to stab an elderly Tory "ran distracted" after the war, "and died so," the young soldier, Potter

Collins, recalled. So did the man who killed a Tory informer and brought his finger back to the widow of the man whose death he had caused; he lost his wits and had to be confined. Jackson's acquaintance fulfilled his vow to kill Tories, slaying over twenty by the war's end. "But," said Jackson, "he was never a happy man afterwards."[18]

If Andy nursed designs of revenge after his uncle's death, he had little time to execute them. A chain of events that began on 10 April disrupted the lives of all the Waxhaw people and led Andy in particular into the most agonizing weeks of his entire life. Sumter once again was raising troops in the Waxhaws. Word had gone out that the Continental army under General Greene was coming into South Carolina, having led Lord Cornwallis on a merry chase all over North Carolina and badly damaged his army at the battle of Guilford Courthouse in March. Now Cornwallis was in Wilmington resting his army, and Greene had plans to move against the British post at Camden. Sumter was preparing to collaborate with him. He was glad to have a definite goal for his men. Recently he had been losing lieutenants, some through death like John Land, others because they were, as he explained in a letter to Greene, "imprudently Going upon private & Disgracefull business"—they were leading their bands against people with whom they had personal differences, or people whose property they wanted to rob under the excuse of calling them Loyalists. No cases of this sort were reported from the Waxhaws, but there were many outrageous examples around Camden and elsewhere in the backcountry.[19]

The Whig fighters of the Waxhaw congregation were to rendezvous at the meeting house in the afternoon of 10 April. Sumter himself would not be there, but it seems evident that the aim of the gathering was to plan concerted action with him and Greene. It was a rainy day. Andy, Robin, Tommy, and Jim were among the Whigs who gathered in the shelter of the trees around the meeting house, on horseback, carrying their knives and guns. They were expecting Billy Nisbet's company and, looking down the road through the mist, thought they could see it coming. As the riders drew closer, the men in front moved aside and revealed the group for what it really was— a troop of uniformed British dragoons, with some Tories in front, dressed in ordinary backcountry costume, to act as a screen. The dragoons, sabers upraised, charged into the crowd before the Whigs had time to react.

In raw terror, the Jackson and Crawford boys spurred their horses through the woods behind the meeting house, where the first leaves were coming out on the trees, down into the valley of Cane Creek, with a couple of dragoons right behind them. At the crossing of the flooded creek there was a muddy patch where Jim's horse got stuck. The others, riding on, could look back and see him being overpowered by a dragoon with a blackjack. They went on, turning up the creek valley. There was a secret bend of the creek deep in the woods where they would be out of sight of any searchers. They got there, dismounted and listened, leaving the horses saddled, prepared to flee again if necessary. They heard no sounds of pursuit, not even a crackling in the dead leaves that covered the forest floor. At length they stripped the horses and tethered them, and settled down to wait until it was safe to come out.

It grew dark. At some point they heard a loud roar. They saw an orange light through the trees, and realized that the meeting house was going up in flames. Their community—what had been their community—was now in British hands, and they were powerless to do anything but sit still and cower. Finally, the three cleared themselves spots on the creek bank, lay down, and sank into a troubled sleep.[20]

CHAPTER NINE

Camden Jail
April 1781

A S IT BEGAN TO GET LIGHT, Tommy, Robin, and Andy awoke. Their joints were stiff, their clothing cold and clammy. Among the bird calls and dewy spiderwebs of a spring dawn, they took stock. The creek was still flooded, the boggy places in the forest still full of puddles. The British were probably still in the area, although there were no noises to reveal their presence. Their own horses and weapons were safe, but they knew nothing of the enemy's movements since last night. Tommy told the Jacksons to wait while he went out to scout.[1]

He did not come back, and after a while, Robin and Andy began getting both hungry and uneasy. If he had been captured, they might be in danger. His house was hardly a mile away; they could go there and check on his whereabouts. Betty would fix them some breakfast, and they could find out what had become of the rest of the militia and plan what to do next.[2]

They and their horses moved carefully through the sodden woods, up the damp creek valley. When they were close enough, they tethered their horses and took a long look at Tommy's cabin from the shelter of the trees. Everything seemed normal. There was a fire burning and apparently no visitors. The two teenagers hurried stealthily to the door and went inside.

The Jackson boys, acting just as they would on scout with the militia, took proper precautions. Besides Betty and her children—six-year-old Jimmy, four-year-old Jane, and a nursing baby—there was another adult, a woman or older man, in the house, whom they asked to go out on the lane to the cabin and serve as sentinel. That way they could eat their breakfast without fear of British interruption.[3]

But this time their precautions were useless. The boys had hardly begun eating when there was a clatter of hoofs in the yard outside. Betty ran to the door as the Jacksons tried to hide, but a group of British regulars burst in, followed by a Tory they knew named Johnson and a gang of his companions. There was no way to escape. Robin and Andy, if they had pistols, were disarmed, while the soldiers forced Betty and her weeping children into a corner and began plundering the house, looking for treasure. The looking glass was smashed, the crockery broken, the baby's clothes ripped off.

The soldiers reached the cabin not by the road, but through the woods, guided by Johnson. They had previously captured Tommy and were now headed for his house. Unfortunately, they crossed Cane Creek at the very place where Robin and Andy left their horses, so they knew the boys were there. The sentinel didn't notice them until they were almost at the cabin.[4]

The officer in charge, a Yankee of some sort, decided to rub his captives' noses in their defeat. He sat on a bench and ordered Andy to clean his muddy boots. Andy, with the boldness his family admired, straightened up. "Sir," he began in his high voice and a faint Ulster accent, "I am a prisoner of war and claim to be treated as such."[5]

The reply was not only feisty but intelligent. Instead of a sullen refusal or a spat curse, Andy focused on the sorest point between British officers and their American adversaries: the status of captured Americans. The British, who called their adversaries "rebels," had been treating them as criminals guilty of trying to overthrow the government. Every American leader from Washington down had protested. There was no British government in America, they said, and British soldiers should treat their American counterparts as prisoners of war. Davie's and Sumter's men, no doubt, talked about what kind of treatment to expect if they were captured, and so on. But for a teen-aged guerrilla to bring up the subject at a time like this was remarkable.[6]

It did him no good, anyway—predictably, it only angered the New York Tory, who drew his sword and brought it down on Andy's head. The boy threw up his left hand to ward off the blow; the blade sliced through the flesh

Young Hickory

of his wrist, his fingers, and into his skull. He dropped to the ground bleeding and in pain. It could have been worse; his fingers were cut to the bone but not severed, and his skull was dented but not cracked by the blow. Either before or after Andy—the sources do not give the sequence—Robin received the same treatment, except that the cut on his head was deeper. Very soon after, the pale, bleeding boys, their wounds crudely bandaged, rode off under guard as British prisoners. Probably the last sound they heard as they left was that of Tommy's cabin going up in flames behind them.[7]

The enemy were determined to round up or kill every Whig in the Waxhaws, and the commanding officer next ordered Andy to guide them to Tommy Thomson's farm, farther down Cane Creek. Andy complied, but chose a way that led them across a field within sight of the house, giving Thomson a chance to swim his horse across the creek and escape.[8]

It may well be, as one biographer suggested, that his captors punished him for that piece of audacity; but all the prisoners fared badly. Later that day, the Jacksons were herded together with the other Whigs captured in the raid. Tommy Crawford was there; so were Tommy Walker, Will McCain, Robin Crockett, and about a dozen others. Most of them were young like the Jacksons, boys who in peacetime would have been apprenticed or in school. Their captors marched them a few miles down the Camden Road, where they spent the night under such tight guard that there was no chance of getting away.[9]

The next two days, April 12 and 13, were an ordeal for the Waxhaw boys, as they marched forty miles to Camden, footsore, hungry, and thirsty, under the threats and sword pricks of the enemy. As they left the Waxhaws they forded several flooded creeks, sometimes in water up to their waists, but were not allowed by the officers to stop and quench their thirst. They passed landmarks they could identify: burned farmhouses, smashed wagons from Gates's retreat the year before, the littered hilltop where the Hanging Rock battle had been fought. On the way, the Tories taunted them with threats of death and physical abuse, which they dared not answer.[10]

They learned the names of their captors. The officer in charge was Captain John Coffin, a Massachusetts Yankee, stiff and soldierly. Under him were three officers, Lieutenant John McGregor, Lieutenant Thomas Walker, and Cornet Joseph Purdy—McGregor a Scot from New York, Walker a Tory farmer, Purdy a New York Tory. One of the three was the man who brought the sword down on Andy's and Robin's heads, but at the distance of two centuries it is impossible to say which; in any case, the officer who cut them had no idea he was doing anything unusual.[11]

Finally, on the evening of the thirteenth, they reached Camden. Most of the boys, Andy included, had been there once or twice before the war with their parents, buying goods at Kershaw's big store, a "Great Mart" for the backcountry of both Carolinas, selling produce in the market, perhaps buying brick or pottery. It had been a thriving little place, with a lawyer, two inns, several shopkeepers, and several craftsmen; but trade stopped when the British came and evicted all the families to turn it into a garrison town. Now it was inconsiderable. "This town lays flat," a Loyalist soldier had recorded the preceding month when he saw it for the first time, "and has but fue Buildings and Very Scatring, but has a very fine Gaol." The three-story brick jail, standing north of town surrounded by a palisade, was a landmark, the stoutest building in the backcountry. Everyone had heard of it; it was where horse thieves, Tories, and marauders were put away securely. It was where they were headed.[12]

Near nightfall they dragged themselves wearily past Logtown, the little settlement of cabins and brickyards north of Camden, and passed through the abatis, the line of sharpened stakes around the jail. There was also a stockade around the building itself, where a British officer registered their names. When he found Andy and Robin were brothers, he ordered them separated; Tommy was separated from them both. There were plenty of different cells; the jail had two or three large rooms in the basement and on every floor, each secured by a heavy door. It could hold several hundred men at need. After the battles the previous summer, it had been full. (The British had taken a thousand captives in the Battle of Camden, and three hundred at Sumter's Defeat.) Now it housed about two hundred and fifty. One was a boy about Andy's age, John Mackey, a noncombatant who had been kidnapped from his home by Tories—the same ones who attacked Captain Land's cabin—because his father was with Sumter.[13]

When Andy entered the cell, one of his first impressions was the overpowering stench. The room was full of dirty, sick men, with no facilities for bathing or relieving themselves. There was only the heavy door and a small window or two to let in air. The Tories who managed the place were unconcerned about sanitary conditions; the prison pen, one Whig remembered later, was like a stockyard. Some men had a particularly repulsive smell. They lay covered with oozing sores, their clothing stuck to them. These, he learned, were smallpox victims, the first he had ever seen. He had heard all his life of smallpox and how dreadful it was; he must have felt like shuddering. He was shut in with the contagion.[14]

Everything about the experience was equally grim. In the cold April nights, the prisoners shivered. At first Andy was better off than most because he had a coat; but then it and his shoes were stolen by one of the Tory jailers, and he shivered too. Many of the men were almost eaten up with lice. The food, Mackey remembered, was "of the meanest quality and the smallest quantity," sometimes stale bread, sometimes the same vegetable scraps that were given to the horses. Assertive as always, Andy complained to a British officer about the amount of food and, as he recalled, succeeded in getting it increased; but the whole garrison, not just the prisoners, was on short rations. Rawdon had meal left for less than two weeks and was anticipating an attack before then from Greene's Continentals, who had stopped shadowing Cornwallis and were in South Carolina, heading straight for Camden. Even officers and their wives were going hungry.[15]

It was a hellish place. Instead of the screams of the damned, there were the constant groans and shrieks of men in the agonies of death, with no attention paid to their suffering. The Tory jailers were like leering devils, constantly taunting their prisoners, threatening them with torture and death, or transfer to Charles Town. That was what happened to many of the prisoners from Camden and Sumter's Defeat, including Tommy's brothers Will and Joey, who were virtually Andy's brothers too. They were taken to Charles Town and handed over to the British Navy, which put them on overcrowded prison ships, floating plague houses anchored off the coast, where the food was wormy and diseases were epidemic. Prisoners sickened and died daily, and were thrown overboard for the sharks. Bad as Camden jail was, most Whigs preferred it to the terrors of the prison ships.[16]

So harsh was the Tories' treatment of the prisoners that it sickened some of the regular British officers, one of whom, a Scottish captain named Campbell, dipped into his purse to supply extra food and clothing for the prisoners and was recognized for it years later by Jackson.[17]

The mood of the prisoners, except those who were ill, was quietly or openly rebellious. Like other men in similar circumstances, they resisted when they could. Some of those in jail with young Jackson, for instance, managed to escape a couple of weeks later, after the battle of Hobkirk's Hill. Andy's protests about the food have already been noted. As his wounds healed, he became more and more the cocky, irrepressible boy his Waxhaw neighbors knew. In doing so, he was not out of line. Coolness in the face of threats or punishment was part of showing one's manhood in the backcountry. Some Whigs in Camden jail, shackled to the floor for trying to escape, had mocked their jailers by playing tunes on their fetters. One group had made playing cards and spent their days gambling. In general, the atmosphere inside the jail was bitterly defiant on both sides. Whig prisoners and Tory jailers knew that a sudden change in the course of the war could reverse their fortunes—and if it did, the outcome for the Tories would not be pleasant.[18]

Andy had been there less than a week when, on 19 April, he and all the other prisoners on the upper floors were herded into the basement. General Greene and the Continental army, 1400 strong, suddenly appeared before Camden; they had a couple of cannon, and the British anticipated they might fire on the jail. They were cramming the prisoners down below, they told them, for their own safety. In the filthy cellar, Andy may have had a chance to see his brother again. Robin's wound was not healing; it was untreated and festering. He also had some sort of intestinal infection. There was nothing Andy could do. They stayed huddled in the basement for a couple of days, and then were returned to the second floor, because Greene had marched around to the other side of Camden and his cannon were not an immediate threat.[19]

The other Whigs and Andy must have discussed avidly what Greene was doing. The Rhode Islander was becoming the kind of hero Sumter had seemed to be the preceding year, tirelessly dogging the enemy, making them pay in time and blood for trying to subdue America. Since the battle at Cowpens in January, Greene had changed the momentum, if not the odds, of war in the South. He led Cornwallis all over North Carolina and inflicted heavy casualties on him at Guilford Courthouse. Now Cornwallis was marching off for reinforcements to Virginia, out of the picture, and Greene was determined to pick off the remaining British posts in interior South Carolina, beginning with the strongest, Camden.[20]

Greene's maneuvering around Camden was meant to keep other British

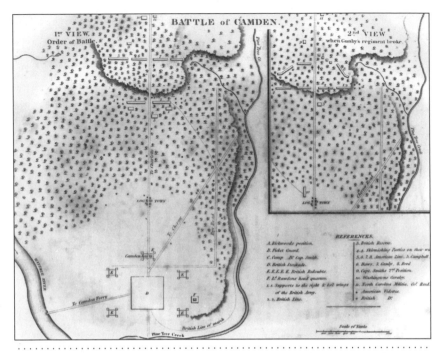

Watching from the top floor of Camden Jail (below the center of the map) on April 25, 1781,
Jackson could follow the progress of the battle over a mile away. This nineteenth-century map
calls it the Battle of Camden; the more common title is the Battle of Hobkirk's Hill.

reinforcements from reaching Rawdon. In the process, however, he had to
ford some deep creeks, not easily crossed with artillery, and decided to send
the cannon away for safekeeping. Continuing his movements, late in the afternoon of April 24 he and his army turned up again on Hobkirk's Hill, north
of the ruins of Logtown, which the British had burned down days before, and
within easy view from the upper stories of the jail. This time, however, he did
not have his artillery, and the British soon learned that fact.[21]

Jackson clearly remembered that afternoon and the following day for the
rest of his life. He and his cellmates watched the Continental army intently,
their best hope of deliverance from the Charles Town prison ships. Toward
evening they saw a soldier come out from the American lines and cross over

to the British. They guessed he was a deserter, and in a few moments their guess was confirmed—unusual activity began among the British soldiers who guarded the fortification around the jail. "Toward sunset," Jackson recalled, "a carpenter with some soldiers came into our room with plank, & nailed up the windows looking toward Genl. Greens encampment; some tories who were with them, abused us very much, told us Green was on their lines without artillery, & they intended to make a second Gates of him, & hang us all. . . . we inferred their intention to attack Genl. Green in the morning or attempt to surprise him before day."[22]

If the British thought the Whig prisoners would submit tamely to having their view blocked, they had mistaken their men. Andy Jackson and another Whig worked all night with a dull razor blade used for dividing their rations to pry out a pine knot in one of the planks. Before daybreak they had a hole an inch and a half in diameter. They took turns putting their eyes to it to see what Greene was doing. Actually, the first action took place out their eastern windows before dawn, when objects were barely distinguishable. Lord Rawdon assembled his whole force, only about nine hundred men, in the far southeast corner of the encampment and marched them silently up a creek valley, under cover of the woods, to the left of the Continentals, on their hill over a mile away. A risk taker like Greene, Rawdon knew he was outnumbered, but he was going to mount a surprise attack.

Through the peephole, Andy could see the British burst from the woods and attack the Continental left. The Continentals were surprised, but they rallied. To the astonishment of the British, cannon boomed at them from the other side. (The weapons had arrived just in time for the battle.) Soon the American cavalry rode to the charge through the smoke. "Never were hearts eleated [sic] more than ours," Jackson wrote, "at the glitter of the americans swords, wielded by the american arm so successfully which promised immediate release to us." But the hope proved false. Complications developed in the American counterattack, and before long the Continentals were retreating. Though sporadic firing went on all morning, until a hard rain in the afternoon ended the action, the battle was essentially over in an hour. Greene's army had not been decimated as Gates's was, but Rawdon had forced them away from Camden for the present. Disappointment and fear for the future gripped the prisoners; some British coming back from the field were so wrought up against the Americans that Andy and his comrades feared they would be taken out and summarily shot or hanged.[23]

As the firing died down, British soldiers shoved a man into Andy's room wearing only a shirt and the drawers used by men who were in the saddle a lot. He was a Continental officer, Captain Jack Smith of the Third Maryland Regiment, and as such might have been entitled to parole; but the British had a report from some women followers of their army that he had killed three prisoners in cold blood after the battle at Guilford Courthouse. They intended to hang him on the basis of this information, which was erroneous. Smith, a big man and a fighter, held Andy's attention as he told of his part in the battle; he had been in the squadron that brought back the cannon. He had just set them up ready for action and was taking a nap in his tent when the British attacked. There was a wild struggle to keep them from getting the big guns. Every other man in the unit was taken or killed, but Smith's cannon were saved.[24]

The following day or the day after, with Greene's army still in the vicinity, the British officers had an opportunity to check the report about Smith with officers of both sides who had been there; it was straightened out, and he was paroled. At the same time, unexpected news of more direct interest came to Andy—the possibility of freedom. Andy Walker, Tommy Walker's big brother, a captain of the Waxhaw Whigs, had managed to capture thirteen British soldiers at the battle, operating independently alongside Greene's army like many of Sumter's Waxhaw followers (Billy Nisbet, for one). Through his sister Jane, a sturdy, black-haired young woman who had already ridden once from Waxhaw Creek with provisions for her brother, he offered to swap his captives for his brother and the other Waxhaw boys.[25]

Jane Walker worked out the exchange with Lord Rawdon, who, sick and tired of the Carolina Irish, stormed at her and drove a hard bargain: thirteen British for seven Waxhaw boys, Tommy Walker and six others, Andy and Robin Jackson among them. The swap took place a day or two later, and Andy walked out of the stinking jail into his mother's arms. Robin was very sick. He had to be held on the horse; Andy, barefoot, walked alongside. They passed the battlefield, which he observed with interest. Farther up the road, at Rugeley's, they passed the Continental army encamped, waiting for Rawdon's next move.

Presumably the whole Waxhaw party started together up the Catawba Path, but perhaps the Jacksons were too slow for the rest of the group, or perhaps the others feared catching something from Robin. Jackson's memories of the return, in any case, stress their aloneness. The day after leaving they were on the road in a drenching rain, just the three of them, chilled and tired, still a few hours from home. Andy became aware that he felt feverish and nauseated as well as wet and cold. Something ugly was invading his body, and from talking with his mother he realized what it had to be. He had smallpox.[26]

CHAPTER TEN

Desperate for Honor
1781–1782

ANDY WAS NOT in jail long enough to witness the complete course of a smallpox infection, which usually lasted about three weeks. He had searing mental images of the different stages, but no picture of the whole disease. No one his age in the Wax-haws—no one who had been born there and had grown up there—had seen a case of smallpox before the war. They heard of it from their parents and neighbors, and of course they dreaded it. "There is no disorder the Americans are so afraid of as the Small Pox, and with good reason as few of them have had it," wrote an immigrant from Antrim. Their fears were justified, for it was by far the greatest killer of the eighteenth century. It was highly contagious; there was no way to stop an infection once it began; and about one of every four people who had it died. That much Andy knew; he did not know the sequence of what was in store for him.[1]

The disease did not "strike in," as the settlers put it, immediately upon contact with an infected person; there was always an incubation period. For eight to twelve days, the victim showed no symptoms at all. But during that time, the virus, Variola major, was colonizing cells in the lungs, replicating thousands of copies of itself, and sending them all over the body. Symptoms began suddenly, as they had with Andy—splitting headache, fever, chills, nausea, and backache. Sometimes there was delirium or three or four nights of terrifying dreams, sometimes convulsions. During this period some victims died, but most lived to see the fever subside and the rash break out.

Flat reddish spots first appeared on the face, then the arms and trunk, finally on the legs, and inside the body. Dozens of painful sores erupted in the mouth and throat, tissues swelled, and the sufferer became hoarse. Over the next several days the rash, thickly spaced all over the body but thickest on the face, turned into pimples, then blisters full of liquid, then open sores running with pus. They burned; the entire skin felt as if it were on fire. This was the period of the sickening odor, when most deaths occurred from internal and external hemorrhage, as the disease tore at the inner organs in the same way it ravaged the skin. After about a week, the eruptions began to subside; now the greatest danger was from secondary infections getting in the open sores. Scabs developed, and one by one the crusts came off. At this point the victim and his family could begin to assess the permanent damage. Sometimes the disease blinded sufferers in one or both eyes, but normally—three-fourths of the time—it just left a collection of pockmarks on the face, sometimes a nuisance, sometimes disfiguring. From then on the victim was immune.[2]

For the first three weeks of May, Andy fought his way through these stages, attended by his mother, in the Crawford house, if it was still standing, or in some outbuilding, some isolated cabin on Major Crawford's plantation. He lay on cowhide or an improvised bed of some sort—when the Tories plundered an area, they generally took or destroyed the beds. The tides of war had brought a Charles Town doctor to the Waxhaws, who helped Betty Jackson tend her son, but no one else came near them. The backcountry Irish customarily shunned the sick to avoid infection, and with a sickness as dreaded and contagious as smallpox, they had good reason to stay away. Andy, Robin, and their mother, then, were largely alone, getting by on whatever food could be picked up in the devastated land. Andy's case may have been relatively benign—he got no pockmarks from it—but at the least he experienced the fever, the burning sensation, the extreme weakness, the pustules and their secretions. He heard, with the remote unconcern of the ill, that Lord Rawdon and the British evacuated Camden and burned the town and the jail. Slowly, somehow, it seemed, the Americans were winning in spite of reverses. At some point, too, he learned that Robin had died.[3]

By May's end, the scabs had dropped off. He was pleased to find that his face was not disfigured. On the heels of the smallpox, he became sick with malaria, what the settlers called "the ague." It was a common enough ailment in the Waxhaws—sporadic chills and fever, and constant weakness. (No one connected it with mosquito bites.) It rarely killed its victims; it would probably persist for months and eventually vanish, perhaps with cold weather. It left Andy, once so tanned and boisterous, weak, pale, and depressed. He and his mother went to live at Major Crawford's.[4]

The course of the war shifted again; the British were now pulling their forces into Charles Town, while Greene was besieging their last interior fort, at Ninety-Six in western South Carolina. The green of the spring wheat and the sprouting corn promised an end to the shortages of food the Waxhaws had been enduring. One day, Andy's mother announced to him that she and several other women, including Mrs. Dunlap, the minister's widow, were going to Charles Town to get through the British lines. They had heard that a general exchange of prisoners was imminent, which meant that many Waxhaw boys held on the poisonous prison ships out in the Atlantic would be released. The women wanted to tend to their health and convey them home to their families. Betty Jackson was particularly concerned for Joey and Will Crawford. Going to Charles Town was her way of trying to reassemble the shattered family she and her sister had shared so long ago, before the war.[5]

She took her leave of Andy in front of the major's house, mounted on horseback, like the other women, for the three- or four-day journey. Both mother and son understood the importance of what she was doing; they also understood the dangers. If for some reason she did not come back, Andy would be virtually alone in the world. Of the Crawfords, only Tommy and young James were left. The McCamies and Leslies were kin, for what that was worth. Major Crawford could be a protector too if he chose, but that was fundamentally his decision and not Andy's. He was not close enough kin to be bound by an obligation to help. So Betty Jackson's last words to her son were about alliances and helpers. "Make friends by being honest," she told Andy, "keep them by being steadfast. Andy, never tell a lie or take what is not yours." Then she added a seemingly unrelated caution for her thin-skinned son: "Never sue for slander. Settle them cases yourself."[6]

This, at least, was what she said as Jackson remembered it—an odd piece of advice in the Waxhaws, where it was usually the church session, not the courts, that handled charges of slander, where there were no lawyers and almost no lawsuits. But whether she really said "sue" or not, the thrust of her message was clear: people were likely to say false and hostile things about Andy, and he was to make them regret it—not to entrust the job to anyone else, but to do it himself. Why this problem was on her mind is not quite clear. Perhaps people in the Waxhaws had said harsh things about her and her sons, although later testimony holds that her reputation and that of her sisters was good. But for her son Andy, protecting his reputation would be a lifelong concern.[7]

There was plenty to occupy him at the major's. With Greene's army harassing the British at Ninety-Six, dwellers on the Wagon Road frequently saw messengers, soldiers, and supplies (not as many as Greene wanted) heading south. The major took full advantage of the traffic. His blunder at Fishing Creek was forgotten, and he was now known as an ex-officer of Sumter's, a generous patriot, whose house was a good place for Whig travelers to put up. He traded with them and prospered. A descendant recalled that the major "became rich during and after the Revolution." In the neighborhood, too, there were still skirmishes going on with the local Tories—though for Andy, weak and exhausted as he was, skirmishing days were over for now.[8]

It was a few weeks later, perhaps around the beginning of July, that the prisoners came back from Charles Town. Will Crawford was among them, gaunt but alive. Joey had died months earlier, shortly after being imprisoned. But that was not the worst news. Betty Jackson was dead, a victim of the "ship fever" (typhus) carried by lice on the bodies and clothes of the prisoners. No doubt she picked it up from one of the boys she was nursing. She died at the home of a carpenter from the Waxhaws, named Barton, who lived outside the city. He made a coffin, and they buried her. Her companions brought her clothes back in a bundle.[9]

It was what she and Andy had foreseen when they parted; it was of a piece with the other wartime disasters that had devoured the family one by one since Hugh's death two years earlier. It was still a hammerstroke. Betty had been the most important person in her son's life—the person who had advised him, admired him, believed in him, encouraged him, protected him against enemies. No one else in the Waxhaws could fill those roles. He would revere her memory and cite her as an authority as long as he lived.[10]

Certain consequences of her death radiated through the rest of Jackson's

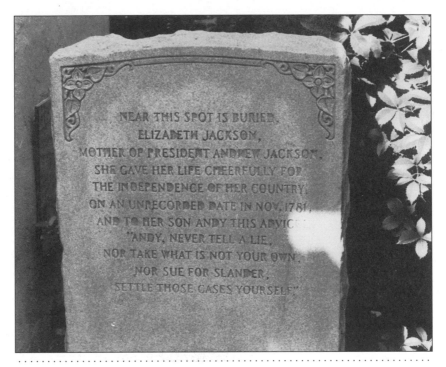

NEAR THIS SPOT IS BURIED
ELIZABETH JACKSON,
MOTHER OF PRESIDENT ANDREW JACKSON.
SHE GAVE HER LIFE CHEERFULLY FOR
THE INDEPENDENCE OF HER COUNTRY,
ON AN UNRECORDED DATE IN NOV. 1781,
AND TO HER SON ANDY THIS ADVICE
"ANDY, NEVER TELL A LIE,
NOR TAKE WHAT IS NOT YOUR OWN,
NOR SUE FOR SLANDER,
SETTLE THOSE CASES YOURSELF"

Betty Jackson's death, which probably took place in June, not November, 1781, is commemorated by this marker on the University of Charleston campus, Charleston, South Carolina.

PHOTOGRAPH BY RICHARD BULLOCK

life. The reverence he felt for his mother he would extend to women in general—at least those of his own color and class. Carolina Irish culture gave young men a lot of latitude in sexual contact with young women. In a culture of small one-room houses, where both sexes slept naked in close proximity, where people bathed together and disrobed together, girls and boys soon learned whatever there was to know about each other's attractions. It was common in both Ireland and America for girls and boys to lie together in the dark conversing and courting, and easy for them to proceed to sexual intercourse if, as an Ulster poet put it, "folk becam obligin." Small wonder, then, that the Anglican missionary Charles Woodmason found ninety-four of every hundred backcountry girls he married to be already pregnant. But Jackson, as

111

. . . .

Desperate for Honor

a teenager, avoided capitalizing on the opportunities the culture gave him. He was "very fond of the girls" on a social level, "and the girls fond of him"; he satisfied his physical needs, it seems, with slaves and prostitutes. Not even his detractors accused him of seducing young women. Andy's conceptions of women, according to a contemporary, were "chivalrous" far beyond the ordinary for a Southern male.[11]

A second consequence was something he shared with many young back-country men who survived the war: a total fearlessness, a sort of fatalistic feeling that the worst had already happened and that there was nothing left to be terrified of. It would lead, in the years just after the war's end, to a marked rise in crime and violence in interior South Carolina, which would ebb as wartime feelings subsided. But for Andrew Jackson the feeling never truly ebbed. As a boy he had simulated fearlessness, in his language and his bearing; now he actually had it. He had lost everything dear to him and had survived; he could survive anything. Situations of extreme risk, once threatening to him, were now welcome; if one can generalize from the experience of some twentieth-century survivors, they may even have given him a little rush of pleasure. In adolescence and manhood, he showed a cool, matter-of-fact willingness, even an eagerness, to take risks, both physical and personal, that made him terrifying to opponents and magnetically attractive to friends.[12]

None of this was instantly apparent in the pale, gaunt youngster who hung around Major Crawford's for the next few months. The major, it seems, had more or less adopted both him and Will Crawford as orphaned relations well worth having. They had been to school, could read and write a decent hand; they would be useful for his next project.

This project was to set up a "public station" on his farm, a warehouse to keep supplies and stores for Greene's army. Major Davie of the Waxhaws, who had become Greene's quartermaster back in December, was surely receptive to the plan. Sometime during the summer it was approved, and by August the public station was in operation—commanded not by the major, however, but by an associate of Joseph Kershaw's from Camden, a smooth-talking merchant named John Galbraith who had long worked with the Whigs and ranked as a militia captain. Galbraith promptly began cutting down trees and building storehouses. He leased two slaves from the major and hired Will Crawford as a commissary to issue supplies to the troops for forty silver dollars a month. Young Jackson may also have received a position as clerk or something similar, perhaps checking in deliveries and issuing receipts from a counter in one of the new log buildings.[13]

Wagonload after wagonload of goods for the army rolled into Crawford's red-mud yard: oats for the horses, wheat and corn for the men. Captain Galbraith checked them in, issuing IOUs to the farmers, payable by the state when the war was finally won. Full of foodstuffs and ammunition, the station became a hangout for Waxhaw men who were not out fighting under Greene, Sumter, or Francis Marion, the other Whig leader in the Low Country. In their hunting shirts and wide-brimmed hats, they lounged around the station joking and drinking whiskey. Some were put on the payroll to drive wagons or guard the storehouses. George McWhorter, Andy's old schoolmate, was a guard; Nathan Barr, an older man who had had smallpox in Camden jail, was on the staff. They and other friends found time to talk with Andy and sympathize with his loss, but there was no one but Will with whom he could share his feelings. Sally, the major's daughter, three years older than he, also tried to make things easier for him. A kind, sensitive girl, she cared for her young kinsman as a younger brother.[14]

At times the station was an exciting place to work. The second week in September, for instance, two units of North Carolina militia encamped there and seriously disrupted its routine. They were headed homeward from Eutaw Springs in the Low Country, where General Greene had brought the British to battle again. Like Guilford Courthouse and Hobkirk's Hill, Eutaw Springs was a narrow defeat for the Continentals, which actually helped them more than the enemy. After the battle, the British forces retired into Charles Town and made no further attempt to hold the Low Country. The North Carolinians, some of whom were from Guilford County and may have been acquaintances of Andy, were tired of fighting, restless, and disorderly. They took down the fences, perhaps for firewood, let the cattle Galbraith had collected escape, and then complained about the lack of provisions. A couple of days after their arrival, their commander, a Frenchman named Malmady, rode up, began storming at them about leaving Camden without his orders, and ordered one of their leaders arrested. A Frenchman in a passion was always a comic figure to the English and Irish, and the Waxhaw people present doubtless savored the scene. The next day the North Carolinians disregarded Colonel Malmady and continued northward.

Cheering news came from Virginia in October. It was said that Lord Cornwallis led his army there into a trap; they were surrounded by American land forces and a French fleet and would have to surrender. In November it was verified; Cornwallis surrendered and the British were ready to talk peace.[15]

Nevertheless, business at the public station continued to grow. New Continental soldiers marched south to replace those whose terms were expiring. That rainy December, a group of paroled British officers from some battle were sent there to be kept under guard. Galbraith lodged them and their servants at Robert Crockett's house—an error in judgment, because one of the officers, John McGregor, had been part of the troop that raided the community in April, and Robin Crockett, Robert Crockett's nephew, had been one of the prisoners taken to Camden jail. On the night of January 11, a band of disguised Waxhaw Whigs, led apparently by Archie McCorkle of Twelve Mile Creek, broke into Crockett's house, threatened the officers with pistols and swords, and robbed them of everything they possessed, down to handkerchiefs, shoe buckles, and clothing. Galbraith, outraged, pursued the robbers, considering the incident a breach of public order. (General Greene agreed, calling them "wretches.") In reality, it was more like a continuation of the Whig-Tory revenge warfare in the spring, with its carefully calibrated violence—robbery, but no personal injury. Andy doubtless applauded it. Most of the perpetrators apparently were not caught.[16]

The station operated through most of 1782, but Andy's connection with it was shorter: he quarreled with Galbraith and left. As Jackson told it many years later, the captain had "a very proud and haughty disposition" and threatened to punish him "for some reason, I forget now what." Andy's immediate response was "that I had arrived at the age to know my rights, and although weak and feeble from disease, I had courage to defend them, and if he attempted anything of that kind I would most assuredly Send him to the other world."

Actually, no other evidence suggests that Galbraith was proud or haughty; other sources portray him as likable, a good companion, "a fine looking prepossessing man"—glib and unscrupulous according to one tradition, but not overbearing. Most likely, Andy was the proud and haughty one. Probably the captain criticized something about Andy's performance at the station—some area where he felt entitled to discipline Andy. Perhaps he threatened to fire him or lay a hand on him. But Andy was no longer a boy; death, disease, and calamity had made him grow up fast. He was an independent young man and acted like one. He could not ignore the threat and intentionally framed his reply to make it clear that he was not afraid of Galbraith's authority. If Galbraith tried to infringe his rights, he warned, he would "most assuredly" kill him.[17]

It may seem a ridiculous threat, but all over the backcountry, in the brutal aftermath of the war, men were being killed for trivial reasons. At any rate, it seriously scared Galbraith, who was no fighter despite his rank, when this pale, sandy-haired, slim Crawford boy promised evenly to "send him to the other world." He complained to the major, who, scared of losing his manager and the lucrative Army business, quickly decided that Andy would have to go. He called him in and explained, in substance, that things were not working out for him at the public station, that it was time in any case for him to learn a trade, and that he was going to live with Mrs. Crawford's uncle, Joseph White, farther down Waxhaw Creek. White's son George was a saddler, and Andy could apprentice to him. The major knew, as did everyone in the community, Andy's love of horses. Saddlery would be a good occupation for him, keeping him in touch with what he liked best.[18]

The major's decision demonstrated Andy's position with sudden clarity. He was a dependent, as his mother had been; in one sense, he had a home, but in another he had none. He had a home in the sense that there would always be someone in the extensive Crawford-Hutchinson connection to provide for him, out of clan loyalty; but there was no one who would take the responsibility of guaranteeing him a permanent place to live. He could be shunted around at the clan's convenience. Maybe he already knew this; if not, the major's announcement might have had an impact on him.[19]

Joseph White and his wife Elizabeth lived in comfort near the confluence of Waxhaw Creek and the Catawba on five or six hundred acres of land, most of it forest. White was a prosperous farmer and perhaps a man of several trades; at his death in 1784, he owned both a set of carpenter's tools and a loom. He also owned at least one slave, a "negro fellow, Bob." He was a Whig; his three oldest sons all fought under Major Crawford, and Joseph Junior permanently ruined his health on the day of Sumter's defeat when he caught a chill while hiding in a creek to elude Tarleton's dragoons. All the boys lived

115

. . . .
Desperate for Honor

with him—Henry, George, Joey, and Hugh. George and Joey, both in their twenties, had learned saddlery during the war and were teaching it to young Hugh, a slight, fair-haired nineteen-year-old; Andy would work for bed and board and learn the basics as well. The Whites were good company, active, hardworking, and honest; a descendant who became governor of South Carolina and grew up among the White clan recalled that as a boy he "thought them the smartest people in the world."[20]

In the shop, a log outbuilding on the White farm, Andy and Hugh learned the various operations. They were varied indeed. One part of the work was finding the wood for the saddletree. The saddle bows had to be forked, so they cruised the woods looking for naturally forked pieces of hardwood that could be trimmed to fit a particular horse's back and then joined together with glue to form a frame (a pot of flour glue bubbled on the fire all day at work). Another part involved obtaining, measuring, and cutting the hide that would cover the frame—a fine saddle was covered in tanned leather, but that was scarce in the backcountry. For the most part they used rawhide. There was equipment for stretching the hide, a variety of knives for trimming it, and an assortment of awls for making holes in it. An apprentice's first task was learning to set the awl and make firm, even stitches in the leather—"twist the thread rather tight, apply just enough wax to make a good thread; use a sharp awl that is filed so as to give four distinct edges," a nineteenth century manual advised a learner, "and if you take pains you will soon be a good stitcher." Then there were girths, bridles, and other furnishings to be cut and trimmed. The shop was cluttered with work materials.

Andy and the White boys, in work aprons, spent the day building saddles or sitting at a bench cutting leather for harness, swapping talk of horses and their gear with men who stopped by on business, as they would at a blacksmith shop. Andy and Hugh became especially close, although their temperaments were very different: Hugh was good-natured and easygoing, a foil for Andy's impetuous, decisive manner. Hugh read a lot and enjoyed using big words in his conversation; Andy preferred riding to reading, and his conversation was simple and emphatic. Some days they all closed the shop and went fishing or got up an impromptu horse race. Nights they went raccoon hunting. It was a pleasant, lazy environment. "I think I would have made a pretty good saddler," Jackson said meditatively years later.[21]

But despite his contentment at the Whites', Andy's real feelings about manual labor are evident in a story the Crawfords handed down from this period, the year 1781 or 1782. Tommy Crawford was building a house, no doubt to replace the one burned by Captain Coffin's troops, with help from all his male relatives and neighbors. Andy, old enough now to do his share, was hewing logs with the broadax—that is, squaring off a felled tree trunk by scoring and then cutting off the round edges. It was tricky, laborious, tedious work, and at one point Andy "threw down his axe and swore that he was never made to hew logs." The comment could have been meant to express humorous exasperation, but the Crawfords read it as more than that. Andy, they inferred, really did not think he was meant to hew logs; he was meant for some grander career. His mother had wanted him to be a minister; he wanted something less high-flown, but still lettered—at least as honorable as the recordkeeping and trading at the public station. Saddlery and horses were not enough. He wanted independence and respect.[22]

After Andy left the public station, a conflict occurred there which he must have followed with great interest. Details are sketchy, but basically there was a falling out between the smooth, plausible Captain Galbraith and the major. Galbraith had been engaging in some kind of financial manipulation. Evidently it was not criminal, for he was never prosecuted for any offense and lived the rest of his short life near Camden, prosperous and respected; he even served as a justice of the peace. But he had incurred some heavy debts and managed to shift responsibility for them onto Will Crawford. Will suddenly found himself liable for a good deal of money, and, to add insult to injury, Galbraith left for Camden without paying him his promised salary.[23]

This all happened in the summer of 1782, as the British army was preparing to evacuate Charles Town, and a welcome peace was about to return to the Carolinas. Apparently the major again applied for help to his old friend William R. Davie, for by October Will was in Salisbury, North Carolina, studying in the office of a lawyer friend of Davie. It was a good spot, safely away from creditors in the Waxhaws and with excellent prospects for the future; Will probably could not have secured it on his own. His departure would not harm the major's affairs in any way; the public station would close now that the war was ending.[24]

Andy Jackson stayed close to all these events; he probably talked matters over with Will as they developed, perhaps expressing with some feeling the thought that he should have killed Galbraith when he had the chance. He rejoiced in Will's opportunity and wished him luck as he set off for Salisbury. In the back of his mind, though, there must have been a little rancor, a bit of envy even at a best friend's success. Will's opportunity by right ought to have been his; he was as quick, as articulate as Will. Andy still had time. He was not yet sixteen. Eventually he too would experience the comforts and pleasures of genteel living in a town.

In fact, he would experience those pleasures the very next year, in 1783— not in Salisbury, however, but in Charles Town.

CHAPTER ELEVEN

The School of Manners
1783–1784

Whites & blacks, all mixed together,
Unconstant strange unwholesome weather,
Burning heat and milling cold,
Dangerous to both young and old. . . .
Mousquetous on the skin make blotches,
Centipedes & large cockroaches.
The water in the wells is bad,
Which makes the inhabitants full sad,
In the streets may be seen
Many whores dressed like a queen,
Some are white, some black, some yellow,
Some are lean, some fat and mellow.
If in your pockets you got pelf,
For colour you may please yourself.
Frightful creatures in the waters,
Porpoises, sharks, & alligators.
No lamps of light, but streets of sand,
And houses built on barren land. . . .
No pleasure here is to be had,
But getting drunk, and that is bad.
Many a bargain, if you'll strike it,
This is Charles Town, how do you like it?

ACK IN THE 1760S, around the time Jackson was born, a visiting sea captain scribbled these verses. Fifteen years later, they were still circulating, though the city, since August 1783, was now "Charleston," by act of the state legislature. (The name may have been changed to reflect the end of royal government, or the change may simply have acknowledged a pronunciation that already existed.) They were popular because they pointed out what was strangest about the

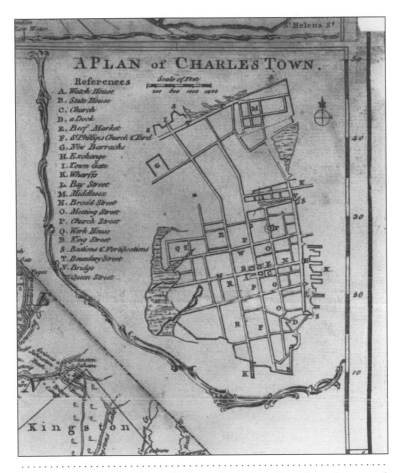

This map of Revolutionary-era Charleston shows the Beef Market in the center of town, the destination for most Waxhaw men, and the adjacent State House, where Major Crawford would have gone to settle his accounts.

place: that a city should exist at all in the rank, unwholesome, tropical environment of the Low Country, with its sultry heat, sand, insects, clouds of buzzards overhead, evil-tasting water, and rotten smells drifting in from the tidal marshes.[1]

Quite as strange, however, to newcomers from the backcountry was the notion of a city itself. They knew only forests and fields, mills and meeting houses, and occasional villages like Camden and Charlotte. Backcountry children had heard of cities—Belfast, Dublin, London—in the songs their parents sang, but not until they came to Charleston could they experience the rows of tall houses side by side, the columned churches and squalid alleys, the carriages and servants of teeming urban life.

For a boy brought up in the Waxhaws, coming to Charleston meant experiencing a succession of strange sights, sounds, and smells from the time he first arrived at the Town Gate on Charles Town Neck. He smelled marshes on either side, bordering the Cooper and Ashley Rivers; ahead was the sandy peninsula, where the city stood behind a heavy crumbling wall built of tabby, a mixture of lime and oyster shells, unlike anything seen in the backcountry. He passed through the gate and looked down King Street, bordered by old, weathered wooden houses. Five church steeples pierced the sky ahead of him. The street was of sand, hard on the wheels of carriages; if the day was windy, stinging clouds of sand whipped through the air. As he rode farther into the city, a mixture of odors assailed him: flowers from the gardens (there was something blooming at almost any season), magnolias, jasmine; at the same time, the smell of decay from the mud flats and from rotting animal carcasses in the streets. He saw numerous black and brown faces, far more than he could have imagined in the backcountry. (Over half the population of 15,000 was African or part African.) Some were servants in livery, some free artisans or peddlers, some whores "dressed like a queen," for the African as well as the European women of Charleston dressed with a stylishness unknown in the interior.[2]

Men from the Waxhaws normally made for the beef market at the center of town, opposite the State House, at the corner of Broad and Meeting Streets. Here was where they sold their cattle and deerskins—a long, low, mean complex of brick buildings, crowded with animals and offal, that contrasted disagreeably with tall, white St. Michael's Church on the other side of Broad. In the intersection, surrounded by an iron fence, stood a statue of William Pitt; it was lacking its right arm, torn off by a cannonball during the war. Ugly as the market was, it was busy all day with traders and merchants, Charlestonians and backcountrymen, making deals, smoking their clay pipes, and often adjourning to one of the surrounding taverns for a glass of rum, which was the drink of choice in the capital. On the way they saw, but rarely exchanged words with, the Charleston gentry, the rich planters and merchants. Male Charlestonians, ruddy and hearty, rode horseback through the

Charles Fraser's 1796 painting of Broad Street, the main street of Charleston, suggests the Georgian elegance of the city. The building on the left was the new courthouse; on the right, St. Michael's Church. In the center was the pedestal for William Pitt's statue.

SOUTH CAROLINA HISTORICAL SOCIETY

streets, sometimes at the "moderate trot" which was the city speed limit and sometimes faster; their women, pale, languid, and dressed in the height of London fashion, rolled by in splendid carriages.[3]

Andrew Jackson experienced all these sensations and more—the salt sea smell of the docks, the smooth burn of West India rum in the throat, the cry of street vendors and the shriek of gulls circling the tall-masted ships—at least once, probably twice, during the years after the Revolution. He and Major Crawford traveled together to Charleston some time "after the peace," that is, probably not long after the British left South Carolina in December 1782. John Ramsey of the Waxhaws recalled traveling with them as far as Camden. He and his brother Alexander spent the night at Gum Swamp above Camden, Andy and the major at the nearby house of Captain William Nettles, a comrade-in-arms of the major.[4]

Ramsey did not give a reason for the major's trip, but it was probably business with the new state government. Major Crawford had ended the war in an enviable position; he was already prospering, and the state owed him a lot of money for the use of his house, timber, and slaves. As early as January 12, 1783, four neighbors appraised the damages done to his property by the public station, and it was probably soon afterward that he headed for the capital to present his claim—even though the act authorizing the payment of claims was not passed until March. Andy, now sixteen, was living at his house again, according to Ramsey, and went with him, perhaps to corroborate his accounts. Now that Galbraith was out of the picture, there was no cause for friction—if there ever had been—between Andy and the major, and a sharp, enterprising, literate lad like him could be useful in a hundred different ways.[5]

There is also the possibility that Andy had business of his own in the capital and required the major's help. The sole survivor of his family, he stood to inherit whatever they had owned. He inherited his father's old land in North Carolina and did not sell it until 1792, but there may have been other bequests; an early biographer speaks of his receiving and dissipating a small inheritance. One early twentieth-century writer, Augustus C. Buell, elaborated a tale of a large legacy from an Irish grandfather, but it is unsupported by other evidence and should be classed as fiction. The story of the smaller inheritance, however, could well be true; there could have been debts owing to the estate of his mother or one of his brothers that could not be collected until after the war.[6]

Another story linking young Jackson and Charleston, vouched for by Jackson himself, seems to support this possibility. "Immediately after the war," it relates, he visited the capital, riding a fine mare. The horse, according to one version of the story, was worth two hundred pounds. If so, chances are good that he bought it with money from a legacy. His occupations at that time, saddler's apprentice and teacher, would not have generated enough money for such a purchase; and in fact, the story observes that, like "many other young men," he "had spent . . . money rather too freely."

This account seems to refer to a visit different from the one with the major. Young Jackson found himself stranded in Charleston, short of money, without an acquaintance in the city he could call on to help him out. Strolling down a street, he "was carried into a place" where a dice game was in progress. The game was called "rattle and snap." Jackson had never played it before, but with his usual cool confidence, he took a seat to place a bet. A gambler wagered two hundred pounds against Jackson's horse. Jackson rolled the dice and won, took his two hundred, paid his bills, and went home. If this episode took place in early 1784, as seems likely, he would have been almost seventeen at the time.[7]

There is evidence, then, for two journeys by young Jackson to Charleston in the years just after the peace—once with Major Crawford and once alone. These were big undertakings for an adolescent, even a healthy teenager on a fine horse. It was a full four days from the Waxhaws to the capital, more if the rivers were high. Camden, where log and frame houses were going up every day to replace those the British had burned, was a day's journey from home. (The jail where he and Robin had been confined was now a charred, crumbling hulk on the outskirts.) From there, the road led through the High Hills of Santee, a rolling country of large farms and plantations, among them General Sumter's, with occasional glimpses of the distant Santee River. As the road, much rutted and broken by wagons, descended into the Santee valley, the face of the country changed ("I find the face of the country more changed in the last fifty miles than in the three hundred before," wrote a Pennsylvanian traveling that way): there were palmettos in the woods, Spanish moss on the trees, and in spring the golden, fragrant sprays of yellow jessamine on the banks and tree trunks. The portions near the river were swampy, and in spring sometimes the road was covered knee-deep in water and mire. It took a day or more to get from Camden to the Santee ferry.[8]

Crossing the muddy Santee on the large raft that carried wagons and horsemen was tedious and time-consuming. Sometimes a traveler had to wait for the river to subside. Generally he ended up spending a night at an inn on one side or the other. On the whole trip, he had to expect to spend three nights at least in a public hostelry, unless he had friends on the way. (Andy and Major Crawford, for example, doubtless spent the second night of their trip at General Sumter's.) Before the war, common travelers like wagoners slept on the road, under their wagons; but crime and violence had increased so much since the peace that it was safer to endure the rough manners, noise, and drunkenness of an inn.[9]

From the Santee to Charleston was roughly fifty miles across the pine woods, marsh, and sandy fields of the Low Country. Few inhabitants remained in these parts—crumbling chimneys and half-burnt houses by the road testified to the number of families forced out by the war. In the spring, a traveler might see columns of white smoke billowing up from several places in the fields as the remaining inhabitants, following Low Country custom, burned off last year's growth to make way for the new grass. It took over a day's ride, generally, to reach the Charleston city wall.[10]

The first time Andy made this long trek, he was in attendance on the major, but the second time he bore the inconvenience and the expense himself. Clearly, some strong attraction lured him back. Most visitors would have agreed that that the main attraction of Charleston was its high society—the company of its planters, merchants, professionals, and their ladies, unmatched in British America for elegance and taste. A Maryland officer on parole in Charleston called the city the capital of "the most polite of all the states." "In all America," declared a supercilious Anglo-Irish nobleman, "there are not better educated or better bred men than the planters. Indeed, Charlestown is celebrated for the splendour, luxury, and education of its inhabitants." Manners in Charleston, according to another European, were more courteous and pleasing than elsewhere in America, and "dress, equipages, furniture, everything denote[d] a higher degree of taste." The prevailing taste was English; games, fashions, and amusements came directly from the Old World. Newspaper columns carried notices of a muff found after a winter ball or a silver corkscrew lost at the race course. No wonder that a visiting Philadelphian in the 1770s was told that "persons coming from the Northward received a polish at Charleston." But offhand, real contact with this glamorous aspect of Charleston life would seem out of the question for young Jackson, a mere "cracker," as Charlestonians called backcountry men.[11]

Nevertheless, the evidence suggests exactly that sort of contact. Henry Lee, who prepared his biography under Jackson's supervision, related that around 1781 many Whig families from Charleston and the Low Country sought refuge in the upper districts, which were now protected by American arms. Among them were "individuals of opulence and refinement," whose manners were accomplished, and habits expensive. In their eyes young Jackson, on account of his misfortunes and his "early spirit and endurance," as Lee put it, was an object of peculiar interest, and their liberal sentiments, elevated carriage, and polished manners made an impression on his mind of deep admiration and lasting respect. To the pleasure of their society, he resigned himself completely.

In other words, the elegance of Charleston society, embodied in a few individuals and families, appeared in the Waxhaws in 1781 and 1782. Naturally enough, it made its headquarters at Major Crawford's, where Andy saw it, was impressed, and found himself accepted by the refugees—perhaps not so much for his "early spirit and endurance," as for his self-confidence, daring, and articulate speech.[12]

Andy already knew a few Low Country people. Isaac Donnom, who hung around the Robert Crawford house and eventually married Sally Crawford, was a Low Country boy who had refugeed to the backcountry with his mother at the beginning of the war. He was a friend of Andy and had ridden with the Whigs west of the Catawba; he also had the Charlestonian social graces. There were other Low Country families on the west side of the river, people of "high-toned" character and "courtly" manners. From 1781 on, Charleston Whig refugee families who had fled early in the war began appearing in the safe areas of South Carolina, biding their time until the British were forced to evacuate; in the fall of 1782, for instance, four such families, the Johnsons, Cochrans, Legares, and Harrises, were spending the season in Charlotte and might easily have ridden down to the Waxhaw settlement.[13]

Early in 1782, the number of Charlestonians in the interior grew radically when the British occupiers expelled a large number of Whig families from the city. These were most likely the "individuals of opulence and refinement" who made Andy's acquaintance in the Waxhaws. The list of those expelled in April reads like a cross-section of the Charleston merchant and professional community, with names like John Paul Grimke, Samuel Prioleau, Joshua Ward, Peter Bacot, Thomas Radcliffe, John McCall, and Daniel Cannon. Not all of these families took refuge in the Waxhaws, but those who did certainly had the resources and the manners to make a splash.[14]

Most likely, the arrival of these fashionable gentry prompted the young saddler's apprentice to drop his trade and join the newcomers in their horseback rides and races, dances and excursions, around the country. But it is probably not true, as Lee suggested, that he threw away his modest inheritance partying with them there. Even supposing that he came into his estate without leaving the Waxhaws—if Betty Jackson had buried a pot of gold coins somewhere—there were just not many places in the war-torn interior to spend large amounts of money.[15]

In the capital, on the other hand, opportunities for big spending abounded—fine tailors, European wines and West Indian rum, sophisticated gambling establishments with games fresh from London, stylish prostitutes, and above all fine horses. Since the late 1760s, Charleston planters had been systematically importing purebred horses from Europe, like the celebrated Arabian Abdallah, sixteen hands high, and using them to improve the American breed. They also brought blooded stock down from Virginia. The backcountry, to be sure, had a few blooded horses, like the major's, but not in numbers like those that ran on Strickland's racetrack, half a mile north of the city wall.

The racetrack was new and exciting to young Jackson. In the backcountry there was plenty of informal racing, but no areas set aside for that purpose. In Charleston, on the other hand, Newmarket and Strickland's race courses were institutions with complex rules and rituals. Newmarket races resumed after the war, in February or April, with a "numerous appearance of genteel company" and enough fine horses for "pretty good sport." A great deal of money changed hands, up to 200 or 300 guineas, and there were elaborate rules about the time and locality for placing bets. It may well have been here that young Jackson acquired his "fine mare." If she was really worth 200 pounds or more, she was a splendid animal indeed. Just before the war, the champion racehorse Flim Nap had been sold for 300 pounds. In 1781 a "bright bay mare, 5 years old, and 14 hands high," a horse of quality, had been offered for sale in Charlestown for 60 pounds.[16]

It was exhilarating for a backcountry boy to run with this crowd—not just for the thrill of racing and judging fine horseflesh and spending lots of money, but because of the constant inevitable competition in appearance and manners, proper dress, "unstudied elegance of air," and "the carriage of polite society," as Lee put it. Young Jackson, observant and quick to pick up new manners, held his own. With the ladies, who insisted on extreme formality, he may have made little progress, but his manners were good enough for the gentlemen. His head for liquor, born of many years spent drinking his uncle's whiskey, also helped, for not everything the young Charleston blades did was elegant. Some of it was as rough and raucous as the backcountry—pranks, practical jokes, "much singing of songs" and "noisy vivacity" at dinner parties in the carpeted homes, with pictures and mirrors crowded on the wall, where gentlemen smoked their pipes, where countless toasts in brandy and rum went round, and the African attendants were instructed to lock the doors to

NEWMARKET RACES, CHARLESTON.
Tuesday, January 10—1st Purse.
Bay horse Romulus, 5 yrs old, belonging to Benjamin Waring
Brilliant, 5 yrs old, belonging to John Mayzant
Duke of Richmond, 5 yrs old, belonging to Henry Britton
Wednesday—2d Purse.
Young Flimnap, 5 yrs old, belonging to Robert Quash
Apollo, 5 yrs old, belonging to Wm. R. Davis
Bucephalus, 4 yrs old, belonging to John Bellinger
5 yrs old, belonging to John Kean
Thursday---3d Purse.
Coxcomb, 4 yrs old, belonging to Robt. Quash
Shadow, 3 yrs old, belonging to John Bellinger
Diomede, 3 yrs old, belonging to Charles S. Myddelton
Marcellus, 4 yrs old, belonging to Chas. Brown
Horses to start each day precisely at two.

☞ Tomorrow being the birthday of our illustrious WASHINGTON, a correspondent hopes all ships, &c. in the harbour, will display their colours in honor of so great character.

The three-day Newmarket Races outside Charleston were the premier racing event of the year, as well as a high point of the social season. Young Jackson would not have missed them if he was in Charleston in February of 1784, as he probably was. ("January" in the South Carolina Gazette *announcement is a misprint.)*

the dining room. "No man was permitted to leave the room," a Low Country man recalled. "The close of the feast found the weaker vessels under the table."[17]

One area in which Jackson could not keep up with his rich acquaintances was the matter of attendants. Every man of any position in the capital, according to a critical Northern visitor, had a slave who literally waited on him, accompanying him everywhere. At dinner parties a slave stood behind each chair. To lack a servant was to be less than a gentleman. But a good slave cost roughly the same as a fine horse; Jackson, a true son of the backcountry and unable to afford both, chose the horse. He wanted to own a slave too, however, as later events in his youth make clear. His inability to measure up to his fellows in this area probably added a sharp edge to his competitive feeling.[18]

Another custom Jackson learned in Charleston, through conversation if not by experience, was a way of handling disputes between gentlemen. In the backcountry, men with scores to settle did so by bare-fisted, down-and-dirty fighting. Not so in Charleston: a gentleman issued a formal challenge to his enemy, in polite, ceremonious language; the two agreed upon weapons, commonly pistols; they met in a secluded place, accompanied by friends, and fired at each other, shooting to kill. Duelling, as it was called, was an English and especially an Irish custom, enthusiastically imported by Charleston gentlemen in the years just before the Revolution. It took root partly because it was imported and partly because the general bloodshed of the Revolution led young men to regard killing and being killed as normal components of life. It appealed immediately to Jackson—it required coolness, courage, and indifference to danger, all of which he had; it was also polished and sophisticated, suitable for the gentleman he wanted to become.[19]

Socializing with the Charleston gentry was an accelerated course in gentility for young Jackson. He was an eager pupil. It gave him great satisfaction to be able to discriminate among imported wines and fine fabrics, to know the proper style of tailoring for a gentleman, and above all, to be able to respond to a genteel person in his own fashion, not to be overawed by anyone he encountered. His mother and perhaps others in his family had suggested from an early age that he had talent and was destined for leadership, and he believed them. It was worth his while, therefore, to learn the manners appropriate for a leader, even if it meant, as Lee put it, "expend[ing] money which he could ill spare, and los[ing] time which he might have devoted to higher purposes."[20]

In sum, it seems that Jackson was in Charleston more than once in 1783–1784, when he was in his middle teens, and that during part of the time he was there he had a lot of money and spent freely. At its end, however, he was alone in the city, with fine manners, a fine horse, and insufficient cash to pay his bills. Perhaps he wore out his welcome with his rich friends when he was unable to go on spending with them in style; perhaps he disengaged from them for his own reasons. One thing is sure: he made no permanent friendships in Charleston. When he strolled into the tavern, staked his horse on a throw of the dice, and won two hundred pounds, he paid his bill and turned his horse's head not toward the town house of some racing companion, but back toward the Waxhaws and his own people.

Despite appearances, however, his destiny in life was settled in his mind. He was a gentleman and was going to live like one. Now all he had to do was to make some money.

CHAPTER TWELVE

The New Acquisition
1784

THERE WAS NO LONGER an academy at Waxhaw Meeting House. The meeting house and the school house were both in ashes, and the members of the congregation were locked in bitter argument about whether they should rebuild them on the same site or in a more convenient location for the residents who had settled after the meeting house was built. In any case, no regular minister was left in the Waxhaws to teach.[1]

The whole community seemed to be withering. Some families had been burned out during the war; some had lost their property, some their men. Much of the old order was passing; Jackson's old master Joseph White and his wife were both gravely ill and would die within the year. Many people were selling their land to move to the rich country across the mountains, or to lands taken from the Native American tribes in Georgia and western South Carolina. Covered wagons and droves of livestock were again common sights on the roads, but now they belonged to families who were moving away. John Simpson, describing his Fishing Creek congregation after the war, summed it up: "Numbers were killed, numbers were gone, and others were ready to go, so that the congregation was reduced to a small number."[2]

Young Andrew Jackson rode into this situation, fresh from Charleston on his fine mare, seeking to pick up the dropped threads of his education. His mother had wanted him educated so that he could become a minister, but he was not going to be one. The church, if it ever had been important to him, was not any longer. He was going to do what Davie had done—get the education of a minister and use it to become a lawyer.[3]

The decision, apparently, was entirely Jackson's. No one in the Waxhaws urged the profession on him or offered to help him as the major helped Will. He came to the conclusion himself that he wanted to be an attorney. How he got to it is worth considering.

The main reason for his decision, undoubtedly, was to improve his status in the world—a compelling reason for a young man who had just been mixing in Charleston society. Already in America, it was accepted that becoming a lawyer was a promising way for a young man to rise out of the lower classes and become a gentleman. A lawyer was a gentleman by definition; he did not have to work with his hands, and he added the honorific "Esquire" after his name.[4]

The thought of the period often made an explicit contrast between lawyers and men who worked with their hands. John Williams, one of the leading judges of North Carolina, and in fact one of the judges who would issue Jackson his license to practice three years later, was said to have begun his career with an incident similar to Jackson's outburst at Tommy Crawford's: he was working at carpentry, grew tired of it, "threw down his rip-saw and declared that he would do no more of that kind of work, but would become a lawyer." Morcell, the hero of George Watterston's 1808 American novel *The Lawyer*, "was ever taught to believe, that I was infinitely superior to all the young men of the neighborhood. I was indeed, the only one acquainted with law." Henry D____, a law student in one of Charles Brockden Brown's fictions, compared himself even more strongly with his acquaintances: "An usher! a clerk! a taylor! Whenever these images occur, some emotion of contempt is sure to bear them company. . . . I am a student of law, whereas they are servile mechanics."[5]

In addition to the image of the lawyer-as-gentleman, there were others that must have appealed to young Jackson. One was the lawyer-as-performer, the man who stood up in open court and spoke boldly and brilliantly for his client. Jackson was, and had been since boyhood, a confident performer, whether in conversation, at the gaming table, or at the track; he enjoyed attention. Another was the lawyer-as-expert, the man who reached into his arcane knowledge and brought out some plea or formula that could change the course of a case, or who simply invoked the correct forms. In the backcountry, many people knew the basics of the law, could draw up a will or a deed, but only an attorney had the power to make a document unchallengeable. With typical lawyer-like superiority, Davie wrote to his brother-in-law Elijah Crockett in the Waxhaws that "[t]he deed you sent was very imperfectly drawn, I have corrected it and signed it, but advise you to have another drawn before this recorded, which I will execute and you can then give me this to be cancelled; this will however answer in case I should die or any other accident." This kind of expertise required a good, accurate memory. Jackson was sure that he had one.[6]

Davie's success was certainly another inducement to study law. The young major's career proved that a boy could leave the Waxhaws and do well. He had become a lawyer, won fame in the war (he was now actually Colonel Davie), married the niece of Willie Jones, one of the most powerful lawyers in North Carolina, and lived in a fine house in Halifax, on the other side of the state, near Virginia. Davie, to be sure, had enjoyed some special advantages— his inheritance from his uncle and his college education at Princeton. But Will Crawford's example showed that these were not necessary. Coming from the same background as Jackson, Will studied law for about two years. In the spring of 1784, around the time Jackson returned from Charleston, he received his license. Thereafter he would ride the circuit as Salisbury lawyers generally did, coming to Charlotte every three months for Mecklenburg County Court, where many people from the South Carolina side of the Waxhaws, Major Crawford among them, occasionally conducted business.[7]

A law license was the passport to this world of opportunities. As Will no doubt told him, in North Carolina the judges of the Superior Court issued licenses. There were no requirements as to age or education; all he would have to do was pass an oral examination, given by the judges, on the basic procedures and terminology of the law. It was not difficult, if he prepared by studying the basic law books carefully and learning the terms. Most judges felt that it took over a year of study to pass, and two or three years was not uncommon, but there was no fixed requirement. The crucial step was finding someone with a good library of law books—multivolume works in complex legalese with Latin and French terms. A practicing lawyer might take him into his office for a fee and let him read these, explaining the hard parts and at the same time giving him practice in writing legal documents correctly; this was the usual preparation, and the one Will followed with a Salisbury lawyer named Spruce Macay (pronounced McCoy). Otherwise, he could find someone with a good collection of law books and study on his own. In either case, he would need to learn Latin to cope with the language; so a decent education was the first requisite.[8]

Jackson talked to his Uncle Crawford and other men he knew in the community and sized up the opportunities. Old Liberty Hall in Charlotte was not a possibility; it had not reopened after the war, and its charter had been moved to Salisbury. A day's ride away on the other side of the river, near the tiny settlement of Winnsboro, was Mount Zion Academy, where his onetime teacher William Humphries now taught. It had a small number of students and seemed to offer a good education.[9]

Slightly closer was a small school, only a year old, in what was called the "New Acquisition," the strip of land that South Carolina had acquired from North Carolina just before the war when the boundary was redrawn. The schoolhouse lay across the Catawba, within the bounds of Bethel congregation, and the school was technically under the charge of Bethel's minister, Francis Cummins; but a heavy-set young minister from Mecklenburg County named Robert McCulloch was the teacher.[10]

Cummins was well known in the Waxhaws. Since the war, he was among the preachers who ministered to the Waxhaw congregation, preaching in either of the two log meeting houses erected by the competing factions, a fact which gave his school, called Bethel Academy, credibility. A number of boys from the Waxhaws were already attending, boarding in the house of a Mrs. Howe, who lived just down the road. She was Isabella Dunlap by birth, originally from the Waxhaws. She rented bed and board in the loft of her log house to academy students.[11]

This was the school young Jackson settled on as a place to brush up his Latin and give himself as much practice with books and study as he recently had in the saddle and at the card table. Exactly when he attended and for how long are unknown, but he boarded with the Howes and pursued, according to his earliest biographer, "a desultory course of studies."[12]

The schoolhouse, according to tradition, was a primitive log building in a shallow valley, downhill from the Howes' house. For some reason, it was not next to the church, as old Waxhaw Academy had been, but about four miles away. Its location was distinctive in yet another way. About two miles down the road was Billy Hill's iron works, the Aera Works, probably the largest industrial enterprise in the backcountry. The British burned it during the war, but now Colonel Hill had it in operation again. Wood smoke from the furnaces drifted over the school at all hours of the day or night, and swaths of red clay and stumps interrupted the forest; acres of trees were cut to keep the furnaces burning. Wagons rattled past on the road to Salisbury, carrying Hill's wares—andirons, bar iron, Dutch ovens, and kettles—for trade with North Carolina merchants. Colonel Hill, spare, energetic, large-nosed, and nattily dressed, was a frequent presence around the meeting house and the academy. Some of his children may have studied under McCulloch, including Billy Junior, who was about Jackson's age.[13]

No roster exists of all the young men and women who went to school with Jackson at Bethel, but a few can be named. Samuel Mayes, a schoolmate, wrote an affidavit for Jackson in Tennessee almost fifty years later in which he recalled that they included "several young men . . . who were intimately acquainted with young Jackson, being boys bread [sic] up in the society of each other." One of the Waxhaw boys may have been the roistering Billy Smith who briefly studied with Andy at Waxhaw Academy. Another was Jackson's ex-schoolmate and ex-teacher James White Stephenson, now in his late twenties. Other students, not from the Waxhaws, included William Cummins Davis, the minister's nephew, in his early twenties, who was preparing for the ministry; and tall, sociable Robin Cunningham of Mecklenburg County, the same age. Young women attended too. Grizzell ("Grizzy") McKenzie, twenty-two, whose family lived within walking distance, was one female scholar. All these students, Jackson included, were grown or almost grown when they studied under McCulloch; indeed, they were virtually the same age as their teacher, young Carolina Irish trying to complete their education in a hurry so that they could get on with their lives. Peggy Stinson, fourteen, from Fishing Creek, was the only younger student whose name is known.[14]

The atmosphere at such an academy would have been noticeably different from that of the backcountry schools Andy had attended before—both more serious and more sociable. More serious, because all the young men had fought in the war. Some, like Stephenson, had been officers; others, like Jackson, only irregulars. But all of them, and the young women as well, had known pain, fear, homelessness, and loss for two years. They had no need for horseplay or artificial excitement. When they sat down with their leather-bound books and homemade pens, they concentrated on the task at hand.

Outside class they were aware that they had other social responsibilities: not only to learn, but to choose a mate and settle down, as society prescribed. Their amusements would have focused on the mingling of the sexes—dances, excursions, church attendance, and the like. Despite their cramped accommodations—half a dozen young men sharing one loft, for instance—they would have concentrated on keeping up pleasing manners and dress. The only scrap of information about their activities, from a question of Jackson's years later to a York County man, fits this assumption: "Can you tell me anything of Dr. John Allison, who married Miss Betsy Hill, while I was at Bethel, going to school of the Rev. Mr. Cummins? He was but 19, she only 17, and they were the handsomenest [sic] couple I ever saw make their appearance."[15]

Jackson's recollection suggests that the academy students regularly attended worship at Bethel. There they listened to dry, pedantic sermons delivered by the Reverend Mr. Cummins in a deep, guttural voice on topics that held little meaning for them, at least for the young men, among whom sophisticated agnosticism was the rage. The opportunity for coming together and dressing up was not to be slighted, however, and much serious love talk took place on horseback riding to and from church. John Allison and Betsy Hill, Billy Hill's oldest daughter, were probably students at the academy and surely members of the Bethel congregation. Their wedding, celebrated with all the fun and frivolity of the backcountry, was evidently a major social event for the students, and their first appearance the Sunday after the wedding, in their finery, was impressive because it embodied the style and the hopes of the young men and women in the congregation.[16]

Of Jackson's progress with the girls at Bethel, there is not a trace of evidence. He was not an aggressive suitor, eager to get a girl into bed, but he enjoyed the social rituals between the sexes, like dancing, and probably performed them with the courtly, polished manners he acquired in the Low Country. There are few traditions about his success with girls in the Waxhaws. He is said to have courted little Peggy Dickey, Moses Dickey's daughter. Polly Massey, a younger sister of his schoolmate Henry Massey, is said to have rejected him.[17]

Another girl whose name was connected with his was Major Crawford's second daughter, also named Polly, and in her case there definitely does seem to have been an attachment, if not a relationship, whose exact nature remains elusive. Many years later, as an old man, Jackson sent her a silver snuffbox he received after the Battle of New Orleans, recalling her "agreeable society." She remembered him for his "noble generosity" as an adolescent, an odd quality to single out in a youngster who had very little to be generous with at that time. One later tradition in the Crawford family held that she rejected him, another that she loved him but that the major vetoed the match. Either version suggests family mythmaking at work, taking the complex reality of a relationship and fitting it into the stock formula of the rejected suitor who makes good. The real relationship remains a mystery.[18]

Jackson's study at Bethel was probably short. His object in attending was basically to practice writing English and Latin, nothing more. At least part of the time in 1784, he was at home in the Waxhaws, living with the major or with the McCamies, occasionally appraising horses for Revolutionary claims and teaching at a school for small children. The school was a few miles north of Waxhaw Creek, in the area where the Porter and Miller families lived. Both families sent children to study with him. Here for the first time he played the leading figure, although on a very small stage. The children stood and bowed when he entered the school; they addressed him with deference all day as he supervised their reading and writing. He broke up their fights, punished their misdeeds, and taught them how to shape their letters. With his forceful personality, Jackson had no problem keeping order in the school, and the money from the parents' fees must have been useful against the time when he would have to leave the Waxhaws to study law. But the main point of his teaching school was surely to show himself to the community as an educated man, not Andy the saddler or Andy the cockfighter.[19]

Once during this time, Jackson went to Salisbury on business. Major Crawford found himself in a financial bind, family tradition has it, as he continued to pay off Will's debts incurred through Galbraith's trickery, and he decided to sell a couple of slaves to raise ready cash. Salisbury, the metropolis of the backcountry, was the market; they would bring a better price there than in Charleston. The major asked Andy, who was unoccupied, to take them there and handle the sale. If problems of legal paperwork arose, Andy could enlist Will's help. So the seventeen-year-old Jackson, mounted on horseback

The New Acquisition

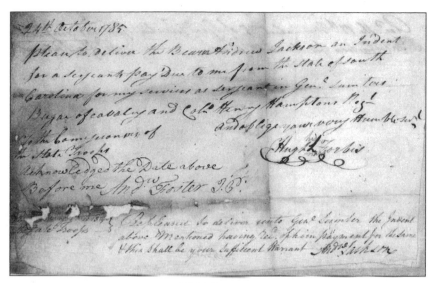

Will Crawford had been in Salisbury two years or more when he wrote this letter to try to get the money he was owed by the State of South Carolina for his expenses and services in the war. In it he referred to his difficulties with John Galbraith, with whom Jackson had also had problems.

SOUTH CAROLINA DEPARTMENT OF ARCHIVES AND HISTORY

and packing a pistol in addition to his best big-city clothes, drove the slaves eighty miles up the dusty Wagon Road.[20]

Jackson duly sold the slaves in Salisbury and had a good chance to talk with Will about legal study, and North Carolina as a place to practice, and living expenses. Will probably urged him to move to Salisbury. It was the seat of the district courts for western North Carolina, and there was a lot of legal business. It also had some genteel families and a reputation for gaiety, with parties, dances, and amusements, attractive to a social animal like young Jackson. There were several large taverns in town, and a racetrack just outside. The cousins could have a high time. It seems clear from the events of the next few years that it was Will's example and his implied or express promise to help Jackson become a lawyer that led him to move to North Carolina.[21]

Anyway, there was no real alternative in South Carolina. Charleston, where most of the courts were located, was too expensive and too sophisticated. During his stay there, Jackson had perhaps gotten acquainted with some Charleston lawyers. They were suave men with great polish, many of whom had studied law in England. He was their equal at the racetrack, but they were too much for him in the courtroom. The South Carolina legislature was moving toward setting up a system of county courts throughout the interior, but there was no guarantee of when that would happen or how long it would take.[22]

Toward the end of 1784, Andy made up his mind. Some people in the community, perhaps among his kinfolk, were critical of the way he had squandered his inheritance, and their attitude may have convinced him to leave. On 4 December he appraised a horse that Jim Crawford lost in the war; before Christmas, he left for North Carolina to learn law. Quite possibly he made no arrangements for doing so, but being Andy Jackson, poised and self-confident, he had no doubt that he would find a way and enjoy himself in the process.[23]

CHAPTER THIRTEEN

Connections
1785

I NEXPERIENCED BUT CONFIDENT, seventeen-year-old Jack
son went to North Carolina in December 1784 to learn the law
with Will Crawford's help. He seems to have attached himself to
Will fairly closely for the next two or three years; one has to say
"seems," however, for there is only one set of documents that
shows where he was or what he was doing at any point in 1785, and they come
from South Carolina.

On October 24, 1785, he and Will were back in the Waxhaws in the company of a thirty-year-old, illiterate veteran of Sumter's army named Hugh
Forbes. Forbes lived in Mecklenburg. He was originally from Guilford Courthouse; he had served in Sumter's forces at the battle of Eutaw Springs and was
entitled to a sergeant's pay. But on October 24, at Foster's store, in the presence
of Andrew Foster, who was now a justice of the peace, Forbes transferred
to Andrew Jackson and James Crawford Jr. his right to an "indent"—a
certificate of compensation from the South Carolina state government—for
one hundred twenty pounds. His price for doing so was "fifty pounds lawfull
money of South Carolina."[1]

Several features of this transaction are hard to interpret; one is why Jackson was involved in it at all. The answer seems to be that the indent had to be
issued by the South Carolina Commissioners of State Troops, who met the
following month at Powell's Tavern, in the sand country below Camden, and

Young Hickory

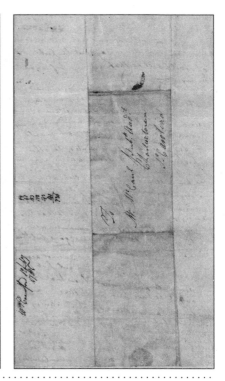

Jackson was only eighteen when he served as intermediary in a complex business deal—
buying an indent (an interest-bearing debt certificate) from Hugh Forbes and reselling it to
Thomas Sumter. The clear handwriting and crisp phrasing of his endorsements
suggest both his self-confidence and his growing mastery of legal language.
SOUTH CAROLINA DEPARTMENT OF ARCHIVES AND HISTORY

that Jackson was the one man in the group with the time to make that trip. Forbes had to farm, as did Jim; Will had to attend to his practice in Salisbury. Jackson was at Powell's Tavern November 17. He picked up Forbes's indent and immediately resold it to General Sumter, one of the commissioners, receiving "full and ample Satisfaction" in return.[2]

Jackson did not record the cash amount of the "full and ample Satisfaction," which is a pity, for that piece of information might explain what these transactions were all about. Clearly, when they bought the right to the indent from Forbes, Crawford and Jackson were engaging in the old and customary practice of buying a long-term obligation by paying its holder ready money at a discount. Forbes gave up his pie-in-the-sky claim to one hundred twenty

. . . .

Connections

pounds in return for fifty pounds in cash. There was a similar trade in indents all over South Carolina at this time. What is not clear is how much Sumter gave Crawford and Jackson for their time and effort in securing the claim and bringing it to him. Perhaps they made a substantial gain on the deal, but later developments suggest otherwise; by early 1786 they were in court suing Forbes for eighty pounds, more than they paid him in the first place. Something clearly went wrong.[3]

Whatever the nature of the transaction, one thing is clear: Andrew Jackson was not studying law continuously during 1785. He was definitely picking up some knowledge of it; his endorsements on the letter and the indent were correctly, even elegantly, phrased. But he may not have been studying full time, and there is reason to believe he was not in Salisbury.

Two traditions assert that he lived in Guilford County for part of the years 1785–1788. Given the strong likelihood that the Jackson family took refuge in Guilford during the war, it would have been natural for him to do so. The lonely little log hamlet at the courthouse, scarred from the battle fought around it in 1781, probably seemed more like home to Jackson than any other community outside the Waxhaws. He had friends there who would be glad to see him again, put him up, and give him what help they could.

One tradition has it that he did his first reading of law—this would have been as an eighteen-year-old, in 1785—at the plantation of Charles Bruce, a neighbor of Robert McCamie who lived seven miles northwest of Guilford Courthouse, renamed Martinville in that year. He, Bruce, and other farmers of the area also fought cocks and raced horses. The story lacks documentary support but sounds plausible.[4]

According to the other account, after receiving his law license—that is, in 1787 and 1788—Jackson lived for a time at Martinville with Tom Henderson and Tom Searcy, two friends who kept a store, and helped them operate it. He and Henderson were as close as brothers, the story goes. Documentary evidence shows that Tom Searcy's brother Bennett was among the party when Jackson left for the west in the spring of 1788.[5]

The second tradition is a little better supported than the first, but its date cannot be right. Tom Henderson no longer lived in Martinville in 1787; when Rockingham County was formed from Guilford at the end of 1785, he was named clerk of court there (the same office he had held in Guilford) and moved up to the new county. If Jackson did stay with him and Searcy and help

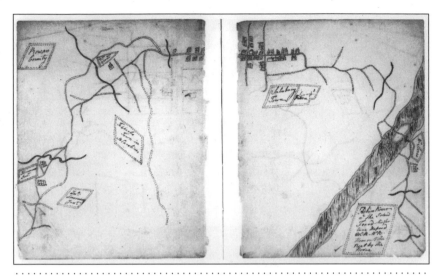

The anonymous author of this journal traveled from Rowan County, North Carolina, to Virginia in 1779, noting the taverns and settlements en route. Guildord Courthouse was merely a fork in the road with a log courthouse and two ordinaries, or taverns.
MCGREGOR AUTOGRAPH COLLECTION, SPECIAL COLLECTIONS DEPARTMENT, MANUSCRIPT DIVISION, UNIVERSITY OF VIRGINIA LIBRARY

with the store, he must have done so in 1785, when he was a newcomer to North Carolina, working for Will Crawford but also looking about for career opportunities. This date would fit comfortably with the Bruce tradition, too. Perhaps Jackson lived with Henderson and Searcy in 1785 and read law casually with Bruce.[6]

There were several components involved in learning the law. One was the drudgery—"useless copying" and learning the forms of legal documents, as the German traveler Johann Schoepf described it in Charleston in 1785. Actually it was far from useless in a profession that set great store by verbal exactitude; an attorney had to be quite sure that his documents were precisely drawn, or he might damage his client's interest through his own carelessness. "You must copy lengthy bills," a young North Carolina lawyer explained to his uncle in 1797, "answers & you must set Richard Roe & John Doe (poor innocent names) to eject, assault, batter and misuse each other and then bring them to justice against their wills." In some states there were bound volumes of legal forms, copybooks in which a beginning law student was expected to go through the volume and copy every form correctly; young John Quincy Adams, in Massachusetts, spent the fall of 1787 in this tedious exercise.[7]

Law students did a good deal of copying in the normal course of their clerical duties, making duplicates of documents that passed through their instructor's office. Some such arrangement, indeed, may have been the basis of Jackson's coming to North Carolina in 1785. His cousin had a growing practice, with more paperwork than he could well handle; Jackson wrote in a neat, legible hand, and could begin learning the forms of legal documents by copying writs and deeds for Will. But it probably did not take him long to master this part of the law, and soon he was ready to move on to the next step, reading law books.

Even in the late eighteenth century, before American state and federal courts began churning out volumes of reports, when most state laws were few and simple, there were many works a beginning lawyer had to master. The library of Spruce Macay, who was to be Jackson's first legal instructor, suggests the abundance of legal writings; in 1791 it held fifty two works on the law, most of them in multivolume sets—Blackstone's *Commentaries,* in four volumes; Bacon's *Abridgment of the Laws,* in five; the *Statutes at Large,* in ten; *The Clerk's Tutor,* in two volumes; and single volumes with titles like Hawkins's *Pleas of Crown, Institio Legalis,* and *The Attorney's Pocket Companion.* Bromfield Ridley, a lawyer who lived in Halifax County, in 1796 left a library that contained twenty-two legal titles, among them Blackstone, *Coke on Littleton, Principles of Equity,* Jacobs' *Law Dictionary, The Law of Evidence,* and *The Yellow Jacket Clerk's Instructions.* Most of these books dealt with the English common law, which was the basis of the North Carolina legal system. Some were quite specialized in their topic. A few, like the *Clerk's Tutor* and *Clerk's Instructions,* were explicitly directed at beginners. Others, like Blackstone, Bacon, and the *Law of Evidence,* were simply basic works that every lawyer, from a novice to an experienced practitioner, constantly consulted.[8]

The practical use of these works is evident from a source like the memorandum book kept by Macay during his service as district judge for the Morgan District of North Carolina. Twice a year he rode west from Salisbury to Morganton and beyond, to hear cases. He carried with him a small book to note the details of the actions and the points of law that would guide his rulings. He always cited his authority: "Confession how to be taken: 2 Hawk(ins) 604," or "Oath of a witness dead or prevented from appearing by the Defendant admitted if sworn to before a Justice or coroner: Law of Evidence 141, 2 H(awkins) P(leas) C(rown) 605." In a rural Pennsylvania county, Jasper Yeates took notes on all cases argued by himself and his fellow lawyers, giving authorities for every point: "2 Bac(on) 141: Will not specifying to be in lieu of Dower, the Widow not excluded," or "2 Bac(on's) Abr(idgment) 594: Fraud defined." Hawkins, Bacon, and the rest were the attorney's basic arsenal; he read them in search of specific ammunition to help him win a case. A beginning lawyer in particular needed to master the authorities, as he was liable to be challenged on any statement he made.[9]

Jackson, then, needed access to the major authorities for slow and careful reading. His cousin could not help him much in this respect. A beginning lawyer himself, with only a year of practice behind him, Crawford had probably accumulated only a couple of books that he used constantly. It would have made sense for Jackson to cultivate the friendship of a gentleman like Charles Bruce, who had a few law books in his library, and take the opportunity to read them regularly.

The best approach in the long run, however, was to sign on with a practicing lawyer and read the authorities under his guidance, because law books were not easy to understand, even for a patient reader. *Coke on Littleton* was notoriously difficult, but even the simpler works could be deeply frustrating. Leonard Henderson, who studied law a few years after Jackson and ultimately became chief justice of the North Carolina Supreme Court, recalled that once when his preceptor was away at court he got stuck on a difficult passage in Bacon's *Abridgment of the Laws* and, finding no one who could explain it to him, lost confidence in his own ability and almost quit the profession. Very likely Jackson, having struggled as best he could with Bruce's books, decided he needed an instructor and asked Macay to take him on. Will doubtless helped persuade Macay; so did Jackson's old Guilford friend, handsome, easygoing John McNairy, who had studied with Macay and was now a lawyer in Salisbury. Toward the end of 1785 or the beginning of the following year, Jackson moved to Salisbury to room with Crawford and McNairy and "enlist into the drudgery," as another law student put it, of Macay's office.[10]

What is interesting about Jackson's stay in Guilford County is his hosts. Henderson, Searcy, and Bruce were more than just friends—they were older men of local influence and power. Henderson, a big, fleshy, cheerful man in his middle thirties, full of jokes and anecdotes, held the lucrative office of clerk of court and owned, besides the store, half the town lots in Martinville. As his grandson put it, he had "accumulated a handsome fortune for those times." One critical local historian has identified him as a central figure in the "courthouse ring" that dominated Guilford County government. He was fond of cards, which may have had something to do with his and Jackson's friendship. His partner and nephew Tom Searcy, a genteel, popular man in his middle twenties, was the son of Henderson's sister Susannah and Reuben Searcy, the clerk of the Granville County court. When Henderson moved to Rockingham County, Searcy succeeded him as clerk of Guilford. Their log store, fragrant with the aromas of bulk tea, black pepper, and coffee, was not only a congenial hangout but a locus of power.[11]

Henderson's influence extended beyond Guilford and Rockingham. He belonged to one of the most influential families in North Carolina. His oldest brother, Richard, who died in 1785, was a prominent judge before the war and the founder of the Transylvania Company, which sent Daniel Boone to begin the settlement of Kentucky. The company failed, but the Hendersons still owned thousands of acres of rich land beyond the mountains. Tom's impressively muscular brother Sam, who also lived in Guilford, was Boone's companion in one of the most dramatic episodes of frontier history, the famous rescue of the Callaway girls from kidnaping by the Indians. Henderson men, generally speaking, tended to be large and vigorous; Henderson women were attractive and assertive.[12]

Charles Bruce was almost equally influential. Scottish-born, a prosperous farmer who owned 3773 acres of land in Guilford and two town lots in Martinville, he served as state senator for Guilford in 1783 and 1784 and was a member in good standing of the courthouse ring. Although he may well have had a law library as the tradition asserts, he did not practice; instead, he made a tidy income surveying and dividing up land confiscated from Loyalists. He was a passionate sportsman; according to a local historian, "he maintained a race track and a stud of racers. He kept deer and fox hounds. . . . He was intensely devoted to the Revolution, as was Jackson."[13]

Behind both Bruce and Henderson was a man more influential than either—whom Jackson must have met if he spent much time with their group—Henderson's brother-in-law Alexander Martin, leader of the courthouse ring, a Princeton graduate who dabbled in poetry. A wealthy lawyer-planter in his forties, Martin had been governor of North Carolina for two

*Alexander Martin, twice governor of North Carolina and a wealthy,
influential man in his part of the state, was a patron of several
of Jackson's closest friends.*

NORTH CAROLINA DIVISION OF ARCHIVES AND HISTORY

years and would shortly become governor again. He lived in the northern part of Guilford County that became Rockingham, on a plantation called Danbury, where he owned more than forty slaves. Tom Henderson's younger brother Pleasant was his private secretary. Martin was also a shrewd land speculator; he owned half of the lots in Martinville, which had been named for him. In some ways, he was not the sort of man Jackson would admire; he had left the Continental Army during the war, accused of cowardice in battle, and was an opportunistic rather than a forceful politician, who preferred to achieve his ends through clever dealing and hospitality. Some North Carolina public figures despised him; Davie called him "Alexander the Little." But he was a man who could be of great help.[14]

In a matter of one or two years, then, this young man from the Waxhaws, through his boldness and his skill with cards and horses, managed to ingratiate himself with some of the most important men in Guilford. The same pattern held true in neighboring counties. Thomas Hart Benton, who met Jackson in Tennessee fifteen years later, was told by him that he "had received hospitality at my father's house in North Carolina." Jesse Benton, his father, was the richest property owner in Orange County, the next county east of Guilford. He lived in an impressive manor house, Hartford, on the Eno River near Hillsborough. He was an educated man, a successful lawyer, and an investor in the Transylvania Company. Presumably, Jackson spent the night at Benton's when he had some business at Hillsborough. Evidently he came recommended by friends who considered him a young gentleman worthy of Benton's acquaintance.[15]

Like Henderson and Searcy, Benton was of Virginia stock, Anglican rather than Ulster Presbyterian. Jackson was comfortable with men of this background; indeed, he seems to have preferred it. A slight majority of his friends in North Carolina were Virginians. The cultural differences between them and his own Ulster Irish were not substantial; moreover, he had known Virginia families in the Waxhaws, like the Masseys and Lands. In the aftermath of the war, when Christianity was a topic of little interest to men his age, the Anglican-Presbyterian difference may not have counted for much. Still, it is revealing that he gravitated to some degree toward the element in North Carolina whose manners were showier, more formal, and more concerned with rank. These were among his concerns too.[16]

The clothes he wore may have contributed to his acceptance. Jackson was always a careful dresser and at eighteen had an acquaintance with Charleston style. He had his clothes made, as was the practice of the time, and undoubtedly they were the best he could afford—buckskin breeches that buttoned at the knee, silk stockings, a dark or striped waistcoat with a row of pewter or silver buttons, and a long coat, cut away in front in the most fashionable manner. Like most men who rode a lot, he wore drawers under his breeches. His long linen shirts were ruffled in the most approved manner, and around his neck he wore a stock, the white cloth band that buckled at the back, with the requisite jabot, or frill, in front. For riding outdoors in cold weather, he wore gloves and a greatcoat of some heavy material, and of course he wore a hat, either a cocked hat or the broad-brimmed "Quaker" hat that had become popular during the war. Unlike the really fine gentry, he did not powder his hair.

The style he aspired to can be compared with the wardrobe of a prosperous Guilford Countian auctioned off at the courthouse in 1787: a set of razors, a pair of gloves, two pairs of worsted stockings, three pairs of breeches, four pairs of silk stockings, four stocks, an overcoat, two coats, three waistcoats, one silver stock buckle, five fine shirts, three handkerchiefs, two waistcoat and breeches, a tobacco box, a penknife, a pair of silver knee buckles, a "fir hatt," a powder horn and bag, a pair of boots, a pair of slippers, and a comb. Jackson had nothing like this quantity of clothing, but he probably owned at least one of everything on the list, even the razors. (At seventeen, he was old enough to have begun shaving at least once a week or so.) Such a wardrobe took money; he bought on credit or paid for purchases with his betting winnings.[17]

Using recollections and secondhand oral accounts, one can paint a rough picture of him when he came to Martinville: notably tall, over six feet; very slender ("slight," was the word people used); carrying himself ramrod straight; and graceful on horseback. His whole bearing was athletic. His hair was light brown ("sandy"); he wore it tied back rather than loose, as some young men did. His eyes were blue. Long-jawed and narrow-faced, he was definitely not handsome—one observer called him "ill-looking"—but he was lively, talkative, magnetic. Even when on his best behavior, he had the quality of attracting attention.[18]

Jackson was adaptable, as he had to be; for the next six years he spent his life in inns or boarding houses, occasionally as a guest in a friend's home, paying his landlord when he had money, or blarneying him into extending credit. He had no home of his own. Usually he had one or more roommates, and of course he was in constant contact with strangers, so he developed the requisite social graces—he danced well, courted the girls, and talked with energy and enthusiasm. He was at ease with people; his conversational skills were as good as they had been when his mother was convinced he should go into the ministry. Occasionally, he betrayed his lack of education. When he was excited his grammar deteriorated, and he never introduced into his speech any of the classical allusions or Latin tags that college-trained gentlemen favored. But many people in Martinville shared these shortcomings. No wit in conver-

This striking portrait of Jackson, thought to have been painted in 1815 by Ralph E. W. Earl, was not discovered until 1941. It shows a younger man than his other well-known likenesses. If accurate, it proves that Jackson, contrary to some traditions, was not red-haired.

HISTORIC CAMDEN REVOLUTIONARY WAR SITE, CAMDEN, S.C.

sation, he was bold and "full of fun." He enjoyed pranks designed to challenge another person, just "to see what would come of it," as he put it. When Jackson was around, there was likely to be a good deal of physical hilarity. Some called him "wild."[19]

Jackson smoked, like most young men in the backcountry. He may have learned the habit in early childhood; there were backcountry boys and girls barely of school age who smoked. He bought his tobacco in twists—tight spirals of twisted tobacco leaves sold in any general store—shredded it, and packed it into his pipe. Probably he favored the long clay pipes common at the time; later, in Tennessee, he would switch to a corncob pipe. Smoking was an approved habit for idle social hours, when young men gathered in front of the fire to plan a hunting excursion or play a game of cards.[20]

Among males he was intensely competitive—not a bad trait for a budding lawyer—in an easy, good-humored, but insistent way. His goal was to be first, whether in an athletic or a social situation. If he could not always win, at least he could dominate. "Overbearing and tyrannical" was the way one Salisbury family remembered him. He was continually challenging other men, often considerably older than himself, for dominance. The Tennessee tradition, however, which held that he "would fight a man at the drop of a hat, and drop the hat himself," probably makes him out to be too aggressive. Bullies, big men who liked to pick fights, especially when they had been drinking, were legion in the backcountry. Jackson was not like them. He was "not quarrelsome," people recalled. He did not start fights; he preferred to assert control by other means.

One of his favorite ways of intimidating others, in maturity, was by pretending to be in a rage. It worked well for him all his life, and probably he used it in his North Carolina years as well; but he had others—verbal behavior, looks, attitudes that evoked "energy, courage, and assurance"—the qualities which naturalists suggest are decisive in determining dominant relationships among human males, as among other species. The Jackson look—steady, withering eye-to-eye contact—saved him from having to use force on a good many occasions. When he did have to use force, however, he responded quickly and often to a degree that left his challenger and his audience open-mouthed.21

An incident from the early years of his law practice makes the point. A "big bullying fellow," much larger than he, stepped on his toes. Jackson considered it accidental and ignored it, but friends whispered to him that the man was picking a fight, and in short order, to make his point, he stepped on Jackson's toes again. He was not, evidently, of high enough social rank for a challenge to a duel to be appropriate; yet Jackson, as a gentleman, was supposed to refrain from fist fights. He solved his problem by seizing a rail from the fence and giving him the point of it "full in his belly." "Sir, it doubled him up," Jackson recalled; "he fell at my feet, and I stamped on him. Shortly the man sat up again," Jackson went on, "and was about to fly at me like a tiger. The bystanders made as though they would interfere. Says I, Gentlemen, stand back—give me room, and I'll manage him. With that I stood ready with the rail pointed. He gave me one look, Sir, and turned away, frightened, a whipped man and feeling like one."[22]

The encounter was typical Jackson; he achieved dominance by one quick recourse to violence, followed by a look and an attitude that conveyed determination. He did not curse or bluster; he simply projected rage. The bully evidently looked into Jackson's blue eyes and saw not only no fear, but no hint of a limit about how far the young lawyer would go to maintain the upper hand.

Andrew Jackson, in other words, at eighteen had mastered the art of making an impression. He was about to make a deep one on Salisbury.

CHAPTER FOURTEEN

Head of All the Rowdies
1786–1787

HE ROWAN COUNTY courthouse stood at the top of a long, gradual hill—a "charming hill," Count Castiglioni called it in 1785—where the two principal streets of Salisbury crossed, oriented northeast and northwest. It was a small, unimpressive frame structure, twenty by thirty feet, somewhat battered from the Revolution, right in the middle of the intersection. Efforts at renovation were made in 1781, but the building was barely usable; during court week in February 1785, court had to adjourn "to meet at Dunn's Big House," presumably because of the bitingly cold weather. In this shabby, unfinished room with its judge's bench, its big window, and its single door, the judicial business of the area, as the count noted wonderingly, was carried on.[1]

Standing by the courthouse, next to the stocks, the whipping post, and other apparatus of justice, a visitor's eye might be caught by a small solitary mountain on the southeast horizon. Dunn's Mountain, it was called, a granite outcropping a few miles away that one English traveler found "beautiful" and "romantic," a popular destination for pleasure rides. The view from it was also beautiful: rich, well-kept farms, dotted with neat, plain log or frame houses. Long dairy barns and an occasional stone building south and east of town betrayed the nationality of the farmers on that side, mostly Germans ("Dutch," as they were called); to the north and west the settlers were mainly Ulster Irish. Both groups shared the town, but tended to socialize only among

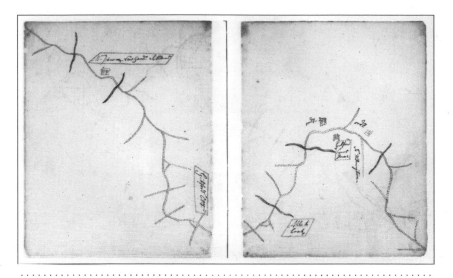

In contrast to Guilford Courthouse, Salisbury in 1779 was by far the largest town in the backcountry.

themselves; indeed, most of the Germans out in the country knew no English and referred to the county seat as "Salzburg."[2]

The town, a collection of ill-matched buildings strung out along the two main thoroughfares and a few cross streets, hardly looked like the metropolis of the backcountry. It was capable of making quite different impressions on visitors, perhaps based on their previous experience. Three Pennsylvania soldiers who passed through it just before Christmas of 1781 registered three varying judgments. One found it "a small, sorry looking place," a second "a remote but tolerable handsome town," and the third "a fine little town " with "two or three Elligant houses." Elkanah Watson in 1785 called it a "pleasant village" and noticed the big stone jail on Main Street. Certainly, there was a range of frame structures, from "Weather Beaton" hovels to pretentious homes with stables and slave quarters in the rear.[3]

Most of the "Elligant houses" William Feltman noticed belonged to families who had been prominent under the British regime. Irish-born John Ross Dunn, of Dunn's "big house" and Dunn's Mountain, was a prominent attorney who had been clerk of court and colonel of the county militia before the war. His frame house, northwest of the courthouse on Innes Street, was a big, impressive dwelling once known for its hospitality, especially at Christmastime; it was still imposing in 1785, though Dunn had died two years earlier. On the main street near the courthouse was another mansion. It had belonged to Hugh Montgomery, another Ulsterman, a prominent merchant of prewar days. He, too, had died during the war, but his family still occupied the house. Other comfortable, well-furnished houses, typically surrounded by neat white fences, belonged to a newer elite of the same kind, merchants and lawyers active in the Whig movement.[4]

The Salisbury gentry led an active social life; in fact, after the Revolution the town was known for its gaiety. A serious-minded young teacher in the later 1780s found that most of the young men his age formed clubs to "eat, drink, joke, and frolic"; they also spent a lot of time dancing. In the 1790s the town council found it necessary to pass an ordinance against racing horses and retailing liquor on the streets. Another sport they prohibited was throwing the "long bullet," a Northern Irish diversion that consisted of tossing a heavy stone or metal ball as far as possible down a street or road. It was fun for young men but hazardous to passersby. According to a visitor during court week in 1795, the people spent "their time in a Laysey manner and gaming considerably Every day and night."

Religion, often a steadying influence on the giddiness of social life, did not play that role in Salisbury, where churches were few and unnoticed. John Brown, in 1795, found "no Publick worship in Town"; the chief Sabbath day activity was attending or trading in the slave market. In February 1785, when Francis Asbury, the Methodist evangelist, came to preach there, he found few listeners, he recorded, because it was court week. Even those few left when he began preaching on the necessity of leading a holy life.[5]

Court week was the climax of Salisbury's civic and economic life. It occurred six times a year, at the four sessions of County Court and the two sessions of North Carolina's highest court, the Superior Court, which traveled around the state. At these times litigants, lawyers, businessmen, slave dealers, and horse traders flocked to Salisbury from all over the backcountry. The atmosphere was intense and festive at the same time. Horse trading, gaming, business deals, and fights took place outside the courthouse as the interplay of deals and negotiations between lawyers, judges, plaintiffs, and defendants

Will Crawford, John McNairy, and "Archibald" Jackson appear as a group in John Steele's store journal. Steele thought all three of them were lawyers; in fact, Jackson was still a clerk in 1786. Note that Crawford picked up the bill for Jackson.

went on within. Superior Court sessions, particularly, attracted lawyers and merchants from all over the state; one of the merchants explained that he came "tho' very little of my Business was in the Courts but with the People at them."[6]

Of course, there was more to Salisbury than the gentry and their slaves. Numerous artisans—carpenters, tailors, blacksmiths, saddlers, even a silversmith—and their families inhabited the town. There were peddlers and small merchants of various kinds, and numerous keepers of taverns, where men from all the other classes went to get drunk. Wagons loaded with goods and materials for these businesses kept the red mud of the streets churned up day in and day out. Their presence lent Salisbury an air of almost urban complexity. It was not Charleston, to be sure, but it was more like a city than any place for a hundred miles around.[7]

Jackson probably became a resident of Salisbury in the winter of 1785–1786, but the first documentary evidence of his presence comes from the following spring. On Thursday, April 27, he, Will Crawford, and John McNairy tied up their horses and strode into young John Steele's store in their riding boots. Evidently they had just arrived back in Salisbury; Rowan's court week was to begin the next Monday. Jackson purchased a quire (twenty-four sheets) of paper, an appropriate item for a law student. It was apparently the first time Steele had seen him, for he got the name wrong in his ledger, "Archibald" instead of "Andrew," but the identity is clear enough from the fact that Steele charged the bill to Crawford's account. Crawford and McNairy had other shopping in mind. Next day each bought a twelve-shilling pair of shoes, wanting to look his best in court. Steele noted "Lawyer" in parentheses after all three names.[8]

Jackson was not a lawyer yet, but he entered Salisbury as a lawyer-to-be, near the top of the social scale. Just as in Guilford, he had connections among the rich and powerful. His instructor, Spruce Macay, was by 1786 one of the wealthiest men in Salisbury. He owned twenty slaves, more or less, including his body servant Guy, a slim, agile young man "of a very black complexion" with a scar over his right eye. He also owned nearly a dozen horses and thousands of acres in Rowan and other counties.[9]

Macay had clinched a place among the ruling gentry of North Carolina in 1785 through his marriage to Fanny Henderson, Judge Richard Henderson's daughter and Tom Henderson's niece. She was attractive and musical, intelligent and energetic, and only three years older than Jackson, whom she must have seen regularly, although no details of their acquaintance survive. He no doubt watched with interest as she made Macay's dwelling fashionable and genteel with mahogany and marble furniture, looking glasses, a pianoforte, and a china press. Through her he kept up contact with his friends in Guilford and Rockingham, and met other Hendersons as well, as her sister and brothers came to stay with her briefly. One of them was probably the only Henderson who did not appeal to Jackson at all: her younger brother Archibald, just his age, a bookish, solemn, self-absorbed teenager who would become one of the leaders of the North Carolina bar in the next generation.[10]

Jackson would study with Macay for over a year, and his studies are the subject of the next chapter, but the reputation he left in Salisbury was not primarily that of a student. When James Parton was interviewing old residents of the village in the 1850s, he heard several tales about him and his roommates, Crawford and McNairy. They were called the "Inseparables." They roomed together at the Rowan House. They were wild, irresponsible law students. (Actually, two of them, Crawford and McNairy, were practicing attorneys, but they acted wild enough to be students.) Between them, they were responsible for a good deal of mischief in the town, but Jackson was the "head of all the rowdies hereabouts."[11]

They were an odd trio in terms of age. McNairy and Crawford were in their middle twenties; Jackson, in his late teens, was the junior rowdy, but later accounts all credit him with the leadership. Perhaps Jackson's later fame led local people to attribute more than actual prominence to him, or perhaps his dynamic personality really did make him the leader.[12]

The three were old friends. Jackson and Crawford grew up together. He and McNairy went back six years, to the time when he and his mother were refugees; the McNairy family lived not far from his kinsman Robert McCamie. McNairy and Will both studied law with Macay, and both began to practice at the same time, in May 1784. They may have roomed together since that time. They often practiced as a team, although each man also took cases on his own. Crawford did two or three times as much business in Rowan County as his friend. Perhaps most of McNairy's practice was near his home in Guilford, and he stayed in Salisbury only part of the time. Some North Carolina attorneys seem to have had rooms reserved in more than one town so that they would always have a place to stay while on circuit.[13]

The Rowan House, run by a genial Englishman, Joseph Hughes, was one of the two best taverns in town, along with Elizabeth Steele's. It stood on the main street, about a block southwest of the courthouse—an ample, two-story frame building with several low buildings attached, where the guest rooms were located. Its accommodations were probably quite comfortable—furnishings in the towns of the backcountry had improved a great deal in the preceding decades, so that genteel guests could count on feather mattresses, curtained beds, looking glasses, and a chamber pot in each room. In the dining area there were tablecloths, curtains on the windows, glassware, and pewter plates. Jackson and his friends may have enjoyed these amenities. They probably shared one bed, however.

The barroom, where food and spirits were served, was a resort for the young men of the town, a place where much of the deviltry in Salisbury was conceived and planned—practical jokes and pranks like stealing gates from private houses, in which Jackson and his friends were avid participants. Here they sat, smoking their long clay pipes, arguing, and drinking—perhaps whiskey ("with which this country abounds," one traveler noted), but more likely rum, the beverage at a high-class tavern, sometimes straight, sometimes in punches or toddies. "The glass circulates freely," commented a visitor to Hughes's establishment. Sometimes local girls showed up for an impromptu dance.[14]

Like any inn, the Rowan House was an eventful place with a large cast of characters. For instance, one of Hughes's numerous slaves, named Judy, who waited on tables, straightened the rooms, and brought male lodgers their shaving water in the morning, recalled being in the Inseparables' room once when the trio had just gotten back from hunting and had gone to dinner. Like many young men's lodging of the time, it was strewn with what a writer of the time called a "litter of guns, books, and greatcoats." Judy was twelve years old. Out of curiosity, she picked up a gun and began fiddling with it. It went off, to her shock, sending a load of buckshot into the ceiling. She ran and hid before the young men could get back to the room to investigate.[15]

That incident, however, was neither the most memorable nor the most destructive of the trio's stay at the Rowan House. One evening, according to a local tradition, the three of them and some friends had a party at the tavern, which became more and more hilarious as the evening went on. "Toward midnight," according to the account, "it was agreed that glasses and decanters which had witnessed and promoted such an evening ought never to be profaned to any baser use. They were smashed accordingly. And if the glasses, why not the table? The table was broken to splinters. Then the chairs were destroyed, and every other article of furniture. There was a bed in the room, and the destroying spirit still unsatiated, seized and tore the clothes and curtains into ribbons. Lastly, the combustible part of the fragments were heaped upon the fire and consumed."[16]

This story sounds as if it gained some color in the retelling. Maybe the orgy of destruction was not quite so extensive originally. The unexpressed assumption behind it is that all three were drunk, or at least groggy enough so that they were incapable of stopping what was, for them, a very costly prank. It is plausible that they were drunk, especially Will Crawford, who had an acknowledged drinking problem. But rum-addled judgment aside, the basic dynamic was the same as in their other activities, horse racing and card playing—simple male competitiveness, seeing who had the nerve to destroy more property than the others. The one who started the competition need not have been one of the roommates; it could just as well have been one of their disreputable friends from the town.[17]

There were several horse racers, card players, and throwers of the long bullet with Jackson and his roommates. One was George Dunn, a man in his early thirties, a son of the late John Dunn of the "big house" on Innes Street. Dunn was a ne'er-do-well who had fought in the Revolution and done nothing since the war. Another boon companion with more money than Dunn—indeed, one of the richest young men in town, who was constantly in court being sued by his creditors—was Hugh Montgomery Jr., a son of the late merchant, a portly young man in his twenties who was often referred to in court documents by a title Jackson wished he had, "Hugh Montgomery, gentleman."[18]

Montgomery's and Jackson's names are linked to an exploit that was remembered years later in Salisbury. Apparently, Montgomery challenged Jackson to a foot race. The idea was laughable on its face, for the lithe, slender law student was probably the fastest runner in town, and Montgomery was too heavy to run fast. But Montgomery proposed equalizing the odds: he would carry another man on his back if Jackson would give him a head start of half the distance. The bet was accepted and money changed hands. It was, again, a matter of sheer masculine swagger, this time with financial gain involved.

The ridiculous match took place on the horse racing course north of town, before a crowd of boisterous onlookers. At the starting signal, Montgomery lumbered down the track clutching and squeezing the man on his back nearly to death, while Jackson, an eighth of a mile behind, ran full tilt to overtake them. It turned out to be a close finish; Jackson won by only two or three yards as the spectators shook with laughter.[19]

All these activities, especially the night of destruction at the Rowan House, unavoidably raise the larger question of how young Jackson got the money to pay for his three years of study in North Carolina, the room and board, the stylish clothes, the dancing schools, the gambling, the destroyed furniture, and the fine horses. The only property he owned, apart from his horse, was the two hundred acres in Mecklenburg he had inherited from his parents, which Jim Crawford was now looking after for him. The income from this land, assuming he rented it, would scarcely have supported his style of life. Major Crawford was giving him no help. The rest of the money had to come from his own efforts. Marquis James, who was sometimes weak on details but understood young Jackson as well as any biographer before or since, was probably quite right in suggesting that respectable Salisbury society "feared that [Jackson] gambled not always as a sportsman who can afford to lose, but as an adventurer who has to win."[20]

There have been recurrent suggestions that Jackson paid part of his way in North Carolina with gambling winnings. One early witness claimed to have seen a ledger book Hughes kept on Jackson, containing charges for room, board, and whiskey, the latter often in large quantities. Jackson, this witness said, partly paid for these items by winning from Hughes in card games, also recorded in the ledger. But these claims deserve close scrutiny. The game Jackson played with Hughes and his cronies was probably all fours, also known as seven-up or old sledge, a lower-class game from England that was very popular on the old Southern frontier. (Conceivably it could have been loo, a century-old gambling game still popular in Virginia and Charleston, or whist; but whist was a game of partnerships rather than individual play, and typically domestic, not found in taverns.)[21]

All fours was a simple, fast-moving game with few opportunities for skilled play: players received six cards each, and then a card was turned up to designate the trump suit. The holders of the high and low trumps automati-

Annals of Gaming. 199

ESSAY XIII.

Containing an Account of the Game of ALL
FOURS *as it is usually played, and the Advantages that may be taken, and Finesses
that may be introduced by those who understand the Manœuvres of the Cards.*

THERE are three principal cards in
this game, which are ace, knave,
and deuce of trumps; the ace reckons
first, as highest, the deuce next, as lowest,
jack or knave, as third, and what is
called the game, as fourth and last; from
whence the game derives its name of All-
Fours.

What is meant by the game as fourth, is
the majority in number after you have
played your cards, reckoning any ace as
four, any king as three, any queen as two,
any knave as one, and the tens express
themselves, by counting for ten each. After cutting for deal you must deal six cards,
three by three, and turn up the thirteenth
card for the trump. If then the eldest of
K 4 hand.

The Annals of Gaming, *printed in London in 1775, advised its readers that
success at All Fours "depends upon chance, that is, if the game is played fair,"
but also warned them that cheating was easy and frequent; "this game is as
dangerous as any upon the cards," it concluded, "to those who are not
greatly upon their guard."*

cally scored a point each; so did the player who captured the jack of trumps, if it was in play, and finally the player who won most honor cards scored one point. The first player to reach seven points in the course of a few hands won the game. With so few cards in play at any given time, there was no way to analyze an opponent's hand or play with calculation, though Jackson and his cronies, familiar with the greasy deck, could probably identify some cards from the smudges on their backs. In other words, it was not easy to win consistently if one was aboveboard.[22]

Cheating was easy in all fours if one had some skill in handling cards; a deft player could turn the jack from the bottom, deal himself more than six cards, or cut skillfully to get the trump wanted. Tricks like these led Mark Twain to declare, in a memorable story, that old sledge as played in Kentucky was not a game of chance. But these were the arts of professional gamblers, card sharps who traveled from town to town in the South and made money from unsuspecting opponents. Such men earned money and a measure of respect, but never qualified for the status of gentleman; if Jackson had been suspected of being one, he would never have been asked to manage a ball, as he was in Salisbury.[23]

Jackson was an avid player, but all the evidence suggests he played primarily for excitement and not for money. Sometimes he lost and sometimes he won. William Cupples, a few years later, trying to reconstruct the specifics of a business transaction, wrote him, "I recollect your gaming at Richmond but not how you broke." Aunt Judy, in one version of her reminiscences, recalled that Jackson "never had no money; he lost it all playin' cyards."[24]

Horse racing and cockfighting were activities in which experience and judgment counted, and it was possible to win regularly without cheating. An early biographer of Jackson stated that he "once bet on a cockfight," and that that was the extent of his involvement in that "low and cruel diversion," but the evidence shows otherwise. Jackson kept the instructions for feeding a gamecock among his papers, and at various times in his later life he took part in cockfights. With the hands-on knowledge of the sport he had since boyhood, it would have been easy for him to keep or at least have an interest in a good game bird. Moreover, in the eighteenth-century South, the sport was hardly considered a "low and cruel diversion." Gentlemen were often among the participants; in Britain, indeed, it was patronized by members of the aristocracy.[25]

But racing horses seems likely to have been more important to him. The owner of a fast horse could make good money locally by matching it against his neighbors' horses, then against those of travelers, and finally against champions in neighboring communities. Probably the most important gap in present-day knowledge about Jackson's career in Salisbury is the number and identity of the horses he owned. Not only were his horses more important to him than anything he was learning of the law (he remained an enthusiastic breeder and racer of horses throughout his long life) but they also may have been his main source of income. George Dunn's older sister Eleanor, who was married to a well-respected German tradesman, Peter Faust, and was no doubt embarrassed by her brother and his wild companions, referred to Jackson as a "rake" whom her husband would have refused to bring into the house; but she conceded that he might have taken him out to the stable to weigh horses for a race and drink a glass of whiskey.)[26]

Eleanor Faust's comment was inaccurate as a specific description—the entrants in races, like horses in general, were classified by age and size, not by weight. Mrs. Faust, not too surprisingly, was a little hazy about what went on in a stable. Like most Southern ladies, she viewed the stable as a center of "slovenly ways," "coarse jokes," and "horse play," as the heroine of George Tucker's early Southern novel *The Valley of Shenandoah* put it, and doubtless avoided it as much as possible. But her focusing on preparations for a race is suggestive. Jackson would have visited Peter Faust not as a technician, to determine a horse's weight, but as a consultant before a race, to "weigh" the animal in a more general sense, assessing its condition and its merits. The implication is that this dynamic, fun-loving nineteen-year-old had established himself in the male community as an expert on horses, presumably because of his own success; as the historian Thomas Perkins Abernathy suggested, "the only obvious conclusion is that he found racing profitable."[27]

One chance piece of information from his Salisbury years tends to underscore this possibility. In the summer of 1787, two men named Andrew Baird and John Ludlow filed suit against Jackson, Will Cupples, and Hugh Montgomery in Rowan court. The charge was trespass on the case, which under North Carolina law could mean almost anything except physical trespass; it meant, broadly speaking, that Jackson, Cupples, and Montgomery had done some specific amount of monetary damage to Baird and Ludlow, either by destruction of property or by refusal to pay money that was due. Baird was a

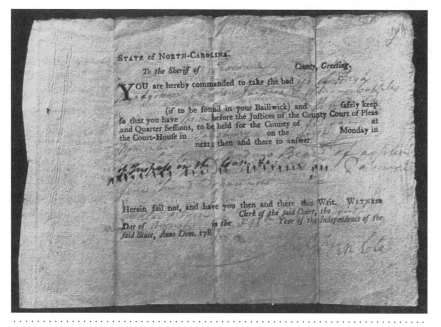

STATE OF NORTH-CAROLINA.

To the Sheriff of _____ County, Greeting.

YOU are hereby commanded to take the body

(if to be found in your Bailiwick) and safely keep
so that you have _____ before the Justices of the County Court of Pleas
and Quarter Sessions, to be held for the County of _____ at
the Court-House in _____ on the _____ Monday in
_____ next; then and there to answer

Herein fail not, and have you then and there this Writ. WITNESS
_____ Clerk of the said Court, the
Day of _____ in the _____ Year of the Independence of the
said State, Anno Dom. 178

The names of Hugh Montgomery, Jackson, and Will Cupples can barely be made out on this
warrant for their arrest in August 1787. It was merely a formality; the case was settled out of
court. The three were charged with "trespass on the case," i.e., some sort of monetary
damage—not actual trespassing.

ROWAN MUSEUM, PHOTOGRAPH BY WAYNE HINSHAW

Wilkes County farmer, and Ludlow appears to have been a horse breeder
from New Jersey who was traveling the South with at least one blooded horse
in tow. That is as far as the facts go, but the possibility immediately suggests
that Ludlow raced his horse, Young Whirligig, against an entry of Jackson
and his friends, that some difficulty ensued, and that Ludlow claimed monetary damages. The sum involved was sizable: five hundred pounds, the price
of a very expensive horse. The case was settled out of court, so there is no
further information about it, but it hints remotely of Jackson's deep involvement with horses and racing.[28]

Two Salisbury men helped Jackson and his friends make bond for this suit,
in the breathtaking sum of one thousand pounds. One was Daniel Clary, a
middle-aged tavern keeper with a large family, the other Henry Giles, a "gentleman" who raced horses and married George Dunn's sister Elizabeth. Nei-

ther man, fortunately, had to put up any money, but their names illustrate how many friends Jackson had in Salisbury, beyond his mentors Macay and Stokes and his comrades McNairy and Crawford.[29]

Perhaps the best-known story of Jackson's activities in Salisbury, unfortunately, came from the memories of Eleanor Faust. She and Jackson were among the participants in a dancing school held in town one winter, the work of a traveling dancing master who enrolled all the young "quality" of the locality, gave a series of balls, and critiqued their dancing style for a fee. The school ended with a ball, and Jackson had enough status to be appointed one of the managers. It was probably to be held, as balls generally were, in the courthouse. The managers sent out invitations, hired the musicians, and provided refreshments. Jackson had the notion of sending tickets to a couple of women in town, a mother and daughter named Molly and Rachel Wood, who led sexually active lives and were outcasts from respectable female society. They may have been prostitutes, as one version has it; perhaps they were just uninhibited amateurs. In any event, Jackson knew them and probably hand-delivered the tickets. He thought it would be fun, as he said, "to see what would come of it." It was fairly typical Carolina male humor.

The ball was duly held, and in the middle of it, the Woods showed up, garishly dressed and conspicuous, with their invitations in order. As Jackson's early biographer told the story, some "confusion ensued." The room buzzed with whispers and gossip as the managers suspended the dancing and tried to persuade the women to leave. They left, but their appearance was the sensation of the evening. Eventually it came out how the Woods obtained their tickets, and Jackson was publicly snubbed by the town's respectable young women. Eleanor Faust's mind was made up, and she did not change it for the rest of her life. The story passed into Salisbury lore and was embroidered; one later version had it that Jackson had scandalized Salisbury society by bringing his mistress to the Christmas ball. Since women in post-Revolutionary America were, as the historian Nancy Struna points out, increasingly "the moral arbiters of male leisure," Jackson promptly lost all credit with the decent part of town society.[30]

If Macay's young wife was among the offended women, the fact might help explain why Jackson, in the middle of his law studies, suddenly left town to study with John Stokes, who lived in the adjoining county of Montgomery, although he practiced in Salisbury. It seems clear that he left Salisbury around this time, the winter of 1787. Judy of the Rowan House remembered that at some point the Inseparables gave up their room with bills unpaid, and that some or all of them decamped. That he left Macay to study with Stokes is well-established, and those biographers who have connected the change with the incident at the ball may well be right.[31]

The reputation Jackson left in Salisbury was mixed. Some slaves in the Macay household apparently remembered him with affection and respect, but their memories have not come down in any detail. To John Steele, Jackson was a young man who paid his bills; he came back to do so before leaving for the west in 1788. He made numerous friends in the town, including some who were willing to pledge large amounts of money for him.[32]

Presumably he had enemies as well, but little is known about them. It seems unlikely that Jackson, with his taste for personal challenge, made it through his three years of law study without an encounter of some sort, but there is no reliable tradition on the subject. (One bogus account of Jackson's years in Salisbury has him involved in four fistfights, improbable on two counts: first, that they violated the code of gentlemanly combat, and second, that in view of his very slim build Jackson probably preferred to fight with a weapon.) Just after he left North Carolina, he issued his first known challenge to a duel, with a degree of assurance that suggested familiarity with the procedure; perhaps, then, he dueled or sent challenges in North Carolina, but there is no evidence of it. The recollections of his years in Salisbury, consisting as they do of the memories of two old women, Eleanor Faust and Aunt Judy of the Rowan House, leave much of his life unilluminated.[33]

Jackson as an old man once let his thoughts stray back, with apparent satisfaction, to his Salisbury days. His comment on them lacked detail, but it would not have pleased Eleanor Faust: "Ah, I was a raw lad then, but I did my best."[34]

CHAPTER FIFTEEN

Law and Masonry
1786–1787

——◦◦◦◦——

PRUCE MACAY was a classic legal type. Well-dressed, dark-haired, with bland, intelligent features, he was discreet, drily witty, and quietly acquisitive. Since his service as judge in the Morgan District began, he had bought up hundreds of acres of land in western North Carolina. A relatively young man, barely thirty years old, he had the advantage of local connections—his family was well-known and esteemed in Rowan County—as well as an education from the College of New Jersey. His practice was by far the largest in Salisbury, and he had been state's attorney since 1779. Macay largely avoided politics, perhaps mindful that it was easy, as another North Carolina lawyer was warned, to "create two enemys for one friend" by seeking office, and concentrated instead on making money. In 1783 he bought a comfortable house two blocks from the courthouse from Adlai Osborne, the clerk of court. His law office, in accordance with standard practice at the time, was a small detached building next to the house.[1]

Macay must have been a good mentor, to judge from the number and quality of the students he attracted early in his career. Davie, McNairy, and Crawford have already been mentioned. When Jackson entered the office, there was already one clerk, a fun-loving, bright local boy named William Cupples. John Steele's ledgers, which show that Cupples purchased six quires of paper between May 1785 and April 1786 suggest that he had already been

A Princeton graduate and a rising lawyer, Spruce Macay was in his
early thirties when he took Jackson on as a law student and clerk. The
date of this protrait, and the artist, are unknown.
COLLECTION OF JO WHITE LINN, SALISBURY, N.C.

with Macay about a year. He and Jackson became fast friends. They worked
together for about a year, then left Macay about the same time and went to
study with John Stokes. The lawsuit mentioned in chapter 14 suggests that by
summer 1787 they owned a horse together, along with Hugh Montgomery,
and in the fall of that year they took their bar examination together. Unlike
Crawford, McNairy, and Montgomery, Cupples was not of Ulster Irish stock;
his family were Virginia Anglicans, and fairly prominent ones; a Cupples had
recently been the Anglican bishop of North Carolina. One could infer from
that background that Cupples had the smooth manners and polished style
that Jackson prized.[2]

Jackson began his serious preparation for the law in Macay's detached office, a little building barely fifteen feet square. It had its own fireplace for cold

Law and Masonry

Spruce Macay's 15' by 16' law office, where Jackson studied, was dismantled in 1876, according to local traditon, for shipment to the Centennial Exposition in Philadelphia and never seen again. This sketch was drawn years later by the daughter of a local woman who remembered the building.

ROWAN PUBLIC LIBRARY, PHOTOGRAPH BY WAYNE HINSHAW

Young Hickory

Salisbury tradition identifies this locally made white pine and
walnut desk with Spruce Macay's office, where Jackson studied. But
its original surroundings would have been less elegant
than the historic home where it now stands.
HISTORIC SALISBURY FOUNDATION

winter days; chairs for Macay, the clients, and the clerks; and at least two large desks for Jackson and Cupples. The desks were like the one preserved in Salisbury and identified (on rather tenuous evidence) as the one Jackson used during his years with Macay: a large, heavy piece, "good cabinetry but not high style," locally made from walnut and Southern white pine, with a slanting work surface and a hinged top. Around the wainscoted walls ran ranks of shelves to hold Macay's law books. When Jackson and Cupples were not busy copying documents for Macay, they were reading in one of these books and copying out extracts for their own use in the bar examination or subsequently in practice.[3]

Among the first works they took down to study, if not the very first, was the four-volume set of Sir William Blackstone's *Commentaries on the Laws of*

England. This was a relatively new work, hardly twenty years old and already recognized as a classic by lawyers on both sides of the Atlantic. Blackstone had taken the whole unwieldy hodgepodge of English common law and reorganized it in a rationalistic eighteenth-century manner, articulating clearly the principles that lay behind centuries of court decisions. If Jackson remembered the sermons he heard as a child, he could comprehend Blackstone, whose orderly, analytical approach—distributing the laws "methodically, under proper and distinct heads; avoiding as much as possible divisions too large and comprehensive on the one hand, and too trifling and minute on the other"—was like the dry rationalism of a Presbyterian discourse. The *Commentaries* featured a small amount of Latin, legal phrases generally translated for the reader's convenience, no obstacle even for a casual student of the dead languages like Jackson. Pithy and lucidly written, it was ideally suited to the law student's technique of copying down passages for rereading and memorization.[4]

Jackson had clearly read the *Commentaries* by the time he left North Carolina in 1788. In Jonesboro, just the other side of the Smokies, in the summer of 1788, he acquired an appendix to the work. It was a short book, of no practical worth for a young lawyer, on the rather abstruse topic of religious liberty in England. Clearly, he bought it because of his respect for the author, either to complete a set he already owned, or to begin stocking his own library with works of the great authority. But in terms of actual utility, he seems to have found more value in another standard work, Matthew Bacon's *Abridgment of the Law.*[5]

Bacon's book was very different from Blackstone's—an alphabetical arrangement of legal topics, crammed under each heading with minute references to cases from English courts. It was very useful in a state like North Carolina, which had formally accepted the English common law as fundamental, and probably quite congenial to Jackson, who had an excellent memory capable of storing many discrete items of legal practice. A tradition from his early days as a lawyer relates that he carried a copy of the *Abridgment* in his saddlebag, wrapped in buckskin, everywhere he rode, and cited it constantly, to the amusement of his fellow attorneys who had a broader knowledge of the law. Certainly Bacon was indispensable in a practical sense: his treatment of trespass on the case, for example (which he called "actions on the case") explained, in order, what persons might bring an action; against whom; for what injuries; after what period of time; and whether action could be brought for fraud or violation of an implied or express warranty.[6]

A would-be lawyer's mastery of these sources, however, was not obtained until he had a chance to see how they were used, in other words, until he had attended court. Court sessions were an integral part of a law student's education. In Salisbury, the County Court of Pleas and Quarter Sessions met every three months, in February, May, August, and November. North Carolina's highest court, the Superior Court, which traveled from one district to another, met for ten-day terms at Salisbury beginning 15 March and 15 September. Jackson and Cupples attended all these, not only to observe the lawyers and judges, but to cultivate acquaintance with possible future clients.[7]

Their future clients would come mostly from the prosperous men of Rowan County, merchants or landowners. It stood to reason: lawsuits, in North Carolina as elsewhere, were mostly about protecting property. The people most concerned with the protection of property were those who had some to lose, in other words, the rich. In one North Carolina county at this period, the richest ten percent of the taxpayers brought twenty-five percent of the lawsuits. Defendants were less wealthy on the average, but above average in wealth for the entire community. The rich gentry, therefore, were often present at court sessions to make sure their interests were safeguarded. People from elsewhere came, too. Colonel Davie's brother Jo, who worked for Billy Hill, was often up from the New Acquisition during Superior Court session with a wagonload of iron, to do Hill's business and look after his interests.[8]

The most frequent parties to suits in Rowan County Court were the estates of prosperous men who had recently died and were suing or being sued for debt. The estate of Hugh Montgomery Sr. was by far the biggest single litigant; Macay handled nearly all its cases. Other estates frequently in court were those of John Dunn, Andrew Boston, and John Oliphant. Most of their lucrative business went to Macay, who also represented the merchant Maxwell Chambers. Next most active were the Rowan County commissioners, who nearly always hired John Stokes. Will Crawford had some regular clients among the most frequent litigants, but they tended not to be so rich as Macay's—tavern keepers Daniel Clary, William Brandon, and Peter Faust. Hugh Montgomery Jr. was frequently in court, but not represented by Macay; Stokes was usually his lawyer. His rich brother-in-law Dr. Anthony

Newman, who had inherited much of the Montgomery wealth, used neither Macay nor Stokes, but entrusted his cases to a bumptious, ambitious lawyer from the country, Billy Sharpe.[9]

County Court also offered opportunities for sizing up attorneys who might eventually be one's rivals. They knew Macay, Stokes, Crawford, and McNairy. Sharpe, who practiced regularly and aggressively solicited clients, sometimes served as state's attorney when Macay was unable to attend. Other practitioners included William Tatham, a likable, articulate man who was too brilliant for his own good—half his time was spent on vast projects for geographies of North Carolina or books on the western Indians—and an obscure local lawyer named Jacob Brown. Alexander Martin sometimes came down from Rockingham to argue a case smoothly and effectively. That was the whole of the Salisbury bar.

At the two sessions of Superior Court, a new set of attorneys appeared in town. These were the big names in North Carolina law, most of them from the cultured eastern part of the state—people like Davie, James Iredell, and John B. Ashe, who could plead eloquently, cite classical authorities, argue obscure points of law, and generally put on a good show when major cases came up. Jackson, however, did not expect to face them as rivals. Under the two-tier North Carolina court system, an attorney could be licensed to practice either in county courts, for five pounds, or in Superior Court, for ten pounds. The qualifications for Superior Court were higher. Jackson's and Cupples's intentions were to apply only for the cheaper County Court license; later, with more experience and more money, they might apply for certification in the higher court.[10]

They watched Macay for cues about how to handle cases—watched him, for instance, interview witnesses and gather evidence for cases. Most cases on the trial docket, they found, were continued to the following term because one of the parties or an essential witness was unable to attend; in May 1786, for example, four out of every five cases were continued. Many others were settled out of court one way or another. Sometimes an attorney had to "confess judgment" when he found he could not make a case for his client. In all, very few cases went to jury trial at any given term, perhaps only three or four. If the verdict went against Macay's client, he could enter a caveat and appeal the whole action to Superior Court, as he did in November 1785 for Joseph

Patterson, charging that the jury was not all freeholders and that the defendant had not been given proper notice of the trial.[11]

An entertaining feature of the court session, not strictly professional, was following the trials of acquaintances who happened to be enmeshed in lawsuits. Jackson's drinking buddies were often in court. George Dunn, at a slightly earlier period, was party to several suits for assault and battery, as both plaintiff and defendant against, among others, Hugh Montgomery's brother-in-law John Blake. By the middle 1780s, he was apparently too poor to play the game of litigation, to sue or be sued; he dropped out of the court records, and one encounters him only in John Steele's account book, where his brother-in-law Henry Giles bought him a blanket. Hugh Montgomery, on the other hand, was often in court being sued for substantial amounts. William Tatham demanded 26 pounds, Jacob Hughey 60, Henry Giles 280.[12]

One major lawsuit that may have had devastating effects targeted Will Crawford. In 1785 one Robert Ellison filed a suit against him for "case," for the considerable amount of 261 pounds, six shillings fourpence. It is difficult to discover this man's identity. There was a rich, litigious man of that name in the South Carolina backcountry; conceivably he sued Will over some matter that originated at the public station in the Waxhaws. In any event, Ellison retained Billy Sharpe; Crawford hired McNairy, Tatham, and Stokes. They delayed and parried Sharpe as best they could until August 1787, when the suit finally came to jury trial, and Crawford lost, with three months' stay of judgment. The financial burden must have been crushing for a young and none-too-affluent lawyer. This outcome may have had something to do with Crawford's apparent decision, around the same time, to leave Salisbury.[13]

Cupples was more successful in keeping his name out of court, except for the Baird-Ludlow suit already mentioned against him, Jackson, and Montgomery, perhaps as joint owners of a horse. But Jackson plunged right into the game of law. In November of 1787, represented by Macay, he joined the lineup of plaintiffs with suits against Hugh Montgomery. Whether this suit represented a breakup in the friendship, whether it was connected with the Baird-Ludlow matter, and how much money Jackson was seeking are questions the sources are too sketchy to answer. The case did not go to trial; it was on its second continuance in the spring of 1788, when Jackson left for the west.[14]

Jackson's action against Montgomery and Baird, and Ludlow's action against him, came after he had left Macay's office to study with Stokes. Whether Jackson's decision to change mentors was at all connected with them or with the other events described earlier is not clear. The notorious incident at the dance may have played a part in his decision, or his friendship with Montgomery may have gone sour. Cupples seems to have made the same switch at nearly the same time. Perhaps he persuaded Jackson, or perhaps he was also involved in the Rachel and Molly Wood incident. Court records raise these possibilities but do not supply enough data to judge between them.

Cupples was part of another important development in Jackson's life, which began around the time he went to study with Captain Stokes. This was his contact with the Masonic Order. Captain Stokes and his younger brother Montfort, who was to become Jackson's close friend, were both Masons. With Alexander Martin, they were among the founders of the North Carolina Grand Lodge of Masonry, set up in 1787 at the meeting of the state legislature in Tarboro; that is, they were already Masonic leaders when the Grand Lodge was established. Cupples probably was a Mason at this time, for fourteen years later he was a leader in the Order. Other friends Jackson respected—Charles Bruce, Tom Henderson, and Bennett Searcy—were members of the brotherhood. So was William R. Davie. This Masonic allegiance of so many of Jackson's friends can hardly have failed to catch his attention.[15]

The Masonic Order was a familiar and on the whole admired presence on the American scene in the years after the Revolution. It was a men's organization, composed typically of wealthy merchants and professional men but with a sprinkling of small storekeepers and craftsmen, that developed in Britain in the early eighteenth century and came to the interior towns of the American colonies around 1750. Its members were supposed to be men of good character. They were initiated into the order by a complicated ritual that they were pledged not to reveal and thereafter attended regular secret meetings for fellowship in their local "lodges." But they also made ceremonial public appearances in their regalia. There were Masonic funerals and in some places Masonic festivals on St. John's Day, June 21. Some symbols of the order were well-known, like the square and compass. There were also signs, tokens, and handgrips known only to members. Their activities stressed virtue and benevolence. It was known that they were obligated to help one another. The Masonic Order seemed a virtuous, uplifting organization without the rowdiness of men's social clubs, without the intolerance and narrowness of traditional Christian churches, an entirely appropriate institution for a new, enlightened republic. It seemed especially fitting that the greatest man in America, General Washington, was a Mason.[16]

Masonry appealed to the Irish love of secret societies and from its first introduction had spread rapidly throughout the island. Irish Masons, indeed, had been instrumental in developing the particular form of the order, so-called "Ancient Masonry," that became dominant in America. Many Masons, therefore, must have been among the leaders of the Ulster Irish migration into the American backcountry; and wherever they put down a settlement, the local members of the order would come together to form a lodge. Theoretically, any new lodge was supposed to have a "warrant" from some supervising body, or Grand Lodge, to guarantee its authenticity; but in America as in Ireland, Masons in a community were apt to set up a lodge, with its own rules and practices, without troubling about a warrant. The Masonic Order, thus, ended up flourishing in backcountry settlements where there were few wealthy men or educated professionals, at least initially.[17]

The Waxhaws apparently was such a place. Some prominent early settlers were Masons: Robert Miller, the first minister of the Waxhaw congregation, Major John Barkley, and Robert Crockett. No Masonic records, and few records of any kind, survive from that era in the Waxhaws, but there are indications that a lodge existed. Jackson grew up familiar with the idea of Masonry as an institution in which leading men of the community, educated men, participated.[18]

In Salisbury he found a similar situation. Old Cone Lodge was established before the war, apparently without a warrant. (When the Grand Lodge of the state was organized in 1787, it was warranted retroactively with the number 9, denoting its order of formation among the North Carolina lodges.) It held its meetings at various local taverns and numbered several leading men among its membership. In one way it differed from the Waxhaws lodge—most of its members were Anglicans of Virginia background. But in essentials, it was the same organization.[19]

What Jackson learned about the inner life of the lodge from his Masonic friends must have seemed attractive. Brothers gathered there to talk, smoke, and drink in moderation, subject to the decision of the lodge leader, or Master. Drunkenness was forbidden; so were obscenities, abusive language, polit-

Law and Masonry

The symbols on this Masonic apron, which was worn in 1793 at the laying of the cornerstone for the University of North Carolina, suggest the complex Judeo-Christian symbolism developed by the Order. It had some attributes of a men's club and some of a church.
GRAND LODGE OF NORTH CAROLINA

ical argument, and religious dispute. Ceremonies were held in costume within the lodge, and with a whole store of ceremonial objects. Candlesticks, painted floor cloths, thrones, and aprons were decorated in the rich symbolic vocabulary that was being created in Masonry around this time: sun, moon, stars, the all-seeing eye of God, the Ark of the Covenant, the pyramid, hourglass, scythe, clasped hands—all of them conveying the need for reason, charity, and benevolence in daily life. Songs stressed the message of Masonic love and brotherhood.[20]

There are reasons for thinking that this message strongly appealed to

Jackson. Later in his life, he became an exceptionally devoted Mason, active in the Order and in defending its values. The beginning of his membership is obscure. His first documented Masonic activity occurred in 1800 in Tennessee; but by that time, the record suggests, he was an experienced and advanced member. Nashville's Harmony Lodge was founded in 1789, the year after his arrival there, but no records of its personnel survive. Jackson could have joined it at any time from 1789 on, or he could have become a Mason in North Carolina and helped to found Harmony Lodge. He was not yet twenty-one, but some lodges admitted members at an earlier age.[21]

Masonry offered several things to young Jackson as he began a career in law: not only the opportunity to fraternize with gentlemen he liked and admired, without the pressures of competitive horse racing, gambling, and drinking, but also, at its best, a genuine warmth and acceptance he found nowhere since his mother's death. The Order was a substitute family of men, kinder and more dependable than the Crawford men had ever been to him. With its ceremonies and its high moral ideals, it served some of the functions of a church to a young man with no strong faith and no church affiliation, and it strengthened the bonds he had already formed with several respectable, powerful men. From the time he became acquainted with Masonry, very probably, he wanted to join, and his friends were glad to invite him.[22]

It is possible, then, that one night at an inn in Salisbury, kneeling in a square drawn on the floor, young Jackson, blindfolded, answered a series of ritual questions with memorized responses, felt the point of a drafter's compass pressed against his left breast, and repeated the oath—"under no less Penalty than to have my Throat cut, my Tongue taken from the Roof of my Mouth, my Heart pluck'd from my Left Breast, then to be buried in the Sands of the Sea . . . my Body to be burnt to Ashes . . . So help me God"—not to reveal the secrets he was about to learn. The vehement sincerity of the language was something Jackson would immediately have understood. It was the same style he used throughout his career. From that night on, he was part of a brotherhood that added both meaning and value to his life.[23]

CHAPTER SIXTEEN

Montgomery to Rockingham
1787

JOHN STOKES cut a startling figure. A huge scar crossed the thirty-one-year-old lawyer's forehead, grazing his eye; there were other scars on his face; the forefinger of his left hand was missing; and his right hand had been replaced by a silver contrivance, sometimes described as a knob. A tall, slender mulatto man, Roger Stapleton, attended him everywhere and took care of his physical needs. It was surprising that he could practice law, and more so that he could do it with wit, courtesy, and kindliness.

The story behind his wounds established an immediate bond between him and twenty-year-old Andrew Jackson. Stokes, a young Virginia captain, was retreating through the Waxhaws with his men in May 1780, when Tarleton's cavalry overtook his unit and hacked it to pieces. He was taken with the rest of the wounded to Waxhaw Meeting House and possibly was cared for by Betty Jackson. When he came to the Salisbury area in 1784 to practice law, he was welcomed as a hero of the Revolution.[1]

Stokes was the right mentor for a couple of young law clerks suffering social ostracism. Although a competent lawyer and a studious man, he was also a bachelor and a horse fancier, fond of a jolly round of drinks. He lived on his family's vast acreage in the woods of Montgomery County, a county without the social pretensions of Salisbury, with his younger brother Montfort (pronounced Mumford), another survivor of the Revolution. Montfort, only a few years older than Jackson, had been held on one of the infamous prison ships, and had just become licensed as an attorney. He was good company for Jackson and Cupples—bright, profane, reckless, and fond of cards. He and Jackson soon became intimate friends.[2]

The Stokes brothers had as much access to public office and power as Macay did, perhaps more. John sat in the Assembly, representing Montgomery County; in 1787 he was elected to the Constitutional Convention in Philadelphia, but did not attend. Montfort, only in his middle twenties, held a key post in state politics—he was a clerk of the Assembly at its December meetings. By 1790 he owned twenty slaves, three of whom he traded to Alexander Martin as part of a deal for a political post. John owned at least nine slaves; in 1788 he married the heiress Elizabeth Pearson and built an attractive mansion on the Yadkin. Montfort, not long after, married Hugh Montgomery's half-sister.[3]

Unlike Macay, who stayed close to home, the captain preferred to ride the circuit. Under his guidance, Jackson and Cupples spent much less time in Salisbury and much more riding from place to place in Salisbury District, which covered a large piece of North Carolina that extended from Virginia to the South Carolina line. It was an area that once would have been called backcountry, but by 1787 it was uncertain what to call it. As the horrors of the war faded into the past, the area was becoming more prosperous and less isolated. It still contained vast tracts of primeval woodland, but all the acreage had been surveyed and had owners. Near Salisbury, some prosperous residents, Virginians mostly, were planning and building generous frame mansions with brick chimneys in a style modeled on coastal Virginia residences. They, and other less prosperous whites, were bringing in more and more slaves. The area struck George Washington as backward when he traveled through it in 1791, but it was thoroughly settled. It lacked the primitive, harsh conditions of the backcountry, and the Indian threat was a distant memory.[4]

Eight counties, centered on Salisbury, made up the district. Each had its own County Court, which heard civil suits where a modest amount of money was in question, plus "all petit Larcenies, assaults, Batteries, and Trespasses . . . Breaches of the Peace, and other Misdemeanors of what Kind soever, of an Inferior Nature." They had no jurisdiction over murder, treason, horse stealing, or large civil suits; these were tried by the Superior Court dur-

181

. . . .

Montgomery to Rockingham

ing its twice-yearly visits to Salisbury. Superior Court contained moments of higher drama than the county courts; only there could a convicted criminal be hanged or have his ears cut off and be branded on both cheeks with the letters H and T, for horse theft. County court judges were limited to fines, whippings, and the stocks in dispensing punishment. Still, most court cases in North Carolina were small, and a Salisbury attorney who attended the county courts regularly had a good chance of finding legal business.[5]

The sessions of the county courts were arranged to facilitate such attendance. Each court met once in a quarter—hence the name Quarter Sessions—during a week set by the state legislature, the General Assembly. No two counties held court on the same week, so that an enterprising lawyer could attend them all. Moreover, adjoining counties tended to hold their courts on successive weeks to make travel from one to the next easy.[6]

A highly motivated attorney, eager for business, could ride the entire circuit, but he needed a stout constitution and a good horse. He had to cover almost four hundred miles in eight weeks. He had to follow wretched roads through seemingly endless forest, into the mountains of Surry County and the sand hills of Richmond County. He had to cross and recross the broad, frequently flooded Yadkin River. Several Salisbury attorneys did not make the complete circuit, but practiced in only a few counties outside Rowan. William Tatham and Jacob Brown practiced in Mecklenburg. Macay had his judgeship to keep him busy, and a very extensive practice in Salisbury besides; he occasionally worked in Surry and Guilford.

Crawford and McNairy, on the other hand, practiced in all the counties of the district whose dockets survive, and probably in all eight. Stokes seems to have had legal business in most of the counties, and by the end of 1787, Jackson and Cupples were in the records of all of them.[7]

For these lawyers, it was not just legal business that made the four-hundred-mile journey attractive. A reminiscent letter from Cupples to Jackson a few years later, describing events that took place on circuit in 1787, made no mention of cases or trials; it described instead a succession of gambling, socializing, and deal making:

> I can recollect as follows. we won of S. Bittles five pounds. my part was paid in cash yours, with a thick set of royal rib. pattern for breeches after that you purchased from Mr. Allen some brown cloth

for a big coat which I think came to about eight pounds. I recollect your gaming at Richmond but not how you broke. but the Sunday after Anson court we were at Mr. Linears [Lanier's] in company with Mr. Crawford when Mr. Allen and yourself made some settlement and you gave this note.[8]

From this and similar sources, one gets a vivid picture of the group—a band of young lawyers, with a few middle-aged men like Stokes, traveling from county to county in a cavalcade. Their manservants attended them, sometimes leading spare horses their masters intended to sell or race, and sometimes leading livestock in which lawyers were paid by clients who lacked cash. Some of them—not Jackson, surely—might be unlucky enough to ride "a chunk of a horse, carrying saddle-bags filled with law books"; others cut a more elegant figure. Their minds were as much on games and amusement as on law and work. They swapped jokes; they kidded each other constantly about their horses, their clothing, their luck at cards, or their athletic prowess; they laughed over juicy bits of testimony from recent trials for fornication, buggery—same-sex activity or sex with animals—or larceny (all misdemeanors). Lawyers saw a good deal of the sordid side of life; it was a common belief in America that too much contact with the law corrupted a man's moral sense. The conversation and the humor of the group were, by the standards of genteel society, indecent.[9]

To some serious young lawyers in other states, this sort of legal fraternizing—eating together, traveling together, bunking together—was wearying in the long run; it afforded no time for reading or serious reflection. But nothing in Jackson's life suggests that either reading or reflection meant a great deal to him. On the contrary, the atmosphere of personal interchange, banter, and competition on the lawyers' fellowship was what he liked best. It foreshadowed the rest of his career—a life surrounded by people, in which study and reading played little part.

The first day out of Salisbury, the lawyers rode a full day's journey to Montgomery, an isolated, thinly settled county bisected by the Yadkin River, whose courthouse was a small, undistinguished log cabin on the river's east bank. Citizens from the west side and their attorneys crossed in a free flat-bottomed ferry operated by a local planter; when the ferry was out of service, or when the Yadkin was high, they had no access to county government.

On either side of the river, log taverns, designated as such by a jug hanging from a pole, served the needs of thirsty litigants and their attorneys in tiny villages called Tindalsville and Henderson, "little shackling [rundown, idle] towns" according to a Mecklenburg County farmer who visited the area fifteen years later.[10]

The legal riders would find lodgings in one of the taverns. Like prudent travelers, they would see that their horses were well-stabled and fed, and then go in search of clients. As in the Waxhaws, there were a few prosperous farmers, men who owned the bottom lands on the Yadkin and its tributaries and perhaps shipped some crops down the river. They turned up at Henderson during court week, concerned about collecting their debts. There the visiting lawyers could cultivate their acquaintance, if not for business then for a friendly game of all fours. But there was little money to be made.

Richmond County, where court met the week after Montgomery, was even less promising. It lay another day's ride to the southeast, the county most remote from Salisbury. Richmond was in the sand hills; the land was poor and so were the people. At the beginning of the war, there had been only one frame house in the entire county. Its new little county seat, the village of Rockingham, was scarcely a village, merely a courthouse, a jail, and a collection of perhaps a dozen log houses. In summer the heat was brutal; in early fall, before first frost, gnats were a constant annoyance. As in several other counties, the new Richmond courthouse sat up on wooden stilts—a small log building with a long flight of steps elevated ten or twelve feet above the middle of the sandy square. One reason for this arrangement, no doubt, was to look imposing; another was to provide a place for farmers from the country to tie up their horses and wagons in the shade or out of the rain. There was good whiskey in Richmond, made by the Scots farmers in the eastern end of the county, but few other attractions.[11]

Anson County, west of the Pee Dee River, where court sat the following week, was a little better. The land was more fertile, and the prosperous farm families were Virginians, with a certain hospitality and style. Many owned slaves. Jackson, Crawford, and Cupples gambled at the home of the wealthy and prominent Lanier family, and at the Ingram family's plantation on the Pee Dee River. Jackson and Cupples won money from a member of the local Bittle family, according to Cupples's reminiscent letter. They also followed the law at the county seat, another new village called, appropriately, New Town, where there was another elevated log courthouse in the center of town, and a good inn, the Buck Tavern.[12]

At times their talk strayed from horse races and recent court cases to professional and political questions. Jackson began to get some idea of the struggles for power and status that preoccupied grown men in North Carolina, for instance, the power struggle involving the Superior Court itself. Beginning in 1786, a faction in the General Assembly had been trying to remove all three judges for misconduct, "undignified bickering" among the judges and "unseemly wrangling between the bench and some of the bar." According to its critics, the judges often started sessions late, adjourned early, imposed high fines and shamefully appropriated some of them, and generally ignored the public's needs at a time when the volume of litigation was higher then ever.[13]

But other motivations were at work, too. In 1786, in the case of *Bayard* v. *Singleton*, the Court made legal history by holding an act of the legislature unconstitutional, possibly the first, certainly the second such decision in American history. Some annoyed legislators wanted to get even by removing the judges who made the decision. Because the North Carolina government was so small, political questions tended to turn into personal quarrels even more rapidly than elsewhere.[14]

Small was a generous term for North Carolina's government. Unlike South Carolina's state government at Charleston, which was solid, imposing, and rather sophisticated, North Carolina's was simple and dispersed. About two hundred men scattered around the state—legislators, clerks, judges, and the governor—governed it in their spare time. They had no permanent seat; since 1782 the Assembly could not agree on a capital. In effect, the capital was whatever village the Assembly chose for its meeting in December, a different one every year. The state records were trundled from place to place in a wagon. It is no surprise that Jackson, whose political views took shape in this setting, came to assume that an elaborate government structure was unnecessary and in most cases undesirable.[15]

Riding through the showers and mud of spring or the heat and storms of summer, the legal travelers on the fourth week of the circuit arrived at Charlotte, where the Mecklenburg County Court met. To Jackson and Crawford, this week was a homecoming; they saw friends and acquaintances from the Waxhaws, including their old friends the Polks, and heard news of their relations. Will and Charley Polk were good company for them, wild, sporting young men who could match them drink for drink at the log cabins that served as inns. The war had not been good for Charlotte's appearance; its buildings looked run-down and neglected—just the courthouse (elevated on brick pillars, with a market area underneath), a jail, three stores, and perhaps a dozen residences, all of logs. A traveler in 1790 called the courthouse "wretched." But the county was fertile, with broad fields of wheat and corn. A lot of transactions in land and slaves were formalized at the County Court, and lawyers and clerks found plenty of business opportunities. And the following week found them in Salisbury at the Rowan court, among familiar faces and situations.[16]

Occasionally, they talked politics. That year of 1787, as Jackson, Cupples, and Crawford made their way around Salisbury District, momentous events were taking place outside the state, but they were so far away that they seemed almost unimportant. Gentlemen from all the states were meeting in Philadelphia to draw up a new constitution for the United States of America. North Carolina sent delegates, among them Davie and Alexander Martin, al though from a local viewpoint, it seemed a totally unnecessary exercise; the people of the state were happy and prosperous and had no need for more government, whatever gentlemen in Massachusetts or Pennsylvania might think. Still, Jackson and his friends doubtless heard reports at first or second hand, from the time the convention met in May, about its progress. Through the summer, they had occasion to talk about the question of a new United States government, whether it would be worthwhile, or whether it would simply mean additional taxes and regulations for North Carolinians.[17]

Another topic that came up frequently, at about the same level of abstraction, was slavery. Since the war, some people in states north of the Carolinas had come to view slavery as wrong because it denied blacks the liberty American Whigs had fought to maintain. In North Carolina the question was less humanitarian and more practical. Many thoughtful men were convinced that it was dangerous to keep importing Africans; their descendants, in the future, led by the same desire for freedom as white Americans, were sure to rebel against their captors and plunge America into war. In 1786 the General Assembly put a heavy tariff on importing slaves in order to discourage a trade "productive of evil consequences, and highly impolitic." But not everyone agreed. A visitor to the state in 1787 reported a conversation with Judge John Williams of the Superior Court, who favored importing more slaves, "frankly declar(ing) that his views were for the present ease and affluence; and said that he admitted that (his) Great Grandchildren wou'd be Slaves," presumably to the victorious blacks.[18]

To young men like Jackson and Cupples, with their fortunes still to be made, the slavery question was quite concrete. They were reminded of it every time they rode from one court to another, for they shared the road with the servants belonging to the more successful members of the party. Captain Stokes was accompanied everywhere by Roger Stapleton. McNairy had his "molatto fellow" Joshua, Spruce Macay his Guy. William Tatham had the man York, whom he bought from Hugh Montgomery. Roger was a free man, Guy and York were slaves, and Joshua's status is unclear; but all four were servants because they had African blood. The service of men like these was more than a convenience; it was a mark of status, a virtual necessity for an ambitious young man. Jackson and Cupples eagerly awaited a chance to acquire their own men. Jackson in particular, heavily involved in horse racing and horse trading as he was, needed the services of an attendant to groom and exercise his horses. Perhaps he worked out an arrangement with his wealthier friends to have this done. It is even possible that he acquired a slave in North Carolina. His first recorded purchase of one, only months after leaving the state, was of a young woman—a choice more easily understood if one assumes he already owned a manservant.[19]

From Salisbury, the lawyers' route led northward to Surry County, where court met on the second Monday of the second month in the quarter. It was a pleasant ride, especially in spring when the peach trees bloomed and clouded the landscape with pink and lavender. Surry, a heavily German county, included the large Moravian settlements at Salem and stretched westward into the foothills of the Smoky Mountains. Its county seat, Richmond, a few miles northwest of Salem, reflected German craftsmanship. The courthouse, on a trapezoidal green, had a stone foundation and a cellar; a neat row of small lawyers' offices, also on stone foundations with stone chimneys and fireplaces, adjoined it. Jackson, Cupples, and Captain Stokes worked in one of these. They probably did a lot of business, for Surry was a large, rich county by backcountry standards, and the Moravians, although they tried to avoid litigation, provided work with their commercial transactions. Several taverns were nearby; Jackson stayed at one kept by a young man named Jesse Lester.[20]

Jackson left an impression in Surry; in fact, local tradition held that he tried his first case there. According to the story, the defendant was a thief, and Jackson took the case on the condition of acquittal or no fee. The client got the whipping post and Jackson earned nothing. But court records lend this story no support. To be sure, many accused thieves were tried in Surry. In the simple economy of the backcountry, people were tried and usually convicted for stealing small items as varied as a petticoat, a brown silk handkerchief, a spelling book, and a bushel of corn. Defending some of them, Jackson would have gone up against State's Attorney Nathaniel Williams, a feisty Rockingham County lawyer who opposed him in court several times in other counties. But Jackson's name is not on the docket for any case in the November term of 1787 or the February term of 1788, the two terms of court he practiced in Surry before he left for the western settlements.[21]

The last two counties on the circuit, Guilford and Rockingham, were familiar territory to Jackson. He once lived, read law, kept store, and raced horses in Guilford, and his friend Tom Henderson was the county clerk in Rockingham, with its new log courthouse still under construction and smelling strongly of fresh timber, weatherboarded in poplar, with brick underpinning, and two fireplaces.[22]

Jackson and Cupples received their licenses together, at the September session of Superior Court in Salisbury. Judges Ashe and Williams gave the examination; no indications exist of how long or searching it was. The session itself was impressive. The judges were on their best behavior, however casual they may have been in the past. Court began promptly at ten o'clock, and by court order, lawyers wore gowns. But to young Lawyer Jackson, as he now could be called, the important thing was the sheet of paper that certified him as "a person of unblemished moral character" with "a competent degree of knowledge in the Law," able to practice before any county court in the state.[23]

CHAPTER SEVENTEEN

The New Country
October 1787–March 1788

A RMED WITH THEIR LICENSES, Jackson and Cupples again made the rounds of Salisbury District courts, beginning with Anson, in October. They took all the requisite oaths, the attorney's oath and the oath of allegiance to North Carolina and its constitution, in open court. They tried no cases, according to surviving records, but they did have other business of their own.

Much of it, as usual, involved horses. In Rowan, they settled the suit against them by Baird and Ludlow. In Mecklenburg, Jackson witnessed the sale of a bay stud horse thirteen hands three inches high, owned by William Picket, to his friend Charley Polk, and may have made money on the transaction.[1]

Jackson probably saw another acquaintance in Charlotte, a merchant named David Allison whose hobby was buying land. A persuasive, well-respected man in his thirties, Allison had a law license but apparently did not practice. He was close to a number of the most influential families in Mecklenburg, including the Alexanders and the Polks; moreover, he was a long-time business associate of the wealthy Blount family of eastern North Carolina, who had substantial land holdings beyond the mountains. Somehow he had gotten to know the three Inseparables, Jackson, McNairy, and Crawford. In 1787 he became a partner with two of them in a scheme that would change the course of Jackson's life.[2]

The New Country

John McNairy, shown here in later years as a judge in Tennessee, was Jackson's closest companion during his law student days. He was instrumental in Jackson's decision to cross the mountains and try out the Tennessee country. The two made the trip together, with a large party of friends, in the spring of 1788.
TENNESSEE HISTORICAL SOCIETY

Someone, possibly Allison, told McNairy that year of a position in the state court system that seemed to be perfectly suited for him. In 1785 the Assembly created a Superior Court in Davidson County, far beyond the mountains in what were called the Cumberland settlements. The first man they appointed as judge resigned the position without ever going to the settlement, and it was open again. It was ideal for a young single attorney willing to travel hundreds of miles through unsettled country. The judgeship would bring honor and a salary; moreover, it would put its holder in a position to make good purchases of land as the country became settled. McNairy was young, but he had friends from the Guilford-Rockingham "courthouse gang" who were well-placed to push his interest: former Governor Martin was now speaker of the Senate, and Pleasant Henderson, Tom's brother, was engrossing clerk of the Assembly. He decided to go after the post.[3]

If he got the judgeship, McNairy expected to benefit not only himself but his friends. Such an arrangement was absolutely normal; in North Carolina or anywhere else, a man in government was expected to use his influence to help his acquaintances. Especially in these wild new settlements, a judge needed support in any quarrels he got into, and he could reward his supporters by giving them court business. Allison could supply McNairy credit through his connection with the Blounts, and in return, McNairy could help Allison and the Blounts with their land transactions. He shared his plan with Bennett Searcy, Tom Searcy's twenty-two-year-old brother, who had studied law, and Searcy agreed to go with him. He also asked Jackson to join the enterprise. Jackson, in turn, may have invited friends of his own: according to John Dunn's descendants in Salisbury, George Dunn accompanied the party and remained in Tennessee for some time. It is not clear that McNairy made any specific promise of help to these men. As things worked out, when they got to the Cumberland, McNairy used his judicial power to appoint Jackson state's attorney for the district, but this appointment may not have been Jackson's reason for joining him. (He also, at a later date, named Allison clerk of court.)[4]

One person McNairy apparently did not ask was his other Salisbury roommate, Will Crawford. He and Will were handling cases together as recently as May 1787 in Rowan Court; but while Searcy and Jackson accompanied McNairy to the west, Crawford stayed east of the mountains. The reasons why are not obvious; the closest thing to a reason is Jackson's mention, a few years later, of Crawford's drinking, evidently a problem that existed for some time. The most one can say with confidence is that the Inseparables, after two glorious years, went their separate ways around the fall of 1787, when McNairy began seeking the judgeship. Some evidence suggests that at the same time Will began moving his base of operations from Salisbury to Mecklenburg, perhaps to be closer to his family. Whether the parting was friendly or bitter is not known, but it must have been harder for Jackson than for McNairy; Will, after all, had been virtually a brother to him.[5]

The judgeship was to be voted on by the Assembly, which met in November at Tarboro, a village in the eastern part of the state. The Assembly also had to consider the question of whether to approve the new federal constitution. (After much debate, they finally referred the constitutional question to a special assembly which would meet the following summer at Hillsborough.)[6]

William Attmore, a visitor from England, happened to be in Tarboro during the session. His journal offers an instructive picture of North Carolina gentry—"Legislators, Planters, and Merchants"—in action. It was an atmosphere that Jackson knew well and enjoyed, although he was probably not in Tarboro for the vote. Besides the meetings of the Assembly, there was a lot of gambling; "a trader of Newbern lost in one night 600 pounds." Social drinking of porter, wine, or rum was intense, and Attmore found that it was "very much the custom in North Carolina to drink Drams of some kind or other before Breakfast; sometimes Gin, Cherry-bounce, Egg Nog &c." (The observation supplies a context for Will Crawford's problem.) Hilarious social occasions were frequent; an acquaintance showed up one morning with a black eye he had gotten at a "jovial meeting" of some legislators after adjournment. He was standing up to entertain the group, he said, when some "of the Company grew riotous, Somebody threw an Orange Skin and hit him in the eye." At times the joviality got violent. Attmore witnessed "a Stout Man in Liquor wanting to fight with another man not so disposed" and trying with insults and gestures "to provoke the quiet Man to strike him first, in order to avoid being indicted for an assault, and as the phrase is here [i e , North Carolina] 'To Quit the Law.'"[7]

Just before adjournment, on December 19 or 20, the legislators finally got around to the western district judgeship. There were two other candidates, both lawyers who seemed more qualified than McNairy, but Martin and Henderson prevailed; their man won the position. (In true North Carolina fashion, however, no one in government bothered to send him an official commission until four months later, when he was saddled up and about to leave for the west.) The news, which must have reached Jackson and McNairy just before Christmas, most likely at the McNairy family's story-and-a-half log home outside Martinville, may have caused the new judge and his friends to hoist a few themselves in celebration.[8]

McNairy had no thought of leaving immediately for the west, not in midwinter. The twisting dirt tracks across the Smoky Mountains, relatively new and untraveled, bristled with obstacles at any season—rushing rivers to ford, steep ascents and descents over long slopes of bare rock, wolves and bears in the forests. One did not attempt them in winter except for an emergency. Moreover, even after crossing the Smokies, he and his party would still be far from Davidson County. Another two hundred miles and another range of mountains, the Cumberlands, separated them from their destination on the Cumberland River.[9]

No, they would wait until spring and spend the time gathering necessary supplies and information about the new country beyond the mountains. In a general way, they already knew what they would find. McNairy, Jackson, and the rest had heard the tales for many years, how the mountains were poor land, steep and rocky, but beyond them lay an earthly paradise, rich, fertile, and unclaimed. In the words of one early writer: "The Fertility of the Soil, and Goodness of the Range, almost surpass Belief; and it is at present well stored with Buffalo, Elk, Deer, Bear, Beaver &c, and the Rivers abound with Fish of various Kinds. Vast Crowds of people are daily flocking to it."[10]

That description was written in 1775, when Jackson was eight years old, by Dick Henderson, Tom's oldest brother, one of the first to try to organize a western settlement. Another Henderson brother, Sam, had traveled to the western country many times. Dick died in 1785, but hefty, blue-eyed Sam still lived in Guilford County, and Jackson probably met him and heard his western stories. "A good woodsman," as his brother Pleasant called him, "acquainted with the Indian manner of fighting from sad experience," Sam loved to recount his tales of adventures, sieges, and battles.[11]

Jackson knew other people who were so impressed with this lush country that they devoted much of their fortunes and energies to it. Some were settlers, like the onetime pastor of the Waxhaw congregation, Thomas Craighead, who had left Carolina for the land beyond the mountains before the war, when Jackson was eleven or twelve. Others, like Thomas Polk and his sons, were simply investors. Since the war, the Polks were deeply involved buying state-owned lands on the Cumberland, or in the Tennessee country, as it was also called. Will went out there to survey and lived in Nashville, the chief settlement, for much of the 1780s. (Craighead also lived there, though Jackson may have been unaware of the fact.) Jackson knew another land dealer, who operated the state land office at Hillsborough for several years, Colonel John Armstrong, a Mason who sometimes met with the Salisbury lodge. From talking with him, Allison, and the Polks, Jackson could have heard not only how fertile the land was but also how much money could be made in buying and selling it. The people he spoke with, in fact, were participants in what later historians would call one of the biggest and most successful land grabs in American history.[12]

In terms of Jackson's own future, the fertility of the new country probably held only a mild attraction for him. A rich tract of land, like a fine horse or a beautiful woman, commanded men's automatic admiration; but he did not plan to be a farmer in the immediate future, and it made more sense for him to look at the Cumberland from an attorney's standpoint. A lawyer could make money in a newly settled region acquiring and selling land as his court contacts gave him opportunity. The better the land, the more trading there would be. It was certainly worth a try, and McNairy's assistance was in effect a free ticket for him to visit the western country and try to make his fortune there.

It would be a mistake to assume, as some biographers have, that he chose the western country because he saw that the settled parts of North Carolina offered him no future. This was not the case for him, nor for McNairy or Searcy. All had good connections in the older counties. There were openings in the east that they were quite capable of filling. Jackson's knowledge of law was incomplete, no doubt, but so was that of many established North Carolina lawyers. John Williams, the Superior Court judge who examined him, was recognized on all hands as an indifferent lawyer, but respected as a judge and an honest man. Jackson did not need to leave Guilford and had no firm intention of staying in the west; his trip to the Cumberland was, as he told his first biographer, "experimental." Although he paid up his debt at Steele's store before he left, he did not request Stokes to discontinue his suit against Hugh Montgomery. On the contrary, it stayed on the Rowan docket for at least a year after his departure, probably because he thought he might return.[13]

One feature of the new country that discouraged some men from settling there may actually have been an inducement for Jackson. This was the danger from the Native Americans. To white people, they were the snake in the western Eden—primitive, murderously hostile, and determined that newcomers should not settle their country. Native American hunters resented white hunters' destroying and running off the game, and many Native American families experienced personal outrages at whites' hands. There was no universal war in the west; some tribes were peaceable, and most Native Americans just wanted to pursue their way of life unmolested.

Still, white settlers were in constant danger of random attacks from occasional war parties. In 1787, the Tarboro Assembly was informed, thirty-three white people were killed in Indian assaults in the Cumberland country. McNairy's predecessor as Davidson County judge, a bright young Halifax County lawyer named John Haywood, hesitated to travel to the Cumberland "for fear of loss of life 'through hostile savages'" and eventually resigned. As late as 1795, Will Cupples was thinking of traveling west of the mountains and nervously wrote Jackson, "I hope you will let no yellow boys ketch me."[14]

Jackson's attitude was very different. A man who met him for the first time in 1788 when he went to Nashville recalled him as an eager fighter from the first, "always ready to pursue a party of Indians that was in doing mischief." Others remembered that he had "a great ambition for encounters with the savages." He not only enjoyed the pursuit, he relished the actual combat; with Native Americans, he was "bold, daring, fearless, and mad upon his enemies." Where other men avoided conflict with the Native Americans, Jackson went out of his way to seek it. Conceivably, this was one of the attractions the western country held for him in the first place: the opportunity to chase and kill hostile Native Americans.[15]

Jackson's rage against Native Americans, if that is what it was, is hard to explain. As far as is known, no member of his family suffered from Native American attacks. To be sure, Susan Alexander thought she remembered the Jacksons' telling her that Hugh was killed by Native Americans, but she was mistaken. There had been no Native American attacks in the Waxhaws for some years before the Jacksons arrived and Andrew was born. The Catawbas were completely inoffensive. In short, it is not obvious why any of the recent Irish arrivals should have feared and hated Native Americans, but it is true that many did. Susan Alexander herself, for instance, hated "those horrid Indians" and reported that the Jacksons did too, "on account of their barbarities."[16]

Perhaps Jackson loathed the Native Americans' "barbarities," but he was not a Native American hater of the pathological kind occasionally met with on the frontier, someone who felt a need to attack or harm any Native American he saw. On the contrary, in later life he negotiated and treated with many.

But growing up in the backcountry among people who had shared first- and second-hand experiences of deadly combat with the Native Americans, he had probably imbibed the attitude expressed by the North Carolina delegates to the Continental Congress when they said that to extinguish the Cherokee nation "would perhaps be no more than the blood of our slaughtered countrymen might call for . . . mercy to the warriors is cruelty to ourselves."[17]

Perhaps it would be most accurate to say that what he enjoyed in Native American warfare was the experience of life-or-death conflict. Since the disastrous year of 1781, one can theorize, violent conflict had become an ineradicable part of the way Jackson looked at the world. Life was not fully satisfying to him if there was no mortal challenge involved. What was poison to some men was medicine to him. The rest of his life suggests that he periodically needed the experience of deadly peril, whether from Native Americans, Tennessee duelists, British armies, or Spanish authorities; time and again he courted it and walked into it. An important part of his decision to try the west, which he himself may or may not have been conscious of, must have been the spice of danger he sensed in the new country.

Traveling west, then, meant for Jackson arming himself with a rifle and a good pair of pistols. He needed money for the journey; he spent the winter months working, taking good care of his horses, and hoping for a good run of luck at cards. After the Christmas holiday, the twenty-year-old Jackson got to work, journeying from one log inn and log courthouse to another through the winds and rains of winter, bantering with landlords and horse-breeding friends, coping with the ups and downs of tavern fare. He carried his copy of Bacon, wrapped in calfskin, and a brief bag stocked with large sheets of the heavy, stiff paper attorneys used, locally manufactured, with the marks of the papermaking mesh still visible on its surface. Smiling and courteous, for a fee he would draw up a writ or a deed, cutting off the length of paper he needed, mixing up some ink, sharpening his quill, and beginning his document in large letters with "State of North Carolina: Anson (or whatever) County."

He may have attended the courts in the southern counties of Salisbury District in January; the documents that would confirm his presence have not survived. He was not at Rowan County Court at the beginning of February, but a couple of weeks later he turned up in Rockingham, where he tried his first recorded case, defending partners Terrant and McClain against a suit by Peter O'Neal for trespass on the case. If this was actually his first case, it was not an encouraging start. His opponent, Nathaniel Williams, outmaneuvered him; Jackson lost and his clients paid twenty-nine pounds.[18]

Various pieces of evidence also place him in Surry, although there is no case on the docket with his name on it. Local tradition had it that he left around this time, owing Jesse Lester some money for his tavern bill. (It added that in 1815 Lester took out the sheet with Jackson's debt on it, crossed it out, and wrote "Paid in full by the Battle of New Orleans.") A few weeks later, just before leaving for the west, he passed through Richmond one more time and drew up a promissory note for Edwin Hickman and David Poindexter, two local landowners, at a time when court was not in session. The fact suggests that he had acquaintances and potential clients in Surry, perhaps because he did some work there.[19]

One place where he definitely worked during the winter term and did substantial business was in Randolph County, just south of Guilford. Randolph was not in Salisbury District—it belonged to neighboring Hillsborough—but its court session was convenient for a Salisbury lawyer; it met the second week in March, when no county court in Salisbury District was sitting. Jackson had probably been at Randolph County Court with Crawford and McNairy several times before. Crawford practiced there regularly, and McNairy on occasion. McNairy was presumably in court at the September term in 1787, when Jesse Stroud, a gambler "of evil fame, name & Reputation and not regarding any decency, or the laws of this State," was caught on the first day of court playing cards for money with his servant Joshua, as well as "a negro boy the property of Archibald Lytle, contrary to all law . . . and to the evil example of all others in like case."[20]

Randolph was in an area not too different from Jackson's boyhood home in the Waxhaws, a thickly wooded part of the backcountry, with rolling hills and a small range of mountains, traversed by two middle-sized rivers, the Deep and the Uwharrie. It was still thinly settled and rather wild. At the court session in 1788, local residents presented several wolf scalps and a wildcat scalp from animals killed in the county, to collect the state bounty on those animals. There were settlers who made their living largely from hunting deer and wild turkey. There were no real towns. The courthouse, a two-story, hip-roofed frame building with a small gallery over the main entrance, stood at a crossroads in the northern part of the county, surrounded by the customary taverns and small offices, in a new settlement called Johnstonville. Like the Waxhaws, the county had been the scene of bitter Whig-Tory fighting during the war. In one way, however, the county seems to have differed from Jackson's community: there were only a few settlements of Ulster Presbyterians, and few meeting houses of any kind.[21]

Society in Randolph contained the same kind of pugnacious men Jackson knew during his childhood. The grand jury regularly indicted men of all social levels for "fiting" or "behaveing in a riotous manner" at other people's homes. In 1785 Nathaniel Williams, the attorney, was fined four pounds for contempt. He apparently failed to learn his lesson, for in 1787, he roughed up the clerk of court, Absalom Tatum, who sued him. Williams promptly countersued for assault. The clash may well have taken place in the courtroom. Other disorderly acts certainly did: Jackson was on hand at the March term in 1788, when Colonel William Moore urged his horse up the steps into the frame building during court session and drew a gun on the sheriff before being subdued. (The judges, asserting their own dignity, fined him fifty pounds and ordered him locked up in the county jail until the fine was paid.) In addition to these violent acts, there was all the backbiting, with accusations of drunkenness, buggery, and theft, that enlivened many a backcountry community. (There were respectable elements, too; Colonel Thomas Dougan, who ran the store across from the courthouse, was a man of influence and culture.)[22]

Jackson presented his license to the court at the December session and must have made a good impression, for the justices of the court, in March 1788, named the tall, cadaverous, smooth-tongued young lawyer as state's attorney. A major step forward in the young attorney's career, the appointment demonstrated that he did not need to emigrate to the western settlements in order to achieve success. It also enabled him to get some private business; in the March term he represented Absalom Tatum in a civil case. The court met on 10 March, and Jackson spent a busy four days preparing and trying cases, although his mind no doubt was constantly reaching forward with thoughts of his western venture. He had three indictments, written in his bold, legible hand, approved by the grand jury, one against William Queen for stealing ten pounds' worth of corn, another against former constable Samuel Graves for feloniously confiscating a brown mare belonging to William Richards. On be-

As county attorney for Randolph County in the 1788 March term, Jackson handled at least
three indictments and prosecuted at least one case—a good record for a young
lawyer admitted to practice only four months before.

NORTH CAROLINA DIVISION OF ARCHIVES AND HISTORY

half of Tatum, he filed suit against the Rockingham County coroner for failing to return a writ. He prosecuted Winger Pearce for profane swearing and being a "Nusence to Society."

The records do not show how much he was paid for these services, but Spruce Macay, in a comparable position a few years earlier, was paid twenty-five pounds per term. A few days after court adjourned, Jackson rode to Salisbury to pay off his account with John Steele, his pockets, if he was lucky, jingling with the British and Spanish coins that North Carolinians still used for currency (accommodating the Spanish ones to the pounds-shillings-pence system) or, if he was less lucky, rustling with the depreciated paper money the Assembly had issued a few years earlier.[23]

Before that visit, however, he returned to Martinville as McNairy's guest. The Saturday after court adjourned, 15 March, was both Jackson's twenty-first birthday and the seventh anniversary of the battle that had been fought at Guilford Courthouse back in 1781. Local tradition says that the young judge-to-be and his friend organized a celebration for that day. Although totally undocumented, it sounds plausible. The War for Independence still loomed large in the collective memory, and one common way of dealing with the mixed memories of suffering, hardship, treachery, and triumph was through public commemorations. At Martinville, where the fields around the town often yielded bones and fragments of weapons from the battle, the need was especially acute. To McNairy, Jackson, and their friends, it was also a good occasion for a set of cockfights, a few horse races, and their inevitable conclusion, a dance in the evening. A speaker to recall the battle and praise its heroes would not be hard to find.[24]

Although it was Jackson's birthday, turning twenty-one may not have been much of a milestone. By most standards he was already an adult; he traded property, took part in lawsuits, practiced a profession, was regarded as an equal by older people. Only a beginner at law, he was a skilled veteran in many of the common male recreations of the era card games, trading and handling horses, raising and fighting cocks; he used them to form friendships and make money. At the same time, he had acquired enough elegance and enough learning to present a respectable front. Women found him charming; a young woman who met him shortly afterward, in Tennessee, recalled his "gay, sprightly disposition and courteous manners." As for the basic adult qualities of endurance and toughness, he had learned them in the hardest school of all.[25]

Not only had Jackson become an adult, he had managed to do so while avoiding the traps that beset many young backcountry men. He gambled, but gambling was not a passion with him. He drank, but steered clear of the addiction to whiskey that wrecked lives in his own family and community. Sex was presumably important to him, but his record in the Carolinas shows no destructive involvement, romantic or carnal, with a woman. Two serious weaknesses marred his character: his thirst for risk, which led him into needlessly dangerous enterprises, and his need to control any situation he was in, which made him an unnerving companion, because he was always calculating, and which sometimes found expression in bullying, feigned anger, and unnecessary enmities.

He was not a great outdoorsman, although like any backcountry male, he

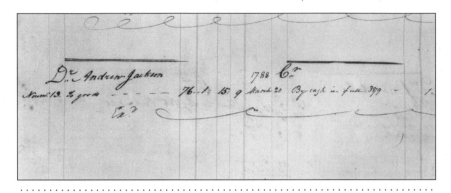

John Steele's ledger shows that Jackson paid up his account in full March 20, 1788, just before leaving for the western country. (It also shows that the storekeeper now had gotten Jackson's name right.)

could handle a night in the woods when necessary. But his life since leaving the Waxhaws had been spent in a succession of inns. Rather than hunt his food, he was accustomed to having it served in a convivial atmosphere. The silences of nature appealed to him less than the conversation of a tavern, and he did not go out of his way to seek wilderness or the simple life. He left the buckskins and homespun of his boyhood behind; he dressed to the limit of his pocketbook, and possibly beyond.

Jackson enjoyed dancing and did it well. As he executed the figures in the smoky, sweaty atmosphere of the dance (if there was one) the night of his birthday, his thoughts were free to run ahead to the new western environment that would soon be his, and the place he might occupy in it. He started with virtually nothing, and had little help, but now his feet were securely on the bottom rung of the legal ladder. If he stayed alert and avoided mishaps, he could soon be in a position to reach his goal—a comfortable, genteel life, enjoyable and leisured, with a good woman; no more. He had strong principles— the Westminster Catechism was burned into his mind, and he subscribed to the Masonic precepts. Within those principles, however, he would not be afraid to take on any man, no matter how much older or more powerful, who stood in his way. Eagerly, confidently, he looked forward to shaping his future.

APPENDIX I

Augustus C. Buell's History of Andrew Jackson
A Note to Researchers and Librarians

ONE SPECIAL DIFFICULTY about researching the early life of Jackson is that there is a body of false material on the subject in circulation. This material, none of it documented in the slightest degree in primary sources, is found in many books on Jackson, including some of the most reputable, but it all stems from one contaminated source, *The History of Andrew Jackson* (1904), by Augustus C. Buell (1847–1904).

Buell, a journalist-turned-biographer of remarkable talent in his line, has been described by the historian Milton W. Hamilton of the New York State Library as "one of the most bare-faced hoaxers in American history." He published four major biographies—of John Paul Jones, Sir William Johnson, William Penn, and Andrew Jackson—and a volume of his own Civil War recollections. All followed the same formula: truth mixed with fabrication, often in the form of "quotes" from nonexistent documents composed in language that sounded historically authentic. His first book, the Civil War memoirs, set the pattern. In it he included quotes from a fictitious service certificate and thrilling, anecdote-filled, first-person accounts of battles in which he took no part. Scores of Union veterans could have proved him a liar, but no one challenged his recollections, and for years they were accepted as vivid fact and used in Civil War anthologies. This reception was probably what gave him courage to proceed in the same line. His method of operation for his four biographies was simple. He carefully read and mastered the existing printed sources; then, whenever he needed an additional name, fact, or colorful anecdote, he simply made it up and attributed it to either a manuscript source, like an ancestor's journal in his possession, or an "obscure" (actually nonexistent) printed source.

All this was set forth in fascinating detail forty years ago, in an article by Hamilton ("Augustus C. Buell, Fraudulent Historian," PMHB 80 [1956]: 478–492). Despite Hamilton's expose, however, Buell's falsehoods have continued to snare some distinguished victims. Within the past thirty years, David Hackett Fischer in *Albion's Seed*, James C. Curtis in *Andrew Jackson and the Search for Vindication,* and the *Dictionary of North Carolina Biography* (James S. Brawley's article on John Stokes) have all repeated some of his misstatements about Jackson and his times. (Overseas researchers are deceived with special ease—for example, D. J. McCartney, in *The Ulster Jacksons*.) Part of the problem is that one of the best twentieth-century Jackson biographies, that of Marquis James, was the work of another journalist-turned-biographer who was not as critical as he might have been and accepted many of Buell's fabrications. The result was to clothe them with the authority of a Pulitzer Prize–winning biographer and thus to prolong their influence.

The purpose of this appendix is to go over the pages in Buell's "biography" (1:21–72) that cover the same time period as this book and point out the errors and fabrications one by one, with a reference to the chapter in this book where a more factual version is given. It is also to urge librarians, as Samuel Eliot Morrison did in a similar appendix to his biography of John Paul Jones (431), to do a service to posterity "by reclassifying as fiction Buell's book . . . and so stamping the title pages." Researchers can save themselves from error by checking the footnotes in Marquis James's book before citing it as a source. Buell's misstatements and inventions are as follows:

pp. 20–21—Buell claims to have gotten this account of the Jackson family's emigration from William Allen of Ohio, who had it from Jackson. Neither of the brothers of Andrew Jackson Sr. mentioned in the account can be identified in other records, and the Catawba Land Company is a fiction; probably Buell invented the whole story. (Chapter 1)

p. 36—Professor Branch and his school. A fabrication; Buell gives no source, and the name Branch does not occur in any record of the Waxhaws. (Chapter 3)

pp. 36–37—Rev. David Humphries. The man's name was William, he was not a minister, and his school closed early in 1779 (Howe, 1:449). (Chapter 3)

p. 37–38 and 40–41—Jackson's recollections of Humphries's school. Fabricated, including the part about his being a "public reader." In fact, most residents of the Waxhaws were literate. (Chapter 3)

pp. 41–42—Hugh Jackson's enlisting in Davie's regiment. Fabricated. Buell appears to have thought that Davie commanded South Carolina troops in the Revolution. In fact, Davie was living in Salisbury, and his men were North Carolinians. (Chapter 3)

p. 42—Davie's "finest plantation in the Catawba Valley" is an anachronism. Years later Davie owned a fine plantation called Tivoli, but at this period he was a young lawyer of modest means. His father was a small farmer and weaver. (Chapter 2)

pp. 45–48—The anecdotes "General Jackson used to relate" of the Kings Mountain battle are fabricated or borrowed. The first may be a borrowing from an unidentified source, but there is nothing to identify it with Jackson. The second is an elaboration of a story told by Jackson in Kendall's biography (45) and repeated in Chapter 8 of this book. All the details added by Buell are false. There is no record of any family named McGary owning land in the Waxhaws; James Crawford's niece Elizabeth was not born until 1791 (Wardlaw, 89); and Martin McGary was not serving under Sumter's command in May 1780. Sumter had no command until June.

pp. 50–51—The footnote about Tories captured by a unit under Davie's command in the early spring of 1781 is false. Davie had no line command from December 1780, when Nathaniel Greene appointed him commissary of the Southern Army. (Chapter 8)

p. 51—"Sands House" should be Land's house; Buell misread his own notes. Jackson was not taken prisoner there, but at Waxhaw Church. He was not taken by Tarleton's dragoons, but by a Loyalist unit. He was held in Camden about three weeks, not two months. (Chapter 8)

pp. 52–53—The whole account of Jackson's Revolutionary experiences given in quotes is a fabrication. Jackson did not serve under Davie at any time in the war. (Chapters 8–9)

p. 54—Joseph White was not a brother-in-law of Betty Jackson; he was no relation to her, although a brother-in-law of Major Robert Crawford. (Chapter 10)

pp. 56–57—The long quotation from Jackson, for which no clear source is given, is presumably a fabrication. That Jackson inherited three hundred pounds from a grandfather in Carrickfergus is not confirmed by any other source. Carrickfergus records show no prominent resident named Hugh Jackson, and the difficulties of transmitting a monetary inheritance across the Atlantic during wartime make the story intrinsically unlikely. (Chapters 10–11)

p. 61—The inheritance and the items Jackson spent it on are all inventions (used in Fischer, *Albion's Seed*, 642). (Chapter 11)

p. 62—Jackson was admitted to the bar at the fall term of Superior Court, not the spring term of circuit court. (Chapter 16)

pp. 62–64—The story of the quarrel with Galbraith is a very considerable elaboration of the mention in Kendall, 67. Details, when they can be checked, are false. Galbraith's given name was John, not Matthew; he was not a Highland Scot, but probably a Camden Quaker; Major Crawford who kept the tavern was named Robert, not Thomas. The whole version is a fabrication, although it rests on a true story. (Chapter 10)

pp. 64–65—John Stokes was a very active practitioner in 1787. He did not live on a fine plantation at that time; two years later, after marrying the heiress Elizabeth Pearson, he built a fine plantation, Cooleemee, in the forks of the Yadkin. No data exist on his law library; but Spruce Macay's library, given in an inventory in 1791, is the largest on record in central North Carolina. (Brawley, "John Stokes," in DNCB, 5:454, repeats Buell's claim about Stokes's library.) Montfort Stokes was John Stokes's brother, not his son. He was clerk of the North Carolina Assembly, not the circuit court. (Chapter 16)

pp. 65–66—"McLeansville" is mistaken for Martinville. Thomas Henderson was not a fellow student at Queen's Seminary. There was a Guilford County constable named Andrew Jackson, but he held his office a few years after the future president had left for the west (Robinson, "Guilford," 64n). (Chapter 13)

p. 66—John McNairy was already practicing law when Jackson came to Salisbury. Bennett Searcy, not Thomas Learcy, accompanied Jackson and McNairy to Tennessee. He was not admitted to the bar with Jackson; no record of his admission exists. (Chapters 13, 14)

pp. 67–69—The long quotation, with its vivid description of Jackson, is fictitious. Griffith Rutherford had no known nephews, and no family named Jarret is known to have lived in Salisbury. Jackson was probably not red-haired; no evidence suggests that he had an Ulster accent when excited. (Chapter 13)

p. 70—McNairy had not been west of the mountains at all when he was appointed judge; court records attest his presence in Rowan County for the two preceding years. (Chapter 17)

pp. 71–72—The supposed quotation from Jackson is not authenticated elsewhere. (Chapter 17)

APPENDIX II

The Jacksons in Mecklenburg County, 1780
Testimonies of Susan Alexander and
Susan Smart

—⁘⊙⊙⁘—

CHAPTER 7 of this narrative relies heavily on the recollections of Mrs. Susan Alexander, which appeared in two installments in the [Washington] *National Intelligencer* in August 1845. (They were reprinted in W. A. Graham, 67–79, which I have used as a source.) This material has long been publicly available and known to every serious Jackson biographer, but most have chosen not to use it. It is, to be sure, a relatively late account, but it comes from a culture in which oral transmission was the standard way of recording history and long-lived individuals often took great care to see that their recollections were well organized and authentic. It deserves more attention than it has received. In this note, I describe Alexander's recollections, argue the case for their reliability, and attempt to deal with some of the difficulties attendant on their use.

In July 1845, just after Jackson's death, Dr. John H. Gibbon, superintendent of the U.S. Mint at Charlotte, North Carolina, sent an article to the *Daily Union*, a Democratic paper in Washington. In his medical capacity he had happened across Alexander, who lived northeast of Charlotte in the Sugar Creek section, and whose existence is verified by the census and other public records (Stafford, 289). She spoke of her Revolutionary experiences, including the encounter with Jackson. Gibbon found her account so interesting that he wrote it up for publication under the title, "Sketches of the Revolutionary War in North Carolina." The Union printed it 11 July; on 1 August the Union's Whig rival, the *National Intelligencer*, reprinted much of it with sarcastic comment on its truthfulness.

The main thrust of the *Intelligencer*'s attack was that Alexander's memories at several points seemed to clash with Amos Kendall's authoritative account of Jackson's early years, published only two years before. Kendall, for instance, had stated that Mrs. Jackson and both her sons fled from the British to North Carolina (Kendall, 30); Alexander recalled only one son. Gibbon went back and reinterviewed Alexander to discuss some of the *Intelli-*

gencer's questions, and her second version, which largely confirmed the first (including the number of sons), with some new material, appeared in that paper 29 August. At that point the newspapers dropped the controversy and went on to more current matters. (W. A. Graham, 67–68)

The Gibbon-Alexander account, thus, began its existence under a cloud of doubt, and later historians have perhaps been reluctant to use it for that reason. But in fact it holds up rather well under scrutiny. The material on early farming and on Mecklenburg County during the Revolution is accurate and impressively detailed; as Gibbon commented, "Mrs. Alexander has herein described persons and dates, the crops and the season, as the best natural evidence to impress the accuracy of her recollections and opinions upon those who are prepared to understand the testimony she offers (Ibid., 79)." As to the story of Jackson himself, the divergence from Kendall's book suggests strongly that this was not fictional embroidering by Gibbon, Alexander, or anyone else, based on a standard biography; if it had been, it would have been smoother and altogether easier to use the accepted version and enhance it with new material. I would argue, then, that this evidence is an authentic account of Susan Alexander's memories, that these memories are generally accurate, and that the disagreements with Kendall need to be considered individually.

The discrepancy that most troubled the Whig editors in 1845 was one of time— Kendall and other biographers stated that the Jacksons fled when Cornwallis advanced from Camden in September, but Alexander maintained that that they arrived at her home in August (W. A. Graham, 74). As I argue in Chapter 7, note 1, Alexander's version, on reflection, seems much more likely. The earlier biographers assumed that the flight was a response to Cornwallis's advance, but since the entire area was in terror of an imminent attack from 19 August on, there seems to be no reason why the Jacksons would have delayed their escape by waiting for an actual troop movement.

The disagreement about the number of Jackson boys in the party is only apparent. Jackson's account, on which Kendall based his narrative, simply states that "we" fled into North Carolina, without specifying who "we" were. Kendall assumed he meant the mother and two sons; he could as easily have referred to his whole family plus the Crawfords; or he could also have meant, as in Alexander's version, himself, his mother, and the McCamies.

The real problem with the Alexander tradition, however, is that of motivation: why should the Jacksons' and McCamies have sought shelter with Susan Alexander's mother, Mrs. Smart? The most likely answer, in view of Ulster Irish custom, is that she was somehow kin to them. Available evidence neither confirms or denies this possibility; the chronicler of the Alexander family knows nothing about Susan Alexander's father James beyond his first name, and not even that much about his wife (Stafford, 290). But she could well have been a kinswoman of George McCamie, who did have relatives in Mecklenburg County.

One John McCamie, who died in Cumberland County, Pennsylvania, in 1766, lived in Mecklenburg for some time and acquired land in Sugar Creek congregation, which he mentioned in his will (typescript copy in files of Mecklenburg Declaration of Indepen-

The Jacksons in Mecklenburg County, 1780

dence Chapter, D.A.R., Charlotte, North Carolina). He was a kinsman of George Mc-
Camie; George was not among his heirs, but frequently appears with him in Cumberland
County records prior to 1765, about the time he appears in the Waxhaws (see Schaumann,
5–6, 43, 65). John left at least one family member in Mecklenburg, his daughter Margaret,
who married first Arthur Alexander and then James Wilson (Stafford, 145–146; Holcomb,
Mecklenburg, 71).

Another early tradition in Mecklenburg County, repeated by Parton in his biography
(Parton, 74–75; cf. Foote, 198–199), held that Jackson and his mother took refuge in Sugar
Creek congregation with the widow Wilson in September 1780. This account need not
conflict with the Alexander narrative; Foote, who was apparently the first to report the tradition, made no claim that the Wilson home was the Jacksons' primary place of refuge,
simply that they stayed there at some point. If Mrs. Wilson and Mrs. Smart were both Mc-
Camie women, then it is natural that the refugees would have spent time at both their
farms, which were near one another in the Sugar Creek area.

In 1954, Neill R. McGeachy, in his history of Sugar Creek Church, suggested (42–43)
that there was no conflict at all between the two traditions. Margaret McCamie Wilson, he
pointed out, was also the widow of Arthur Alexander and had a number of older children
with that surname; Susan could have been one of those, perhaps the one referred to in
Alexander's will as Ann. (Susan Alexander, as other records make clear, had the surname
Alexander before she was married to John Alexander [Stafford, 289].) In this way Jackson
and his mother could have stayed with both the Wilsons and the Alexanders, inasmuch
they were staying at the same house.

Though ingenious, McGeachy's conjecture is unconvincing. The conflicts between
Alexander's story and the evidence about Margaret Wilson's family are simply too numerous:

1. Alexander gives her mother's name in 1780 as Mrs. Smart (W. A. Graham, 64),
   her mother, presumably, having remarried. Margaret Wilson did not remarry
   after James Wilson's death in 1776; she was still named Wilson in 1802 when her
   will was drawn up (Mecklenburg County Will Book G, p. 47).
2. Alexander mentions "brothers" in the army (W. A. Graham, 73). Margaret
   Wilson had only one son, Elias, by Arthur Alexander. Her other sons were too
   young to be in the war (Stafford, 145–146).
3. Alexander states that her mother was pregnant with her last child in 1780 (W. A.
   Graham, 73); see conflict 1.
4. Alexander states more than once that her father's name was James Alexander
   (*Daily Union*, July 11, 1845; Stafford, 289). Margaret Wilson's husband was named
   Arthur Alexander (Stafford, 145).
5. Alexander says her father was in the army (*Daily Union*, 11 July 1845). Arthur
   Alexander died in 1763 (Stafford, 145), and James Alexander presumably had died
   if her mother was now Mrs. Smart. She must have been referring to her
   stepfather, Smart.

Any one of these discrepancies can be explained away, but together they are weighty enough to sink McGeachy's hypothesis. One statement he made in his history, moreover, has been positively harmful: he referred to "Susannah Wilson" as Margaret Wilson's daughter. This name, manufactured to suit his theory, has no documentary support in James Wilson's will, Margaret Wilson's will, or any other source I am aware of.

My approach, however, is broadly similar to McGeachy's; I accept both traditions, Wilson and Alexander, as authentic, and suggest another way of harmonizing them—both women were McCamies. Margaret Wilson's grandson told James Parton that she was George McCamie's sister (Parton Notebooks, 1:189), which is unlikely in view of John McCamie's will, but certainly they were close relatives. Some undiscovered piece of genealogical evidence may throw more light on the connection between the Alexander/Smart and Jackson/McCamie families; in its absence, I maintain that my conjecture fits the evidence as well as any previous one.

This is an appropriate place to mention another piece of evidence on the Jacksons' flight that many biographers, notably Marquis James, have used, and to explain why I have not done so. It comes from an account collected by Daniel Green Stinson, a South Carolina antiquarian of the 1840s whose work is the basis of Ellet's South Carolina accounts in *Women of the American Revolution*. His work is generally quite reliable, within the limitations of oral tradition, and I would willingly use this evidence if I could make it fit with the rest of the existing data; but being unable to do so, I have had to discard it.

The account is based on the recollections of Susan Barnett Smart, a long-lived woman who in 1780 was unmarried and living at her father's house southwest of Charlotte. (Marquis James and others have confused her, understandably, with the equally long-lived Susan Alexander, who was married in 1780 and living northeast of Charlotte.) She related that in the summer of 1780 she saw a sunburned, sallow youth riding past their house alone on a tired horse. He was from the Waxhaws. She asked if he knew Major Crawford, and he replied, "To be sure I do; he is my uncle." He gave his name as Andrew Jackson and said that the British were on their way to Charlotte. She inquired about the Whigs' activities. "We are popping them occasionally," he replied and went on his way ("Carolina Woman"). (The version of this story given in Parton, 73, with slightly different wording, seems to have been an elaboration of Susan Barnett Smart's narrative that Parton heard from a woman in the Dunlap family of Charlotte. There is no reason to suppose it more authentic than the printed version in "Carolina Woman," and good reason to suppose it less so. Cf. Parton Notebooks, 1:147–148.)

This story must pertain to September, when the British were advancing on Charlotte; indeed, it ought to belong to the period after September 21, the date of the engagement at Walkup's farm, since before that time the Whigs were quite unorganized and not "popping them occasionally," or at all. In that context, the picture it presents of an unaccompanied Jackson, riding as a traveler or messenger, is striking and a bit unlikely. Jackson himself, in describing his activities at that time, always uses the pronoun "we" ("on the advance of Cornwallice we again retired & passed charlott in Mclenburge county," AJ Pa-

pers, 1:5, or "on the advance of Cornwallis, we again fled to No Carolina," undated memorandum on the Revolution, AJ Papers) in such a way as to suggest that he and his mother,
and whoever else made up the party, were acting generally as a unit. Moreover, the road
the Barnetts lived on was not the Wagon Road (although Parton, 73, states that it was), but
the Old Saluda Road farther west (L. D. Spratt, DM 11VV290), not a direct route from the
Waxhaws to Sugar Creek. It is hard to imagine what business could have brought AJ there
by himself. One is tempted to suggest that Susan Barnett remembered the wrong Jackson,
and that it was Robert who was riding from the Waxhaws.

At a slightly later period of the war, AJ may well have been riding alone fairly frequently on the road past the Barnetts' (see Chapter 8).

APPENDIX III

Andrew Jackson's First Twenty-One Years
A TIMELINE

1767	born March 15 in Waxhaw community; lived in house of James Crawford.
1774 or 1775	briefly attended an "English school" near home with his brothers.
1776–1779	attended Latin school (academy) at Waxhaw Meeting House; lived with Robert Crawford.
1779 or 1780	(possibly) attended one term at Liberty Hall Academy, Charlotte, North Carolina.
1780	
June 1	assisted in care of wounded Virginia troops at Waxhaw Meeting House.
June 3 or 4	fled into North Carolina with Crawford relatives for fear of British invasion.
June 12 or 13	returned to South Carolina.
August 6	present at the Battle of Hanging Rock.
August 19 or 20	fled to Mecklenburg County, North Carolina, with his mother and other relatives, to avoid British invasion; stayed at home of Susan Alexander.
Sept. 25 and 26	fled to Guilford Courthouse, North Carolina, with his mother and other relatives, to escape British; may have stayed at house of Robert McCamie.

. . . .

Andrew Jacksons First Twenty-One Years

1781

Jan. or Feb.	returned to Waxhaw community with his mother.
March	involved in shootout with Tories at Captain John Land's cabin.
April 10	ambushed at Waxhaw Meeting House.
April 11	arrested by British, wounded, and taken to Camden jail with brother Robert and others.
April 25	witnessed Battle of Hobkirk's Hill from jail window.
April 28 (approx.)	released from Camden jail, walked forty miles home with his mother and brother.
May	was ill with smallpox most of the month; his brother died.
June	went to live with Robert Crawford; his mother died.

1782

| *early months of year* | worked, probably without pay, at government station on Robert Crawford plantation. |
| *later in year* | left Crawford's, went to live with Joseph White and learn saddlery. |

1783	traveled to Charleston with Robert Crawford on business, probably in the spring; lived with various relatives.
1784	traveled to Charleston again, alone, probably early in the year; spent some time there. Later attended one term of Latin school at Bethel Academy in the New Acquisition. Later taught one term of English school in the Waxhaw community.
December	Left the Waxhaw community and went to North Carolina to study law with William Crawford.
1785	probably lived at Guilford Courthouse much of this year, helped with storekeeping, and read law books. In October and November he was back in the Waxhaw community, and took part in a trade of veterans' land certificates.
1786	early in the year, or perhaps later in 1785, moved to Salisbury, North Carolina, to study law under Spruce Macay. Stayed there until early 1787, living at the Rowan House.

1787

| *February or March* | left Macay to study law under John Stokes; lived at Stokes's plantation in Montgomery County, North Carolina; rode the circuit of central North Carolina courts. |
| *August* | with two friends, was sued for 500 pounds by a horse dealer. The case never went to trial. |

September 26	admitted to the bar to practice in the lower courts of North Carolina; probably went to Guilford Courthouse (Martinville) to live with John McNairy.

1788

February	argued his first recorded case, in Rockingham County, North Carolina.
March	served as state's attorney at quarterly court session in Randolph County, North Carolina.
March 30	drew up a deed in Surry County, his last recorded law transaction in North Carolina.
April	with John McNairy, Bennett Searcy, and others, left North Carolina for the Tennessee country.

Notes

————⦿⦿⦿————

The primary source for the events of Jackson's early life is, of course, Jackson himself. He recounted many of them at various times in his long life, in letters and interviews, with his customary vividness. These recollections, along with traditions collected by nineteenth-century researchers, form what one might call the standard package of information about his early years. They have been written up by generations of biographers including, in the twentieth century, such excellent ones as Marquis James and Robert V. Remini. Many are reproduced in *The Papers of Andrew Jackson,* now being published by the University of Tennessee Press. I have made full use of them, as will be evident to any Jackson scholar; I have also gone through the notebooks of James Parton, Jackson's great nineteenth-century biographer, in the Houghton Library at Harvard.

In a few instances, this book adds new information to what is known about Jackson's youth. Most of it comes from new sources that are peripheral—an affidavit here, a storekeeper's ledger there—and serves only to augment the traditional account. But two pieces deserve more detailed mention. The uncompleted campaign biography of Jackson by Henry Lee Jr., written in 1828 under Jackson's general supervision, hitherto extant only in manuscript form, has recently been edited by Mark A. Mastromarino and published by the Tennessee Presidents Trust. No previous biographer has used this work, which is, as Mastromarino says, "a major source of many of the episodes of Jackson's early life." Most of the new material in it was subsequently incorporated into Amos Kendall's 1843 biography without credit to Lee, sometimes with alterations of phrasing or emphasis. Comparing Lee's version with those of the other biographers who wrote during Jackson's lifetime, Kendall and Reid, brings out a few suggestive differences with the traditional account, especially with regard to Jackson's contact with Charleston and Charlestonians after the Revolution.

The other significant new primary source is a thorough and well-documented genealogical work by a descendant of the South Carolina Crawford family, Mary Frances Thomas Veach's *Sorting the Waxhaw Crawfords*. Incorporating written family histories from the nineteenth century, it sheds some new light on Jackson's relationship with the Crawfords, his adoptive family, and with other evidence, shows that his break with his South Carolina kin came slightly later than earlier biographers have supposed. When he left the Waxhaws in 1784 he was not striking out on his own; he was going to North Carolina to study with a Crawford cousin. His separation from his relatives came in 1788, for reasons that are not quite clear, when he left for Tennessee while William Crawford stayed east of the mountains.

In one instance, I have attempted to rehabilitate a source—Susan Alexander's recollections, published shortly after Jackson's death. Some earlier biographers have used them; some have ignored them because of doubts about their reliability. In my view, they are probably quite reliable, and offer a unique perspective on Jackson in his early teens. I argue the case for them in Appendix II.

Source material on the Waxhaws, the scene of Jackson's childhood and war-torn adolescence, is more abundant than one might think, although few primary source documents have survived from this era; there were few government agencies and no local newspapers. I have used sources on the Waxhaws not tapped by any previous Jackson biographer—the autobiography of James Potter Collins, the entertaining diary of John Osborne, the Joseph Kershaw account book, the recollections of Maurice Moore, the Revolutionary tales collected by Lyman C. Draper, and valuable church and family records collected by genealogists. The oral histories collected by Daniel Green Stinson and used by Elizabeth Ellet in her *Women of the American Revolution* are full of revealing glimpses of everyday life.

The recent upsurge of scholarly interest in the backcountry, led by historians like Rachel Klein and Daniel Thorp and archaeologists like Kenneth Lewis, has also been a great help. The picture of Revolutionary-era life in the Waxhaws presented here is not as rich in detail as it would be for a nineteenth-century community, but I think I can safely say that it is more complete than any previous account.

Like Jackson's great nineteenth-century biographer James Parton, I have also used sources from Northern Ireland to deepen the reader's understanding of the Waxhaws. The fact is that Jackson spent his earliest years in an immigrant community which was as much Irish as it was American; I felt I had to use Ulster sources as a way of understanding the cultural assumptions that the Waxhaw people brought with them. Researching this book, therefore, has meant rewarding contact with scholars in Belfast and Cultra, Northern Ireland; it has also meant getting involved in the fascinating and endlessly evolving debate about the Scotch-Irish and their significance in American history. In this book, I have avoided the term "Scotch-Irish," too much encrusted with misunderstandings and misstatements, and used instead "Irish Protestant," "Ulster Irish," or, following eighteenth-century usage, simply "Irish."

Notes

For the North Carolina backcountry, where Jackson spent his later adolescence, legal records are abundant and help to sketch a picture of the society. Another source I have used for this portion is a biography of young Jackson by Archibald Henderson, the well-known North Carolina historian, that was serialized in newspapers in the 1920s but not published in book form. It contains a useful mix of local history and tradition. In this portion of my book, I have focused on a development not noted by previous biographers: Jackson's growing association with men of Virginia background, substantially different from his backcountry origins, and his gradual self-transformation into a Virginia-style gentleman.

PREFACE

1. The document that substantiates this anecdote, Jackson's second note to Avery, is reproduced in AJ Papers, 1:12. The story in its complete form is a matter of oral tradition, passed down in the Avery family; it is retold in M. James, 47–49. A slightly different version, also from the Avery family, is in Isaac Thomas Avery, Jr., "Waightstill Avery," DNCB, 1:70–71. For additional information, see Chapter 16, note 10.

CHAPTER ONE

1. The emigration of Andrew Jackson (hereafter AJ)'s family from Ireland to Carolina is at the beginning of all the early biographies: Reid and Eaton, 9–10; Lee, Biography, 1; and Kendall, 9–10. (Parton, 39, 46, follows Kendall.) Reid's account, the earliest, gives 1765 as the date; some other authors, such as Lee, suggest a date a year or two earlier. The ages of Hugh and Robert Jackson are not given exactly in any of these sources but can be estimated from the fact that Hugh, the elder, was considered barely old enough to fight, that is, sixteen or seventeen, when he died in battle in 1779.

2. The earliest biography of AJ states that his parents landed at Charleston on their journey to the Carolina backcountry (Reid and Eaton, 9). Both major twentieth-century biographers, Marquis James and Remini, have rejected this assertion and argued that the family came via Pennsylvania, the route of most early Irish immigrants. Their reasons are given by James, pp. 365–366. But James's reasoning no longer seems as good as it once did. Part of his argument was that the Crawfords resided in Pennsylvania before coming to the Waxhaws, and that Andrew and Betty Jackson probably came with them; but this contention was based on an undocumented article in a 1920 D.A.R. magazine. Current understanding of the Crawfords' migration suggests that they came directly from Ireland to America in the 1760s and could as easily have come via Charleston as via Pennsylvania (Veach, 131). James's other point, that the Jacksons' and Crawfords' names would have appeared in Council Records if they had entered through Charleston, is based on a misunderstanding. The Council records list only immigrants who were applying for bounty land; those who intended to buy their own would not have registered with the Council. Accordingly, I have accepted the Reid version.

The Jacksons and their kinfolk probably sailed from Larne, the port for all of eastern Antrim (Dickson, 103–104). In the few accounts of family members' emigration that specify the port of departure, Larne is the port mentioned (Walter Clark Manuscripts, 3:332).

On South Carolina's offer of land and the reasoning behind it, see R. J. Dickson, 56–57; Woodmason, xxii and note; and Meriwether, 241–242. The bounty ended in 1767; Dickson estimates that it attracted perhaps three thousand settlers over the whole period, but Meriwether (257) calculates that by the end of 1765 less than a thousand bounty settlers had arrived in the colony, suggesting perhaps that the Jacksons emigrated at the beginning of a large wave of settlers. After 1771, economic conditions in Ulster occasioned a larger migration (Ibid., 225).

3. R. J. Dickson, 2–18; Leyburn, 171–173; Gailey, *Scotland*, 4–6, 32–33. The literature on the Scotch-Irish, who in this book are called generally Ulster Irish or Irish Protestants to avoid the misleading implications of the traditional name, is vast, but, until the 1960s, of little value (and not always of value since). Earlier American writers were largely interested in creating a distinguished ancestry for themselves and praising the attainments of Ulsterfolk and their descendants in the United States. Earlier British writers were mostly partisans in the vituperative religious-political debate that continues to torment Ulster. The first start—and it was only a start—toward a dispassionate historical treatment of Irish Presbyterians in America was James Leyburn's *The Scotch-Irish* (Chapel Hill: The University of North Carolina Press, 1962.)

Since Leyburn, however, there has been an increasing stream of scholarly writing that has broken free of stereotypes to illuminate the complexity of the Irish migration, the way in which it changed over time, and the varied strands that composed it. Not all the Irish migrants who settled the backcountry were Presbyterian; indeed, not all were religious. Sources such as Howe, 1:336, and Woodmason, 42, document that among the Irish backcountry settlers there were Roman Catholic families (who seem to have conformed to the Presbyterianism of the majority), and Eid, 221, propounds "the possibility that most colonial Scotch-Irish were Christians characterized in varying percentage with residual pre-Christian beliefs [for] whom a label like Presbyterian (or Catholic) is misleading."

Good studies exist of the Ulster Scots in Ireland and of the Southern backcountry and Appalachian culture. In this note, however, I want to acknowledge my debt to the studies of the actual migration whose comparison of the two cultures has done most to shape my account: David N. Doyle, "Ireland, Irishmen, and Revolutionary America"; E. Estyn Evans, "The Scotch-Irish in the New World" and "The Scotch-Irish: Their Cultural Adaptation," especially good on material culture; Blethen and Wood, "From Ulster to Carolina," who stress particularly the versatile and practical nature of the Ulster emigrants; Dickson, "Ulster Emigration to Colonial America"; and Keller, "What Is Distinctive about the Scotch-Irish?" It will be evident that I disagree with some of the contributors to Blake, *The Ulster-American Connection,* but it is a serious and stimulating book. David Hackett Fischer's impressive *Albion's Seed* is related only imperfectly to this study of the Waxhaws, where the North British and Lowland Scots presence was negligible, and as I point out elsewhere, several of its references to Jackson's life are inaccurate; but its powerful synthesis has influenced my thinking at many points.

. . . .

Notes

The term "Scotch-Irish" was far less common than "Irish" in eighteenth-century America for emigrants from Ulster. When it was used, its implications were not necessarily favorable; two of the examples cited in Blake, 2–3, are derogatory. It seems to occur most often in references to the Ulster emigrants brought to backcountry North Carolina in the 1750s by the Ulster governor Arthur Dobbs; cf. Leyburn, 215, and the John Brevard diary, 19 September 1791. Theodorus Swaine Drage, an Anglican clergyman, used the term in a letter to Benjamin Franklin March 2, 1771 (Franklin Papers, 18:42), about the people of Salisbury, North Carolina, but on the following page, referring to the same people, he called them merely "Irish." The fact suggests that he saw no important difference between the two designations.

In South Carolina I have found one example of "Scotch-Irish" applied to the Ulster people, again derogatory. The intemperate Anglican missionary Charles Woodmason referred (50) in 1768 to "the Northern Scotch Irish" as "certainly the worst Vermin on Earth," contrasting them with an Anglican Irish "Gentleman." The British military during the Revolution, as one might expect, called them simply "Irish"; Tarleton, 86, described the Waxhaw community as "a settlement of Irish." But more importantly, so did the settlers themselves: in Moore (87–88), J. Johnson (347), and Stuart (entry of 27 March 1828), settlers using what was patently a broad Scots dialect are called simply "Irish." Lathan's oral tradition gives the story of a backcountry Whig, Bob Kilpatrick, who was aggrieved by a British soldier's holding a piece of dried cow dung to his nose and inviting him to "smell old Ireland." Finally, visitors to the Carolinas before the end of the Revolution generally used the term "Irish."

4. Murphy, 10, estimates her birthdate as shortly after 1740. On her personality and spinning skills, see Susan Alexander's recollections, Graham, 72; on her family background, Parton, 47–61. The old slave Phyllis, interviewed by Parton, described her as a "stout woman" (Parton Notebooks, 1:167), but since both meanings of "stout"—"strong" and "fleshy"—were in use in the early nineteenth century, it is hard to be sure which she meant. That she was physically tough emerges clearly from this narrative. It is unlikely that her family lived in Carrickfergus, where the linen trade played only a small part in the economy (Gill, 166n); they probably lived in the country nearby.

5. Among previous Jackson biographers, Kendall, Parton, and Remini have based their account of Andrew Jackson the immigrant on a document in the AJ Papers, LC (reproduced in Bassett, 1:4) not in AJ's handwriting, which purports to give the facts about him and his three older brothers in Ulster. To my knowledge, however, no one has been able to corroborate any of its assertions about the Jackson family. The other major biographer, Marquis James, also used A. C. Buell's fraudulent biography as a source and cannot be relied on. Kendall additionally stated, without giving a source, that AJ's paternal grandfather was Hugh Jackson, a linen draper of Carrickfergus. No such name appears in Carrickfergus sources, and as the preceding note points out, there were few or no linen drapers in the town. Lee, whose manuscript biography Kendall used as a source, described him (1) as a soldier in the garrison of Carrickfergus Castle during the siege of 1701. (This date must be a misprint for 1761. There was a "siege of Carrickfergus" in 1760 with which most people in Ulster were familiar; it occurred when the French attacked the castle, and is, in fact, re-

ferred to in Reid's biography as an occasion when the Jackson boys' grandfather suffered hardships of some kind.) Lee also stated that the condition in life of his son, Andrew Jackson the immigrant, "though not opulent or exalted, was . . . independent."

There are other versions, including a letter in the AJ Papers, LC, from one Robert Jackson, who claimed to be AJ's paternal uncle, which describes the Andrew Jackson family accurately but gives data about Andrew's brothers that is irreconcilable with the document cited at the beginning of the paragraph. With evidence so conflicting and tenuous, the only fair conclusion about AJ's father can be that nothing beyond his name is reliably known.

6. The most thorough account of the Hutchinson sisters is in Murphy, 8–15b; see also Lessley, 352–355. The sister not named in the text is Grace, who emigrated to the Waxhaws a single woman (possibly with the Jacksons) and was married there to James Crow, one of the "bounty Irish" settlers. On Robert Crawford and his background, see Veach, 105, 152–153. On migration by clans, see Fischer, 662–664.

7. Pettus, *Waxhaws*, 1–11, offers a complete account of the beginnings of the Waxhaw settlement. As she suggests (3), the bounds of the Waxhaw congregation were probably an important factor in defining the extent of the settlement; Presbyterians in the colonies laid particular stress on observing the bounds between congregations (J. G. Craighead, *Seeds*, 282.) Pettus, however, does not delineate the limits of the Waxhaw congregation, so that one must fall back on her other definition, suggested also by Meriwether (137): the waters of Waxhaw and Cane Creeks, with their tributaries. By this definition, the Waxhaws extends some distance into North Carolina. McNeely, 7, suggests that it embraces the two southwesternmost townships of Union County (then Mecklenburg). It principally covers the northwestern third of Lancaster County, South Carolina.

The population of the Waxhaws around 1770 was estimated at 120 families, or perhaps 600 or 700 people (Howe, 1:363; cf. Bridenbaugh, 127–128).

8. Kendall was the first biographer to state that the Jacksons and Crawfords emigrated together; Veach, 131, refines this statement on the basis of land transactions to suggest that Robert Crawford came before 1763, and James Crawford and his family in 1765. On Jane Crawford's feeble health, see Kendall, 12. I do not wholly accept Veach's list (129–130) of James and Jane Crawford's children. The four boys are well-documented, Thomas and James in the deeds cited by Veach, and Joseph and William in AJ's letter to James H. Witherspoon, 11 August 1824, in the Jackson Papers, LC. (For William Crawford there is a good deal of other evidence, which is discussed in Chapter 12.) Thomas and James seem to have been older, born before 1760; the ages and birth order of William and Joseph are uncertain. Of the girls, Elizabeth is mentioned in M. James, 26, but this story is taken from the corrupt and unreliable Buell biography (see Appendix I for details). There is no other mention of her or her supposed husband Martin McGary. As Veach points out, the existence of the other two girls rests on traditional claims, unconfirmed by any contemporary evidence.

9. Gill, 157–160; D. Dickson, 179; Crawford, "Change," 187–188; Stephenson, 2.

10. Importance of milk and milk products in Ulster: Young, 51, 184–186; Lucas, 19–24,

30–31; M'Skimin, 257–259; Gailey, *Scotland*, 20; Twiss, 30. In Carolina: Woodmason, 52, 151; Moore, 13–14, 41; Lathan; Stinson, 214–215; E. T. Clark, 1:751; H. M. Wilson, 193–194; Scott, 13; J. P. Collins, 61; Osborne diary, 21 July 1802. On grazing cattle in the woods, see Saye, 58; Ellet, 119, 210; T. Clark, 38, 43; MacMaster, 130; D.G. Stinson to Lyman C. Draper, 5 September 1873, DM 9VV307; Pettus, 15–16; Moore, 20; McNeely, 8; Silver, 173–180; Stedman, 217n.

11. Miller, 67, 69, 72; Pococke, 21; Crawford, "Change," 190; Howe, 1:428; Doyle, "The Irish and the Christian Churches," 181–183; Pettus, 25. Doyle, 189, points out the essentially political rather than spiritual nature of Ulster Presbyterianism.

Irreligion and its consequences were a common worry of both clerical and lay commentators on America; see Butler, 33 (seventeenth-century Maryland); Smyth,1:132 (eastern North Carolina); and, closer to the Waxhaws, Hanger, 403–404, and Reese, 68–70, 74. With no minister, one North Carolina Presbyterian divine warned, people were left "in gross ignorance of their duty to God and man." (McCorkle Sermons, No. 7)

12. Affidavit of Thomas Stephenson, 30 July 1828, in Bassett 3:416–417; Joseph F. White to Lyman C. Draper, undated, DM 15VV 416–417.

13. The route between Charles Town and the backcountry is described in detail at the beginning of Chapter 11. On marketing practices in the Ulster linen industry, see Gill, 142, and Crawford, "Towns," 143–148.

14. The quotation is from Schoepf, 2:172. For the reaction of a traveler encountering the Low Country for the first time, see Reeves, 21:475–476. Health is discussed in Smyth, 1:204–205; Oxley, 391; Silver, 193; O'Hara, 170; and Schoepf, 2:217. For a practical example, see the experience of the British army, plagued by fevers after it moved inland from Charles Town in the summer of 1780 (Cornwallis to Charles Balfour, 13 September 1780, Cornwallis Papers).

15. Landrum, 1–2; Watson, 296; Clitherall diary, April 16, 1776. The main road that ran from the Waxhaws to Charleston is referred to by a variety of names. Lewis, "Economic Development," 94, correctly calls it a northern extension of the Catawba Path; it was, equally, one of several southern branches of the Great Wagon Road, which ran south to Charlotte, North Carolina, and there divided (Rouse, 71, 138). Woodmason, 34, called it simply the "Great Road." In contemporary documents, it was sometimes called the Camden-Salisbury Road or the Charleston-Salisbury Road. To Waxhaw residents it was above all the road to Camden, the nearest trading center, and in this book I generally refer to it as the Camden Road to reflect that image.

16. On the general living conditions of the emigrants before they left Ulster, see Mogey, 7–8; R. J. Dickson, 2–18; Gailey, *Scotland*, 21–22; Gerlach, 49; Gill, 157–160; Crawford, *Domestic Industry*, 1, 5–14, 24–26, 37–38; Crawford, "Towns," 143; B. Collins, 141; Akenson and Crawford, 17; Young, 52–53; and Stevenson, 486.

The OED (2:5) defines "cabin," applied to a dwelling, as a "permanent human habitation of rude construction. Applied esp. to the mud or turf-built hovels of slaves or impoverished peasantry." The citations given for it prior to 1750 come largely from Ireland. On Irish log cabins in America, see Glassie, "Cabin," 341–345, 353, 355, 365, 368–369; Evans,

Irish Folk Ways, 69, 86; E. T. Clark, 1:751; Meriwether, 165; Crozier, 320; Evans, "The Scotch-Irish: Their Cultural Adaptation," 79–80; and Castiglioni, 150, 165. Evans, "Relics," 34, mentions the use of shingles in Armagh. Lane, 63, 64, 66, has photographs from North Carolina. Woodmason, 16, referred to "open Logg Cabbins" in an area not far from the Waxhaws, a reference that some historians, such as Bridenbaugh, 139–140, have interpreted as three-walled log pens; but perhaps a more plausible interpretation is that the cabins lacked filling between the logs; they were "open" as corncribs were open.

17. Examples of clapboarded log cabins can be seen at historic reconstructions such as Brattonsville, South Carolina, or the Greensboro, North Carolina, Historical Museum. The McNairy house, at the latter place, is an example of a log house onto which a second story was later added (interview with William Moore, director of the Greensboro Historical Museum). The distinction between "cabin" and "house" is implicit in statements like J. P. Collins, 14: "[T]he good man furnished my father with a house, or rather a cabin." Richardson's house is described in Howe, 1:417. It even had a name: "Poplar Spring." (B. P. Robinson, Davie, 17) Barnett's house: Stinson, 214.

"Here are frame Houses and Brick Chimneys," wrote Abishai Thomas in 1794 to stress how rapidly Knoxville, Tennessee, had developed (Faulkner, 139). On chimneys in the backcountry, see Davidson, *Scotch-Irish*, 7; cf. Henderson, 326. No eighteenth-century brick construction survives in the Waxhaws, but brick was in use elsewhere on the Great Road before the Revolution, such as, Camden (Lewis, "Economic Development," 100–101), Charlotte (Blythe and Brockmann, 22), and Guilford Courthouse in North Carolina (Baroody, 9, 37–41). It was made at Logtown, just north of Camden, a few years later; two American officers from Greene's army in 1781 hid behind "a small Brick Oven" to spy on the British defenses (Mathis, 104). Brick fragments were used as filler in the York County house of Colonel William Bratton, traditionally built in 1776 (Wilkins, Hunter, and Carrillo, 21); bricks underpinned the house of a tailor who lived some miles farther west (J. P. Collins, 17). Both these houses were in areas somewhat remote from the main commercial routes. All things considered, it seems probable that some Waxhaw houses of the same era had brick chimneys or ovens. Glazed houses were rare in the backcountry in 1760 (Meriwether, 165) and were still rare a quarter of a century later (Moore, 41); cf. H. L. Watson, 17.

18. Restorations of eighteenth-century backcountry farms like the one at Historic Brattonsville, York County, South Carolina, include most of these outbuildings. To judge from J. P. Collins, 66, the most common were the smokehouse and the separate kitchen. A still house is discussed more specifically in Chapter 3. On slaves' housing, see Beck, 127.

On elimination, see Glassie, *Ballymenone*, 758; Mogey, 36–37. Using the woods rather than building a privy was not a uniquely Irish preference, however. William Drayton, a wealthy Charlestonian who traversed the predominantly English areas of coastal North Carolina in 1786, did not notice a single "N[ecessary] house" in the entire state.

19. Merrell, 186, 193ff., 199, 210–11; D.S. Brown, 254; Pettus, *Waxhaws*, 35; Smith, 1:184–194.

20. Revill, 17–23, summarizes the facts about James Crawford's property. On Mc-

Camie, see statements of James and Thomas Faulkner, Walter Clark Mss., 3:312, 315. Jackson's land was also claimed by another settler, Thomas Ewing (see Remini, AJ1, 3–4). The plats of land grants in the South Carolina Archives that are labeled "Irish" and come from the Waxhaws all pertain to lands on the south side of the settlement, for example, John McCrory, Henry Stimson, Agness Wilson, Daniel Wilson.

21. On the boundary problem, see Meriwether, 250. Evidently a trail had been blazed along the line, or part of it; Charles Woodmason followed it in 1768 (Woodmason, 33).

Robert Crawford's land purchase was recorded in Mecklenburg County (Revill, 17–19).

22. M. James, 367, n14; Walter Clark Mss., 3:331. As Remini, AJ1, 427, n9, points out, early biographies do not agree whether Andrew Jackson Sr. died before or after the birth of his last child. Like Remini, I think it is more plausible to assume that he died before.

23. The case for South Carolina is presented at length by Herd, the North Carolina case by Harris. M. James, 368–374, in a closely argued footnote, compares the two cases and comes down on the South Carolina side, while confessing, "My opinion is that neither party has proved its case." The quote is from Harris, 5.

24. Had AJ not been fighting with a South Carolina volunteer group in spring 1781, he would not have been seized and taken to Camden, with the disastrous consequences narrated in Chapters 9–10. Had he not gone to Charles Town on government business in 1783, he would not have had the formative experiences described in Chapter 11.

CHAPTER TWO

1. Moultrie, 552–553.

2. AJ, in his letter of recollections to Amos Kendall, July 19, 1843, AJ Papers, said the house was three-quarters of a mile west of the road. Many backcountry houses were located at the end of such lanes; other examples are in Chapters 7 and 8.

3. Partitioned-off rooms, an early amenity in a log house, appear in the McNairy House in Greensboro and are mentioned in J. P. Collins, 63, as a feature of a York County house in the 1780s.

4. Affidavit of Thomas Stephenson, 30 July 1828, Bassett, 3:416–417; Logan Mss., DM 16VV 287–288.

5. Kendall, 12.

6. Veach, 129, 132. M. James (8) states that James was a distiller but gives no source. Much of his information on the South Carolina period of AJ's life came from A. S. Salley of the South Carolina Historical Commission and deserves a presumption of accuracy; I have followed him here.

Another statement by James (16), however, that Crawford owned land extending to the Catawba and operated a grist mill, is contradicted by existing deeds, according to Nancy Crockett, a longtime researcher of early landowners in the Waxhaws; a third (6), that Crawford owned slaves as early as the 1760s, is at least dubious. I have found no evi-

222

Young Hickory

dence suggesting that he owned slaves at any time. In 1790, neither of James's sons in the Waxhaws, Thomas and James Jr., held any slaves at all (Heads of Families, 23).

Marquis James was interested in portraying James Crawford as a prosperous farmer, but all the available evidence suggests he was considerably less so than his brother Robert. That Crawford served in the militia is clear from the "James Crawford" file in SC-AA. He was not, however, the Lieutenant James Crawford mentioned in George White's pension application, NA. That was his son (see Chapter 6 for fuller discussion). One building from his farm, a log smokehouse, survived into the twentieth century (Pettus, "Andrew Jackson Memorial").

7. The local historian Daniel G. Stinson estimated (to Lyman C. Draper, September 5, 1873, DM 9VV307) that in 1780 only one-twentieth of the land in that part of the backcountry had been cleared. On Crawford's land, see Harris, 30. On forests and grazing cattle, see Saye, 58; Ellet, 119, 210; T. Clark, 38, 43; MacMaster, 130; D. G. Stinson to Lyman C. Draper, 5 September 1873, DM 9VV307; Pettis, 16; Moore, 20; Landrum, 1–2; McNeely, 8; Silver, 173–180; and Stedman, 217n. The records of Charles Burnett's estate sale in 1762 (Anson County, North Carolina, Will Book 1, p. 283) refer to a "gang of hogs." On hogs running wild, see J. P. Collins, 54.

8. Lumpkin, 140; Blethen and Wood, 21; E. Wilson, 303; Silver, 96–97; Klein, 51–56; and Theodorus S. Drage to Benjamin Franklin, 2 March 1771, Franklin Papers, 18:40. See especially the figures given by Klein, 26–27, in which probate records show that at least 52 percent of backcountry households owned guns, and as Klein points out (24), these figures understate the extent of ownership. The conversation with the hunter is from Castiglioni, 150. Hunting was popular in Ulster, too (see Young, 43; Akenson and Crawford, 51). Sources such as Biggar, pp. 82, 98–99, 151, 158–159; the quotation from Sheridan in Bliss, 166; and D. Kennedy, 149, suggest that many households in Ulster in the 1760s owned firearms.

9. Parton, 64. Doddridge, 123, recalled that boys on the frontier received their first rifle around the age of twelve or thirteen, and the sources cited in Sajna, 98–99, 130–131, confirm this age for Ulster Irish Pennsylvania. Daniel Boone received his first rifle at this age (Faragher, 15). South Carolina fathers at the present time often introduce their sons to deer hunting at age nine or ten, and some a good deal earlier. Cf. Ramsay, South Carolina, 2:405: "Children are . . . early equipped for the chase with a dog, a gun, and a horse. Boys not more than ten years old can show with pride the deer they have killed."

10. A good idea of the volume of traffic on the Wagon Road can be gotten from Thorp, "Business," especially the pages (400–402) on trade between Charles Town and Salisbury. On cattle drives, see Merrell, 179; Tompkins, 1:22; Reitz et al., passim. On cow pens, see Dunbar, 125–128. On "New Pensilvaney," see Joshua Gordon "Witchcraft Book," [12]. On "Virginny," see Bliss, 217. Thomas Blair's pension application, NA, referred to the river as the "Catawby."

11. The estate sale of Charles Burnett, in 1762 (Anson County, North Carolina, Will Book 1, p. 283), lists nine pounds' worth of flour, about the value of a horse, as being purchased by "Mr. Kersha." William Moultrie ("Journal," 552) noticed large wheat fields in the

Waxhaws in 1772, as did Cornwallis in 1780 (to George Turnbull, September 11, 1780, Cornwallis Papers). Andrew Walker: James G. L. Huey to George Huey, 19 June 1884, in Huey, 3.

12. On the origins of Waxhaw Presbyterian Church, see Howe, 1:288–290, and Pettus, 25–27. In the text, and to some degree in the notes, I have tried to be scrupulous about the terms used in colonial and Revolutionary South Carolina for places of worship. According to John Drayton (Cohen, 267) only those of the Anglicans were called "churches"; the rest were referred to as "Meeting Houses &c." Woodmason, 14, understood that more than a thousand people attended services on a typical Sunday, but this was merely a rumor he heard; hundreds is far more likely. Cf. Saye, 57.

13. Other Presbyterian places of worship in the South Carolina backcountry are described in Howe, 1:338, 422, 427, 433; the dimensions and floor plans of Presbyterian meeting houses in the Cumberland Valley of Pennsylvania, where many early Waxhaw settlers came from, are in Nevin, 37–38, 59, 140, 174, 182 184. Robert and Jean Miller's deed is cited in Pettus, 26.

14. Twelve tunes: Stevenson, 196–197; Patrick, 111, 121, 133; Simpson, 549. On Elizabeth Jackson's Bible, see Howe, 1:539. On communion service, see Pettus, 23–24; Howe, 1:508; Buck and Buck, 17.

15. Pettus, 26–30; Robinson, Davie, 22.

16. Howe, 1:509; Craighead, 282; J. P. Collins, 15–16. A list kept by John Simpson of his pastoral visits in 1774–1775 (copy in the South Caroliniana Library) suggests how seriously this responsibility was taken. On shorter Catechism, see Parker and Smith, 72–73. On "Question-book," see Akenson and Crawford, 51, 81.

17. Howe, 1:416–420.

18. Ibid., 1:420; Robinson, Davie, 19–24.

19. Hugh's and Robert's attending common schools: Reid, 10. AJ also attended an "English school," according to some of the recollections gathered by James Walkup for the birthplace controversy in the 1850s. Probably it was the same one. George McWhorter, who claimed to have been his schoolmate, lived near Walkup's mill; another account named Israel Walkup and James and Henry "Mass" (probably Massey) as fellow students (Harris, 35, 37). Parton interviewed another former schoolmate he identified as "Mr. Ewing" (Parton Notebooks, 1:186–187) but Parton often got names slightly wrong, and the man was probably a member of the Huey family who lived in the vicinity. The Massey family, from Brunswick County, Virginia, lived on Waxhaw Creek (Henry Massey pension application, NA). Henry Massey was Hugh Jackson's age; James was apparently older (Massey Family File, York County Library). A school attended by these boys would probably have been on the north side of Waxhaw Creek not far from the McCamies'—an easy walk for all three Jackson boys. The Walter Clark Manuscripts, 3:332b, contain a map of the neighborhood that shows all these places.

Walkup is a name with numerous spellings, including "Wahab," "Waughup," and "Wauchope," and no standard one. The central consonant must have been a guttural on the order of the Scottish "ch."

This is probably an appropriate place to explain my handling of proper names in the text. I usually refer to the men and boys of the Waxhaw community by nicknames rather than full names, because it seems to me that to use the full names—Thomas, Andrew, Hugh, Robert, William—is to misrepresent the texture of life in the Waxhaws, to make it unnecessarily pompous and stately. In upcountry South Carolina, then as now, boys and grown men were commonly referred to by diminutives—Tommy, Andy, Huey, Bob or Robin, Billy or Will. A spy's account to Lord Cornwallis in 1780 (Wickwire and Wickwire, 243) conveys the flavor of backcountry conversation: "I went as far as Fishing Creek, & there Billy McDaniel's wife told me that she saw Dicky Thomason who said he saw young Tommy Rigdom that just came from camp." James Knox of Mecklenburg County was known as "Jimmy Knox the blacksmith." (John Rosser to Lyman Draper, 13 September 1873, DM 13VV12) Recollections in the Walter Clark Manuscripts (3:324, 332) refer to AJ's brother "Huey" Jackson and his boyhood friend "Charley" Findley. Colonel William Hill, a Revolutionary leader of local importance who appears in Chapter 5, was called "Billy" Hill (Moore, 22), but AJ's fellow law student William Cupples (see Chapter 13) went by the nickname Will. The nickname for Robert could be either Robin or Bob. I have felt free to use these nicknames except in a few cases of high-status men like Thomas Sumter and William Richardson Davie, to whom there is no positive evidence that nicknames were ever applied.

The sources rarely depict backcountry common schools in any detail. Caldwell, 66, and Scott, 14, stress physical punishment. J. P. Collins, 15, notes the yearly schedule. Stevenson, 216–217, and James Orr's poems in Akenson and Crawford, 31, 51, describe Ulster schools of the late eighteenth century and their reliance on the Bible and the Catechism. The quoted material is from the papers of John Allen, a schoolmaster in Orange County, North Carolina, in the 1780s (Harry L. Watson, 19).

As Esmond Wright observed (Blake, 4), the Presbyterian Irish were committed to education. In County Down, the common people were described as "anxious" for their children to be educated (Stevenson, 216–217). Bastards in Guilford County, North Carolina, were routinely "bound out" to a master with orders that he teach them reading and writing as well as a trade (B. P. Robinson, "Guilford," 62). "It would have broken my heart if I had not known how to read," testified a Mecklenburg County woman. "It is a terrible loss not to know how to read." (Graham, 72) Arnow, in *Flowering*, 169–170, paints a similar picture for the early Tennessee frontier. By age twelve, a contemporary of AJ who lived west of the Catawba "had learned to read English pretty well and write a fair hand, and gained a tolerable knowledge of arithmetic." (J. P. Collins, 16)

One would expect, then, a high rate of literacy in the Carolina backcountry, and this seems to be the case. The lowest figure suggested for the number of literate adults in a given backcountry community is slightly over half (C. G. Davidson, *Scotch-Irish*, 11), the highest 98 percent (Fischer, 716). A careful investigation in Guilford County, North Carolina, found 86 percent literacy among all signers of legal documents, and 91 percent among men (Hughes, *Guilford County*, 21). The historian of the early South Carolina backcountry estimated 80 percent or 90 percent of settlers could sign their names (Meriwether,

177). Anecdotally, much can be inferred from casual mentions of reading, like that of a backcountry adolescent visiting a neighboring settlement for the first time, who took up "an old book that lay close at hand, and was perusing the same." (J. P. Collins, 29) An account of the Waxhaws by a descendant of early settlers stresses the literacy of the early settlers, shown by the number of eighteenth-century books passed down as family heirlooms, especially religious books (McNeely, 10).

20. Parton, 64; Harris, 35.

21. George McC. Witherspoon to Lyman Draper, March 20, 1874, DM 12VV 380–381, states that Thomas Crawford lived on the waters of Cane Creek. No source gives a date for his birth; Veach (129, 135) conjectures a date between 1745 and 1750. In 1774 his father deeded him part of the family land on the Wagon Road (Ibid., 132); it seems likely that this deed was connected with his marriage to Elizabeth Stephenson. Her gravestone in Waxhaw Church graveyard gives her birthdate as 1753. James Crawford, born in 1775, who is buried near her, was probably her oldest son, though not cited as such by Veach, whose list of children (134) begins with Jane, born 1777. Fischer, 675, mentions the early age at marriage in the backcountry.

22. That Thomas lived on Cane Creek rather than near his father suggests that he and his wife were living on Stephenson land, just as they buried their dead in the Stephenson plot at Waxhaw Church. Nancy Crockett, my source for the fact that the Stephensons lived on Cane Creek, argues that John Stephenson, who objected to his son's going off to Charles Town to fight because of "the demoralizing influence of camp life" (Kegley, 46), would not have tolerated a riotous wedding feast. My view is that standards change; behavior that now seems wild may have seemed safe and acceptable when it had the sanction of long tradition. On John Stephenson an elder, see Howe, 1:421.

This account of wedding festivities is drawn mainly from Moore, 27–28, and the Osborne diary, 2–3 April, 12 May 1801, both of which describe weddings near the Waxhaws a few decades later, in York County, South Carolina, and Union County, North Carolina, respectively. Barkley, 32–35, provides an Ulster parallel. I have also used Finley, 71, whose Irish Presbyterian author spent his childhood in the Waxhaws. "Making an appearance" in an Irish settlement in North Carolina was called "coming out," but the custom was the same (Rankin, 104). I have added a detail or two from Doddridge, 102–106, which deals with English Tidewater settlers from Maryland and Virginia in frontier Pennsylvania. Although these settlers were not Irish, their customs appear to have been influenced by the Irish, in the use of whiskey and the practice of the "infare" (see EDD 3:318); of course, they simply may have been broadly similar. "Plantation" was used of any farm; cf. Davies, 319, for an example from Pennsylvania, or Feltman, 11 December 1781, for one from North Carolina. J. P. Collins, 21, describes boys' games at a frolic.

23. Of Jane Crawford very little is known. She signed a document in June 1774 with the name "Jennet" (Lancaster County Deed Book H, 100); by 1780 she had died (Murphy, 10). Her burial place is unmarked and unknown. Death and burial customs seem to have been very similar in Ulster and in settlements of Ulster people in North America. On Ulster, see James Orr's "The Irish Cottier's Death and Burial" (Akenson and Crawford, 29–30,

110–111); Pococke, 14; M'Skimin, 263; and Lunney, 8. On settlers in America, see Ford, 241; and Moore, 42. On "big house," see M. Williams, 39. On sitting around hearth, see Evans, *Irish Folk Ways*, 93. "Discoursing" girls was a term used frequently in the Osborne diary (e.g., February 11, April 15, May 7, May 23, September 26, October 6, 1800); it referred to conversation intended as a prelude to a physical relationship—what the Ulster settlers' twentieth-century descendants in South Carolina call "talking trash."

On superstition in Ulster, see Moore, 42; Akenson and Crawford, 111; Howe, 1:408, 417; McSkimin, Carrickfergus, 259; and Wilson, 133.

24. Any Irish accent might be called a brogue, as Doyle, *Ireland*, 249, points out. Woodmason, to be sure, renders the speech of the Carolina Irish in an eighteenth-century stage Irish accent (150, 154), but this seems consistent with his frequent stereotypes and exaggerations in other areas. More typical is the sentence of an Irish immigrant cited by Moore (87): "Och, but yees a braw company wi' ye!" There were and are several Ulster accents; the broad Scots occurs typically on the north and east coast (Braidwood, 6; Crozier, 312). Speakers of other accents might caricature the broad Scots (Monahan, 32) or describe it as "disagreeable" (Akenson and Crawford, 32) or hardly intelligible to strangers (Stevenson, 244, 282). It is far from certain that all the Ulster immigrants in the Carolinas spoke in broad Scots, but some definitely did. "The family speak very broad," noted Enos Reeves of an Irish Presbyterian household in Guilford County, North Carolina (Reeves, 467). Not only did the immigrants bring over an accent, but they preserved it, or a familiarity with it, for a long time. A man born in Lancaster County in 1836 recalled hearing an old neighbor woman who had been born in South Carolina in 1769 read a book written "in Irish dialect." (Mosher, 77). James Parton, researching his biography in the Waxhaws in 1859, thought he detected traces of a brogue in some people he interviewed (Parton Notebooks 1:183).

25. Norris W. Preyer acutely observes in his Postscript to *Hezekiah Alexander and the Revolution in the Back Country* (Charlotte: Author, 1987), 191, that Irish Protestants have acquired two distinct and contradictory images in early American history. Some contemporary observers described them as industrious, others lazy; some called them pious, others licentious and rowdy; some saw them as cohesive, others as anarchic. Twentieth-century historians have used one image or the other, according to the evidence they preferred to focus on. Preyer suggests that both may be right, that there were two groups, and asks, "Were the seventeenth- and early eighteenth-century Scotch-Irish immigrants a more cohesive and religiously motivated group than those who came toward the middle of the eighteenth century?"

South Carolina Presbyterian history would certainly suggest so. The wave of immigrants that began in the 1760s and their comparative lack of "piety and devotion" are well attested from several backcountry Presbyterian congregations (see Howe, 1: 336, 340–341, 406, 428, 439). Woodmason, who commented (42) on the new surge of immigration in 1768, thought early in his ministry (38) that the newcomers were better behaved than the earlier Irish settlers, but later (60) he called them "the Scum of the Earth, and Refuse of

Mankind" and asserted (96) that the "Cohees," or Pennsylvania Irish, were far more pious and orderly. Arthur Young, in 1779, found a general consensus in Ulster that the emigrants of the 1760s and early 1770s had been "idle," "worthless," poor, and Presbyterians, or at least "Dissenters." (38, 50). The Belfast News Letter, referring apparently to the emigrants of the 1760s, called them "the very meanest of the People" (M. A. Jones, 13). The nominal Presbyterianism of the emigrants tells little about their behavior, for the temper of Ulster Presbyterianism had changed in the course of the eighteenth century. The historian of the church affirms that from about 1750 attendance at religious functions had been shrinking, that the agrarian uprisings of the 1770s in Antrim and Down offered "humiliating evidence that religion was losing its hold upon the hearts and minds of the population," and that two decades later "drunkenness, profane swearing, and Sabbath-breaking were fearfully prevalent" among Ulster Presbyterians (Reid, 3:338, 341n, 383). By the 1770s, in other words, it was quite easy for people to be Presbyterian and idle, worthless, and rowdy.

To be sure, there were still instances in these years of Presbyterian congregations going to America under the leadership of their minister; Stephenson's Scotch-Irish Migration offers an example of such an exodus in 1772. But evidence on both sides of the Atlantic suggests that the bulk of the Bounty Irish were freelance, unorganized, and, compared to earlier migrants, irreligious.

CHAPTER THREE

1. Attendance at Humphries's academy: Reid, 10. That AJ went to stay at Robert Crawford's when he began school there is well-supported by the evidence. The best piece comes from AJ himself. In a letter to Robert Mills, July 8, 1827 (Bassett, 3:371), he mentioned Major Crawford, "who lived there [i.e., the crossing of Waxhaw Creek] when I was growing up and at school," and continued, "I lived there for many years." Given the context, there is little doubt that "there" refers specifically to the Robert Crawford place. The question is which years, exactly, made up the "many years." It is known that AJ's earliest years were spent on the James Crawford place. It is also known that after his mother's death in 1781 he lived intermittently at Robert Crawford's before leaving for North Carolina in 1784. But for most of those three years he was living elsewhere, for reasons explained in Chapters 10, 11, and 12. So the "many years" probably also included a period before his mother's death, specifically the years he was going to school at the meeting house.

Other pieces of evidence strengthen this deduction. Aunt Phyllis, a slave of Robert Crawford's, recalled that AJ had boarded there with two other young men while he was attending school (Walter Clark Manuscripts, 3:317); she also remembered treating him for the "big itch." (Parton, 60) Robert Crawford's descendants believed that he had not only lived on the place, but had been raised there (George McC. Witherspoon to L. C. Draper, March 14, 1871, DM 12VV369).

The obvious question is why he should have done this — why he should have moved only a mile down the road to attend a school that was three miles away. Aunt Phyllis's recollections supply a possible answer. He was to room with two other academy students; they could help each other with their studies and concentrate on their lessons in a way that he could not have done if he had been living on the James Crawford farm. It is for this reason that I suggest that William Crawford, who is known to have attended the school (Howe, 1:541, 582), accompanied him.

2. On Presbyterian academies, see Keller, 80–81. Caldwell, 66, is the source of the term "dominie," and shows how freelance academies, in addition to those conducted by ministers, flourished in the region (69, 72). Pettus, 31, gives the early history of the Waxhaw Academy.

3. Except for Adair and Brown, the students named are mentioned in Howe, 1:582. Adair's attendance is confirmed by AJ in a handwritten note on Adair's pension application, NA. Brown's studying the classics "at a school in the Waxhaw congregation" is from Saye, "Cedar Shoal Church." As Brown was born in 1763, the school must have been Humphries's. A variant account in Howe, 1:616, gives a date of 1782, which is impossible; the schoolhouse had been burnt the previous year, and the school was not reorganized until 1784 or 1785. AJ intended for ministry: Reid, 10.

4. Wardlaw, 88–89, 93–94; Reeves, 471. AJ to James Witherspoon, August 11, 1824, Jackson Papers, LC, mentions his early "sincere regard" for Sarah Crawford. On Phyllis, see Parton, 60.

5. R. Friedman, 16, 23, 30; Leyburn, 152–153; Newman I. White,VI, 226; Stevenson, 418, 440; Twiss, 89.

6. R. Friedman, 20, 53, 59, 60, 94–95; Parton notebooks, 1:169; Newman I. White, VI, 226; *North Carolina Folklore*, 4 (December, 1956):17. Doddridge, 119, mentions an ointment of sulfur and lard as a homemade frontier cure for the itch; if Phyllis did not use pokeweed, this was probably what she used.

7. Barkley's tavern is mentioned in Moultrie, 552, W. L. Smith, 75 ("an indifferent house") and Brevard diary, September 30, 1791. Robert Crawford's house, though not mentioned as a public house in any surviving source, had its share of distinguished visitors—Lord Cornwallis in 1780 (Cornwallis to George Turnbull, September 11; to Nisbet Balfour, September 15, 1780, Cornwallis Papers) and President Washington in 1791 (Henderson, 277)—presumably because it was accessible and large. The slave Phyllis recalled "many boarders" there (Parton Notebooks, 1:168). Andrew Pickens, from whom Crawford bought the property, had operated a store, so that there was probably a suitable building on the site.

A good idea of the volume of traffic on the Wagon Road can be gotten from Thorp, "Business," especially the pages (400–402) on trade between Charles Town and Salisbury. On cattle drives, see Merrell, 179; Tompkins, 1:22; Reitz et al., passim. On cow pens, see Dunbar, 125–128. On Andrew Walker, see James G. L. Huey to George Huey, June 19, 1884, in Huey, 3.

For the concept of the gentleman in America, see Bushman's excellent discussion, pp. 30–99 and 182–186. Isaac's formulation for Virginia (131) seems equally correct for the Carolinas: "Appropriate demeanor, dress, manners, and conversational style were essential.

These traits—specially if accompanied by a familiarity with the sources of sacred, Classical, or legal learning—gave a presumption of gentility, but the status of gentleman could be confirmed only if one unmistakably possessed the means of personal independence."

The presence of genteel clothes and accoutrements in the pre-Revolutionary backcountry—at least along the Wagon Road—is evident from Lewis, 139, and Tompkins 1:24. Joseph Kershaw's account book for 1774–1775 gives data about the Waxhaws in particular; some residents like Henry Foster, John Barkley, and John Barnet were ordering broadcloth and fine linen for shirts, waistcoats, and coats. One cannot be sure what these men wore every day, but these were certainly their Sunday clothes. (Linda Ballard of the Ulster Folk and Transport Museum helped me interpret these accounts.) For an overview of genteel American men's clothes at this time, see Warwick, Pitz, and Wyckoff, 154–155, 159–161, 170–171.

8. Bridenbaugh (170) argues that gentlemanly status could not be created within the backcountry, but could be (and rather often was) imported from the coast, based on wealth, education, or family connections. Charles Woodmason, with his customary hyperbole, sized up the inhabitants of Camden when he first arrived among them in 1766 (6): "No genteel or Polite Person among them—save Mr. Kershaw an English Merchant settled here." Two years later, ill in a remote part of his district, he lamented (38), "How hard the Lot of any Gentleman in this Part of the World." He did describe several backcountry residents as "gentlemen," but mostly because they were Anglicans or agreed with his religious views (17, 42, 134, 135). At one point (52), he made it clear that, from his perspective, gentility in the backcountry was relative, describing how a prominent local man of Anson County, North Carolina, "treated me very genteely (in their Way)."

James Clitherall, a few years later, found a similar want of gentility in the Waxhaws, at least at John Barkley's tavern (Clitherall diary, April 16, 1776), and Enos Reeves in 1782 found the girls of the Waxhaw settlement, except for Sarah Crawford, "the greatest Contrast to Gentility that could possibly have been Presented." (Reeves letterbook, Letter 240). Barkley signed more than one document with a mark (Stub Entries, 3:151, 153, 154, 157). But there was certainly some learning and politeness in the Waxhaws. Gaston read the Charles Town newspaper, brought from Camden, every week (Ellet, 157); Crawford expressed himself with clarity and vigor in his letter to the South Carolina state auditor 20 March 1785 (SC-AA). In a deed to Thomas Land in the 1770s, Waxhaw resident Robert McClanahan identified himself as a "Gentleman" (Anson County Deeds, B:431).

On Davie and his father, see B. P. Robinson, *Davie*, 38–39, 117; Pettus, 19; and Ellet, 171. Arnow, *Seedtime*, 350–357, describes everyday dress on the Cumberland frontier of the 1780s.

Crudity was no monopoly of the Irish-settled parts of the backcountry; British plebeians were similar no matter which island they came from. Smyth, 1:131–133, contains examples of spectacularly ungenteel behavior from predominantly English eastern North Carolina.

9. Warwick, Pitz, and Wyckoff, 154–171. Boys' clothing is discussed in more detail in Chapter 4. The "old, heavy, wool hat" mentioned by the nineteenth-century historian of

Salisbury, North Carolina (Rumple, 172), is best described in Smyth 1:180. The brim was exceedingly broad; two Revolutionary anecdotes from the South Carolina backcountry concern persons who were shot or almost shot because the hat they were wearing concealed their sex or race (DM 9VV206, 13VV143). When men went bareheaded, it was usually in an emergency situation, (J. P. Collins, 37).

10. Lightwood: Ginns, 12. Evans, *Irish Folk Ways*, 90, has drawings of several sorts of light holders in use in Ulster. The poor in County Down did not use candles: McClelland, "Miscellanea," 69. Candle making required a good source of beeswax or tallow, plus available labor; in the backcountry it was practical only on a large or well-organized farm. Humphries's later school, where he is said to have taught from 1779 to perhaps 1800, when he sold his lots in the town, was Mt. Zion Academy in Winnsboro (Howe, 1:449), 505. Taking off one's shirt in order to fight was a gesture from a time when clothing was harder to replace than it now is; it is mentioned in, such as, Monahan, 55 ("Andy Black . . . had off his cloths to fight with me"). On cornbread as snack, see Ginns, 56.

11. Lambert, 78–85; Howe, 1:449; McMaster, 57, 59–60.

12. Kegley, 44–46, 49; J. M. C. Montgomery to AJ, March 20, 1814, in Bassett, Correspondence, 1:482. Affidavits from Thomas and Nathaniel Stephenson are in Ibid., 3:416–418; both knew AJ from boyhood, though neither claimed specifically to have been a schoolmate.

13. A strand of oral tradition in Mecklenburg County held that AJ briefly attended Liberty Hall at some point in his youth. Susan Alexander heard that he did (W. A. Graham, 78); Parton, in the 1850s, was assured that he had (Parton Notebooks, 1:143–144, 152, 191). The tradition gives no dates and no details about his schoolmates, and there is no support for it in the early biographies, but one other piece of evidence gives it some credibility. The Reverend Cyrus Hunter told Parton (1:66) that his father Humphrey Hunter had been a schoolmate of AJ and related his father's impressions as given in the text. The claim seems a little hard to believe, in that Hunter was twelve years AJ's senior, but it is just possible; Hunter, like other young backcountry men interested in the ministry, pursued a sporadic, often interrupted course of studies until he was in his middle twenties. Archibald Henderson, after comparing the lives of the two, concluded (and I would agree with him) that if they were schoolmates it must have been at Liberty Hall in 1779 or 1780 (Henderson, "AJ," October 10, 1926), when Hunter was twenty-four and AJ was twelve. The reliable local historian Chalmers G. Davidson concluded that AJ studied at Liberty Hall "at least a few weeks." (Davidson, "Independent Mecklenburg," 125) Liberty Hall's closing is mentioned in an 1810 essay by Adlai L. Osborn, reproduced in Newsome, "Miscellany," 406.

14. "Learned his letters": William Harbison to Lyman Draper, March 5, 1873, DM 4VV38. AJ's reading: Remini, 7–8, 428 note 6. On fluent speech and preaching, cf. Howe, 1:343n. On Betty Jackson's fondness for Hugh, see Graham, 71, 76. On lack of money, see Reid, 10.

15. Parton, 65, 66–67. Compare Twiss, 32, on the Irish fondness for talking nonsense.

16. George McC. Witherspoon to Lyman Draper, 14, 20 March 1871, DM 12VV369, 371. On Robert Crawford, see note 4. His educated vocabulary and command of language

are evident from his letter to the South Carolina State Auditor, March 20, 1785, in SC-AA. Will Crawford is described in more detail in Chapters 12 and following.

17. Gault and Leighty, 7; Glassie, *Ballymenone*, 464.

18. This description is based mainly on Parton, 64, 73, 110–111, and the Parton Notebooks, 1:156, 167. For the early portraits, see Barber, 36, 39, 47–48. Some twentieth-century biographers have used Parton's data to depict the young AJ either as a young psychopath, inarticulate and "choked with rage" (Rogin, 42), or as a backwoods bumpkin, "cantankerous and extremely defensive," whose underlying pathology was masked, like that of a Flannery O'Connor character, by "mimicry and crude levity" (Curtis, 8). Neither approach is tenable, even in terms of the little evidence that exists. Parton's account suggests that AJ was a boy favored by the adults of his community, from whom good things were expected; in no way the dull, slobbering bully that Rogin portrays. Curtis seems to blame AJ for the mores of the backcountry; crude levity and an appetite for fighting were part of Carolina Irish male behavior and in no way unique to AJ.

My efforts to find a definition of the "water-rush" have been unsuccessful, but the question of AJ's slobbering deserves a little more attention, because Rogin (44) made it part of his arraignment of AJ, warning darkly of "disturbances in the parasympathetic nervous system." Gardner's article, Rogin's source on this point, states inaccurately (405) that AJ "was a drooler" all his life, "from infancy to manhood." The article cites only two specific occasions: one (409) during his fifties, when AJ was dosing himself with large quantities of mercuric chloride, or calomel, one effect of which is increased salivation (Johnsen, 934), the other (405) the recollection of Aunt Phyllis. It could well be that AJ as a child was also being dosed with calomel and producing more saliva than he could handle. It hardly seems necessary to mention that Jackson spent much of his adult life in the highest circles of Southern and national society, and that if he had had a chronic problem with excessive saliva it would have been commented on frequently.

19. On bedbugs, cf. the account of William Tennent in 1775 when visiting at the house of a prominent man in the backcountry: "After a sleepless and wet night, I was shocked by the blood and slaughter of my calicoed shirt and sheets in the morning." (Gibbes, 1:228) For a parallel from Piedmont, North Carolina, at a later date, see Ginns, *Rough Weather*, 24–25.

20. Arnow, *Seedtime*, 351, 364, 368–369, 383; Doddridge, 92–93. Trousers and overalls are mentioned in Parker, 70; Woodmason, 32, 61, 143; Arnow, *Seedtime*, 353–354, Smyth, 1:180; and the Osborne diary, 29 September 1800.

21. Glassie, 342; Meriwether, 174; and cf. Ginns, *Rough Weather*, 12, for a parallel from late nineteenth-century Appalachian culture, which was in many ways a lineal development of Carolina Irish culture. Grits and mush are ably discussed in Arnow, *Seedtime*, 394–397; see also Smyth, 1:43, and Moss and Hoffman, 9, 94. On eating out of one dish, see Reeves, 469–470. There are comparable instances from Ulster (Young, 186) and Appalachia (Ginns, *Rough Weather*, 6). China: Baroody, Appendix 1.

22. Importance of milk and milk products in Ulster: Young, 51, 184–186; Lucas, 19–24, 30–31; M'Skimin, 257–259; Gailey, *Scotland*, 20; Twiss, 30. On breakfast in Carolina, see

Woodmason, 52, 151; Moore, 13–14, 41; Lathan; Stinson, 214; Doddridge, 82, 88; E. T. Clark, 1:751; H. M. Wilson, 193–194; Scott, 13; J. P. Collins, 61; Osborne diary, July 21, 1802. Woodmason, 34, found eggs available fairly often in his travels, but cf. Arnow, *Seedtime*, 419, and Louis-Philippe, 78.

23. J. P. Collins, 69, gives the impression that morning prayers were frequent in back-country Presbyterian families. On Scottish and Irish psalmody, see Turner, 37; Patrick, 145–146; and Reeves, 467.

24. Arnow, *Seedtime*, 396–397, 408–409, 422; Ginns, *Rough Weather*, 34; Ellet, 89. Trash pit: cf. Baroody, 71–72.

25. For flax culture in Ireland, see Crawford, Irish Linen Industry, 5–14. Goodrich, 10, goes over the same process in Appalachian culture, and cf. Ellet, 133. From Jennet Linn's letter to John Linn, May 3, 1779 (CCGSB, 4:74), it is evident that flax was sown in April in the Waxhaws; Goodrich, 10, states that it was on Good Friday. Swingling flax is mentioned in a letter from Francis Ross Miles to L.C. Draper, April 16, 1874, DM 13VV148. On flax in the house, see Graham, 65, 73; Howe, 1:535; Caruthers, Old North State, 64. On Betty Jackson and her background, see Parton, 47, 59, 61. Graham, 72, also comments on her excellence as a spinner.

26. Allaire, 18; Cash, 48.

27. Chiggers and seed ticks: Gregorie, 192; Woodmason, 57–59; Castiglioni, 149.

28. Osborne Diary, January 3, March 17, July 16, August 19, December 15, 17, 1800; January 12, April 25, 1801; January 20, 1802. Thorp, 404–405, found a similar seasonal pattern in colonial Rowan County, North Carolina.

29. My sources for the distilling process, roughly in order of usefulness, are Russ Roberts, 6–8; Cratis Williams, "Moonshining," 11–14; Connell, 3–7; *Ridley* v. *Williamson*, Middle Tennessee Supreme Court Records, TSL; and entries of January 7, 20, 27, 28, February 4, 7, 10, 14, 19, 1800, Osborne diary. See also Newsome, "John Brown's Journal," 291. Heavy drinking by women is mentioned in J. P. Collins, 70, and in the minutes of the church trial of Agnes Carr for intoxication (Holcomb, *Fishing Creek*, 8–19). Particularly revealing in the case of Carr is the comment (10) that "at certain other times, she had taken more than was for her good," which suggests that moderate drinking by women was accepted. On drinking by children, see Scott, 13; J. P. Collins, 20, 37; cf. Struna, 246. For the use of "groggy" to mean "drunk," see Osborne Diary, passim.

30. Astley, 11–12; Parton, 1:105, 111; Robert Crawford account, SC-AA; Haines, 55; Tylden, 227; Caruthers, *Old North State*, 175; Ellot, 104. Arnow, *Flowering*, 193–200, contains much on the importance of horses in early backcountry society.

31. Buttermilk: Ellet, 287; Moore, 87; Arnow, *Seedtime*, 408. An encounter between a band of Whig refugees and a group of local Tories in late May 1780 quite near the Waxhaws is described in Tarleton Brown, 15–16.

The importance of slaveowning in the backcountry is spelled out in H. L. Watson, 29ff. On Africans' adaptation to European tools and work routines, see Boles, 44–47. The list of escaped slaves recaptured and in the Camden jail in *South Carolina Gazette,* 11 December 1775, suggests how many of the slaves in backcountry South Carolina were directly from Africa and what they generally wore. How difficult it could be to discipline slaves is obvious from the fragmentary diary of twenty-one-year-old Samuel Mathis, who lived near Camden (Kirkland and Kennedy, 400ff.); see especially the entries of March 1, 17, 19, 28, 30 and April 3, 1781. On the odor, see Smyth, 1:39, and Jordan, 459, 460n, 492, 518; on the Bible and slavery, see Jordan, 91–98.

Slaves were relatively rare in the Waxhaws in the 1770s; probably less than one family in five owned them, though many others wanted slaves. Klein, 20, records that the demand from the backcountry for slaves increased markedly just before the war. Some families, like that of AJ's uncle George McCamie, had only one (Graham, 71); James Kennedy's 1779 will mentions two (Book N–L, Camden District, p. 69); and Robert Dunlap's inventory in 1774 mentions only one "Negro Wench." (Charleston Free Library, Misc. Records, Vol. 98, p. 1)

A comparison with the Federal census figures of 1790, nine years after the fighting in the Waxhaws was over, by which time slave ownership had surely increased, provides a basis for comparison: 27 percent of families in the Waxhaw area of Lancaster District owned slaves in 1790 (63 of 236); one-third of them (twenty-two families) owned only one slave. Slaves made up 13 percent of the non–Native American population, the same proportion Klein found in Long Canes and Edgefield. (I used Heads of Families, 23–24, beginning with the George Dunlap household in the second column on 23 and ending with Peter Galaway in the second column on 24.)

Apart from Simpson, the largest documented number of slaves belonging to a single owner in or near the Waxhaws before 1780 is Thomas McElhaney's eleven in 1776 (McDow, 33–35). (Smyth, 1:199, mentions a large slaveholder west of the Catawba whom he loosely credits with fifty slaves, the Barnetts' neighbor Thomas Neill in Mecklenburg County is said to have had thirty or forty; but neither number has documentary support and both appear much larger than the largest holdings in the area as late as 1800; see Pettus, *Waxhaws*, 86–87.)

32. On AJ as a slaveholder, see Chapter 16; Remini, AJ1, 56, 133; and Remini, AJ, 45.

33. Arnow's discussion (*Seedtime*, 397–404, 411–414) of meat and vegetables in eighteenth-century Tennessee generally corresponds with the data available from the Waxhaws in scattered references like J. P. Collins, 20, 30, 63, and Woodmason, 13, 34, 36. She suggests (407) that food preparation was partly a matter of social class: main dishes in the homes of the prosperous were more apt to be roasted, but common settlers fried their food. A twentieth-century observer of Appalachia found both meats and vegetables prepared in deep fat (Karpeles, 147). Moss and Hoffman, 45–47, 95, stress boiling and stewing as methods of preparation. On greens, see ibid., 14.

34. On Sabbath observance, see Pettus, 23–24. "Wandering on the sabath": entry of May 7, 1802, Osborne Diary; cf. J. P. Collins, 15–16, 19. On visiting ministers, see Howe, 1:421, 430–431. On dressing up for church, see Ellet, 121–122; Howe, 1:434.

35. The evidence for AJ's free and casual use of the name of God in his speech is abundant for all stages of his life (Parton Notebooks 1:192; Remini, 3:396). By several accounts, swearing was prevalent in the backcountry (Woodmason, 98; Tompkins, 1:26), but not all

men swore to the same extent. An oath—calling upon God—was serious business, and Thomas Young, in contrast to AJ, recalled that he had not used an oath until the Revolution, when he swore to avenge his dead brother (J. Johnson, 446). In J. P. Collins's recollections of his youth in the backcountry, only one man, an aggressive trifler met by chance at a tavern, is depicted as a habitual swearer (62–63). Intuitively, one would suspect an inverse correlation between swearing and piety, but the Southern white male character is complex enough to accommodate both; cf. Francis Asbury's account (E. T. Clark, 1:777) of crossing a river in North Carolina with several young men "who sometimes prayed and sometimes swore."

The phrase "hell of a fellow" was one of W. J. Cash's most useful and widely recognized contributions to Southern studies (Cash, 48). Cash described the attitude in ibid., 44, in words that apply fairly well to AJ, and place his attitude in a cultural context: "bald, immediate, unsupported assertion of the ego . . . of which the essence was the boast, voiced or not, on the part of every Southerner, that he would knock hell out of whoever dared to cross him."

36. A sample of frolics in the Waxhaws and the kind of activities that went on at them can be found in the Osborne Diary, entries of January 1; April 18; May 7; September 3, 23, 25, 27, 1800; March 20; April 3; June 17; July 11; and September 15, 1801.

William Crawford, James's son, had a drinking problem (AJ to Robert Hays, November 1792,7, AJ Papers, 1:151. On the identity of the William Crawford mentioned in this letter, see Chapter 12, note 21.) So did William White Crawford, James's grandson (Veach, 141).

37. Bassett, *Correspondence*, 1:2; B. W. C. Roberts, 306–309; Akenson and Crawford, 51.

38. James Crawford Jr. and Christiana White were married, according to a nineteenth-century descendant, "not long before the commencement" of the war (Veach, 138). (This statement would mean the commencement of the war in the Carolina backcountry, in May 1780.) A deed of land to James Jr. from his father, March 1, 1780, probably marks the approximate date (Ibid., 132).

CHAPTER FOUR

1. Crittenden, "Communication," 382; Ellet, 99, 157; Joseph Kershaw Account Book, passim.

2. George McC. Witherspoon to Lyman C. Draper, March 20, 1874, DM 12VV379; John Reid Ms., 1; Floyd, 2.

3. Lambert, 45–46, 50.

4. General military situation: Lee, *Memoirs*, 124-125; Moultrie, 356–367. On moving to North Carolina, J. P. Collins, 17–18, gives an example. On fighting only on horseback, see Gregorie, 186–187; Wickwire and Wickwire, 486; Merrens, 261. On Montgomery's company, see Nathan Barr account, SC-AA. On Crawford's company, see George White pension application, NA; Moss, 214. On Dunlap's company, see records of many men of Dunlap's company in SC-AA, compiled by Nancy Crockett, which show service from May

to June 12, 1779; this would presumably have been in the Charles Town campaign. On Davie, see Pettus, 45. There is no documentary evidence to show that Hugh Jackson served under Davie rather than his Uncle Crawford, but many historians, such as B. P. Robinson, *Davie*, 35, have made the statement.

5. Lee, *Memoirs*, 125–130. The service of Dunlap's company ended June 12; I assume, therefore, that they were back in the Waxhaws by the time the battle of Stono Ferry took place.

6. McCrady, 384–391; Nathan Barr account, SC-AA; Kendall, 14. AJ to T. H. Wither-spoon, December 12, 1836, stated that his father and brothers were buried in the Waxhaw Church graveyard; either Hugh's body was brought back from Charleston, or, more likely, he died on the way back.

7. Graham, 71, 76.

8. McCowen, 1–7.

9. Undated manuscript in AJ's hand, Jackson Papers, 1:5. On kidnapping boys, see Turnbull to Cornwallis, June 15, 1780 both in Cornwallis Papers, 30/11/2. A comparable report about the Hessians is in J. Graham, 73.

10. Jackson Papers, 1:5. AJ did not date this incident, but it must have taken place after the battle, on May 29, and Tarleton states (Tarleton, 32) that his forces remained on the site until the evening of May 30 and then marched back to Camden. Tarleton and some of his men must have made this excursion up to the Catawbas on May 30, while the remainder of his troops rested after the battle.

11. The best summary of Buford's Defeat, or the Buford Massacre, as the engagement is called, is in Power, 5–10.

12. Ellet, 158; Howe, 1:537. On young women's dress, see Woodmason, 61; Reeves letterbook, Letter 239. On women's dress in general, see Fischer, 732.

13. James B. McLaughlin to Amos Kendall, February 14, 1843, AJ Papers. Other witnesses recalled survivors who had lost one arm or both, one leg or both (Ellet, 229). Susannah Barnett and her mother are said to have fed six men who had only two arms among them (Stinson, 214).

14. No single account exists of events in the Waxhaws in the early part of June 1780, but evidence from a variety of American and British sources makes it possible to reconstruct them with some accuracy. Tarleton and his prisoners returned to the British post at Camden "a few days" after the battle (Tarleton, 32), say June 1 or 2; Lord Cornwallis arrived at Camden June 1 to begin the next phase in the pacification of South Carolina (Bass, *Dragoon*, 84). That phase, clearly, was the taking of oaths of allegiance, or "paroles," as Cornwallis and the other military men called them.

Many inhabitants of the Waxhaws gave their paroles (Tarleton, 86, 119). AJ recalled it this way: "The first movement of the British after Buford's defeat was by Losley & Tarleton up to the Waxhaws, taking the paroles of the people and getting written protections" (undated memorandum on the Revolution, AJ Papers, LC). Tarleton said the paroles were taken "during the stay of the volunteers of Ireland [a Loyalist infantry unit]" (Tarleton,

86). Evidently, then, Tarleton on his parole-taking errand was accompanied by a military force of some size.

Other American sources make it possible to date this movement. North Carolina authorities, fearful that the advance might mean an invasion of their state, ordered General Griffith Rutherford to make a stand at Charlotte with the militia, which he did on June 3 and 4 (B. P. Robinson, *Davie*, 42); some American historians credited this massing of troops with causing the British to retreat (Lee, *Memoirs*, 167). Tarleton's return to the Waxhaws, then, came on the Saturday and Sunday following Buford's Defeat, possibly because Sunday was the easiest day to assemble a large number of inhabitants at a central location.

None of the above sources states where Tarleton and his troops encamped, but W. D. James, 21, records a tradition that a large British force came up to the Waxhaws early in June and camped at Robert Crockett's. An oral tradition recorded in Draper Mss., DM 9VV379, has it that Lord Rawdon, whose visit is described in the next chapter, camped at Crockett's, but Rawdon's letter to Cornwallis written while on this expedition is dated from "Lesslie's House, Waxhaw" (Cornwallis Papers, 30/11/2), so perhaps the tradition really referred to Tarleton's visit a week before.

For a description of the oath, see Paul H. Smith, 131.

15. Undated memorandum in AJ's hand, AJ Papers; Ramsay, 127; B. P. Robinson, *Davie*, 42. AJ knew the Polks from boyhood and affirmed that they were all Whigs (Garrett, 188). On the family, see J. Johnson, 84–85.

16. Rawdon to Cornwallis, 11 June 1780, Cornwallis Papers, 30/11/2; J. Graham, 217; Lambert, 99; Hilborn and Hilborn, 185. "Leonard" may have been Captain Samuel Leonard of the first battalion of New Jersey Volunteers (M. J. Clark, 3:175, 358). George Turnbull to Cornwallis, June 15, 1780, Cornwallis Papers, implies a little about British practice in taking provisions: "I have given no Receipts for any Provisions as yet. But I fear it will be necessary on some occasions to give a Receipt."

17. Rawdon to Cornwallis, June 11, 1780, Cornwallis Papers, 30/11/2; Lambert, 118; Murphy, 10; Harris, 30; Boatner, 918–919; Merrell, 193ff.; J.P. Collins, 24. There were numerous tales of Ulstermen in the British forces who recognized people among the Carolina Irish as former neighbors, for example, Veach, 138. One instance involving Rawdon, although not in the Waxhaws, is given in Ellet, 273.

18. Rawdon to Cornwallis, June 11, 1780, Cornwallis Papers, 30/11/2.

19. Ibid. A few weeks later, Rawdon was more aware of the abundance of foodstuffs; see same to same, July 2, 1780, Cornwallis Papers, 30/11/2. Woodmason, 34, 107.

20. Klein, 58, 60, 62, 64–68, 102; Jennet Linn to John Linn, May 3, 1779; CCGSB 4 (September 1981):74.

21. Rawdon to Cornwallis, June 11, 1780, Cornwallis Papers, 30/11/2; J. Graham, 217; B. P. Robinson, *Davie*, 41.

CHAPTER FIVE

1. AJ's limited service in the Revolution has occasioned a good deal of writing, much of it fanciful. Marquis James, 22, observes that AJ's own accounts of it are "brief and mod-

est"—a description that would probably apply to the service itself—with the exception of his capture and imprisonment, narrated in Chapters 8–9, which AJ recalled in vivid detail. The basic fact is that AJ, at thirteen, was a couple of years too young for effective military service. His first biographers (Reid and Eaton, 10–11) give the impression that he rushed into arms as soon as the war extended "its ravages into that section of South Carolina, where he then was"; but they create that impression by ignoring 1780 entirely and jumping forward to 1781. AJ, the reader is told, enlisted "at the tender age of fourteen," that is, in March 1781; his first action was the encounter at Waxhaw Church in April, where he and Robert were captured. All this is true (see Chapter 8), but for 1780 his participation is unsupported by evidence. Buell's statements (1:52) that Davie made AJ a mounted orderly and gave him a pistol are fabrications; see Appendix I.

2. William Crawford's Revolutionary claim in SC-AA shows service from April 20 to June 21, 1780 as "sentinel," a position that suggests he may have been considered too young for the duties of a cavalryman or infantryman. There may be some fudging as to the dates, for between the surrender of Charles Town May 12 and the assembling of Sumter's troops around June 14 there was no official South Carolina force. But if he was telling the truth, he may have been serving with a North Carolina unit for part of this time, as George White of the Waxhaws did (pension application, NA). Other Revolutionary claimants from the Waxhaws stated they had served during roughly the same time period, from April to June 1780.

3. "York Tories": James Hemphill to Lyman C. Draper, October 2, 1874, DM 4VV85. Turnbull's actions can be followed in his correspondence with Lord Cornwallis, Cornwallis Papers, 30/11/2. On Huyck, see Samuel C. Williams's note in Winn, 43:204–205n. Daniel G. Stinson's sources consistently gave the name as "Hook" (Ellet, passim), as did Potter Collins (24–27); Joseph Gaston (C. G. Davidson, Gaston, 16–18) recalled it as "Hoik," perhaps an attempt to reproduce the Dutch pronunciation. Turnbull, in his letter to Cornwallis 19 June, spelled the name "Huik."

Huyck's raid is one of the few reliably dated events in this chapter. Accounts of it are in the Charles Lewis affidavit, John Simpson Papers, SCL; Simpson's own account, in Howe 1:510–512; and Turnbull's letter to Cornwallis, 15 June 1780, Cornwallis Papers. Ellet, 226–227, is based on oral tradition. The arrest of William Martin, however, is a deduction. It is known (Stephenson, 21; Ellet, 165) that Martin was arrested and confined for six months in Rocky Mount and Camden, that is, he was arrested before August 1780, when the post at Rocky Mount was abandoned. It is also known (Ellet, 124–126) that he preached against collaboration with the British the Sunday after Buford's Defeat, which would make his arrest a matter of urgency. Taken together, the two facts suggest that it was probably at this time that Huyck arrested Martin.

4. Ellet, 179, 226; Woodmason, 34, 45, 105; Ramsay, *Revolution*, 136.

5. Contemporaries on both sides, such as the American Ramsay (*Revolution*, 116) and the Englishman Stedman (2:198–199) agreed that the proclamation of June 3 drove many Americans into armed resistance. So have later historians such as Lambert, 97, and R. M. Brown, 75. For a balanced discussion, see Paul H. Smith, 131–133. Rawdon enforced the policy energetically; see his letter to Cornwallis June 22, 1780, Cornwallis Papers, 30/11/2.

6. Pension applications of Jacob Patton and George White, NA; Winn, 43:203; Weigley, 14–15; Lee, *Memoirs*, 174–175; Sam McCalla to Lyman C. Draper, January 2, 1873, DM 14VV436–443.

7. Bass, *Gamecock*, 51–52, 55–57; Hill, 8; Winn, 43:203–204. The branch was Clem's Branch, famous in the history of the American resistance in South Carolina (Louise Pettus, "Clem's Branch," *York Observer*, July 22, 1990).

8. M. James, 20. The following Waxhaw men and their dates of enlistment are from the Revolutionary claims in SC-AA. The list is not inclusive; it contains only those who gave precise dates and who served at some time under Robert Crawford. But it probably reflects the general trend.

APRIL: George White, the 15th.

MAY: Henry Foster, 8. Josiah Cantey, 12. Thomas Thomson, 25.

JUNE: William Nisbet, 2. John Nisbet, 4. Benjamin Thomson, 7. William Crawford, as adjutant, 21. Thomas Crawford, 23. Robert Carnes, Henry Coffey, James Craig, John Craig, James Crawford, James Dunlap, Henry Foster Jr., Peter Galloway, John Gillespie, John Lessley Jr. [AJ's cousin], John McMurry, Alexander Montgomery, Robert Montgomery, Moses Stephenson, Henry White, Hugh White, 25. Robert Davis, 26. John Foster, 29. Andrew Foster, Archibald McCorkle, Abel Nilson, 30.

JULY: John Baird, Elijah Crockett, John Dunlap, Allen Hood, Robert Montgomery, 1. James McIlwain, Robert McIlwain, 6. Ralph Smith, 14. Hugh Montgomery, 23.

New River: Gregorie, 79. Davie states in his memoirs (B. P. Robinson, *Sketches*, 8) that New River and the Catawbas "reinforced" his contingent of North Carolina troops then stationed on upper Waxhaw Creek. He makes the same statement about Major Robert Crawford and his company; but Crawford, by August, was clearly serving under Sumter (see the next chapter), and most of the men in his command, in their Revolutionary claims, described themselves as followers of Sumter. The truth would seem to be that the chain of command in the Waxhaws was fluid. Officers who served under Sumter, including New River, were essentially independent commanders, each of whom could operate at will, as Hill and Winn did in Huyck's defeat, or put himself and his men at the disposal of another general officer. New River and Crawford were both camping with Sumter and reinforcing Davie.

9. Reid and Eaton, 10–11; J. Graham, 72. As for provisioning the patriot forces, the accounts of James Dunlap and William Massey in SC-AA show, respectively, 300 pounds of beef delivered to Davie on July 1 and 200 pounds delivered to Robert Crawford on June 20. (The early date of the latter delivery, if correct, suggests that Major Crawford assembled his company several days before formally joining Sumter.) On Rawdon's anger, see Rawdon to Cornwallis, July 2, 1780.

10. On exercises, see Bass, *Gamecock*, 57. On shortage of powder, see Ellet, 178. On melting pewter, see Ramsay, *Revolution*, 130. "Careless and slovenly": W. A. Graham, 235. On supplies, according to John Adair's pension application, NA, Sumter's men "were to

find their own horses and arms, cloathing and all necessaries." "Poor hunting-shirt fellows": J. P. Collins, 26. On numbers, see Turnbull to Cornwallis, July 6, 1780; Rawdon to Cornwallis, July 7, 1780, Cornwallis Papers, 30/11/2.

11. B. P. Robinson, *Sketches*, 8.

12. Pettus, 47; Ellet, 171; B. P. Robinson, *Davie*, 117; Harrison, 26, 1776–1783.

13. Two sources exist for the event described in these paragraphs, the unconsummated attack on the British at Waxhaw Creek ford: a brief mention in Colonel Richard Winn's notes (43:204) and a much more detailed account by Joseph Graham, based partly on Davie's recollections (W. A. Graham, 233). Winn's version is short enough to be quoted in its entirety: "About the seventh or eighth of July, being informed that a body of British was on their way from Camden towards the Waxhaws, [Sumter] went with his whole force to meet them. But after passing the Waxhaws, finding the information not correct, retreated." Graham's version gives all the detail related in the text. But in one respect, the two are irreconcilable: Winn places the action on July 7–8, Graham on the nineteenth and twentieth of the month. I have followed Winn as to the date and need to explain my reasons for doing so, because previous historians who have used this material, notably Blackwell P. Robinson in his excellent biography of Davie, have followed Graham.

In the first place, there is little doubt that the two writers are describing the same incident: a false alarm of a British advance, preparations to meet the British at or near Waxhaw Creek, disappointment, and subsequent dispersal of troops—deliberate according to Winn, unplanned according to Graham. It strains credibility to suppose that this sequence of events happened twice in the same month.

British sources suggest that Winn's date is more likely correct. Rawdon did order an advance of troops to the Waxhaws on July 3, under Captain Kinloch, but they withdrew before July 6 because of the threat from Sumter's force (Rawdon to Cornwallis, July 2, 1780; Turnbull to Cornwallis, July 6, 1780, Conwallis Papers, 30/11/2). After July 7 Rawdon was wary of sending a large body of troops to the Waxhaws, both because of Sumter and because he was unaware of DeKalb's whereabouts and did not want to weaken his force at Camden (Rawdon to Cornwallis, July 7, 10, 1780, Cornwallis Papers, 30/11/2). Winn's date, therefore, seems closer to the truth, though it may be a day or two off.

This conclusion is buttressed by the fact that Graham's narrative is very casual about dates. Examples of clear misdating are the burning of Hill's Iron Works, which Graham (232) places on July 9 and which actually happened on June 19; Graham's statement (233) that Sumter's troop strength swelled to five hundred on July 12, the day of the battle at Williamson's plantation, which actually took place while Sumter's troops were dispersed; his assertion (237) that Sumter crossed the river at Land's Ford on August 2 after the battle at Rocky Mount, the actual date of the crossing being the fifth; and his putting Cornwallis's arrival in the Waxhaws on September 20 (248), when letters show it was nine days before that date. For Graham to be two weeks off in the date of the incident, therefore, is not unlikely; indeed, it is typical.

14. Winn, 43:204; Hill, 8–10; Bass, *Gamecock*, 60.

15. Accounts of Huyck's Defeat are in Hill, 9–10; Winn, 43:204–206; J. P. Collins, 25–

27; Turnbull to Cornwallis (2 letters), July 12, 1780, Cornwallis Papers, 30/11/2; J. Johnson, 336–338; and Howe, 1:516–517.

16. Allusions to DeKalb's approach are in Rawdon to Cornwallis, July 7, 31, 1780, Cornwallis Papers, 30/11/2. Sumter wrote DeKalb a letter July 17 to discuss possible strategies (Bass, *Gamecock*, 62–63). On Davie's raid, see B. P. Robinson, *Sketches*, 9–11, and Hunter, 103.

17. Winn, 43:207.

18. Lee, *Memoirs*, 176, and B. P. Robinson, *Sketches*, 11, mention the conference, the numbers of men, and the joint departure. Bass, *Gamecock*, 64, assigns the date of Sunday, July 30 for the attack on Rocky Mount, I believe correctly; Rawdon to Cornwallis, July 31, 1780, Cornwallis Papers, 30/11/2, the most nearly contemporary source, gives that date. Lee's date of July 30 for the conference, then, is off by one day.

Backcountry men's unwillingness to serve except on horseback was an object of surprise to many British; see Cornwallis to Lord George Germain, August 20, 1780, Cornwallis, 503; Rawdon to Cornwallis, March 7, 1781, Cornwallis Papers, 30/11/69; and the remarks of George Hanger quoted in Wickwire and Wickwire, 426. John Adair, describing his service in his pension application, remarked that for him and his neighbors it was "absolutely necessary that they should act on horse back."

As for the weather, heavy rains and swollen creeks are consistent features in the military action of the next few days. A huge downpour terminated the action at Rocky Mount July 30, and the following night was stormy (Hill, 12; Winn, 43:208). The "late heavy rains" just before August 3 flooded Fishing Creek, Rocky Creek, and the Catawba (Winn, 43:209; Rawdon to Cornwallis, August 3, 1780, Cornwallis Papers, 30/11/3). By August 5, the Catawba, though still flooded, was subsiding (DM 9VV202). On the Whigs' feeling that they were doing God's work in the war, see the comment by William Hill, significant and perhaps representative, on Huyck: "The ill behaviour of the enemy made an impression on the minds of the most serious men in this little band and raised their courage in the belief that they would be made instruments in the hand of Heaven to punish the enemy for his wickedness and blasphemy." (Hill, 9)

19. The traditional date for this action is August 1 (e.g., McCrady, 624), but the evidence seems compelling that it took place July 30. Davie's account of the action in his memoirs (B. P. Robinson, *Sketches*, 12) stressed that he took pains to attack on the same day as Sumter, and Rawdon's letter cited in the previous note establishes that Sumter attacked on the thirtieth. Rawdon makes no mention of Davie's attack, then or later.

20. The battle at Rocky Mount is described in Rawdon to Cornwallis, July 31, 1780, Cornwallis Papers, 30/11/2; Sumter to Thomas Pinckney, August 9, 1780, copy in DM 5VV159; B. P. Robinson, *Sketches*, 11; and Hill, 11–12. Winn, 43:207–209, adds the detail that Sumter, after breaking off the attack, delayed his retreat until August 3 because of the flooded creek.

21. "Gamecock": Bass, *Gamecock*, 60. On reinforcements from Hanging Rock, see Winn, 43:209. On Direction Rock, see Steen, 34. The crossing is described in Sumter to Thomas Pinckney, August 9, 1780, copy in DM 5VV159; and cf. the oral tradition related by

Notes

D. G. Stinson in DM 9VV202. The fact that Sumter, Davie, and their officers were able to get together to confer on August 5 despite the flooded river (B. P. Robinson, *Sketches*, 13) indicates that the Catawba was passable by a man of sufficient daring or skill; the problem lay in moving a whole army across it.

22. Pension applications of Thomas Blair and John Adair, NA; B. P. Robinson, *Sketches*, 13. The men's anticipation before Hanging Rock is apparent in the traditional ballad about the battle quoted in Ellet, 188. On the Crawfords' taking care of the Jackson boys, see the parallel scene in J. P. Collins, 25, where a teenage boy is welcomed into a guerrilla band with the comment, "We will try to take care of you and not let the Tories catch you."

CHAPTER SIX

1. According to the Virginia Almanack for 1780, moonset was at 10:40 p.m. on August 5. Sumter (to Thomas Pinckney, 9 August 1780, DM 5VV159) reckoned his strength at 600 men at the time of Hanging Rock; from the context, it is clear that he must have meant 500 of his own men and perhaps 100 North Carolinians. Winn, 210, estimated Whig strength at 500 but may not have included the North Carolinians. Davie (B. P. Robinson, *Sketches*, 13) recalled 500 North Carolinians and only 300 South Carolinians, but this figure seems highly unlikely. Hill, 12, recorded that no man in the force had over five rounds of ammunition at the time, a statement corroborated by Ramsay, *Revolution*, who states (2:130) that Sumter's men sometimes had only two or three rounds on the eve of battle, and (2:137) that before Hanging Rock no man had more than ten.

2. Winn, 210.

3. The distance from Land's Ford to the site of the Hanging Rock battle near Heath Springs is eighteen miles in a direct line; horsemen riding slowly should have been able to reach the camp in four or five hours. Thomas Blair, in his pension application, recalled that he "marched" (i.e., rode) all night; Winn, 210, said the halt was made about two hours before daylight. Probably, then, the Whigs did not leave Land's Ford until well after dark.

4. AJ recalled (Kendall, 25) that Lieutenant James Crawford was wounded at the battle of Hanging Rock; Veach, 138, makes it clear that this was James Crawford Jr. James Crawford Sr. certainly fought in the Revolution and indeed lost a horse at Sumter's Defeat (SC-AA), but there is no mention of his being an officer.

5. Davie's account (B. P. Robinson, *Sketches*, 13) is the best.

6. Sumter to Pinckney, August 9, 1780, DM 5VV159; B.P. Robinson, *Sketches*, 13–14.

7. Winn, 210. Both Sumter, in his letter to Pinckney, and Winn, 211, cited 1400 as the number of British and Tory troops, Sumter "from certain accounts" and Winn "from the best information." Most subsequent historians have followed them. Still, using Winn's own figures, it is hard to see how they arrived at the total. Winn reckoned 300 British regulars in the camp, with 300 more after the reinforcement from Rocky Mount came back, for a total of 600. The North Carolina Tories, he said, numbered 500. The total enemy force, thus, would seem to have been 1100 or so.

8. Several details in this paragraph refer forward to anecdotes later in the chapter: the green leaves to the story of Alex Walker in note 11, the officers' coats to Jim Crawford in note 18 (for Sumter's coat, see Gregorie, 105, and Bass, *Gamecock*, 89), the bayonets to Dick Wright in note 15, as well as Alex Walker in note 11. Weller, 121, contends that the use of the bayonet among Southern partisans was rare, but evidence in this and the next chapter, note 10, suggests that it may have been a bit more general than he believes. (See also Cousar, 52.) On carrying balls in the mouth, see Winn, 211; and Ellet, 196. J. P. Collins, 52, adds that another purpose of the practice was to prevent thirst. An advertisement in the *South Carolina Gazette,* June 14, 1783, mentions a slave brought to the battle by his owner, Josiah Jordan of North Carolina; Jordan was killed and the man joined the British forces.

On the general approach to the battle, Winn, 210, is the fullest account. Davie, (B. P. Robinson, *Sketches*, 14) unaccountably states that the troops went off to the left of the Wagon Road, when it is clear from the map that he must have meant the right.

9. Benjamin Thomson, according to his pension application, was sixteen when he fought at Hanging Rock; Samuel McCreary (Ellet, 170) was fifteen or sixteen. On the other side, a Tory lad named Gibson, who died in the battle, was sixteen (Inscriptions, 30). AJ's inability to describe the battle is mentioned in James B. McLaughlin to Amos Kendall, February 27, 1843, AJ Papers, Tennessee State Library. This disclaimer did not stop Kendall, 25, from portraying AJ as a member of Davie's corps and a participant. On the other hand, the story of Lieutenant James Crawford, recounted later in this chapter, which first appeared on the same page of Kendall's biography, must have come from AJ himself. It reads very much like the account of an eyewitness and is my principal reason for asserting that AJ was present at the battle, though not as a combatant.

10. In these three paragraphs, I recount the course of the Battle of Hanging Rock twice: first as a series of noises, then as a set of troop movements and attacks. I have not tried to give a full, authoritative account. (The best account is in Buchanan, 133–136.) Of the primary sources on the battle, Sumter's letter to Thomas Pinckney, on Horatio Gates's staff, is by far the best, having been written only three days afterward, on August 9. (It is reproduced in Bass, *Gamecock*, 72–73.) It gives only one view, however, of a multifarious set of operations which were largely out of the commander's control, and needs to be supplemented by the recollections of Colonels Richard Winn (210–212) and William Hill (12–13). William R. Davie's reminiscences (B.P. Robinson, *Sketches*, 14–15) contain surprising errors and should be used with care. There is no account from a British participant, but memoirs like Stedman, 201–203, give a good sense of the reports and secondhand versions that were floating around the British army. It is Stedman, 202, for instance, who points out that Bryan's Tories were as poorly armed as Sumter's Whigs, and who (203) estimates American casualties at 100; Sumter's count was 20 killed, 40 wounded, and 10 missing.

One early version of the battle should be mentioned for its inaccuracy: that of William D. James, Marion's biographer, in the 1828 Camden Journal, which revolves around the struggle for possession of a British "fort" or "stockade." No other source mentions any such fortification in the camp. James is also alone in saying that the battle "lasted the greater part of the day and the enemy lost 800 men." In fact, the battle lasted three or perhaps four hours, and British casualties, though greater than the American losses (Sumter estimated 260 killed or wounded), were nowhere near James's figure. (A typescript of his account is in the Hough Collection, Lancaster Public Library.)

On the Native American ("Indian") warwhoop, see also Ellet, 137.

11. DM 9VV29; Ellet, 189.

12. C. G. Davidson, Gaston, 18; Ellet, 189; DM 14VV455.

13. DM 11VV292.

14. Winn: DM 16VV14–15, 37. Hill: ibid., 16VV47–48. Sumter: Bass, *Gamecock*, 70. The quotation is from W.A. Graham, 225.

15. Kendall, 25; Veach, 138. Veach's account tentatively identifies the battle as Guilford Courthouse, but the story is evidently the same as the one in Kendall related by AJ. The detail of the pocket handkerchief is from a letter of George McC. Witherspoon, DM 12VV369. As J. P. Collins, 40, shows, it was possible to make a litter for moving a wounded man to a safe place; the Crawfords' failure to do so suggests that James must have seemed dead or dying.

16. Sumter to Pinckney, August 5, 1780, DM 5VV159; B. P. Robinson, *Sketches*, 16.

17. Will's lost horse is in his Revolutionary account in SC AA.

18. The family story, reproduced in Veach, 138, mentions Betty Jackson and Christina Crawford, the British soldier, and the Tory's maltreatment. AJ's shorter reminiscence (Kendall, 25) merely states that Crawford's friends found him alive the next day where they had left him, but that a Tory kinsman had stolen his coat. Crawford's own claim in SC-AA makes no mention of his wound but suggests that he served in Sumter's cavalry continuously, "for ye most part following his fortune." I assume, then, that after convalescing he rejoined Sumter in the fall when his operations resumed.

The hospital set up by Davie in Charlotte is mentioned in Ellet, 229; Stinson, 214; J. Graham, 234; and Kendall, 27. Ellet, 169, adds that some wounded were taken to the Waxhaw Meeting House. The mass influx of women and children the day after a battle is described in, e.g., J. P. Collins, 53.

Catawbas' participation in the battle: D.S Brown, 269n.

19. Peaches were in season during August (W. A. Graham, 77) and were eaten both by Gates's troops marching toward Camden (Ramsey, *Revolution*, 139) and by Sumter's men retreating after Camden (Notes from Alexander J. Bradley, DM 14VV210). Wheat was harvested in the Waxhaws from July 1780 (Rawdon to Cornwallis, July 2, 1780, Cornwallis Papers) to September (Cornwallis to George Turnbull, September 11, 1780, Cornwallis Papers). Roasting ears were considered emergency rations (e.g., Ellet, 131; Cyrus Hunter to D.G. Stinson, December 1875, DM 15VV284-285) but were enjoyed just the same (W. A. Graham, 77). The song about Sumter is reproduced in Gregorie, 143–144.

20. Bass, *Gamecock*, 75.

21. Ibid., 78; J. Graham, 234; B. P. Robinson, *Sketches*, 19. The names of the Waxhaw captains are those recorded in the Revolutionary Accounts in the South Carolina Archives as having served under Crawford.

22. For a fuller discussion of this question, see Appendix II.

23. Kendall, 27; B. P. Robinson, *Davie*, 56.

24. For the circumstances of the Battle of Camden, see Davis, 75–99, and Lumpkin, 60–67. The pursuit of the Americans by Tarleton and the Tories is recounted in Seymour, 7; Stedman, 2:209, and W. Gordon, 106. Jacobs, 25, describes the retreat of a group of Maryland troops. Sixteen months later the road was still littered with smashed and abandoned wagons (Tilden, 216). Gates: SRNC, 22:94–95; John Finley pension application, NA.

25. Kendall, 27.

26. Gregorie, 101–102; Stedman 2:212; Bass, *Gamecock*, 82–85.

CHAPTER SEVEN

1. Two memoranda in the AJ Papers, one of which is reprinted in AJ Papers, 1:5, give AJ's summary of his family's flight. Both tell essentially the same story: "on the advance of Cornwallis, we again fled to No Carolina." Cornwallis's actual advance north from Camden began September 7 (memorandum of John Money, aide to Cornwallis, Cornwallis Papers, 30/11/3), but it is likely that AJ and his family fled from the anticipated advance rather than the actual one. From August 18, the date of Sumter's Defeat, the inhabitants of the Waxhaws expected a British invasion and fled to avoid it (pension applications of Archibald McCorkle and Thomas Brown, NA). Susan Alexander's recollections, described more fully in Appendix II, state positively that the Jackson party arrived at her family's house outside Charlotte rather early in the month of August.

2. The source is Susan Alexander's recollections. See Appendix II for a full discussion.

3. Gregorie, 101–102; Bass, *Gamecock*, 82–84; notes of Alexander J. Bradley, DM 14VV210; recollections of Major Joseph Pagan, DM 11VV322; Joseph F. White to Lyman Draper, December 13, 1870, DM 15VV90; Sam McCalla to Lyman Draper, DM 14VV455. The records in SC-AA show that all four Crawford males mentioned lost horses at Sumter's Defeat. The James Crawford mentioned must be James Sr., as his son had been severely wounded only two weeks before. From AJ's own testimony (to James H. Witherspoon, August 11, 1824, AJ Papers) it is known that William and Joseph Crawford were captured, presumably at Sumter's Defeat. No later battles are mentioned in the records of either man, and Joseph died in prison in October. Other Whigs besides the major escaped by swimming the river, for instance William Nisbet, who turns up again in Chapter 8 (Nisbet, 143).

4. B. P. Robinson, *Sketches*, 21. To many backcountry people the defeat was shattering. A woman from west of the river recalled, "I seemed to fear nothing after the disastrous defeat of Sumter" (Ellet, 280). On the British attitude toward slaves see Tarleton, 88–89; Frey, 120ff.; and Cornwallis's order of September 27, 1780 "for Marking all Negroes belonging to the Army, with the Number of the Regt. or the Initial Letters of the Department that employs them . . . & [to] flog out of the Encampment all those who are not Mark'd agreeable to Orders." (Newsome, "Orderly Book," 276).

5. Elizabeth Russell White was said to have had a purse of guineas brought from Ire-

land (White Family Papers); Ellet, 182, mentions a Waxhaw family with a few gold guineas hidden in a cloth. An agreement between two members of the Nisbet family of Salisbury, North Carolina, enumerates 225 half johannes coins buried in a pewter flask under the house, the same number in a tin canister under the hearth, silver dollars under the stair in a "bagg," and several other similar items (Agreement between William and David Nisbet, 1788, Nisbet Papers). Susan Alexander (W. A. Graham, 78) conjectured of the Jacksons, "I think they had hid many of their things in the woods, as many bodies did." British soldiers sometimes searched for such valuables by poking the ground with iron ramrods (Caruthers, *Caldwell*, 223). For other examples of hiding valuables, such as salt and linen, see Caruthers, *Old North State*, 158, and J. P. Collins, 65.

6. J. P. Collins, 49; Crittenden, "Travel," 243; W. Gordon, 108. The Feltman diary, December 20, 1781, gives an instance of flooding in Twelve Mile Creek that halted travel, just as Alexander Noble, twenty years earlier, had been stranded in the same area "with Reain and the Waters being high." (quoted in Pettus, 20)

7. W. A. Graham, 71.

8. Ibid., 71; Wickwire and Wickwire, 194–195; Ramsay, *Revolution*, 154; Stedman, 2:213–214; B. P. Robinson, *Davie*, 63.

9. Parton, 74–75; W. A. Graham, 72–73. A small photograph of a building identified as the Wilson place appears in Alexander, 1:87. According to Stenhouse, however, the location of the building is now unknown.

10. Parton, 75; Parton Notebooks, 1:190, 192; W. A. Graham, 73.

11. W. A. Graham, 71–72.

12. Howe, 1:537; memorandum of John Money, Cornwallis Papers, 30/11/3; Cornwallis to George Turnbull, September 11, 1780; to Nisbet Balfour, September 23, 1780, ibid., 30/11/80; Bass, *Dragoon*, 106.

13. Cornwallis described these Tory units as "Volunteer Companys of our Militia" in a letter to Nisbet Balfour, September 21, 1780, Cornwallis Papers, 30/11/80. For their raids, see Ellet, 271; Bruin, 4; and Dunlap, 140.

14. B. P. Robinson, *Sketches*, 21–23.

15. Ibid., 24, recounts the British advance on Charlotte. Susan Alexander recalled that the Jacksons and McCamies left on September 24 or 25, as the British advance from the Waxhaws began (W. A. Graham, 77.) Their plan was to go around behind the British army (Ibid., 74), for Mrs. Jackson wanted "with all intenseness" to get home (Ibid., 78). It turned out, however, to be impracticable; British and Tory troops covered all the roads that led to the Waxhaws, and some were still stationed in the Waxhaw community (Cornwallis to Archibald McArthur, September 29, 1780, Cornwallis Papers, 30/11/80). Evidently, then, they changed their plans and fled north, passing through Charlotte as AJ recalled (AJ Papers, 1:5). Kendall, 30, whose biography was prepared with AJ's cooperation, is the source for their going on to Guilford.

16. Kendall, 30, mentions Mr. McCulloch as the Jacksons' intended host. There was indeed a famous McCulloch in Guilford County, Henry Eustace McCulloch, the Londoner who held title to much of the best land in the county; but by 1780 he had been declared a

Tory, his lands were forfeit to the state, and he was not in America (B. P. Robinson, "Guilford," 61; Reeves, 468–469). Apart from him, I have found no McCulloch in the county. Susan Alexander's guess is in W. A. Graham, 78.

17. On Rachel Caldwell, see Caruthers, *Caldwell*, 203. She actually had two sisters, Jane and Nancy, who were married to Dunlaps, and Caruthers does not specify which one he means. Both were from the Waxhaws, however. Betty Jackson was closer to Nancy than to Jane. On Robert McCamie, see Eisele, 1–5. His name, sometimes misspelled as McKemic or McKinnie, appears more than once on the Fred Hughes Guilford County map and in Kearny, passim. The W. C. Rankin Papers contain marriage bonds for a James McKemie (1779) and Liz McKemie (1782) in Guilford County, with a note suggesting that James may have been a brother of John McCamey of Carlisle. The executor of John's will was his son Robert McCamey, but I have no documentary proof that the Robert McCamie in Guilford was that son, only the fact that both men lived in North Carolina, that the name is quite uncommon, and that Robert of Guilford had the social status to make him an appropriate executor.

Sparks, 146, recalled having heard, possibly from AJ himself, that AJ and his family had moved to Guilford County at some time.

18. The dates of AJ's undocumented stay in North Carolina are naturally approximate. Many Waxhaw settlers returned to their homes in January of 1781 (Archibald McCorkle pension application, NA; John Barkley receipt, January 30, 1781, Stub Entries, 3:150; Robert Crawford document, January 16, 1781, quoted in M. James, 26). This movement coincided with Cornwallis's departure from South Carolina in pursuit of the Continental army (Weigley, 33–35), and thus corresponds with AJ's recollection: "When Cornwallace passed on leaving [South] Carolina we again returned to our place of Residence" (AJ Papers, 1:5). By early March he was definitely back in the Waxhaws; see Chapter 8 and notes.

On Charlotte, see Blythe and Brockmann, 22; Moultrie, 553. On Davie's stand at the courthouse, see B. P. Robinson, *Sketches*, 71–72.

19. W. Gordon, 108; William Davidson to Horatio Gates, September 26, 1780, Davie Papers; SRNC, 14:651, 778; Crittenden, "Travel," 248–249, 256–257; Parton Notebooks, 1:163; E. Watson, 294; W. A. Graham, 76.

20. SRNC, 14:777–778, 786; Reeves, 469; Smyth, 1:175; Tilden, 215; B. P. Robinson, *Davie*, 75–77. On crossing the Yadkin, see Crittenden, "Travel," 243–244; Reeves, 468; E. Watson, 294; Hunt, 5; Tilden, 215; and "Anonymous Itinerary," 289. Chamberlain, 1–2, describes the river.

21. "very bad" road: Caruthers, *Old North State*, 116. Guilford Courthouse: B. P. Robinson, "Guilford," 63; manuscript by Katherine S. Hoskins in Hughes Papers; SRNC, 14:394. John L. Durham, historian at Guilford Courthouse National Military Park, helped me envision the exact site where the courthouse stood. General William Davidson estimated the number of the militia at 430 (Ibid., 14:655). The decision to store the weapons there implies that Dent's store, like most backcountry stores, was a stout, reasonably secure building. The anonymous Virginia–North Carolina map of 1779 shows two ordinaries at the court house.

22. SRNC, 14:608, 711. Gallup, 31, cautions that the word "nakedness" in descriptions of troops' clothing is not always to be taken literally.

23. Feltman diary, December 8, 9, 1781; Reeves, 467; Rankin, 19, 21, 210; Foote, 233.

24. The Buffalo Church records are loose, unnumbered pages, some with dates and others without. I designate the pages from which I drew the cited material by the name of the accused and the date, when given. James Coots; James Barr; Francis McNairy, 1777; Catherine Moreland, 1773; George Parks, 1780; Sarah Ewing, 1780; Alexander Tasy, 1783.

25. Reeves, 467; Baroody, 78, and Appendix I; Hughes, *Guilford*, 25–26, 47–49; "Anonymous Itinerary," 288; Feltman diary, December 11, 1781.

26. Eisele, 1–5.

27. The surviving court records do not begin until 1781 (B. P. Robinson, "Guilford," 61), but court was held in November 1780, as shown by a deed cited in Kearney, 101, which was proved at November Court of that year. On court sessions as public theater, see A. M. Roeber's article "Authority, Law, and Custom."

28. Francis McNairy: see the cases relating to him in the Buffalo Church records. John McNairy in 1827 said that he had known AJ more than forty-five years (Heiskell, 296), that is, their acquaintance began before 1782; however, AJ's law study in North Carolina began late in 1784. He must have met McNairy, therefore, when he and his mother lived in Guilford as refugees in 1780–1781. McNairy's career is in North Carolina, 4:178. John McNairy is not on the militia rolls, but his father was a captain (Hughes, *Guilford*, 11) and John was paid after the war for services to the state during the Revolution (SRNC 17:544). Bruce: Stockard, 39; Hoskins, 116–118; and the xeroxed typescript on the Bruce family in the Hughes Papers.

29. Weigley, 21–22, 25–26; B. P. Robinson, *Davie*, 84, 87; B. P. Robinson, *Sketches*, 28–29; Kirkwood, 12; Gregorie, 117.

30. Lambert, 166–167.

CHAPTER EIGHT

1. There are two accounts of the gun battle at John Land's. One is AJ's, dictated to James B. McLaughlin in January 1843 and preserved in a memorandum in the Jackson Papers; the other, from Garden, 424–425, is the recollection of John Mackey, a boy who was being held prisoner by the Tory band during the attack. They provide complementary versions of the incident, one from outside the cabin, one from inside. Most of my narrative comes from AJ's account, which clearly states that Land's cabin was west of the river, not on the east side of Land's Ford, as portrayed in some accounts.

2. Garden, 424, gives the date of the incident as 2 March. This is supported by the casualty list in Agee, "Annuities," 112, in which John Land's death, a few weeks later, is dated in March. Land, incidentally, was a Virginian and a connection of Sumter, a brother-in-law according to one account (Steen, 34). On the reason for the end of the attack, Mackey (Garden, 424–425) mentioned the death of Yarborough as a factor; the other two reasons are from AJ's version. Littleton Isbell, a colorful character, is described in Daniel G. Stinson to

Lyman C. Draper, October 18, 1873, DM 9VV343–344. On bullets in mouth, see J. P. Collins, 52.

3. That Crawford "afterward died of the wound" is from AJ's recollection to McLaughlin, memorandum, January 1843, AJ Papers, LC. Crawford's deed is in Holcomb, Lancaster County, 64; it was sworn before John Drennan, a fellow officer in the Whig militia. By the summer of 1781, Crawford definitely had died; see AJ to J. H. Witherspoon, August 11, 1824, AJ Papers, LC.

4. B. P. Robinson, *Davie*, 84, 87; Robert Crawford account, SC-AA; Davidson, Gaston, 28. J. Johnson, 380, vividly described the burned and abandoned cabins between Charlotte and Camden as they appeared two years later.

5. J. P. Collins, 23. Klein, 102, suggests that the Tory bands included many people who were renegades and outcasts from backcountry society—horse thieves, mulattos, and the like. There may well have been a certain amount of class hostility in their destroying the books and amenities of their Whig victims. (See also Klein, 60–62, and Ellet, 211.) Certainly the Loyalists as a whole evoked contempt from some leading Whigs; Davie described them as "poor indolent creatures, who adopted their principles just to change their situation" (to William Smallwood, 11 November 1780, in Balch, 164–16). But there were also people of substance among them, like some of those cited in the next note.

6. Daniel Harper: Saunders, 394; Floyd, 2; Cousar, 55; Palmer, 362–363. John Hutchinson: note dated September 15, 1780, Cornwallis Papers, 30/11/3. Sally Featherston: Alex Bradley notes, DM 14VV228; D.G. Stinson to Lyman C. Draper, May 16, 1872, DM 9VV59. Johnson: Kendall, 49. Loyalists in Simpson's congregation: Howe, 1:513. Inscriptions, 30–31, lists several headstones from a "Tory cemetery" near the Waxhaws. For an example of Tory neighborhoods, see J. P. Collins, 32. Hiding in swamps: Gray, 145.

7. Ellet, 231. Archibald McCorkle in his pension application (NA) recalled that he and other Waxhaw Whigs who returned had to defend themselves "from the ferocious attacks of their loyal neighbors."

8. The best description of this kind of warfare by a participant is J. P. Collins, 29–65. Officers' reaction: Reeves, 474; Royster, 277.

9. O'Hara, 171, 173.

10. Moore, 43; C. G. Davidson, *Gaston*, 16; Howe, 1:536; Jefferies, 3; Hugh Coffey account, SC-AA. Ellet, 3:228, quotes a contemporary ballad: "The Tories took their neighbors' worth,/ and away a whig must go." Whig destruction of Tory property: J. P. Collins, 66–67. For contemporaneous destruction of the same sort in Ulster, see e.g., Elizabeth, Countess of Moira, to Francis, Earl of Huntington, February 4, 1771, in Bickley, 3:153; La Tocnaye, 221; and Biggar, 158–159. An exceptional instance of physical violence toward a woman is in Ellet, 3:202.

11. Gregorie, 113–117; Bass, Gamecock, 85ff., 135; M. Elder to Lyman C. Draper, June 9, 1873, DM 9VV246. Major Thomson is referred to in many Revolutionary accounts in SC-AA, such as Nathaniel Cousar, Thomas Cousar, John Craig, and James Dunlap. For his being a blacksmith, see Rodman, 53–55. On the Nisbet brothers, see Nisbet, 107–108, 143.

On Andrew Walker, see Huey, 3. On Frederick Kimball, see Moss, 534; D. W. Brown to Lyman C. Draper, July 6, 1873, DM 12VV228.

12. J. P. Collins, 34.

13. Ibid., 36. Susannah Spratt Grier's recollection of AJ's hiding out with his friends at Spratt's slaughter pen is in Thomas Grier's pension application, NA. (Spratt's slaughter pen is mentioned in John Bigham to Nathaniel Greene, December 12, 1780, in Greene Papers, 5:684.) Quite possibly her recollection was exaggerated or distorted, but there is certainly nothing improbable in a Whig band's riding thirty miles to elude Tory opponents. The group Potter Collins was in rode such distances routinely; cf. p. 64.

As mentioned in Appendix 2, if AJ did ever ride past Susan Barnett's house and have the encounter she described, it was probably in this time period, February–April 1781.

14. Polk, 1:45–46. The Polks claimed to have heard this story from AJ himself. It is hard to place in time. The claim that the pursuing cavalry were led by Tarleton is hard to take seriously, since Tarleton spent very little time in the Waxhaws after June. Possibly it happened later in the summer of 1780, when AJ was a noncombatant but was accompanying Polk for some reason; but the spring of 1781 seems more likely.

15. J. P. Collins, 27, 36 37, 40, 46; Garden, 425.

16. K. M. Brown, 21 30; J. Johnson, 446; Wade, 97; Kendall, 45.

17. Ellet, 234; Stinson, 215–216.

18. D. G. Stinson to Lyman C. Draper, May 7, 1873, DM 9VV210; notes from Logan Mss., DM 16VV323; J. P. Collins, 56; Kendall, 45.

19. Gregorie, 150; Greene Papers, 8:xli; Sumter to Greene, April 7, 1781, Ibid., 8:65–66; R.M. Brown, 76–81; The [Charles Town] *Royal Gazette* April 17, 24, 1782.

20. The main source for this ambush at the meeting house, which brought on the most traumatic events of AJ's early life, is AJ's own reminiscences, written up in Reid and Eaton, 11–12, and amplified in Kendall, 48–50. Two other brief reports exist: an item from the *Royal Gazette* of Charles Town, 23 February 1782, in DM 16VV438, and a letter from Sumter to Greene, April 13, 1781, in Greene Papers, 8:91.

CHAPTER NINE

1. Kendall, 49.

2. Parton, 1:88.

3. The very first biography of AJ, that of Reid and Eaton, contained the story of his capture and imprisonment, the most exciting event of his early life (12). When it was reissued in 1824, it contained an additional paragraph, added presumably at AJ's request, stressing the boys' stealth and caution and demonstrating that their capture was due to bad luck, not carelessness (lviii). Evidently this part of the story was important to AJ, and I have tried to follow his emphasis.

The sentinel appears out of nowhere at this point in the narrative. It was either another militiaman, elsewhere unmentioned, who came out of the woods with the Jacksons, or a noncombatant adult. My choice in the text is merely a guess. For Thomas Crawford's family, see Chapter 3, note 31. The baby is mentioned in Kendall, 50.

4. Reid and Eaton, 12; Kendall, 49–50.

5. As Remini (*AJ*, 429) points out, AJ's exact words are unknown, but their content is agreed on; this quote is James Parton's approximation 1:89. On the identity of the officer, see note 11, below.

6. Metzger, 158–159.

7. Reid and Eaton, 12; AJ to Amos Kendall, January 9, 1844, AJ Papers, LC. That the British burned Thomas Crawford's house is nowhere recorded; but an oral tradition (George McC. Witherspoon to Lyman C. Draper, March 20, 1874, DM 15VV381) has Crawford building a new house after the war's end, and it is a matter of record that the British burned several dwellings ("Official Correspondence," 8).

8. M. James, 27–28; map from Kendall, reproduced in AJ Papers, 1:8.

9. According to Parton, 90, there were twenty-three prisoners in all. Reid and Eaton's account, 10, mentions eleven prisoners taken at the church. At least three more were added the next day: the Jackson boys and their Crawford cousin. The official correspondence on both the British and American sides mentions captives but gives no numbers. Thomas Walker is mentioned in Huey, 5. Mathis, 1:209, gives the name of another captive as "W. McCain," who is probably to be identified with the William McCain also mentioned in Huey, 5. Robert Crockett is mentioned in Crockett, 3–4. Huey, 3, characterizes most of them as "mere boys." Nathan Barr may have been another prisoner; see Chapter 10, note 13. AJ recalled (James B. McLaughlin to Amos Kendall, January 2, 1843, AJ Papers, 1:7) that a cousin was captured with him and Robert. According to Parton, 90, it was Thomas Crawford. The oral tradition recorded in Veach, 138, maintains that it was James Crawford, but this tradition is inaccurate in many details and may be in error here. Kendall's version, 49, which came directly from AJ, states that James was captured the day of the attack and Thomas the following day, but mentions only one cousin's being taken to Camden. Since the Jacksons were taken at Thomas's house, I think the preponderance of the evidence favors Thomas; but I have no explanation why James was not taken too.

According to Sumter's scouts, the British "began to Retreat on Wednesday night." (Greene to Sumter, April 13, 1780, "Official Correspondence," 9).

10. Kendall, 51; "Anonymous Itinerary," 289–290.

11. Sabine, 218–220; M.J. Clark, 3:178–179, 183, 185, 190, 202–207. AJ in his recollections mentioned "Major [actually, at this time, Captain] Coffin" ("Jackson's Capture," AJ Papers, 1:5), so he clearly knew the identity of that officer. He did not name the officer who struck him, which suggests to me that it was not Coffin but one of his subordinates. The violence of the act in any case seems inconsistent with Coffin's character as described in Sabine.

12. Rawdon to Nisbet Balfour, April 15, 1781 ("Coffin returned the night before last. He killed fourteen of the Enemy, & took a few"), Cornwallis Papers, 30/11/5, makes it possible to date AJ's arrival with some precision. Prewar Camden, including Kershaw's pottery manufacture, is described in Schulz, "Hinterland," 93–95, and Schulz, "Rise and Decline,"

30, 105–106. Stedman, 2:193–194, lists the goods the British took from Kershaw's store in 1780. K. Lewis, Camden, 23, gives background on Kershaw, some of whose store ledgers are in the State Historical Society of Wisconsin. On "Great Mart," see Avery, 256. On eviction of families, see Mathis, 110. On Camden in 1781, see Benjamin Ingraham diary, entry of March 15, 1781, in Thomas, 95. On jail, see Kirkland and Kennedy, 1:204; K. Lewis, "Jail," 7.

13. The jail and its environs are carefully described in K. Lewis, "Jail," 6–8, 26, 31–32. I accept his conclusion that the interior jails built by the colonial authorities in the 1770s were all on the same plan, and that the jail at Camden was therefore essentially identical to the one at Ninety-Six. The number 250 for the prisoners is AJ's estimate, in his reminiscences to James McLaughlin (McLaughlin to Amos Kendall, January 2, 1843, AJ Papers, 1:7), on which I have drawn for some other details in this paragraph. Prisoners at Camden and Fishing Creek: Boatner, 168, 369. John Mackey's story is in Albert G. Mackey to Lyman C. Draper, January 16, 1874, DM 15VV262–263; and Garden, 425. Logtown appears in some detail on the map in Gunby, opposite page 77, and is mentioned in the Clitherall diary, April 13, 1776, and Kirkland and Kennedy, 1:209. See also Schulz, "Rise and Decline," 30.

14. Kirkland and Kennedy, 1:207. AJ (McLaughlin to Kendall, January 2, 1843, AJ Papers, 1:7) recalled the smallpox, which had been a problem in the garrison at least since the preceding fall. In November of 1780 an officer mentioned its prevalence among the Africans he had detailed to construction work (George Turnbull to Cornwallis, November 2, 1780, Cornwallis Papers 30/11/3). John Adair, who was in Camden jail from August 1780 to March 1781, had smallpox (Ellet, 273). Alexander Fleming of the New Acquisition died there of smallpox (Howe, 1:339), as did James Smith, a political prisoner from Rowan County, North Carolina (Rumple, 110–111).

15. Ellet, 247; McLaughlin to Kendall, January 2, 1843, AJ Papers, 1:7; Samuel McCalla to D. G. Stinson, June 6, 1841, DM 9VV76. Parton, 90, describes AJ's complaint about the food and says that it was stale bread once a day. Another prisoner (Rhyne, 55) remembered scraps of pumpkins. The quote is from Albert G. Mackey to Lyman C. Draper, January 16, 1874, DM 15VV262. On the general shortage of food in Camden in April, see Rawdon to Nisbet Balfour, April 13, 1781; Cornwallis Papers, 30/11/5; and Davie to Greene, April 11, 1781, Davie Papers. At least one prisoner is reported to have died of starvation in Camden jail (Ellet, 132).

16. AJ's own recollections, in AJ Papers, 1:5, 7, feature examples of savage Tory treatment. Kirkland and Kennedy, 1:209, contains a memory of Tories' threatening prisoners with hanging or actually stringing them up for fun. Prison ships: Ibid., 1:206; Francis Ross Miles to Lyman C. Draper, January 8, February 14, 1874, DM 13VV143. AJ's fellow prisoner John Mackey was taken to Charles Town when the British evacuated Camden and placed on a prison ship (Albert G. Mackey to Draper, January 16, 1874, DM 15VV263).

17. Eliza Campbell Evans to L. C. Draper, December 14, 1874, DM 15VV82–85; AJ to Sam Houston, c. August 8, 1824, AJ Papers, 5:431.

18. Rhyne, 55; Kirkland and Kennedy, 1:208; Ellet, 264.

19. AJ to Sam Houston, c. August 8, 1824, AJ Papers, 5:431; Weigley, 49; Mathis, 104–105.

20. Weigley, 33–49, has an excellent discussion of Greene's strategy in the spring campaign of 1781.

21. Mathis, 104–106; Guilford Dudley pension application, NA.

22. "Jackson's Imprisonment," AJ Papers, 1:5. There was and is some doubt in Camden about whether it was really possible for AJ to have viewed the battle from the jail, even from an upper floor, because of the topography. Kirkland and Kennedy, 1:209, comment on the difficulty but go on to add that another Revolutionary veteran, Will McCain of the Waxhaws, claimed to have witnessed it from the same floor. Very likely he was in the same cell with AJ; indeed, he may have been the prisoner who helped AJ cut a hole in the plank. Albert G. Mackey to Lyman Draper, January 16, 1874, DM 15VV263, confirms the boarding up of the windows, with the comment, "You damned rebels, you shall not have the pleasure of seeing your countrymen."

23. "Jackson's Imprisonment," AJ Papers, 1:6; Kirkland and Kennedy, 1:209; Howland, 103. Hard rain: Samuel Mathis diary, in Kirkland and Kennedy, 1:402.

24. "Jackson's Imprisonment," AJ Papers, 1:6; Mathis, 108–109. Guilford Dudley's pension application, NA, refers to John Smith as Capt. Jack Smith.

25. Mathis, 109; Reid and Eaton, 13; Huey, 3, 5.

26. Huey, 5; "Jackson's Imprisonment," AJ Papers, 1:6; McLaughlin to Kendall, January 2, 1843, Ibid., 1:7. AJ's accounts of his return home, in the two sources last cited, contain puzzling sentences and unresolvable contradictions. He was exchanged "with six others" (1:5), and given the unsettled state of the area it would have seemed almost necessary for the released prisoners and their families to travel home as a group; but there were "only two horses in our company when we left Camden" (1:6), according to AJ. The second assertion makes it sound as if the rest of the company abandoned the Jacksons. One can make up any number of scenarios, none verifiable, to explain why. The evidence may be to some extent defective. AJ's statement that the "distance to the nearest house to Camden where we stopped that night was forty five miles" (1:6) is surely a misquote of some sort. Forty-five miles was about the distance to the Waxhaws, but there were many houses in between; and the journey would have taken two days with AJ on foot. AJ said (1:6) that the rain and exposure caused the smallpox to "strike in" (i.e., appear); in other words, he had no symptoms before the end of the return trip. As he remembered, they appeared during or immediately after the rain.

CHAPTER TEN

1. Hopkins, 3–4, 41–42; Rhyne, 25.

2. Hopkins, 3–6; Shurkin, 25–26, 36–37. "Strike in" is AJ's terminology, from James McLaughlin to Amos Kendall, January 2, 1843, in AJ Papers, 1:7.

3. Remini, *AJ1*, 430, note 13, points out the absence of pockmarks in AJ's portraits. Robert Jackson's death is mentioned in James B. McLaughlin to Amos Kendall, January 2, 1843, in AJ Papers, 1:7. The doctor who helped AJ is called "Dr. Tongue" in one source

(Kendall, 58) and "Dr. Bond" in another closely related source (McLaughlin to Kendall, March 15, 1843, AJ Papers, LC). Neither name is common in the Carolinas, and I have found no physician, military or civilian, of either name in the surviving records. There was, however, a family named Tonge, of professionals and shopkeepers, in Charles Town and nearby St. Paul's Parish at the time of the Revolution. They are referred to with some frequency in Moore, *Abstracts of Wills*; McElligott, *Charleston Residents*; and SCHGM. If AJ's helper bore the rare surname of "Tongue," he was probably a member of this family; hence my reference in the text to "a Charles Town doctor." On shunning the sick, see Woodmason, 38. On Rawdon's evacuation of Camden, see W. Gordon, 193; B. P. Robinson, *Sketches*, 111–114.

4. For a good short description of malaria in South Carolina, see Weir, 40–41.

5. Ramsay, *Revolution*, 2:288–289, and W. Gordon, 223–224, mention the general exchange of prisoners, including those of the militia, in June. The Waxhaw militiamen would certainly have been involved, and this fact helps to date Mrs. Jackson's departure for Charles Town. (Compare M. James, 31, who places her death in November 1781, and Remini, AJ, 19, who suggests that she did not go to Charles Town for several months after AJ's illness. Reid and Eaton, 10, on the other hand, state that she died only a "few weeks after Robert," a timetable that agrees with this account.) Particulars of her visit, including some of the other women who made up the party, Nancy Dunlap and a Mrs. Boyd, were given by AJ on two occasions: AJ to J. H. Witherspoon, August 11, 1824; and James B. McLaughlin to Amos Kendall, January 2, March 15, 1843, all in Jackson Papers, LC. The letter of January 2 is also the source for his residence at Major Crawford's. The affidavit in John Ramsey's pension application, NA, also mentions that AJ lived at Major Crawford's after the war, but it probably refers to a slightly later period; cf. Chapter 11, note 4. The military situation in June is described in Lambert, 170–173.

6. Remini, AJ1, 24, argues that Mrs. Jackson and her companions most likely traveled on horseback, despite a tradition that they went on foot; I agree. I use the version of her parting words given in Sparks, 148, as Marquis James, 396, did; I found his reasoning persuasive. (Besides, the other version he mentions, that of A. F. Buell, is probably invented; see Appendix 1.)

7. Betty Jackson's reputation became an issue in the presidential campaign of 1828, and AJ collected testimony at that time from some Tennesseans who had lived in or near the Waxhaws in the Revolutionary era and knew her or knew of her then (affidavits of Thomas Stephenson, July 30, 1828; Samuel Mayes, July 31, 1828; and Nathaniel Stephenson, 1 August 1828, in Bassett, 3:416–418). They all told the same story—that she had a "fair . . . character for virtue and piety" (417) and a reputation "as good as any other person in that neighborhood" (418). The Stephenson brothers were aware of the Hutchinson sisters as a family grouping and evaluated them as such—the sisters had all married "respectable, clever men" (418) and all their families had good characters, "especially the women"(417). The last statement could be construed as an indirect reference to James Crawford's drinking; cf. Chapter 4, note 27.

Both Stephensons also went out of their way to note that Betty Jackson was a woman "of not much property" (417)—differentiating her economic status from that of her brother-in-law James Crawford. These comments may provide a clue to her fear of slander. Despite the security and mutual aid of the clan system, wealth was an important determinant of respect in the backcountry (Fischer, 754–758); families without wealth were apt to be slighted. Betty Jackson may already have experienced some slights.

8. Joseph F. White to Lyman C. Draper, December 13, 1870, DM 15VV90–91, relates the family tradition of Robert Crawford's becoming rich during and after the war. A battle with Tories on Waxhaw Creek in August 1781 is reported in George McWhorter's pension application, NA; William Barkley reported guarding Tories on the Catawba in the same year (Moss, 44).

9. Mrs. Jackson's death was related by AJ to biographers and correspondents several times (Reid and Eaton, 10; James McLaughlin to Amos Kendall, January 2, March 15, 1843; AJ to James Witherspoon, August 11, 1824, AJ Papers, LC). None of these accounts gives a specific cause of death, but Lee's biography (5), prepared under AJ's supervision, attributed her death to a "fever prevailing in the lower country." Later biographers have suggested, very plausibly, that the fever was probably related to the epidemic diseases that ravaged the prison ships (see Ramsay, Revolution, 286, 288). Remini, AJ1, 24, identifies "ship fever" with cholera, but a more likely identification is typhus; see Zinsser, 169, 219–221, which also spells out how typhus was transmitted from ship to shore.

Joseph Crawford's death is mentioned in his file, SC-AA. It took place in October, presumably October 1780.

10. For AJ's lifelong devotion to his mother's memory, see Parton, 1:68, and Parton notebooks, 1:37. A central thesis of Rogin's Fathers and Children, articulated on page 46, is that Mrs. Jackson's death in Charles Town filled AJ with a rage that shaped his behavior for the rest of his life, a "buried rage at his mother for dominating him, abandoning him, and denying him nurture." Rogin states his case with some rhetorical passion, but no evidence supports it. Nothing suggests that either AJ or any of his contemporaries regarded Mrs. Jackson's mission to Charles Town as an abandonment, nor that she denied him nurture, nor that he ever felt that sort of hostility toward her.

11. On Ulster cultural patterns, see Akenson and Crawford, 104; Evans, Irish Folk Ways, 86, 283; Willes, 39; Twiss, 49; Young, 200; Woodmason, 32, 39, 99–100, 117; Fischer, 653. Gillis, 30–34, indicates that this free association was a general British pattern, not merely Irish. The Osborne diary, written in the vicinity of the Waxhaws two decades after the Revolution, has abundant information on the same courting and sex patterns; see, for example, the entry for September 30, 1800: "I aimed for company with his wifes Daughter after we all went to bed for past time up I gets & goes to the girls bed But I'll swer if Osbourn order me off to my Bed again the first time ever I was Served So." (The "Osbourn" in the quotation was a kinsman of the diarist.)

Remini, AJ1, 25, excellently summarizes AJ's attitude toward women. AJ's conduct as a young man in Salisbury, North Carolina, is the subject of several interviews in the Parton notebooks, e.g., 1:106, 116, 133. The tradition in Salisbury was that he chased "yellow women," such as mulattoes (Brawley, "Isn't It Time"), and a story from his Salisbury days, narrated in Chapter 14, makes clear that he was acquainted with loose white women as well. "Chivalrous": John Overton, quoted in Parton, 1:149.

12. In the text I have described AJ's risk-taking behavior in terms of conscious, explanatory concepts ("fearlessness," "fatalism"). Psychiatrists who deal with the same kind of material are more apt to describe its irrational, involuntary aspects. Survivors of trauma often feel a compulsion to expose themselves to physical risk (Herman, 39–41), perhaps because reenactment triggers a surge of endogenous opioids, chemicals that enhance mental well-being (van der Kolk, 73). Lee's biography, 9–10, gives a good example from AJ's early manhood of deliberate exposure to physical danger. I extend the concept a bit, however, to encompass social as well as physical risk. Two stories from AJ's residence in Salisbury—the tale of the ball he managed and that of smashing the furniture, both recounted in Chapter 14—suggest that he had an indifference to social consequences (loss of reputation, ostracism, legal action) that only the very rich could afford in the eighteenth century. It seems plausible that his willingness to court social "danger" is another aspect of his risk-taking behavior, perhaps attended with the same compulsive and/or pleasurable features. (I am indebted to Dr. C. Y. Wemple of Washington, D.C., for help on this point.)

On crime after the war in South Carolina, see Nadelhaft, 128–129.

13. The earliest reference I have found to the public station at Crawford's is in the pension application of George McWhorter (NA), who stated that he began work there in August 1781. William Crawford began working for Galbraith September 2 and continued through May 3, 1782 (SC-AA). There are no references after May, and by the beginning of 1783 the station was definitely closed; Major Crawford was calculating the costs he had incurred in connection with it, including the hire of his slaves and the trees felled for the buildings. He claimed twelve months' hire for the slaves, perhaps an indication that the station closed around August or September (SC-AA). Most references to it in the audited Revolutionary accounts come from the fall of 1781 and refer to Captain Galbraith or "Kilbreth" as being in charge; see, for instance, the accounts of John Crockett, John Foster, William Galloway, and Robert Montgomery, all in SC-AA. Galbraith's own account in the same collection places him in Camden in spring 1780. He lived near Camden after the war as well (Holcomb, *Lancaster County*, 38) and was appointed a tobacco inspector there in 1784 (*South Carolina Gazette*, 29 April 1784). On his character, see note 17.

There is no evidence that AJ worked at the station, and indeed he may have been too weak to work; but he was certainly resident at the major's, and his qualifications were as good as Will Crawford's. Galbraith seems to have felt entitled to discipline him verbally, a fact that suggests he was working under Galbraith's supervision. Both AJ and Will Crawford had mastered a fancy "official" signature by the early 1780s, as documents in the Robert Crawford file, SC-AA, show—Crawford's ending with an elaborate double loop on the final "d," AJ's with a large open loop on the final "n," somewhat different from his adult signature.

14. Nathan Barr account, SC-AA; George McWhorter pension application, NA. Wardlaw, 93–94, makes clear AJ's feeling of esteem and gratitude for Sarah Crawford.

15. Weigley, 65–69; Malmady to Greene, September 28, 1781; Galbraith to Greene, September 29, 1781, Greene Papers. For background on Malmady, see Lassenay, 1:44.

16. Robert Crockett account, SC-AA. Tilden, 215–216; "Anonymous Itinerary," 289; and Feltman, December 20–24, 1781, are three accounts by members of a Pennsylvania military unit that passed through the Waxhaws that winter. Tilden and Feltman mention the British officers; all mention the rainy weather. For the incident with the prisoners, see Galbraith to Greene, January 18, 1782; John Strong et al. to Greene, January 12, 1782; and Greene to Galbraith, January 28, 1782, all in Greene Papers.

17. The only source for AJ's quarrel with Galbraith is his own recollection, in James McLaughlin to Amos Kendall, January 2, 1843, AJ Papers, 1:7. Galbraith is mentioned in the Reeves diary, April 9, 1782, and in George McC. Witherspoon to Lyman C. Draper, March 20, 1874, DM 12VV380. The "rich Highland brogue" with which M. James, 33, credits Galbraith is, unfortunately, an invention of the twentieth-century biographer A. C. Buell; see Appendix I. In fact, Galbraith was no Scot, but probably a Carolina Quaker; see the next note.

18. On homicide in the backcountry after the war, see Nadelhaft, 128–129, illustrated by Drayton's encounter ("Back Country," 3–4) with a tavernkeeper near Orangeburg who had killed two of his neighbors "as cooly [sic] . . . as if they had been Bucks or Wolves." North Carolinians recalled a similar period, with a high rate of murder, after the war's end (Caruthers, *Old North State*, 191). Galbraith had already received death threats in connection with the incident of the British prisoners (Galbraith to Greene, January 18, 1782, Greene Papers).

As for his nonviolent response, there is evidence to suggest that the captain was a Quaker who owed his rank merely to military convenience. Galbraith was a Quaker name in New Garden and Wilkes County, North Carolina, from which Quaker emigrants went to Camden. There was a large Friends meeting in Camden, the records of which have been lost; but Galbraith's name appears frequently in surviving legal records with that of a Camden Quaker named Millhouse.

19. A later reminiscence by AJ, in an account heavily laden with early Victorian pathos (Kane, 56), describes his situation after his mother's death as having "no home" and "no friends." That depiction is plainly exaggerated for effect, but if there is a kernel of truth in it, it may be AJ's awareness that there was no place for him in any family circle in the Waxhaws. He was a member in good standing of the Crawford clan, but no particular family took him in. Later reminiscences of this period suggest that he may have stayed at various times with George and Peggy McCamie (James Craig letter, 1858, Walter Clark Mss., 3:312) and Thomas Crawford (George McC. Witherspoon to Lyman C. Draper, March 20, 1874, DM 12VV381) in addition to the Whites.

20. South Carolina Deed Abstracts, 4:21, 34; Joseph White will and inventory, March 13, 1784, Kershaw County Will Book A1, 262; Wardlaw, 95–98; SC-AA #8432, Joseph

. . . .

Notes

White; Joseph F. White to Lyman C. Draper, December 13, 1870, DM 15VV91; A.S. White account, 1909, White Family Papers, SHC. Henry White may not have been alive by 1782; he was definitely dead by the time Joseph White wrote his will in 1784. The family tradition is that he drowned in the Catawba.

Hugh White wrote AJ at least one letter a few years later, recalling the "intimacy that subsisted between us in our puerile State" (White to AJ, September 9, 1797, AJ Papers, 1:149). Since White is credited with no more than a common school education, the flowery, Latinate language suggests his intelligence as well as the esteem in which he held AJ.

21. There seems to be no source for the craft of saddlery in the eighteenth-century American backcountry, so I have used eighteenth-century urban sources (Garsault, Stockham) and balanced them against nineteenth-century sources from the American West (Rice and Vernam), with additional details from elsewhere, like an eighteenth-century saddler's bill in the John Steele Papers. On saddle construction, see Tylden, 112–113, 126. On use of natural hardwood, see Rice and Vernam, 16, 75. On rawhide, see Ibid., 16. On flour glue, see Garsault, 102; apron: Stockham, 110 (illustration). On girth, surcingle, padding, see Frederick Allemong bill, March 6, 1787, John Steele Papers, SHC. On equipment, see Salomon, 238–239, 256. On apprentice's duties, see C. C. Martin, 77–78. A good description of Hugh White in maturity is in A. S. White's reminiscences, White Family Papers, SHC. On coon hunting, see cf. J. P. Collins, 71.

22. George McC. Witherspoon to Lyman C. Draper, March 20, 1874, DM 12VV381. Apprenticeship was generally unpopular among American boys after the war; contrasted with the sweeping rhetoric of the Revolution, it was thought of as a form of "bondage" (Rorabaugh, 36).

23. The story of Galbraith's "bad conduct" with the Crawfords is in George McC. Witherspoon to Lyman C. Draper, March 20, 1874, DM 12VV380. For his failing to pay Will Crawford, see William Crawford account, SC-AA. Crawford family tradition had it that he "ran away and went back to Europe," but in fact he went no further than Camden, where he died in 1792 (Holcomb, Kershaw, 7, 38; Lancaster, 15–16).

24. Will Crawford's name first appears in the Salisbury records as witness to a marriage bond October 9, 1782; within the next ten months he witnessed nineteen more (Rowan County Marriage Bonds, marriage of John Eller and Susanna Eller). One other bond with Crawford as a witness, for the marriage of John Giles and Rachel Williams, was dated January 10, 1782, but this date cannot be correct; according to Crawford's account in SC-AA he worked at the public station until May 1782. Probably the clerk misdated the year, as sometimes happens in January documents. The lawyer he studied under was probably Spruce Macay; I say this because most witnesses for marriage bonds in these years were somehow connected with Macay—others who frequently witnessed were John Macay and Fanny Macay. Crawford was admitted to practice in May 1784. He is further discussed in Chapter 12, note 21.

CHAPTER ELEVEN

1. These verses were quoted by a Hessian soldier in 1781–1782 (Kipping, 19), but the original form was written by a Captain Martin in 1769 (Merrens, 230–231). A comparison of the two versions shows that the Hessian or some British military man made some minor changes and added several couplets dealing with matters of interest to the occupying forces, like prostitutes and taverns. I follow the version given in Kipping, except that in the sixth line I have restored "centipedes" from the original in place of an unintelligible word used by the German. On the change of the city's name, see Fraser, *Charleston*, 169.

2. Rogers, 58, 83, 88; R. A. Smith, 40, 49, 53; Schoepf, 2:164, 166, 222; Ryan, 209–211, 219; Merrens, 283; Fraser, *Charleston*, 175, 177; Ezell, 34; Kipping, 18; Thomas, 102–103.

3. Merrens, 267, 283–284; R.A. Smith, 51, 56; Reitz et al., 1–6; Schoepf, 2:165, 219; Ryan, 211, 221; Ezell, 25; Thomas, 102; *South Carolina Gazette,* 3 June 1783.

4. John Ramsey pension application, NA; William Nettles pension application, NA. Ramsey refers to Nettles as a major, but Nettles's own application suggests that captain was the highest rank he reached.

5. Robert Crawford file, SC-AA; Brimelow, 1.

6. On AJ's land in North Carolina, see AJ Papers, 1:3–4 and note. Reid and Eaton, 13–14, describes his inheritance as "small," but "sufficient . . . to have completed his education." His next biographer, Henry Lee, reproduced these words almost verbatim (Lee, 5). The account of Augustus Buell (1:56) has been accepted by several other twentieth-century biographers (e.g., M. James, 34) but seems completely unfounded; see Appendix I.

7. The story of AJ's visit to Charleston and his wagering his horse in a dice game exists in two slightly different variants. Published the year he was elected, it was described as an incident "never heretofore recorded" (Laval and Bradford, 4–5). Presumably AJ himself was the source. In 1843, AJ told James B. McLaughlin the same story, with a few differences of nuance (McLaughlin to Amos Kendall, February 14, 1843, AJ Papers, LC). In the later version, the gambling took place at the tavern where AJ was staying with acquaintances. In the first, more suited to a campaign year, AJ wandered into the place by chance and knew none of the people involved. In the text I have combined elements of both. "Immediately after the war," "like many other young men," "rattle and snap," and the identification of the horse as a mare are from the McLaughlin letter. "Carried into a place" and the amount of the wager are from Laval and Bradford. I have made one change. Laval and Bradford give the amount as two hundred dollars, which cannot be right; currency in Charleston was still reckoned in pounds in the 1780s (Schoepf, 2:222). If the figure of two hundred is correct, the monetary unit is certainly pounds.

The Laval-Bradford version is vague about the time of the incident, but suggests that it took place late in AJ's youth, when he was looking for a place to settle; the McLaughlin version places it immediately after the war. It can hardly have happened after the beginning of 1785, when AJ went to North Carolina to study law and cast his fortunes definitely with that state; and obviously it happened after the British evacuation of Charles Town in December 1782. In other words, it belongs somewhere in the years 1783 and 1784.

More specific dating is impossible, but it is tempting to try to fit the story into the general sequence of events in the Reid-Eaton biography for these years (13–14): AJ (1) received a small inheritance, (2) spent it unwisely, (3) went back to school briefly, and (4) departed for North Carolina. This story seems to fit naturally into phase two, spending the inheritance. One could suggest either that AJ and Major Crawford went together to Charleston with AJ's legacy in hand, and that the major subsequently left his young kinsman in Charleston to fend for himself, while he returned to the Waxhaws; or that both returned home together, and AJ later visited Charleston on his own. To me the latter seems more likely. Like Marquis James (377), I would conjecture that the second visit took place in winter or spring, when the social season was at its height, that is, in late 1783 or early 1784.

8. Schulz, "Rise," 38; Drayton, "Back Country," 30–31, 36; Reeves, 475–476.

9. Drayton, "Back Country," 36–37; Clitherall diary, 10–13 April 1776; E. T. Clark, 1:536; D. S. Brown, 87; Crittenden, "Travel," 248–249; Nadelhaft, 128–129.

10. Drayton, "Back Country," 31, 37; Coke, 104.

11. R. A. Smith, 82, Ryan, 219–220, Fraser, Charleston, 171, William Heth to O. H. Williams, August 6, 8, 1780, Williams Papers, Maryland Historical Society; Hanger, 405; Schoepf, 2:168–169, 222; Fraser, Patriots, 29; South Carolina Gazette, February 26, April 13, 1784.

12. Lee, 5. This paragraph has no parallel in the Reid-Eaton biography, which Lee was using as his main source on AJ's youth; one must conclude that Lee got his information from the general himself. Certainly, Lee, as a scion of a leading Virginia gentry family, would have found AJ's initiation into genteel manners especially interesting.

13. Wardlaw, 83; Moss, 261; Moore, 35–37, 41–42; Johnson, 84, 377.

14. Barnwell, 8–10.

15. Lee, 5–6: "To the pleasure of their society [i.e., the Charlestonians in the Waxhaws] he resigned himself completely. . . . In the indulgences of this expensive society . . . he expended money which he could ill spare." No visit to Charleston is mentioned.

16. Schoepf, 2:169; Fraser, Charleston, 171; R. A. Smith, 56; Irving, 34–35, 38, 41–42, Pt. 4, p. 12; Ramsey, South Carolina, 402–403; Royal Gazette, 13 June 1781; South Carolina Gazette, 12 April 1783, 7 February, 8 April 1784.

17. Lee, 6; Rogers, 72–73; Grayson, 59–61, 66; Ford, 190–191.

18. Ford, 142–143, 189. The rough equivalency in cost of a horse and a slave is mentioned in a document, dated May 10, 1791, in folder 297 of the Lenoir Family Papers, SHC; and cf. Struna, 171. For AJ's early interest in owning a slave, see Chapter 17.

19. The basics of the code duello are given in Truman, 48–52. For its importation into Charleston, see Ulmer, 2, 7, and Grayson, 62–63. Wyatt-Brown, 351–357, is excellent on the social overtones of duelling at a slightly later period.

20. Lee, 5–6.

CHAPTER TWELVE

1. Howe, 1:540–541. AJ's endorsement on John Adair's pension application, NA, states that the British burned both the meeting house and the school house. Leslie, 22–23, describes an earlier schism within the Waxhaw congregation, around 1776, not corroborated in any other source. In mid-1784 the congregation reunited under a new minister, the Pennsylvania-born Robert Finley, who was first mentioned as minister in William Barnett's will in September, 1784, but was not formally installed until 1785 (Sprague, 2:58–61).

2. Howe, 1:514. Klein, 115, mentions the economic hardship in the backcountry just after the war.

3. Reid and Eaton, 14, and Lee, 6, mention AJ's choice of the legal profession at the same time as his decision to go back to school. His attitude toward religion is discussed further in Chapter 13.

4. Farmer, "Bar Examination," 170. The use of "Esquire" for attorneys is pervasive in North Carolina court documents of the period.

5. Ashe, *Biographical History*, 3:428; Bloomfield, 172, citing Watterston, *The Lawyer,* and Charles Brockden Brown, *The Rhapsodist and Other Uncollected Writings.* It is worth noting that Williams, although esteemed as a man, was not thought of as an especially competent lawyer; but he had all the status that went with the profession.

6. Attorney-as-performer: L. Friedman, 270. Davie's ringing defense of the Tory Samuel Bryan in 1782 (B. P. Robinson, *Davie*, 156–158) is an example. A lawyer of that generation recalled that all an attorney really needed was "a good voice" and "a fluid utterance" (Bloomfield, 141). On the widespread public knowledge of legal forms, see Ashe, "Social Conditions," 206; the sample deed at the beginning of the Dickey account book is an example. Davie's letter to Crockett, September 22, 1789, is in the Davie Papers, SHC.

7. The account book of an unknown Salisbury attorney in the Macay-McNeely Papers, SHC, shows that he was employed several times by Robert Crawford of the Waxhaws at Mecklenburg Court in 1763–1765. William Crawford first appeared in a record in Salisbury in October 1782 (Rowan County Marriage Bonds, marriage of John Eller and Susanna Eller) and was admitted to the bar there May 4, 1784 (Minutes of the Rowan County Court of Pleas and Quarter Sessions).

8. Farmer, "Legal Practice," 266. Farmer, "Bar Examination," 163, mentions the lack of an age requirement. Battle, 195, makes it evident that 21 was a customary age for being licensed; but it was not a minimum, as demonstrated by cases like that of John Sitgreaves of New Bern, who was licensed at age 19 in the 1770s and was a clerk of the State Senate by age 21 (Gertrude S. Carraway, "John Sitgreaves," North Carolina, 5:353). On the lack of a requirement for the period of preparation, see Farmer, "Bar Examination," 160, and Reed, 84. The sketch of Richard Henderson in the Henderson Family Papers ("A short although a correct sketch of the Henderson family," 6) shows that some judges felt that more than a year was needed to prepare; Henderson, however, passed his examination after only a year of study. Self-preparation is mentioned by Wettach, 8, and exemplified in the careers

of John Haywood in North Carolina (DAB 4:466 and Thomas Hart Benton in Tennessee (Benton, 21–23).

Marquis James's contention (37) that Spruce Macay's last name was pronounced "McCoy" receives support from various manuscript sources in which the name is so spelled, such as Parton Notebooks, 1:103, 105; a letter of attorney, October 6, 1787, in the Macay-McNeely Family Papers, SHC; and an entry in the minutes of the Rowan County CPQS, November 6, 1783.

9. Howe, 1:449, 505–506; Brawley, *Old Rowan*, 10; Newsome, "Miscellany," 406.

10. Howe, 1:601–602. McCulloch was remembered by one man in the Waxhaws as "the man that taught Genl A Jackson his letters" (William Harbison to Lyman C. Draper, March 5, 1873, Draper Mss. 4VV38) and by another as "the last classical teacher of Andrew Jackson" (Ellet, 205).

11. Sprague, 3:458–461; Howe, 1:632–633, 651. Whitley, 5, 6, 10.

12. Reid and Eaton, 14. The South Carolina Historical Commission's marker at the site of the Howe cabin gives a date of 1779 for AJ's attendance at the school. This is clearly an error; the school was not founded until 1782 (Whitley, 6).

13. Whitley, 8, 9, 17; Howe, 1:601–602; Ferguson and Cowan, 117–119. Entries from the John Nisbet Papers in the Southern Historical Collection show that, as early as May 1783, Hill had the furnace back in operation and was trading Dutch ovens, andirons, sad-irons, and kettles for linen, corn, bacon, and flour from a Salisbury merchant.

14. Certificate of Samuel Mayes, July 31, 1828, in Bassett, *Correspondence*, 3:417. William Cummins Davis: Howe, 1:602n, 2:66. James W. Stephenson: Howe, loc. cit.; William Smith: Howe, loc. cit.; Moore, 58, where Smith is said to have attended Joseph Alexander's school at Bullock's Creek. This is probably a mistake for Bethel Academy, as no other evidence suggests that he studied at Bullock's Creek. Robert Cunningham: Sprague, 2:58, 61. Grizzell McKenzie: Moore, 56–57; Dulin, 62. Margaret Stinson: J. Johnson, 460–461; Mount, 14–17.

15. On the accommodations at boarding schools, cf. the recollections of John Chesnut, who attended Mt. Zion Academy in 1787: "The accommodations were very deficient. The scholars occupied lofts in different boarding-houses. There were eight of us in that part of the house we lived in. I recollect, well, that William C. Pinckney . . . with his friend Benjamin Ferguson, occupied the loft of a recitation building, a log-house, about twenty by twenty-four feet." (O'Neall, 2:168)

16. Cummins: Sprague, 3:418–421; Howe, 1:632–633, 651. The popularity of agnosticism in the South at this time is mentioned in E. T. Thompson, 1:126. A writer from coastal North Carolina remarked after the war that religious principles were "rather unfashionable" (Dickson, 40). On freethinking in the Charlotte-Mecklenburg area, see Alexander, 281, and Tompkins, 1:78.

17. Peggy Dickey: Fleming, 42–43, is the basic source. Fleming gives the impression that her marriage to Joseph D. Kilpatrick, who prevailed over AJ for her hand, took place in Salisbury; but a careful reading of the text and notes shows that both Dickey and Kilpatrick were from the Waxhaws and were married there in 1786. Her grave marker in the

Third Creek Presbyterian cemetery (McCubbins file, Rowan County Library) suggests that she was born about 1772; to be interesting to AJ in 1784 and marriageable in 1786, she must have been slightly older. The same records show that her first son was named Moses; the name suggests strongly that she was a daughter of Moses Dickey of the Waxhaws.

The Polly, or Mary, Massey story is supported by oral tradition (M. James, 36. In the list of Massey children given in Starr, 4, she was the fifth child, younger than Henry, who was born in 1762.

18. O'Neall, 2:411; Wardlaw, 93–94. The correspondence between AJ and Mary Crawford Dunlap is reproduced in Bassett, *Correspondence*, 4:359, 382–382.

19. Harris, 34; Parton, 99; Herd, 48. Vignettes of schoolteaching are from Arnow, *Flowering*, 143–144, 179, 189. Compare the experience of John Brown of the Waxhaws in Ellet, 3:235. After the war he intended "to pursue a course of study," so he "enlarged his means by teaching school."

20. George McC. Witherspoon to L. C. Draper, March 20, 1874, DM, 12VV380. Witherspoon claimed to have seen AJ's receipt for the slaves, which was lost during the Civil War. A woman writing from Salisbury in the summer of 1783 commented to her sister-in-law that slaves sold "very high at present" (Margaret Balfour to Eliza Balfour, August 17, 1783, in Caruthers, *Old North State*, 82).

21. William Crawford turns out to have been a pivotal, indeed familial figure in AJ's early career. Since the publication of Parton's nineteenth-century biography, students of Jackson have known that he had a roommate and close friend named William Crawford in Salisbury while he was studying law (Parton, 104–105). If they had looked into Parton's notebooks, 1:135, they would have found a statement from one Salisbury informer that he and Crawford were especially close. Some people in Salisbury understood that AJ and Crawford were closely related, though they did not know the exact kinship (Henderson, "Jackson," 8). But no biographer has posited a family relationship between AJ and Crawford, for a very good reason: in the only surviving letter in which AJ referred to Crawford, he called him simply "my old friend" (to Robert Hays, November 2, 1797, AJ Papers, 1:151).

Yet the evidence is overwhelming that the William Crawford who practiced law in Salisbury from 1784 through the early 1790s was in fact AJ's first cousin, who grew up under the same roof with him:

1. A letter in the file of AJ's cousin William Crawford in SC-AA was written from Salisbury in 1785.
2. The signature on the letter closely resembles that on a legal document in the John Steele Papers, a note of hand to William Houston dated April 27, 1787 in Salisbury and witnessed by Crawford.
3. A tradition existed in the Waxhaws that AJ's cousin William Crawford studied law after the war (Howe, 1:582).
4. A descendant of Major Crawford in the 1880s believed that AJ had gone to Salisbury to live and study law with a "Mr. Crawford." (Andrew J. Witherspoon to New Orleans Picayune, in *New York Times*, October 23, 1881).

5. A Crawford family history written years later by a descendant of James Crawford Jr. but not made public until recently, states that AJ and William Crawford studied law together with a third companion who later became prominent in Tennessee (erroneously identified, in this tradition, as John Overton; it was actually John McNairy), and that William Crawford died young (Veach, 138). The account is worth quoting: "Andrew Jackson and Overton, and William Crawford, brother to James, having studied law together, commenced practice. William Crawford soon died and Jackson and Overton came to Tennessee together."

6. When AJ first appeared in the records of the Salisbury merchant John Steele, he charged his purchase to Crawford (Entry of April 27, 1786, Vol. S-1, John Steele Papers, SHC).

In view of all this, the really puzzling question is why AJ referred to Crawford as "my old friend" (admittedly a strong term for AJ) rather than "my cousin" or "my kinsman." The rest of the letter to Hays supplies a possible explanation: Crawford, it goes on to say, "has entirely left of[f] Drink and I am in hopes will profit by his imprudence." By 1797, that is to say, Crawford had a drinking problem of long standing. It is possible that an exasperated AJ decided not to claim kinship with a cousin who could lead him into troublesome obligations.

In any case, it now appears likely that AJ came to Salisbury because his cousin, from whom he anticipated help, was there already. Crawford's drinking problem may already have been developing, and he may have been of less help than AJ expected; I explore this question further in Chapter 16, note 17.

In view of the Jackson Crawford connection, the story reported by Parton 1:101—that AJ first applied to study with Waightstill Avery in Morganton and was turned away for lack of a place to board—seems questionable, and I have omitted it from the text. For a young man of limited resources, the help of a kinsman would be clearly preferable to that of a stranger, even a well-respected stranger. A kinsman could give more help in an informal way for less money and free board to boot. I argue in Chapter 13, indeed, that AJ may not have begun formal legal study until a year after he arrived in North Carolina. Parton's only source was oral tradition in the Avery family.

22. Salisbury: Corbitt, 50–51; Parton, 109; Rumple, 181. Charleston lawyers: Reed, 68, 76n, points out that in the years just before the Revolution thirty-five graduates of the Middle Temple in London were from South Carolina, proportionately more than in any other colony. Only one was from North Carolina. On the evolving court system in South Carolina, see Klein, 135–142.

23. M. James, 36–37.

CHAPTER THIRTEEN

1. Hugh Forbes account, SC-AA; Hugh Forbus pension application, NA.

2. Forbes account, SC-AA; Gregorie, 210.

3. Fifty pounds, the amount given in Forbes's receipt, was a comparatively high price to pay for a South Carolina indent worth one hundred twenty pounds. By 1785 investors had come to doubt South Carolina's ability to pay off its war debt, and the average selling price of an indent had declined to less than 25 percent of face value (Brimelow, 5). Crawford and AJ paid Forbes a considerably better rate, about 40 percent.

Two later documents in the Mecklenburg County Civil Action Papers, NCSA, probably concern the same matter: a warrant requiring Forbes's appearance at April court in 1786 to answer a suit, brought by Crawford and AJ, for breach of covenant, and a bond for his appearance at July court in 1787. The amount Crawford and AJ sought in both instances was eighty pounds. On the later document, AJ's name has been lined through, perhaps a sign that he was withdrawing from the case. I have found no later documents bearing on it. The whole affair and its outcome are so murky that I have decided to omit it from the text and merely note the obvious—that the deal went sour in some unspecified way.

4. Stockard, 39; Hoskins, 116–118.

5. Partin, 1:114; Hughes, *Guilford County*, 5–7; Remini, *AJ1*, 35. Hamilton Jones, a personal friend of the Hendersons, talking with James Parton two generations later, assured Parton (Parton Notebooks, 1:107) that AJ and Pleasant Henderson had been as intimate as brothers when AJ lived at Martinville; probably he meant Pleasant's older brother Thomas, since Pleasant lived not at Martinville but at Danbury with Governor Martin (see note 6).

6. Hughes, *Guilford County*, 14, 121; B. P. Robinson, "Guilford," 64. On AJ's legal practice in the winter of 1787–1788, see Chapter 17.

7. Schoepf, 2:216; Charles Wilson Harris to Dr. Charles Harris, November 27, 1797, Charles Wilson Harris Papers, SHC; Adams, 2:298 and note; entries from May 27, 1785 to April 17, 1786, Journal No. A, Steele Papers, SHC.

8. Bloomfield, 141; Account Book, folder 17, Macay-McNeely Papers, SHC; Weeks, 214 note.

9. Spruce Macay memorandum book, 1786–1794, NCSA; Miscellaneous Legal Papers, 1780–1790, Jasper Yeates Collection, HSP.

10. On the challenge of reading Coke, see Adams, 2: 331, 372–373. The source of the story about Leonard Henderson is Judge W. H. Battle; see the loose notes on Henderson in the Henderson Family Papers, SHC. "Enlist into the drudgery": Charles W. Harris to Dr. Charles Harris, May 8, 1797, Charles Wilson Harris Papers, SHC.

11. Dalton, 4–5; "A short . . . sketch of the Henderson family," 6–8; Henderson, "Samuel Henderson," 31, 36, all in Henderson Papers, SHC; Charles D. Rodebaugh, "Thomas Henderson," North Carolina, 3:107; Faragher, 73–76, 106ff., 132–139.

12. "Guilford's First Real Estate Boom Launched Back in 1781," clipping from *Greensboro Daily News*, July 5, 1928; Dalton, 5; "A short . . . sketch of the Henderson family," 4, all

in Henderson Papers, SHC; Hughes, Guilford County, 5–7, 14, 68. Hughes, 6, errs in saying that Thomas Searcy left the county and went west in 1788 with AJ; Searcy was still clerk of court in 1790 and appears in Guilford County records as late as 1796 (Guilford County Marriage Bonds, NCSA, record of Hugh Braly and Ruth Dreskell, July 26, 1796).

13. Hughes, *Guilford County*, 7, 84, 120–121; Hoskins, 116–118. Hoskins lived on the farm that had belonged to Bruce (Henderson, "Andrew Jackson," 7 November 1926).

14. Harrison, 1748–1768, 137–140; Wheeler, *Sketches*, 1:181; B. P. Robinson, *Sketches*, 35. For a hostile view of Martin, see Hughes, *Guilford County*, 5–7, 107–108. AJ evidently had confidence in Martin's probity; ten years later it was to Martin that he revealed the evidence that led to the exposure of the Glasgow land frauds in North Carolina (Bassett, *Correspondence*, 1:39n). Pleasant Henderson's life is sketched in Charles D. Rodenbough, "Pleasant Henderson," DNCB 3:104–105, and in the folder bearing his name in Henderson Papers, SHC.

15. Benton, 736; Chambers, 6–9.

16. Of the people not related to AJ who became his friends in North Carolina, John McNairy, David Allison, Spruce Macay, Hugh Montgomery, George Dunn, and Daniel Clary were of Irish Presbyterian descent. John Stokes, Montfort Stokes, Will Cupples, Thomas Henderson, Thomas Searcy, Bennett Searcy, Jesse Benton, and Henry Giles were Virginia Anglicans. Alexander Martin, although of Ulster stock, was Anglican (Rumple, 303).

17. On men's fashionable dress in this era, see Warwick et al., 213–218; for the backcountry, Arnow, *Seedtime*, 350–359; and for Salisbury, Rumple, 173–174. The wardrobe belonged to Jesse Steed and is from the Minutes of the Guilford County CPQS, December 12, 1787. A few purchases of cloth by AJ are mentioned in Vol. S-1, Steele Papers, SHC. Will Cupples to AJ, August 19, 1795, AJ Papers, 1:67–68, seems to refer to a transaction paid for partly by credit and partly by gambling winnings.

In the eighteenth century, males began shaving at a later age than is typical today. For example, Lieutenant Francis Brooke of Virginia, not yet nineteen, was unable to grow the whiskers and mustache officers were asked to wear for a Native American treaty signing in the 1780s (Brooke, 52). For the frequency, once a week, compare Samuel Henderson's practice, mentioned in Faragher, 132.

On powdered hair in the 1790s as a mark of status, see Bailey, 56.

18. Unfortunately, the most vivid description of AJ in Salisbury is fiction—"Nancy Jarret"'s account in Buell, 1:67–69. It has found its way into standard biographies such as M. James, 38, 40. See Appendix I. My description in the text is based on the recollections of "Aunt Judy" and the granddaughters of Eleanor Dunn Faust in Parton Notebooks, 1:116, 119, 133.

The most prominent distortion of AJ's appearance is the statement in Buell that he was red-haired, a description that has been taken up by many later writers. Buell was probably elaborating on Parton's description of his hair as "reddish-sandy" (1:111); but Parton's own notebooks fail to support this assertion. "Aunt Judy" described him as "a tall, slight young man with sandy hair," the Misses Beard as "slight, bony, freckled, [and] sandy-

266

Young Hickory

haired." The earliest portraits of AJ as an adult show his hair as dark brown. "Aunt Judy" also told Parton that she did not remember AJ's wearing his hair long or loose.

19. Parton 1:107; Parton Notebooks 1:39, 82, 106, 115–116; on AJ's lapses in grammar, see also Benton, 736.

20. Goff, 304. On the use of tobacco in the backcountry, see Woodmason, 88, and Allaire, 28; compare Karpeles, 152, on the use of tobacco among children in twentieth-century Appalachian culture, in many ways a lineal descendant of the earlier backcountry culture.

21. Allison, 14; Parton, 1:106; on "energy, courage," see Ardrey, 93. On AJ's feigned rage, see Remini, 1:32–33; on his need to dominate, Ibid., 3:402.

22. Parton Notebooks, 1:85–88. On the prohibition against fistfights, see Rule V of the Code Duello, in Truman, 50.

CHAPTER FOURTEEN

1. Castiglioni, 174; Brawley, "Courthouse"; Brawley, "Footnotes," 7 March 1965; Minutes, Rowan County CPQS, 7 February 1785.

2. The stocks are mentioned in the minutes of the Court of Pleas and Quarter Sessions for February 4, 1784. John Steele did the woodwork and iron work for a pillory in May 1787 (entry of May 12, Vol. S-1, Steele Papers), but it is unclear whether this was repair work or new construction. On Dunn's Mountain, see Smyth, 1:175–176; Chamberlain, 3. On the countryside, see Reeves, 468; Coke, 108; Feltman diary, entries of December 13–15, 1781. On German buildings, see Castiglioni, 173; Hood, 46–47. On the Germans and Irish, see Chamberlain, 4. On German speech, see Gehrke, 1–3.

3. Entries for December 14, 1781 in Tilden diary, Feltman diary, and "Anonymous itinerary"; Newsome, "John Brown's Journal," 291; Watson, 294. The crude drawing in the Virginia–North Carolina map suggests the heterogeneity of the buildings in Salisbury in 1779, as does the more precise Sauthier map of 1770. Both show one cross street, and by 1780 clearly there were more (Rumple, 155, 157).

4. Carole Watterson Troxler, "John Ross Dunn," DNCB 2:120–122; Linn, "Hugh Montgomery," 1592–1593; Rumple, 158. I deduce the existence of fences around Salisbury dwellings from the fact that AJ and his "rowdies" were accused of carrying off gates (Parton 1:106).

5. Parton, 109; Caldwell, 79; Rumple, 180; Newsome, "John Brown's Journal," 294; E. T. Clark, 1:481–482.

6. Court week is described generally in Ashe, "Social Conditions," 205, Mecklenburg court specifically in Clitherall diary, April 17, 1776. Ownby, 43–45, has a good description of court week in the late nineteenth-century South. The quotation is from William Blount to John Steele, July 10, 1790, Wagstaff, 1:68.

7. Lewis, 232–233, provides an impressive list of artisans in Rowan County during the late colonial and Revolutionary eras (not all of them, of course, in Salisbury). Her discussion on 214–215 and 220–222 stresses the relatively diversified character of the region.

. . . .

Notes

8. Entries of 27–28 April 1786, Vol. S-1, John Steele Papers.

9. For Macay's wealth, see Linn, *Tax Lists*, 312–313, and the 1791 inventory of Macay's possessions in the Macay-McNeely Papers (account book, folder 17). The 1790 census credited him with nineteen slaves (SRNC, 26:1040); the account book lists twenty. Guy, who is listed among them, is described in Morgan District, North Carolina Superior Court of Law and Equity, Slave Records, 3:30. He appears in Ledger A, Steele Papers, under date on November 16, 1785, doing an errand for Macay.

10. Harrison, 1769–1775, 506–507, mentions the pianoforte, which is not, however, in the account book referred to in the previous note, from which the other items are drawn. On Fanny Macay and her family, see "A Short . . . Sketch of the Henderson Family," 8; Battle, "Leonard Henderson," 195; "Archibald Henderson," 12; and Dalton, 2, all in the Henderson Papers. Archibald is undoubtedly the moody young Henderson referred to in Caldwell, 78–81; the citation from Dalton also refers to his suicide attempt.

11. Parton, 1:104 105.

12. William Crawford's exact age is hard to determine. The date and place of his death are unknown, so no tombstone exists; he did not marry, so nothing can be inferred from marriage records. It seems clear that he was a little older than AJ, he fought in the battles of 1780 and AJ did not, and he lost a wagon at Buford's Defeat (William Crawford file, SC-AA). These data would seem to make him at least eighteen in 1780. A conjectural birthdate would be 1762. His admission to the bar in 1784 is consistent with these other facts; he would have been twenty-two then, probably about the average age for beginning lawyers.

13. Lawrence, 3–5. McNairy's six appearances in the list of witnesses to Rowan County marriage bonds in 1783 and 1784 strongly suggest that he studied with Macay in those years, for the same reasons given in Chapter 10, note 24—that witnesses to these bonds in the 1780s were typically people connected with Macay's law practice (Rowan County Marriage Bonds, RPL). Moreover, when Macay bought the house where he was going to live and practice from Adlai Osborne in 1783, McNairy witnessed the deed (Minutes of Rowan County CPQS, February 4, 1783).

For almost every case in the Rowan County Court of Pleas and Quarter Sessions's trial docket for 1786–1787, the name of the attorney or attorneys for both litigants are given, designated by abbreviations. A tabulation of the appearance of each attorney's name reveals the following caseload for the five busiest attorneys during the two-year period: Spruce Macay (Mc), 565 cases; Crawford (C), 361; William Sharpe (Sh), 208; John Stokes (St), 206; McNairy (McN), 192.

Waightstill Avery, as a beginning lawyer in 1769, rented lodgings in both Charlotte and Salisbury, with a deduction for periods when he was absent (Avery, 253).

14. On Hughes and the Rowan House, see three writings by the Salisbury historian James S. Brawley: *Views*, 23; *Brief History*, 120; and "History's Footnotes," *Salisbury Post*, May 10, 1959; also Rumple, 165. Hughes's ordinary (i.e., tavern) license for 1785 is noted in Linn, *Tax Lists*, 62. He owned fourteen slaves in 1792 (Ibid., 313), and twenty in 1790 (SRNC, 26:1039). John Steele described him as an "Innkeeper" in his entry of March 31, 1785, Vol. S-1, Steele Papers; the same account book contains many purchases connected

with tavern management—two tea trays, a pair of plated buckets, six tumblers, three bowls, and a hundred pounds of sugar. Thorp, "Taverns and Tavern Culture," 682–684, has an excellent discussion of tavern furnishings in the late colonial period; in "Taverns and Communities," 81–82, he discusses what drinks were consumed. On the tavern as a breeding ground for pranks in early America, see Wright, 66–69. "With which this country": Reeves, 469. "Girls" was the term used in Tilden, 231; they were presumably not from the highest social set, since Tilden and his friends had just danced with some genteel young women at a dancing school and had escorted them home. "The glass circulates" is in Ibid.

15. Parton, 1:106; Henderson, " Andrew Jackson," October 17, 1926. "litter of guns": Austen, 250.

16. Parton, 1:108.

17. AJ to Robert Hays, November 2, 1797 (AJ Papers, 1:151, mentions that Crawford had "entirely left of[f] Drink and I am in hopes will profit by his imprudence."

18. According to Parton, 1:106, George Dunn, a member of AJ's "roystering set," was an uncle of his informants, the Misses Beard. According to Salisbury genealogists, he was connected with the Beard family in two ways: his sister Susan was married to John Lewis Beard, and his niece Mary Faust was married to John Beard (communication from M. J. Fowler, January 2, 1997). The Misses Beard with whom Parton spoke were daughters of Mary Faust Beard. Years later when George Dunn was aged and poor, "with no family or profession," it was Susan Dunn Beard's son-in-law Charles Fisher who was responsible for securing the old man a pension (Minutes, Rowan County CPQS, August 20, 1818, August 25, 1820). The pension application (National Archives, S41515) gives Dunn's birth year as about 1752 and relates his Revolutionary service. None of the Dunn heirs seem to have been wealthy. John Dunn Jr., who described himself in 1786 as "Eldest Son & Heir at law" of John Dunn (Deed Book 10:430), in the same document called himself a "labourer." Yet the Dunn estate, handled by AJ's mentor Spruce Macay, brought in over 1300 pounds (Minutes, Rowan County CPQS, May 9, 1789)—all of which perhaps went to satisfy creditors. George may have been the most penurious of the heirs; in September 1787, for instance, his brother-in-law Henry Giles bought him a blanket (entry of September 1, 1787, Vol. S-1, Steele Papers).

Hugh Montgomery Jr. was wealthy. His father left him all his land on the New River in Virginia (Linn, "Hugh Montgomery," 1594). In 1787 he sold a slave to the lawyer William Tatham (Minutes, Rowan County CPQS, August 11, 1787). He was sued eleven times in the years 1786 and 1787, and at least two of the suits, documented in the Civil Action Papers, Rowan County, NCSA, address him as "Hugh Montgomery, Gentleman" (writs of Henry Giles and William Tatham, May 1787, Civil Action Papers; Trial Docket, Rowan County CPQS, 1786–1787). He is described in Parton, 1:107. The inventory of Hugh Montgomery Sr., including a harp, two writing desks, various silver items, and 98 deer skins, with a total value just over 27,000 pounds, is bound into the back pages of Minutes, Rowan County CPQS, 1800–1807.

19. Parton, 1:107. A very similar race among young Charleston blades is described in Grayson, 60.

20. Friedman, 278; Arnow, *Flowering*, 313–314; M. James, 38.

21. Parton, 1:109, mentions the ledger, but he did not actually see it; it was said to be in the possession of a man in Lincolnton, North Carolina (Parton Notebooks, 1:126–127) and to contain accounts of AJ's winnings at cards and horse races. Brawley, "History's Footnotes," May 10, 1959, adds that AJ rolled dice with Hughes, but this seems to be a local historian's elaboration of a good story; AJ rarely gambled with dice after his experience in Charleston with rattle and snap. On all fours, see Brawley, *Rowan County*, 30; Parlett, 259; and note the entry in Newsome, "John Brown's Journal," 294. Bailey mentions loo frequently (56, 166, 168), but all fours is the game from which almost all his examples of cheating (167–169) are drawn. On whist, see Parlett, 219–221; Spruill, *Life*, 108; and note.

22. R. F. Foster, 286–291; Parlett, 185–187, 257–259.

23. Some cheating techniques specific to all fours are described in R. F. Foster, 291–292; general late eighteenth-century techniques in Bailey, 67, 167–169. The Mark Twain story is "Science vs. Luck"; see Twain, 64–66. Bailey, 66–67, explained the distinction between a sportsman and a gambler, a distinction which was of importance in his own life, roughly contemporary with AJ's. Bailey's experience while in his twenties was not unlike AJ's in Salisbury; cf. Ibid., 64: "Although my reputation has suffered much from being reputed a libertine and not a fit associate for the virtuous and genteel part of society, yet at this place [Sweet Springs, Virginia] I have been honored with the management of their balls, an evidence that I was at all times competent to be a gentleman."

24. Cupples to Jackson, August 19, 1795, in AJ Papers, 1:67; Henderson, "Andrew Jackson," October 17, 1926.

25. Lee, 24; Remini, *AJ1*, 134; Cox, 120, 122.

26. Examples of making money from the possession of a fast horse are in Bailey, 61 and 186ff. On AJ's continuing involvement with horse breeding and horse racing, see e.g., M. James, 112–114; Benton, 736; Parton, 1:110–111; and Peyton, December 5, 1872, January 9, May 8, 1873. Conceivably AJ and Cupples owned a horse together; in his letter of August 19, 1795 (AJ Papers, 1:67) Cupples reminded AJ that in 1786 or 1787 they had jointly won eight pounds from a man named Bittles in Anson County. Moreover, they were joint defendants in the 1787 suit, which may have involved a horse. Judy of the Rowan House told Parton that AJ "had fine horses." (Parton Notebooks, 1:116) This evidence suggests locating AJ among what Struna, 171, calls "entrepreneurs on the sporting scene" who emerged in the late eighteenth century—people who devoted their time and talent to making money from the upper-class fondness for horse racing as a leisure pursuit. Eleanor Faust's comment is in Parton, 1:109.

27. Tucker, 2:73; Abernethy, 123.

28. Recognizance Bond, October 28, 1787, in AJ Papers, 1:11; Warrant, "Wm. [sic] Ludlow & Andw Beard vs. Hugh Montgomery and others," August 1787, Rowan Museum, Salisbury, North Carolina. A bill of sale dated August 22, 1787 for a ten-year-old stud horse named Young Whirligig, sold by Baird and Ludlow, is in the Lenoir Family Papers. This document gives the residences of both men. The full-blooded stud horse Whirligig, pre-

sumably the sire of this horse, was imported from England in 1773 and stood at stud in both New Jersey and North Carolina (F. Harrison, 2:203).

29. The 1790 census return in SRNC, 26:1039, lists Clary's children and slaves. His tavernkeeper's license is referred to in Minutes, Rowan County CPQS, November 8, 1783 and February 9, 1788. A deed to William Nisbet, November 3, 1787 (Deed Book 11:505) refers to Giles as a "gentleman." His marriage to Elizabeth Dunn was on June 19, 1786 (Rowan County Marriage Bonds). John Steele, on November 3, 1787, paid him one-fourth "of the purse Race by agr[eem]ent"; three days later Giles purchased, through Steele, a bay horse for forty pounds (Vol. S-1, Steele Papers). In 1792 he owned six slaves (Linn, *Tax Lists*, 313).

30. Struna, 173; Parton, 1:107–109. W. O. Foster, 270n, mentions a ball held at the courthouse in the 1790s.

John Steele's account book has an entry February 12, 1787, the only one of its kind in the three-year period of AJ's sojourn in North Carolina, for an eighteen-shilling subscription "to part of a ball." The date suggests a Washington's Birthday ball; the general's birthday was already an established holiday for social events. The entry sounds a cautionary note about the "Christmas ball" in the text. Only the Misses Beard's memory vouches for the date of Christmas, and of all features the date of a ball is perhaps the most easily forgotten. A Washington's Birthday ball in 1787 would fit in very well with the other elements of this story.

A search of the few surviving records about Salisbury in the 1780s reveals little about Molly and Rachel Wood (as Parton's informants recalled their names). A Mary Wood (Molly?) was one of several women charged with assault at the August 1786 term of County Court (Minutes of Rowan County CPQS, August 11, 1786) and tax lists show women named Mary and Rachel Wood living in the part of the county east of the Yadkin at various times during this period—1778, 1787, and 1795 (Linn, *Tax Lists*, 158, 274, 366). Whether these women would have crossed the river and come into town for a ball is questionable.

31. Aunt Judy's recollections: Parton, 1:106. Every biographer of AJ, from the very first (Reid and Eaton, 14) has recorded that he began law study with Macay and completed it with Stokes. Local historians, such as, Brawley, "Footnotes to History," *Salisbury Post*, July 22, 1962, have attributed the change to the scandal at the ball. Ely and Brown, 320, date the beginning of AJ's study with Stokes in March 1787; that date would fit nicely with the Washington's Birthday ball conjectured in note 12, but there is no direct evidence.

32. Lee, 7; Ledger A, 43, Steele Papers.

33. The bogus account is from *Salisbury Post*, September 19, 1971, based on a purported eighteenth-century diary which I have not seen but which, from internal evidence, must be fictitious. The duel is AJ's challenge to Waightstill Avery, narrated in M. James, 47–49. It is worth noting that Bailey, whose status often fell a little short of gentility, had many fistfights in his career but only one duel (Bailey, 70–75).

34. Parton, 1:108.

Notes

CHAPTER FIFTEEN

1. The best sketch of Macay's life and background is Harrison, *Princetonians, 1769–1775*, 505–509; see also DCNB, 4:119. His portrait is owned by Mrs. Stehle Linn, Salisbury. Letters that illuminate his personality are in SRNC, 17:181, and Southern Historical Association, Publications, 3 1899:133–134. His lands in 1791 are listed in his Account Book, Folder 17, Macay-McNeely Papers, SHC. On his practice, see Chapter 14, Note 4. He had 565 cases in 1786–1787; his nearest competitor had 361. The distribution of cases among attorneys in Rowan County is similar to Waldrup's findings for Chowan County in eastern North Carolina (148–152). The comment on attorneys in politics is from Daniel Anderson to Duncan Cameron, February 9, 1798, Cameron Family Papers, SHC.

2. Cupples's personality is apparent from his letter to AJ, August 19, 1795, in studying with Macay, from 1785 to 1787. He appears as a witness of Rowan County marriage bonds five times between October 1785 and February 1787, and purchases by him are recorded in John Steele's papers, Vol. S-1, six times from May 27, 1785 to April 17, 1786. Additionally, he and AJ witnessed a deed for the sale of a slave December 1, 1786. Cupples's close relation with John Stokes is shown by the fact that he mentioned their joint affairs in his will (Linn, *Wills*, 62). The Reverend Charles Cupples, who was probably Will's uncle, officiated at the baptism in 1781 of two nephews of John Stokes, for whom Stokes stood godparent (McRee, 1:467–468). Cupples's will, dated March 2, 1800, mentioned land he owned in Montgomery County (Linn, *Wills*, 82).

3. Parton, 103; Raynor, "Is This Andy Jackson's Desk?" *Salisbury Post*, October 7, 1984; Raynor, Piedmont Passages, 17–22.

4. Adams, 2:300, 328; Boorstin, 3–4; Blackstone, 1:120.

5. Ely, 434 note. The full title of the book AJ bought was *An Interesting Appendix to Sir William Blackstone's Commentaries on the Laws of England*. The book reproduced a correspondence between Blackstone and Joseph Priestley discussing religious liberty for dissenters in England.

6. Chroust, 2:63; Bacon, 1:44–53. Some lawyers, like John Quincy Adams's mentor Theophilus Parsons, criticized Bacon's work for its lack of intellectual content (Adams, *Diary*, 2:384). The tradition that AJ relied heavily on Bacon's authority is the starting point for an anecdote about his first recorded duel, in the summer of 1788, which is told in Henderson, "Andrew Jackson," November 7, 1926, and M. James, 47–49. The anecdote, passed down in the family of AJ's opponent Waightstill Avery, hangs on a pun on the word "bacon." It seems almost too pat to be believable, but as Henderson pointed out, a cryptic reference in Parton, based on AJ's own words, (1:162–163n) supports it.

7. Corbitt, 50–51.

8. Waldrup, 147–148. Waldrup also found (154–155) that about one-third of all civil actions involved a prosperous plaintiff suing a less prosperous defendant for money due; poor individuals sued rich ones much less often. Most of the time, both parties to a suit were about equal in wealth. The most common suit in the lower courts was an action for trespass on the case, in other words a suit to recover money due for damages or by contract (Ibid., 178).

Joseph Davie appears in John Steele's Journal No. A on September 23, 1786 and March 16, 1787, both dates during the session of Superior Court (Steele Papers, SHC).

9. The top twelve litigants in the Rowan County Court of Pleas and Quarter Sessions in 1786–1787, whether as plaintiff or defendant, were as follows: Hugh Montgomery's executor, 58 cases; John Brevard, 24; Rowan County commissioners, 21; William Wray, 15; William Brandon, John Dunn's administrator, and John Oliphant's executor, 14 each; Maxwell Chambers, 13; Andrew Boston's administrator, Peter Faust, Daniel Clary, and Anthony Newman, 12 each (Trial Docket).

Clary: Minutes, Rowan County CPQS, February 9, 1788. Brandon: Rumple, 181. Newman: Rumple, 180; Linn, "Hugh Montgomery," 1594, 1604–1605. William Sharpe: North Carolina, 5:321–322.

10. The roster of lawyers in Salisbury is compiled from the Trial Docket, Rowan County CPQS, 1786–1787, where each is denoted by an abbreviation. A few others turned up very occasionally—Reuben Wood of Randolph County, and "A," probably Waightstill Avery of Morganton. For more on Sharpe, see Rumple, 111–112; DNCB, 5:321–322; and Minutes, Rowan County CPQS, August 8, 1786. On Tatham, whose brief stay in Salisbury happened to coincide with AJ's, see Williams, "Tatham," and Davie to Macay, July 13, 1785, in the Davie Papers, SHC, which contains an engaging reference. On Davie's performance in court, see B. P. Robinson, *Davie*, 156–158, 173–175. Waldrup, 350, describes the licensing of lawyers. Cupples received his county court license in 1787. On December 28, 1790, he returned to court and received his Superior Court license ("Return of Monies Received for Attornies Licenses . . . by the Hon.ble Samuel Spencer, Deceased, 1788–1792," Miscellaneous Records, Superior Court, Morgan District, NCSA).

11. Continuances: Waldrup, 224. The trial docket for 1786–1787 shows that at most terms of Rowan County Court about ninety percent of cases were continued; only May 1786 and May 1787 had a lower rate. The John Steele Papers contain a note from Macay, September 28, 1786, summarizing an interview with a witness in a suit for debt. Macay's caveat in the case of Thompson v. Patterson, November term, 1785, is in the Rowan County Civil Action Papers, NCSA.

12. Dunn: Minutes, Rowan County CPQS, May 9, 1782, November 8, 1783; Case #55, Trial Docket, February 1785; entry of September 1, 1787, Journal No. A, Steele Papers. The warrants for Montgomery are in Rowan County Civil Action Papers, NCSA; those of Tatham and Giles are for the May term of 1787, that of Hughey for the November term of 1787.

13. A Robert Ellison lived in Fairfield County, South Carolina, and was a man of some prominence (McMaster, 57). He appears often in the Fairfield County Court minutes from 1786 on, suing for the value of property or horses he sold (e.g., Holcomb, *Fairfield*, 12, 13, 22, 24, 45, 55, 64). After Ellison's victory, Crawford contended with more suits. At the November 1787 term, John Morrison filed suit for forty-five pounds against him, with Montgomery and John Brevard as codefendants, and won his case in 1790. Another suit, by the administrators of John Nesbit, cost Crawford and others fifty-five pounds (entry of No-

vember 3, 1790, Minutes, Rowan County CPQS). This spate of suits may indicate that Crawford was a more vulnerable target than previously; it coincides with a sharp drop in the number of cases he handled in Rowan County. From May 1786 through May 1787, Crawford averaged about fifteen new cases at each term of court. After that time, the number of new cases he handled dropped abruptly into single digits per term. (Trial Docket, Rowan County CPQS, 1786–1787 and 1788–1790). Together, the data suggest a personal or professional crisis of some sort, but direct evidence is lacking. See Chapter 17, note 5.

14. In *Jackson* v. *Montgomery*, Stokes represented Montgomery, and McNairy put up bail for him. That these men continued to be friendly with AJ increases the likelihood that the suit did not reflect a serious breach between the two parties. The case continued over several terms and was dismissed in February 1789 (Trial Docket, Rowan County CPQS).

15. Parramore, 88, 92; Haywood, 24; Shute, "Old Cone," 10; Speidel, 55, 66, 72; Hughes, 84; Denslow, 80; Nocalore, 1:44, 49.

16. Bullock, 56–57, 98–99, 105 106; Huss, 84–85.

17. P. Robinson, 5–6, 9, 11; Bullock, 87–89. For the autonomy of local lodges in Ulster, see Leighton, 27, 133, 143; for the corresponding phenomenon in America, Allen E. Roberts, 47. A good example of Masonry's spread into the interior is the lodge at Carlisle, Pennsylvania cited by Huss, 293: it was warranted in 1792, but at that time eleven Masons were already living in this small backcountry town.

18. Pettus, 97–98.

19. Haywood, 12, 21; Shute, "Old Cone Lodge," 9–12. Parramore, 85, points out that Masonry's hierarchical structure was apt to appeal more to Anglicans than to Presbyterians or Baptists; and in fact, almost all of AJ's Virginia Anglican acquaintances in note 9 were certainly or probably Masons (seven out of nine), but none of the Presbyterians were. Huss's study of the Carlisle lodge (249) points up a similar conclusion; in the heavily Ulster Irish area around Carlisle, only 16 percent of the Masons whose religion could be identified were Presbyterian. In Pennsylvania as in North Carolina, the Masonic order was supported mainly by Anglicans (Ibid., 59).

20. Rules of conduct for a contemporaneous North Carolina lodge are in Shute, "Washington Lodge," 56–60. Shute, "McCauley Apron," gives a reading of the symbols on a ceremonial apron worn by a North Carolina Mason in this period. Compare the symbols and decorations from an Ulster lodge as given in Simpson, 28, 57–60, and cf. Bullock, 129: "Lodges offered moral instruction without sectarian divisions, a symbolic language of social distinction that did not depend upon local associations, and (not least of all) a means of creating and justifying a space for the relaxed sociability of eating, drinking, and singing."

21. Bryson, 33–34; Denslow, 76, 77, 79, 87. A. B. Andrews Jr., a Mason who did a careful study in 1921 of AJ's Masonic affiliation, pronounced himself "not able to conclude that Jackson joined the order before he left North Carolina." (Bassett, *Correspondence*, 1:59) That statement still holds; AJ joined the order before 1800, but whether in North Carolina or Tennessee is speculative. For what it is worth, Henderson, "Andrew

Jackson," October 31, 1926, cites a tradition that Robert Searcy, younger brother of AJ's traveling companion Bennett Searcy, who arrived in Nashville after AJ, was the first Mason in Nashville.

22. Parramore, 41, alludes to the muted competition for the allegiance of prominent men between the churches and the Masonic order: "Many Masons felt strongly that the codes of conduct encouraged by their order were the most demanding of any system devised by the mind of man. Herein lay the source of the difficulties between Masonry and the organized church of that era."

23. Bullock, 16–17, cites this oath from a 1730 expose of Masonic rituals in England. The ritual in Old Cone Lodge may have varied from this model in detail, but the essential content was the same.

CHAPTER SIXTEEN

1. The description of Stokes in M. James, 39, incorporates family tradition James heard from a descendant and thus qualifies as a semiprimary source; see also Brawley, "Old Judge John Stokes' Home," *Salisbury Sunday Post*, June 20, 1971, Brawley files, RPL; Samuel E. McCorkle Sermons, No. 7. Stokes to James Iredell, March 26, 1784, Charles E. Johnson Collection, NCSA, mentions his decision to reside in Salisbury. For Roger Stapleton, see Minutes of Rowan County CPQS, November 6, 1789. For Stokes's Revolutionary experience, see W. D. James, Appendix, 5–6.

2. Stokes was a relative newcomer to Salisbury, having been admitted to practice in 1784 along with Crawford and McNairy (Minutes, Rowan County CPQS, May 4, 1784). He was immediately appointed county attorney to fill in for Macay, but not until 1786 did he wind up his affairs in Halifax, where he had served in the same position (Minutes, Halifax County CPQS, February 1786). For the family's lands in Montgomery County, see Lassiter, 406. In 1786–1787 he represented Montgomery in the state legislature (Ashe, *Biographical History*, 7:447). On the roughness of the area, see Robert Bailey's account (56–60) from the 1790s, of being intimidated and nearly robbed by "five large vulgar looking men" at an inn on the road from Charleston to Salisbury in what must have been either Anson or Montgomery County.

In some accounts of AJ's life, Stokes is credited with a large, elegant plantation in Rowan County. He did indeed have one, but only at a slightly later period of his life, after his marriage in 1788 to Betsey Pearson, the daughter of the wealthy Richmond Pearson.

Stokes's personality is difficult to assess. Marquis James's account (39), based partly on the statements of a descendant, stresses Stokes's conviviality, but other contemporary sources like S. E. McCorkle's sermon (No. 7, McCorkle Sermons) and Charles Caldwell's elegy, quoted in Henderson, "Andrew Jackson," October 17, 1926, dwell on his Revolutionary heroism and civic virtue. A letter, March 27, 1787, in the James Iredell papers suggests a generous, warm-hearted man with a penchant for extravagant language. Another (Stokes to Iredell, March 26, 1784, Charles E. Johnson Collection, NCSA) mentions his fondness for buying books. In 1787 Stokes bought a brown horse from John Steele and sold

Steele a bay mare (Ledger A, 5, Steele Papers); given Steele's serious interest in horse breeding, these transactions suggest a similar interest on Stokes's part. Montfort Stokes's personality and his relationship with AJ are described in W. O. Foster, 239, 259, 270–271.

3. James S. Brawley, "John Stokes," DNCB, 5:241; Parramore, 92; Lassiter, 406; Ely and Brown, 388; W. O. Foster, 239–240; Rumple, 244; "Old Judge John Stokes' Home," clipping from *Salisbury Sunday Post,* June 20, 1971, in Brawley files, RCL.

4. Henderson, *Washington's Southern Tour,* 326.

5. Iredell, 299, 310. Superior Court: McRee, 2:158–159. No records of the Salisbury District Superior Court for this period survive, but the flavor of the sessions can be appreciated in the minutes of the Hillsborough District Superior Court, transcribed and published by Haun.

6. In other states, the circuit court—judges, clerks, and other officials—moved from county to county with the lawyers (L. Friedman, 270–271; Calhoun, 62–63); in the North Carolina system, however, only the lawyers moved. The eight counties of Salisbury District at the end of 1787, in the order in which their courts met, were Montgomery, Richmond, Anson, Mecklenburg, Rowan, Surry, Guilford, and Rockingham (Corbitt, 50–51). Each county in the sequence was adjacent to the one next after it. This arrangement took shape only in 1786, with the rescheduling of Mecklenburg's court date (Iredell, 600); dates of sessions in the other counties are from the Act of 1785 (Ibid., 548).

7. The exact riding distance on the circuit, by my calculations, beginning and ending at Salisbury and going from courthouse to courthouse in the order given above, is 377 miles. AJ and Cupples's admissions to the bar appear in the minutes of Rowan County CPQS, November 6, 1787; Surry County CPQS, November 13, 1787; Guilford County CPQS, November 20, 1787; and Rockingham County CPQS, November 27, 1787. Tompkins, 1:68, gives the record of AJ's admission in October 1787, with Cupples and Alexander McGinty, at Mecklenburg County Court. That Anson County's was the first court AJ visited after obtaining his law license is clear from the endorsement on the license, dated "October Session" 1787 (AJ Papers, 1:10).

The transfer of Richmond County into the new Fayetteville District was enacted by the Assembly in late 1787 (Iredell, 626–627) but it had been in the works for some time, prompted by complaints from Richmond County residents about the long journey to Salisbury.

Crawford, Stokes, and McNairy are listed in the CPQS trial dockets for Surry and Rockingham, the only counties outside Rowan in which the dockets have survived. Crawford is mentioned in the minutes of Mecklenburg County CPQS, January 30, 1788. McNairy practiced in Guilford (CPQS minutes, May 1786) and Anson ("List of Suits, Deeds, Ordinary License, Marriage License, etc., 1787," Anson County miscellaneous papers). Stokes, likewise, practiced in Guilford (Stockard, 36) and Anson, to judge from the wills given in McBee, 118, 122. Stokes, Tatham, and Brown were admitted to practice in Mecklenburg April 16, 1784 (minutes, Mecklenburg CPQS). Macay is in the minutes of Guilford CPQS for May 1786, and in the docket of Surry County CPQS for the Febuary 1787 term. All the foregoing legal documents are in NCSA.

8. Cupples to AJ, August 19, 1795, AJ Papers, 1:67–68. Bassett (AJ, 1:12) takes "Richmond" in Cupples's letter to refer to the seat of justice in Surry County, at the other end of the district; but the mention of "Anson court" almost in the same breath makes it far more likely that he was referring to Richmond County, adjacent to Anson. If so, then Cupples was most likely recounting events prior to 1788, for Richmond County was tranferred into the new Fayetteville District by act of the Assembly in late 1787 (Iredell, 626–627). "Mr. Allen" may well have been William Allen, who was one of Cupples's executors in 1800 (*North Carolina Mercury*, September 23, 1800).

9. Calhoun, 60–61; Bloomfield, 171. Cf. Meehan, 26–28. "chunk of a horse": Maurice Moore to Lyman C. Draper, October 7, 1870, DM 14VV157. The term "buggery," used here and in Chapter 18, embraced both male-male sex and sex with animals; prosecutions for the latter were far more frequent, but in conversation the verb "bugger" could refer to either activity. For examples from a Pennsylvania county culturally similar to central North Carolina, see notes on *State v. McSherry* 1782 and *State v. Connor* 1786 in Miscellaneous Papers, Jasper Yeates Papers, HSP; for an example from North Carolina, see affidavit of Jacob Lineberger, February 26, 1789, Randolph County CPQS, Criminal Action Papers.

On North Carolina legal humor, a stray document produced two generations later by a group of circuit-riding lawyers in western North Carolina, in a much more proper and straitlaced era (Tweed, 10–25), is suggestive. The balky old horse ridden by one of the group had just died, and they memorialized the deceased with a mock address that alluded (24) to some of his behavioral and physical (including genital) peculiarities, and a verse (21) part of which ran:

> *Sometimes upon his onward course,*
> *He'd make a sudden pause,*
> *And strain and strain, as if he had*
> *Some mighty pregnant cause.*
> *Go on! old Ball, the Judge would say;*
> *Stop! says Ball, a bit;*
> *I'm full of corn and fodder too, and*
> *I must have a s—.*
> *The master's wrath rose further yet;*
> *He threatened castigation.*
> *But Ball stood firmly on his rights*
> *Until a pissication.*

If this is a fair sample of Victorian legal humor, then one can imagine that the humor of the early national period was even more pungent.

10. Wright, 52; Entry of January 5, 1802, Osborne Diary; Lassiter, 5–13.

11. Huneycutt and Huneycutt, 1–2, 14–15, 35, 42, 157, 159, 203.

12. Medley, 64, 66, 205; Cupples to AJ, August 19, 1795, AJ Papers, 1:67. Lanier and Bittle families: McBee, 118 and passim; Bentley, 20; Ingersoll, 114.

13. Frank Nash, "John Williams," Ashe, *Biographical History*, 3:433; Robinson, *Davie*, 175–176; McRee, 2:141, 154. On the postwar increase in litigation, see Waldrup, 110.

14. Lefler and Newsome, 243; Robinson, *Davie*, 166–169.

15. Lefler and Newsome, 244; Ashe, "Social Conditions," 213.

16. Charlotte after the war: Blythe and Brockmann, 98; Tompkins, 1:68; W. L. Smith, 74. On William and Charles Polk, see J. Johnson, 84–85, and Thomas Taylor interview, DM 16VV27.

17. Lefler and Newsome, 262–265.

18. Ibid., 254; Attmore, 38–39. On the general expectation of an eventual slave uprising, see Jordan, 388–393, and cf. Frey, 225–228. Jordan stresses the period after 1791, when the Saint-Domingue revolt gave new point to Southern whites' fears, but the apprehension existed for years; Charles Woodmason in 1768 (94) described the Africans as an "Internal Enemy . . . [who may] surprize us in an Hour when We are not aware," and Jefferson's forebodings in Notes on Virginia (163), written in the 1780s, are the classic statement on the subject.

19. AJ Papers, 1:15. The slave was a teenager named Nancy; her purchase was witnessed by David Allison, who is discussed in Chapter 18. There is no evidence that AJ owned a slave while in North Carolina, but the lack of evidence is not conclusive, county court records in Salisbury District are far from complete. Joshua is mentioned in the indictment against Jesse Stroud, September Sessions 1787 in Randolph County, Criminal Action Papers, NCSA. York: Rowan County Deed Book, 11:48, NCSA.

20. Fries, 645–649; remarks of Hon. William C. Hammer, Congressional Record, June 18, 1926, 11570; Minutes of Surry County CPQS, May 13, 1790. Bassett, *AJ*, 13, erroneously locates Lester's tavern (he spells the name Lister) in Martinville. I infer Lester's youth from the fact that he was married May 20, 1787, during court week (Holcomb, Surry County, 122).

21. M. James, 40; Surry County Criminal Action Papers, NCSA.

22. Farmer, 164; L. Butler, 21.

23. AJ Papers, 1:10. The license was issued September 26, 1787. "Lawyer Jackson": cf. the mention of "Loyer Lock," in entry of January 6, 1802, Osborne Diary.

CHAPTER SEVENTEEN

1. Minutes, Mecklenburg CPQS, October 27, 1787. William Picket, the seller of the horse, does not seem to have been a Mecklenburg man—his name does not appear in local records. AJ could have served as his agent in conveying the horse in Mecklenburg, possibly profiting from the trade. As for the buyer, there were three possible Charles Polks in Mecklenburg in 1787: William Polk's brother, "Devil Charley"; his uncle, Captain Charles Polk; and his first cousin, "Civil Charley" (Angelotti, 14–19). Given AJ's friendship with William Polk, "Devil Charley" would seem a bit more likely than the other two. The purchase, moreover, would fit with "Devil Charley's" reputation as a careless roisterer who spent inordinate amounts of time in gaming and drinking (J. Johnson, 84–85).

2. Not much is known about David Allison. He may have been from Guilford County originally—a man of that name appears in Guilford County marriage bonds in 1782, as a bondsman for the marriage of Robert Erwin and Livy McCamey (Marriage Bonds, NCSA). In the same year a David Allison witnessed a large number of transactions in Guilford County land confiscated from Tories (Guilford County Deed Book 2, NCSA). From 1782 to 1788, however, he was mainly in Charlotte, where he owned property (Minutes, Mecklenburg County CPQS, 12 July 1782) and served on grand juries (Ibid., December 31, 1785). For his connection with the Blounts, see John Nelson to John Gray Blount, August 17, 1783, in Blount Papers, 1:85, and Remini, *AJ1*, 51–52. He was evidence for Charles Polk Jr. in a 1787 lawsuit against Barbara Ayers (Mecklenburg County Civil Action Papers, NCSA). When AJ and his friends became acquainted with him is not known, but when he was admitted to practice in 1788 in Washington County, AJ stood security for him (Ely and Brown, 354; Remini, *AJ1*, 109), and William Crawford was his security in a case before Mecklenburg Court January 30, 1788 (Minutes, CPQS). I have found no evidence of his practicing in the eastern counties.

3. Haywood, 211–212, 243.

4. Marquis James adopted the idea of a Guilford County historian, Katherine Hoskins (M. James, 41, 378) that AJ's initiative was behind McNairy's decision to seek the judgeship. It has some plausibility, for McNairy was an easygoing, basically conservative young man, not likely on his own to remove to the west. But although the initiative may not have been McNairy's, it does not follow that it was AJ's. Allison is a more likely possibility; through his connection to the Blount family, he had large financial interests beyond the mountains, and he benefited directly from McNairy's position. In 1789 McNairy appointed him clerk pro tempore of the Superior Court (Fulcher, 1).

According to John Overton's narrative, reproduced in Parton, 1:149, McNairy, AJ, Searcy, and "perhaps" Allison came to Nashville together at the end of 1788. There were probably others in the party, but their names have not survived. George Dunn's participation is mentioned in Parton Notebooks, 1:135. Though unsupported by other evidence, the claim could be true. Dunn was not a conspicuous person, and his name might easily have been forgotten by people outside his family. He later returned to Salisbury and died there, impoverished, in 1824 ([Salisbury] *Western Carolinian*, February 17, 1824; Rowan County CPQS minutes, August 20, 1818; J. Watson, 173).

McNairy had no statutory power to appoint a state's attorney, but the power was customary for district judges and he doubtless assumed that he had it on that basis; see Ely, "Legal Practice," 423.

5. Crawford's name continues to appear, with decreasing frequency, in the records of the Rowan County Court at least through 1791. On the other hand, the amount of fees he collected at each session of Mecklenburg County Court went up over the same period (County accounts of executions, Mecklenburg County miscellaneous papers, NCSA). In October 1788, Hugh Montgomery filed suit against him in Mecklenburg County, which suggests that he was living there by that time (Mecklenburg County Civil Action Papers, NCSA). In 1790, however, he asked the Mecklenburg County Court for six months' notice

before a case was tried in which he represented one of the parties; the request indicates that he expected to be away from that area for some time (Minutes, Mecklenburg County CPQS, October 27, 1790). He is not identifiable anywhere in the 1790 U.S. Census of North Carolina nor in any tax list from this period. Cupples managed to stay in contact with him after AJ's departure, and a postscript to his 1795 letter to AJ (AJ Papers, 1:69) suggests that both men were concerned about him and felt that he needed help: "The last time I saw Mr. Crawford about four weeks ago he promised to call on me in one week from that time on his way to Nash Ville. I encouraged him all I could."

For the convenience of future researchers, I should add that the attorney William Crawford who appears in the Salisbury records later in the 1790s is not AJ's friend, but his first cousin, Major Robert Crawford's son, who married a North Carolina girl, practiced in Salisbury for some years, and left a family which still is well-known in the area (Veach, 104, 123–124).

6. Lefler and Newsome, 267.

7. Attmore, 37–41.

8. SRNC 20:262, 270; 21:358–359. The other two contenders were Howell Tatum, a well-connected Halifax attorney ten years older than McNairy, and Josiah Love, who was mentioned a few years later as owning an excellent law library. Both men migrated to the Cumberland despite their disappointment and became good friends of AJ (Ely and Brown, 374–375, 388; Hofmann, 23, 64, 375).

The McNairy House, or to be precise an eighteenth-century log house long identified with the McNairy family, is now an exhibit at the Greensboro Historical Museum. For more details on it, see Weatherly, passim.

9. On the difficulties of travel over the Smokies, cf. Newsome, "John Brown's Journal," 307, and E. T. Clark (Francis Asbury made the crossing only a few days before McNairy and AJ), 1:568–569, 630–631, 752–753.

10. D. Davidson, 1:143.

11. Mark F. Miller, "Richard Henderson," North Carolina, 3:105–106; Arnow, Seedtime, 310; Arnow, Flowering, 158n; Henderson, "Samuel Henderson," 31–38; "A Short . . . Sketch," 6, Henderson Family Papers, SHC.

12. The western land scheme is thoroughly detailed in Abernethy; for Armstrong's involvement, see 49–52. The main beneficiaries were the Polks and David Allison's protector William Blount, who later became AJ's patron as well; see Ibid., 118, 127–128. Armstrong as a Mason: Haywood, 20–21. Craighead: Harrison, Princetonians, 1769–1775, 466; J.G. Craighead, 60; Arnow, Flowering, 181. Polk: Polk, 1:46; Sellers, 19.

Abernethy, 122, suggested that AJ visited the western country in 1787, a year before definitely moving there. His basis was a petition of that year from numerous "transmontane residents" which included the name "Andrew Jackson" (SRNC 22:708); but Abernethy made no attempt to verify that this was AJ's signature, and in view of AJ's frequent legal appearances in Salisbury District throughout that year, a trip over the mountains seems quite unlikely.

13. Remini, AJ1:34–35, refers to AJ at this period as "drifting around the state" and

"getting nowhere"; Ely, 423, states that he left North Carolina largely because he "found it difficult to attract clients." The "drifting" to which Remini refers was the normal travel around the circuit practiced by younger lawyers. As for the difficulty in attracting clients, most young attorneys understood that their first couple of years would be a "starving time" until they developed a clientele (Farmer, 170); AJ's experience seems neither unusual nor cause for discouragement. On the contrary, he secured an appointment as state's attorney in his first six months of practice.

John Williams: Ashe, *Biographical History*, 3:429. "merely experimental": Reid and Eaton, 15. *Jackson* v. *Montgomery* was dismissed in February, 1789; Crawford paid 4 pounds, eleven shillings court costs (Trial Docket, Rowan County CPQS, NCSA).

14. "John Haywood," DAB 14:466; Haywood, 216–231; Cupples to AJ, October 31, 1795, AJ Papers, LC. Arnow, *Seedtime*, 282–306, gives a thorough account of Native American attacks on the early Tennessee frontier.

15. Robert Weakley to James B. McLaughlin, February 25, 1843, AJ Papers, LC; Remini, *AJ*1:45.

16. Graham, 71, 76.

17. For some examples of pathological hatred of Native Americans, see Faragher, 95–96. Hatley, 180–201, is excellent on backcountry attitudes toward Native Americans in this era; the quote is from p. 193.

18. Trial Docket, Rockingham County CPQS, February, 1788, NCSA.

19. The promissory note drawn up by AJ was listed in the catalog of the American Art Association, April 8, 1926. For further data on Hickman and Poindexter, see Register, 150, and Ratcliff, 2:93, 159. For the story of the debt to Lester, see Bassett, AJ, 1:12, where Bassett notes that AJ himself said that he passed by Jesse Lester's front door, that is, through Richmond, on his way to the western country in 1788.

20. The indictment against Stroud is in Randolph County, Criminal Action Papers, NCSA. March 11 was the first day of the court session in 1787. Blair, 8, mentions Crawford's practice but, oddly, fails to mention McNairy.

21. Blair, 4, 10, 27, 44; Caruthers, 13, 33, 57, 64ff.; Martin, 4.

22. Blair, 6, 9, 10, 22. Grand jury presentments, March 1787 and December 1787; warrant for Elender and Sarah Taylor, August 2,1787; affidavit of Jacob Lineberger, February 26, 1789, all in Randolph County Criminal Action Papers, NCSA.

23. AJ's indictments, signed "An.w Jackson, Atto. for County," are in the Randolph County Criminal Action Papers for March, 1788. (See also AJ Papers, 1:11–12, and Ely, 423.) The phrase "Nusence to Society" is from the grand jury presentment of December 1787. Macay's salary in 1780 was one hundred pounds for acting as county attorney at four terms of court (Minutes, Randolph County CPQS, 13 March 1780). On currency in North Carolina in the 1780s, see Ashe, "Social Conditions," 204; Tompkins, 2:93–94; and Minutes, Rowan County CPQS, November 6, 1782. The John Dickey daybook, a merchant's account book from Rowan County in 1785–1786, was kept in terms of guineas, shillings, and pistoles. "Specie tickets"—paper I.O.U.'s for gold and silver—were also in use; see Henry Giles's note to John Steele, August 28,1787, Steele Papers, SHC.

24. Bones were still being turned up on Guilford battlefield in the nineteenth century; cf. Caruthers, *Caldwell*, 237. Robinson, "Guilford," 53, relates the tradition of the 1788 celebration. For comparison, see the sermon (#1) of Samuel E. McCorkle, preached at a patriotic celebration in Rowan July 24, 1786, McCorkle Sermons, DU.

25. Heiskell, 319.

Bibliography

—◦⦿◦—

ABBREVIATIONS USED IN THE BIBLIOGRAPHY

CCGSB	Chester County (South Carolina) Genealogical Society Bulletin
HSP	Historical Society of Pennsylvania, Philadelphia
NA	National Archives, Washington, D.C.
NCHR	*North Carolina Historical Review*
NCSA	North Carolina State Archives, Raleigh
PMHB	Pennsylvania Magazine of History and Biography
SCAH	South Carolina Department of Archives and History, Columbia
SCHM	*South Carolina Historical Magazine*
SHC	Southern Historical Collection, University of North Carolina, Chapel Hill
W&MQ	*William and Mary Quarterly*

MANUSCRIPT SOURCES

Accounts Audited, Revolutionary War Claims, SCAH

Adair, John, pension application, NA

"Anonymous itinerary of the Pennsylvania Line from Pennsylvania to South Carolina, PMHB 36 (1912):273–292

Anson County, North Carolina, Miscellaneous Papers, NCSA

Anson County, North Carolina, Will Books

Baroody, John C., "Archaelogical Investigations at the Site of David Caldwell's Log College, 1980," mimeographed copy, Greensboro, North Carolina, Public Library.

Blair, Thomas, pension application, NA

Brawley, James, Collection, Rowan Public Library, Salisbury, North Carolina

Brevard-McDowell Papers, SHC

. . . .
Bibliography

Brown, Thomas, pension application, NA

[Bruin, Lillian McCain], "McCain Family History of Union County, North Carolina, and Lancaster County, South Carolina," typescript, n.d., Camden Archives, Camden, South Carolina

Buffalo Presbyterian Church, Greensboro, North Carolina, session book, c. 1770–1790, Presbyterian Historical Center, Montreat, North Carolina

Cameron Family Papers, SHC

Carr, James O., ed. and comp., "The Dickson Letters," mimeograph copy, South Caroliniana Library

Charleston (South Carolina) Free Library, Miscellaneous Records

Charleston Inventories, Vol. CC, SCAH

Clark, Walter, Manuscripts, NCSA

Clitherall, James, Diary, SHC

Cornwallis, Charles, 1st Marquis, Papers, Public Record Office, London (microfilm)

Crockett, Nancy, "John Crockett, Revolutionary War Patriot," typescript, n.d., Camden Archives, Camden, South Carolina

Crockett, Nancy, comp., Old Waxhaw Graveyard, mimeograph copy, Lancaster, South Carolina, Public Library

Davie, William R., Papers, SHC

Dickey, John, store account book, 1784–1786, Perkins Library, Duke University

Draper, Lyman C. , Manuscripts, State Historical Society of Wisconsin (microfilm)

Drayton, William, "Remarks on a Tour through the Back Country of the State of South Carolina, 1784," ms. in South Carolina Historical Society, Charleston

Drayton, William, "Journal of a Tour by Sea & Land from Charleston to New York, and from New York through the States of Jersey, Pennsylvania, Delaware, Maryland, Virginia & N. Carolina to Charleston, 1786," South Carolina Historical Society, Charleston

Dudley, Guilford, pension application, NA

Dulin, John R., comp.,"York County, South Carolina, Cousins," typescript, York County Library, Rock Hill, South Carolina

Dunn, George, pension application, NA

Eisele, Florence Leclerq, "Hays-McKemie Families," typescript, 1956, in HSP

Feltman, William, Journal, May 1781 to April 1782, HSP

Forbus, Hugh, pension application, NA

Gordon, Joshua, manuscript volume, 1784, South Caroliniana Library

Greene, Nathaniel, Papers, Clements Library, Ann Arbor, Michigan

Grier, Thomas, pension application, NA

Guilford County, North Carolina, Court of Pleas & Quarter Sessions, Minutes, 1784–1788, NCSA "Guilford County Marriage Bonds," 3 vols. (typescript, NCSA)

Halifax County, North Carolina, Court of Pleas and Quarter Sessions, Minutes, November 1784–May 1787, NCSA

Harris, Charles Wilson, Papers, SHC

Henderson Family, Papers, SHC

Horn, Stanley, Collection, Tennessee State Library

Hough Collection, Lancaster (South Carolina) Public Library

Hughes, Fred, Papers, Guilford College Library, Greensboro, North Carolina

Iredell, James Sr. and Jr., Papers, Perkins Library, Duke University

Jackson, Andrew, Papers, Library of Congress

Jefferies, John, "Reminiscences of the Revolutionary War," in Jefferies Family Papers, South Caroliniana Library

Kershaw, Joseph, Account Book, 1774–1775, State Historical Society of Wisconsin (microfilm)

Kershaw County, South Carolina, Camden District Will Book

Lancaster County, South Carolina, Deed Books

Lancaster County, South Carolina, Probate Records

Lenoir, William, Papers, SHC

Massey Family File, York County Library, Rock Hill, South Carolina

McBee, Mary Wilson, "Anson County, North Carolina, Abstracts of Early Records," typescript, 1950, Charlotte-Mecklenburg Public Library

McCamie, John, will, copy in possession of Mecklenburg Declaration of Independence Chapter, Daughters of the American Revolution, Charlotte, North Carolina

Macay and McNeely Family Papers, SHC

Macay, Spruce, Notebook, 1786–1794, NCSA

McCorkle, Archibald, pension application, NA

McCorkle, Samuel Eusebius, Sermons, Perkins Library, Duke University

McCubbins, Pauline, Collection, Rowan Public Library, Salisbury, North Carolina

McWhorter, George, pension application, NA

Mecklenburg County, North Carolina, Civil Action Papers, NCSA

Mecklenburg County, North Carolina, Court of Pleas & Quarter Sessions, Minutes, 1785–1791, NCSA

Mecklenburg County, North Carolina, miscellaneous papers, NCSA

Morgan District, North Carolina, miscellaneous records, NCSA

Morgan District, North Carolina, slave records, NCSA

Murphy, Marion Emerson, "Early Leslies in York County, South Carolina," 3rd ed., typescript in possession of Nancy Crockett, Lancaster, South Carolina

Nettles, William, pension application, NA

Nisbet, John, Papers, SHC

Osborne, John, Diary, typescript, Union County Public Library, Monroe, North Carolina

Oxley, Joseph, Journal, HSP

Parton, James, Papers, Houghton Library, Harvard University

Patten, Jacob, pension application, NA

Ramsey, John, pension application, NA

Randolph County, North Carolina, Court of Pleas and Quarter Sessions, Minutes, 1784–1792, NCSA

Randolph County, North Carolina, Criminal Action Papers, NCSA

Bibliography

Rankin, W. C., Papers, SHC

Reid, John, "Original Copy of the Life of Genl Andrew Jackson as far as written," ms. in Tennessee Historical Society Miscellaneous Papers, Tennessee State Library

Reeves, Enos, Journal, Perkins Library, Duke University

Ridley v. *Williamson*, Middle Tennessee Supreme Court records, Tennessee State Library

Rockingham County, Court of Pleas and Quarter Sessions, Trial Docket, 1786–1788, NCSA

Rockingham County, Court of Pleas and Quarter Sessions, Criminal Action Papers, NCSA

Rodman, Ida McDow, "The McDow Family in America," typescript, 1953, Camden Archives, Camden, South Carolina

Rowan County, North Carolina, Civil Action Papers, NCSA

Rowan County, North Carolina, Court of Pleas and Quarter Sessions, Trial Docket, 1784–1788, NCSA

Rowan County, North Carolina, Court of Pleas and Quarter Sessions, Minutes, 1786–1792, NCSA

Rowan County, North Carolina, Deed Books

Rowan County, North Carolina, estate inventories, bound with Court of Pleas and Quarter Sessions minutes, 1800–1809, NCSA

Rowan County, North Carolina, Marriage Bonds, 2 vols. (typescript, Rowan Public Library, Salisbury, North Carolina)

Schaumann, Merri Lou Scribner, comp., Tax Lists—Cumberland County, Pennsylvania, mimeographed copy, HSP

Simpson, John, Papers, South Caroliniana Library

Stafford, Alvah, Alexander Notebooks (typescript, 1985, Charlotte/Mecklenburg County Public Library, Charlotte, North Carolina)

Starr, Catherine Massey, "Henry Massey: A Soldier in the Militia—South Carolina Line, Revolutionary War," typescript, Lancaster, South Carolina, Public Library

Steele, John, Papers, SHC

Stokes, Montfort, Papers, NCSA

Stuart, Cyrus, Diary, Special Collections, Clemson University

Surry County, North Carolina, Court of Pleas and Quarter Sessions, Trial Docket, 1787–1788, NCSA

Surry County, North Carolina, Criminal Action Papers, NCSA

Thomson, Benjamin, pension application, NA

Washington, George, Papers, Library of Congress

White, George, pension application, NA

White Family, Papers, SHC

Yeates, Jasper, Papers, HSP

PRINTED PRIMARY SOURCES

[Adams, John Quincy], *Diary of John Quincy Adams,* ed. David Grayson Allen, 2, March 1786–December 1788 ("The Adams Papers, Series I, Diaries; Cambridge, Mass.: Belknap Press of Harvard University Press, 1981)

Agee, Jean C., comp., "Annuities for Persons Hurted [sic] in the Service of the State," CCGSB, 8 (Sept. and Dec., 1985):82–89 and 109–117

Allaire, Anthony, Diary of Lieut. . . . ("Eyewitness Accounts of the American Revolution"; New York: Arno Press, 1968; first published 1881)

Astley, Philip, *The Modern Riding-Master* (Philadelphia: Robert Aitken, 1776; 1st published London, 1774)

Attmore, William, *Journal of a Tour to North Carolina,* ed. Lida Tunstall Rodman ("James Sprunt Historical Publications," 17, No. 2 [1922])

Austen, Jane, *Northanger Abbey* (New York: Alfred A. Knopf, 1992; first published 1817)

[Avery, Waightstill], "The Diary of Waightstill Avery," *North Carolina University Magazine,* 2nd series, 4 (1855):246–257

Bacon, Matthew, *Abridgment of the Laws* (5 vols.; Dublin: Luke White, 1793)

Bailey, Robert, *The Life and Adventures of . . .* (Richmond: J. & G. Cochran,1822)

Balch, Thomas, ed., *Papers Relating Chiefly to the Maryland Line during the Revolution* (Philadelphia: Printed for the Seventy-Six Society, 1857)

Barnwell, Joseph W., ed., "Letters to General Greene and Others," SCHM 17 (January 1916):3–13

Bassett, John S., ed., *Correspondence of Andrew Jackson* (7 vols.; Washington: The Carnegie Institution, 1926–1935)

Battle, William H., "Memoir of Leonard Henderson," *North Carolina University Magazine,* 9 (November 1859):193–202

Bentley, Elizabeth Petty, comp., *Index to the 1800 Census of North Carolina* (Baltimore: Genealogical Publishing Co., Inc., 1977)

Benton, Thomas Hart, *Thirty Years' View,* 1 (New York: D. Appleton and Company, 1854)

Bickley, Francis, ed., Report on the Manuscripts of the Late Reginald Rawdon Hastings, Esq., of the Manor House, Ashby de la Zouch, 3 (London: Historical Manuscripts Commission, Twentieth Report, 1934)

Blackstone, William, *Commentaries on the Laws of England in Four Books,* 12th ed. (London: A. Strahan and W. Woodfall, 1793)

Boyd, Julian P., ed., *The Papers of Thomas Jefferson* (26 vols. to date; Princeton, N. J.: Princeton University Press, 1950–)

Brooke, Francis Taliaferro, *A Narrative of My Life* (Richmond: MacFarlane & Ferguson, 1849)

[Brown, Tarleton], *Memoirs of Tarleton Brown* (Barnwell, S.C.: The People Press, 1894)

Caldwell, Charles, *Autobiography of Charles Caldwell, M.D.,* ed. Harriot W. Warner (New York: Da Capo Press, 1968; first published 1855)

Caruthers, E.W., *A Sketch of the Life and Character of the Rev. David Caldwell, D.D.* (Greensboro, N.C.: Swaim and Sherwood, 1842)

Bibliography

Chesney, Alexander, *The Journal of . . .* , *a South Carolina Loyalist in the Revolution and After,* ed. E. Alfred Jones (Greenville, S.C.: A Press, 1981?; first published 1921)

Clark, Elmer T., ed., *The Journal and Letters of Francis Asbury* 3 vols.; Nashville: Abingdon Press, 1958)

Clark, Murtie June, *Loyalists in the Southern Campaign of the Revolutionary War,* 1, 3 (Baltimore: Genealogical Publishing Company, 1981)

Clark, Thomas D., ed., *South Carolina: The Grand Tour, 1780–1865* (Columbia: University of South Carolina Press, 1973)

Clark, Walter, ed., North Carolina State Records (26 vols.; Winston and Goldsboro, N. C.: Nash Publishers, 1895–1906)

Cohen, Hennig, "Drayton's Notes on Pickering's List of Americanisms," *American Speech,* 31 (December 1956): 264–270

[Coke, Thomas], *Extracts from the Journals of the Rev. Dr. Coke's Five Visits to America* (London: G. Paramore, 1793)

[Collins, James Potter], *Autobiography of a Revolutionary Soldier* ("The American Military Experience"; New York: Arno Press, 1979; first published 1859)

Cornwallis, Charles, 1st Marquis, *Correspondence,* ed. Charles Ross, Esq. (2nd edition; 3 vols.; London: John Murray, 1859)

Davies, Alun C., "'As Good a Country as Any Man Needs to Dwell In': Letters from a Scotch Irish Immigrant in Pennsylvania, 1766, 1767, and 1784," *Pennsylvania History,* 50 (October, 1983): 313–322

Dorman, John Frederick, comp., *Virginia Revolutionary Pension Applications* (29 vols. to date; Washington: 1957–)

Ellet, Elizabeth F., *The Women of the American Revolution,* 3 (New York: Charles Scribner, 1856)

Ely, James W. Jr., and Theodore Brown Jr., eds., *The Legal Papers of Andrew Jackson* (Knoxville: University of Tennessee Press, 1987)

Ezell, John S., ed., *The New Democracy in America: Travels of Francisco de Miranda in the United States, 1783–1784* (Norman: University of Oklahoma Press, 1963)

Finley, James B., *Autobiography, or, Pioneer Life in the West* (Cincinnati: Methodist Book Concern, 1855)

[Ford, Timothy], "Diary of Timothy Ford, 1785–1786," SCHM 13 1912:132–147, 181–204

Fries, Adelaide L., ed., *Records of the Moravians in North Carolina,* 2 ("Publications of the North Carolina Historical Commission"; Raleigh: Edwards & Broughton Printing Company, 1925)

Fulcher, Richard C., *1770–1790 Census of the Cumberland Settlements: Davidson, Sumner, and Tennessee Counties* (Baltimore: Genealogical Publishing Company, 1987)

Garden, Alexander, *Anecdotes of the Revolutionary War in America* (Charleston: A. E. Miller, 1822)

Garsault, Francois-A. de, "L'Art du bourrelier et du sellier," in *Academie des Sciences, Descriptions des Arts et Metiers,* vol. 16, Les Arts du cuir (Geneva: Slatkine Reprints, 1984; first published 1774), 1–147

Gibbes, Robert W., ed., *Documentary History of the American Revolution* 3 vols.; Spartanburg, S.C.: The Reprint Company, 1972; first published 1855)

Ginns, Patsy Moore, *Rough Weather Makes Good Timber: Carolinians Recall* (Chapel Hill: The University of North Carolina Press, 1977)

Ginns, Patsy Moore, *Snowbird Gravy and Dishpan Pie* (Chapel Hill: University of North Carolina Press, 1982)

Graham, Joseph, "General Joseph Graham's Narrative of the Revolutionary War in North Carolina in 1780 and 1781," in *The Papers of Archibald D. Murphey*, ed. William Henry Hoyt ("Publications of the North Carolina Historical Commission"; Raleigh: E. M. Uzzell & Co., 1914), 212–311

Graham, William A., *General Joseph Graham and His Papers on North Carolina Revolutionary History* (Raleigh: The Author, 1904)

[Gray, Robert], "Colonel Robert Gray's Observations on the War in Carolina," SCHM, 11 (1910):139–159

Grayson, William J., *Witness to Sorrow*, ed. Richard J. Calhoun (Columbia: University of South Carolina Press, 1990)

Hanger, George, *The Life, Adventures, and Opinions of Col. George Hanger, written by himself*, 2 (London: J. Debrett, 1801)

Haywood, John, *Civil and Political History of the State of Tennessee from Its Earliest Settlement Up to the Year 1796* ("The First American Frontier"; New York: Arno Press, 1971; first published 1823)

Heads of Families at the First Census of the United States, 1790: South Carolina (Baltimore: Genealogical Publishing Company, 1966)

Hill, William, *Colonel William Hill's Memoirs of the Revolution* (Columbia: The Historical Commission of South Carolina, 1921)

Hofmann, Margaret M., *Genealogical Abstracts of Wills, 1758 through 1824, Halifax County, North Carolina* (Weldon, N.C.: The Roanoke News Company, 1970)

Holcomb, Brent, comp., *Kershaw County, South Carolina, Minutes of the County Court, 1791–1799* (n.p.: privately printed, 1986)

Holcomb, Brent, comp., *Lancaster County, South Carolina, Deed Abstracts, 1787–1811* (Easley, S.C.: Southern Historical Press, 1981)

Holcomb, Brent, comp., *Marriages of Surry County, N. C., 1779–1868* (Baltimore: Genealogical Publishing Co., 1982)

Holcomb, Brent, *Probate Records of South Carolina, 3* (Easley, S. C.: Southern Historical Press, 1979)

Holcomb, Brent H., and Elmer O. Parker, eds., *Early Records of Fishing Creek Presbyterian Church* (Greenville, S.C.: A Press, 1980)

Howland, H. R., "The Second Battle of Camden, S.C.," *Potter's American Monthly*, 4 (Feb., 1875):99–104

Hunt, Gaillard, ed., *Fragments of Revolutionary History* (Brooklyn: The Historical Printing Club, 1892)

Iredell, James, *Laws of the State of North-Carolina* (Edenton, N.C.: Hodge & Wills, 1791)

Bibliography

Jacob, John J., *John J. Jacob Narrative* (Cumberland, Md.: J. M. Buchanan, 1826)

Jefferson, Thomas, *Notes on the State of Virginia,* ed. William H. Peden (Chapel Hill: The University of North Carolina Press, 1954; first published 1787)

Johnson, Joseph, *Traditions and Reminiscences, Chiefly of the American Revolution* (Charleston: Walker & James, 1851)

Kearney, Timothy, *Abstracts of Guilford County Deeds* (Raleigh: Privately printed, 1993)

Keith, Alice Barnwell, ed. *The John Gray Blount Papers* (2 vols.; "Publications of the State Department of Archives and History"; Raleigh: State Department of Archives and History, 1952)

Kipping, Ernst, *The Hessian View of America, 1776–1783* (Monmouth Beach, N. J.: Philip Freneau Press, 1971)

Kirkwood, Robert, *The Journal and Order Book of Captain Robert Kirkwood . . . ,* ed. Rev. Joseph Brown Turner (Port Washington, N.Y.: Kennikat Press, 1970; first published 1910)

Lancaster County Historical Commission, *Inscriptions from Old Cemeteries In Lancaster, South Carolina* (Lancaster: Tri County Publishing Company, 1974)

La Tocnaye, Jacques Louis de Bougrenet, Chevalier de, *A Frenchman's Walk in Ireland, 1796–7,* trans. John Stevenson (Belfast: McCaw, Stevenson, & Orr, Ltd., 1917)

Laval, J., and S. F. Bradford, *Cabinet* (Philadelphia: P., K., and C., 1829)

Lee, Henry, *Memoirs of the War in the Southern Department of the United States* (New York: University Publishing Company, 1869; reprinted 1969)

Linn, Jo White, comp., *Abstracts of Wills and Estate Records of Rowan County, North Carolina, 1753–1805* (Salisbury, N.C.: The author, 1980)

Linn, Jo White, *Rowan County, North Carolina: Tax Lists, 1757–1800* (Salisbury, N.C.: Privately printed, 1995)

Louis-Philippe, king of France, *Journal de mon voyage de l'Amerique,* ed. Suzanne d'Huart (Paris: Flammarion, 1976)

Macay [McCoy], Spruce, "Letter to Major Mountflorence," n.d. [1782?], *Publications of the Southern Historical Association,* 3 (1899):132–135.

McElligott, Carroll Ainsworth, *Charleston Residents, 1782–1794* (Bowie, Md.: Heritage Books, Inc., 1989)

MacKenzie, Roderick, *Strictures on Lt. Col. Tarleton's History* (London: The Author, 1787)

McRee, Griffith J., *Life and Correspondence of James Iredell* (2 vols.; New York: D. Appleton and Company, 1857)

Martin, C. C., *The Harness-Maker's Complete Guide* (Chicago: Jefferson Jackson, 1891)

Mathis, Samuel, "Battle of Hobkirk's Hill," *American Historical Record,* 2 (March, 1873):103–110

Merrens, H. Roy, ed., *The Colonial South Carolina Scene: Contemporary Views, 1697–1774* (Columbia: University of South Carolina Press, 1977)

Moore, Caroline T., comp., *Abstracts of the Wills of the State of South Carolina, 1760–1784* (Columbia, S. C.: Privately printed, 1965)

Moore, Maurice, *Reminiscences of York,* ed. Elmer O. Parker (Greenville, S. C.: A Press, Inc., 1981)

Moultrie, William, "Journal . . . while a Commissioner on the North and South Carolina Boundary Survey, 1772," ed. Charles S. Davis, *Journal of Southern History,* 8 (November, 1942), 549–555

Moultrie, William, *Memoirs of the American Revolution* (2 vols.; New York: David Longworth, 1802)

Newsome, A. R., ed., "A British Orderly Book, 1780–1781," Pts. 3–4, NCHR 8 (July, 1932):273–298, 365–392.

Newsome, A. R., ed., "John Brown's Journal of Travel in Western North Carolina in 1795," NCHR 11 (October, 1934):284–313

Newsome, A. R., ed., "A Miscellany from the Thomas Henderson Letter Book, 1810–1811," NCHR, 6 (October, 1929) 398–410

"Official Correspondence between Brigadier-General Thomas Sumter and Major-General Nathaniel Greene," Charleston, S. C., *Year Book, 1899* (Charleston: Lucas & Richardson, n.d.), appendix

Pace, Antonio, ed., *Luigi Castiglioni's Viaggio* (Syracuse: Syracuse University Press, 1983)

Paltridge, George H., comp., "List of Pensioners for the Year 1787," *Virginia Magazine of History and Biography,* 50 (1942):163–168

Parker, Joel, and Smith, T. Ralston, *The Presbyterian's Hand-Book of the Church* (New York: Harper & Brothers, 1861)

Peyton, Bailie, "Reminiscences of the Turf," *Rural Sun* (Nashville, Tenn.), October 31, November 21, December 5, 1872; January 9, March 13, May 8, 1873

Ratcliff, Clarence E., comp., *North Carolina Taxpayers, 1679–1790* (Baltimore: Genealogical Publishing Co., Inc., 1987)

Reese, Thomas, *An Essay on the Influence of Religion in Civil Society* (Charleston, S. C.: Markland & M'Iver, 1787)

[Reeves, Enos], "Extracts from the Letter-Books of Lieutenant Enos Reeves, of the Pennsylvania Line," PMHB 21 (1892):466–476

Register, Alvaretta Kenan, ed., *State Census of North Carolina, 1784–1787* (Baltimore: Genealogical Publishing Co., Inc., 1987)

Robinson, Blackwell P., ed., *The Revolutionary War Sketches of William R. Davie* (Raleigh: The North Carolina Division of Archives and History, 1976)

Rogers, George C. Jr., ed., "Letters of Charles O'Hara to the Duke of Grafton," SCHM, 65 (July, 1964):158–180

Ryan, Frank W. Jr., "Travelers in South Carolina in the Eighteenth Century," *Charleston Year Book,* 1945 (Charleston: Walker, Evans, and Cogswell, 1948)

Salley, A. S. Jr., ed., *Documents Relating to the History of South Carolina During the Revolutionary War* (Columbia: The Historical Commission of South Carolina, 1908)

Salley, A. S. Jr., ed., *Stub Entries to Indents Issued in Payment of Claims Against South Carolina Growing Out of the Revolution* (9 vols.; Columbia: South Carolina Historical Commission, 1910–1939)

. . . .

Bibliography

Saye, Rev. James H., "Personal Reminiscences," CCGSB, 8 (June, 1985): 56–58

Schoepf, Johann David, *Travels in the Confederation*, ed. Alfred J. Morrison (2 vols.; Philadelphia: W. J. Campbell, 1911), 2

Scott, Edwin J., *Random Recollections of a Long Life* (Columbia, S. C.: Charles A. Calvo Jr., 1884)

Seymour, William, *A Journal of the Southern Expedition, 1780–1783* ("Papers of the Historical Society of Delaware," 15; Wilmington: Historical Society of Delaware, 1896)

[Shaw, John Robert], *John Robert Shaw: An Autobiography of Thirty Years, 1777–1807*, ed. Oressa M. Teagarden (Athens: Ohio University Press, 1992)

Showman, Richard K., and Dennis M. Conrad, eds., *The Papers of General Nathanael Greene* (9 vols. to date; Chapel Hill: The University of North Carolina Press, 1976–)

[Smith, William L.], "Journal of William Loughton Smith, 1790–1791," *Proceedings of the Massachusetts Historical Society*, 51 (1917–1918): 20–88

Smith, Sam B., and Harriet Chappell Owsley, eds., *The Papers of Andrew Jackson* (6 vols. to date; Knoxville: The University of Tennessee Press, 1980–)

Smyth, John F. D., *A Tour in the United States of America* ("Eyewitness Accounts of the American Revolution"; 2 vols.; New York: Arno Press, 1968; first published 1774)

South Carolina Deed Abstracts, 4 (Easley, S. C.: Southern Historical Press, 1984)

Sparks, W. H., *The Memories of Fifty Years* (Philadelphia: Claxton, Remsen, & Haffelfinger, 1870)

Stedman, Charles, *The History of the Origin, Progress, and Termination of the American War* (2 vols.; Dublin, 1794)

Stephen, George, *The Adventures of a Gentleman in Search of a Horse* (London: Saunders & Otley, 1845)

[Stinson, Daniel G.], "A Carolina Woman of the Revolution," *Godey's Lady Book*, 52 (January–June 1856: 213–217

Stockham, Peter, ed., *Early Nineteenth-Century Crafts and Trades* (New York: Dover Publications, Inc., 1992; first published 1807)

Stokes, George T., ed., *Pococke's Tour in Ireland in 1752* (Dublin: Hodges, Figgin, and Co., 1891)

Tarleton, Banastre, *A History of the Campaign of 1780 and 1781, in the Southern Provinces of North America* (London: T. Cadell, 1787; reprinted 1968)

Tilden, John Bell, Diary, PMHB 19 (1895):51–63, 208–233.

Truman, Ben C., *The Field of Honor* (New York: Fords, Howard, & Hulbert,1884)

[Twain, Mark], *The Complete Short Stories of Mark Twain*, ed. Charles Neider (New York: Bantam Books, 1958)

Tweed, Gilbert, "Some North Carolina Mock Orations," *North Carolina Folklore*, 3, no. 2 (December 1955): 20–26

Twiss, Richard, *A Tour in Ireland in 1775* (London: privately printed, 1776)

Wagstaff, H. M., ed., *The Papers of John Steele* ("Publications of the North Carolina Historical Commission"; 2 vols.; Raleigh: Edwards & Broughton, 1924)

Watson, Winslow C., ed., *Men and Times of the Revolution; or, Memoirs of Elkanah Watson* (Elizabethtown, N. Y.: Crown Point Press, 1968; first published 1856)

Willcox, William B., ed., *The Papers of Benjamin Franklin,* vols. 18–19 (New Haven: Yale University Press, 1974–1975)

[Willes, Edward], *The Letters of Lord Chief Baron Edward Willes to the Earl of Warwick, 1757–62,* ed. James Kelly ("Studies in Irish Archaeology and History"; Aberstwyth, Wales: Boethius Press, 1990)

Williams, Samuel C., ed., *Early Travels in the Tennessee Country* (Johnson City, Tenn.: The Watauga Press, 1928)

Williams, Samuel C., ed., "General Richard Winn's Notes—1780," SCHM 43 (1942):201–212, 44 (1943):1–10

Woodmason, Charles, *The Carolina Backcountry on the Eve of the Revolution: The Journal and Other Writings of Charles Woodmason, Anglican Itinerant* (Chapel Hill: University of North Carolina Press, 1953)

Works Progress Administration, Calendar of the O. H. Williams Papers in the Maryland Historical Society (Baltimore: The Maryland Historical Records Survey, 1940)

Young, Arthur, *A Tour in Ireland,* ed. Constantia Maxwell (Cambridge: University Press, 1925)

SECONDARY SOURCES

Abernethy, Thomas P., *From Frontier to Plantation in Tennessee* (Chapel Hill: The University of North Carolina Press, 1932)

Akenson, Donald Harman, and W. H. Crawford, *Local Poets and Social History: James Orr, Bard of Ballycarry* (Belfast: Public Record Office of Northern Ireland, 1977)

Alexander, John B., *The History of Mecklenburg County from 1740 to 1900* (Charlotte, N.C.: Observer Print. House, 1902)

Allison, John, *Dropped Stitches in Tennessee History* (Nashville: Author, 1897)

Angellotti, Mrs. Frank M., *The Polks of North Carolina and Tennessee* (Columbia, Tenn.: James K. Polk Memorial Association, 1984; first published 1923–24)

Ardrey, Robert, *African Genesis* (New York: Atheneum, 1961)

Arnow, Harriette Simpson, *Flowering of the Cumberland* (New York: The Macmillan Company, 1963)

Arnow, Harriette Simpson, *Seedtime on the Cumberland* (New York: The Macmillan Company, 1960)

Ashe, Samuel A. Stephen B. Weeks, Charles L. VanNoppen, eds., *Biographical History of North Carolina* (8 vols.; Greensboro, N.C.: Charles A. Von Noppen and Co., 1908)

Ashe, S. A., "Social Conditions in North Carolina in 1783," *N. C. Booklet,* 10, no. 4 (April, 1911), 200–222

Barber, James G., *Andrew Jackson: A Portrait Study* (Washington: The National Portrait Gallery, 1991)

Bibliography

Barkley, John, "Marriage and the Presbyterian Tradition," *Ulster Folklife*, 39 (1993): 29–39

Bartlett, T., and Hayton, D. W., eds., *Penal Era and Golden Age: Essays in Irish History, 1690–1800* (Belfast, 1979)

Bass, Robert D., *Gamecock: The Life and Campaigns of General Thomas Sumter* (New York: Holt, Rinehart, and Winston, 1961)

Bass, Robert D., *The Green Dragoon* (New York: Henry Holt and Company, 1957)

Bassett, John Spencer, *The Life of Andrew Jackson* (2 vols.; New York: The Macmillan Company, 1916)

Beck, Monica L., "'A Fer Ways Off from the Big House': The Changing Nature of Slavery in the South Carolina Backcountry," in Crass et al., eds., 108–186

Betts, Albert D., *History of Methodism in South Carolina* (Columbia, S. C.: The Advocate Press, 1925)

Bigger, Francis J., *The Ulster Land War of 1770* (Dublin: Sealy, Bryers, and Walker, 1910)

Blair, J. A., *Reminiscences of Randolph County* (Greensboro, N. C.: Reece & Elam, 1890)

Blake, John W., ed., *The Ulster-American Connection* (Coleraine: The New University of Ulster, 1981)

Blethen, Tyler, and Curtis Wood Jr., *From Ulster to Carolina: The Migration of the Scotch-Irish to Southwestern North Carolina* (2nd ed., Cullowhee, N.C.[?]: Western Carolina University, 1986)

Blethen, Tyler, and Curtis W. Wood, "A Trader on the Appalachian Frontier," in Mitchell, 150–165

Bliss, Alan, *Spoken English in Ireland, 1600–1740* (Dublin: The Dolmen Press, 1979)

Bloomfield, Maxwell, *American Lawyers in a Changing Society, 1776–1876* (Cambridge, Mass.: Harvard University Press, 1976)

Blythe, LeGette, and Charles R. Brockmann, *Hornet's Nest: The Story of Charlotte and Mecklenburg County* (Charlotte, N. C.: Public Library of Charlotte and Mecklenburg County, 1961)

Boatner, Mark M. III, *Encyclopedia of the American Revolution* (3rd ed.; Mechanicsburg, Pa.: Stackpole Books, 1994)

Boles, John B., *Black Southerners, 1619–1869* ("New Perspectives on the South"; Lexington: The University Press of Kentucky, 1984)

Boorstin, Daniel J., *The Mysterious Science of the Law . . .* (Boston: Beacon Press, 1958)

Braidwood, J., *The Ulster Dialect Lexicon* (Belfast: Queens University, 1969)

Brawley, James S., "Another Jackson Proof Uncovered Here," *Salisbury Post*, November 10, 1974

Brawley, James S., *Old Rowan: Views and Sketches* (Salisbury, N. C.: Rowan Printing Co., 1955[?])

Brawley, James S., "The Rowan County Courthouse," *Genealogical Society of Rowan County, North Carolina Magazine*, 6 (June, 1992):46–48

Brawley, James S., *Rowan County: A Brief History* (Raleigh: North Carolina Department of Cultural Resources, 1974)

294

Bridenbaugh, Carl, *Myths and Realities: Societies of the Colonial South* (Baton Rouge: Louisiana State University Press, 1952)

Brimelow, Judith M., *Accounts Audited of Claims Growing Out of the Revolution in South Carolina* (Columbia, S. C.: Department of Archives and History, 1985)

Brooke, Peter, *Ulster Presbyterianism: The Historical Perspective, 1610–1970* (New York: St. Martin's Press, 1987)

Brown, Douglas S., *The Catawba Indians* (Columbia: The University of South Carolina Press, 1966)

Brown, Keith M., *Bloodfeud in Scotland, 1573–1625: Violence, Justice, and Politics in an Early Modern Society* (Edinburgh: John Donald Publishers Ltd., 1986)

Brown, Richard Maxwell, *Strain of Violence: Historical Studies of American Violence* (New York: Oxford University Press, 1975)

Bryson, William J. Jr., *A Celebration of Jackson Lodge Freemasonry* (Lancaster, S. C.: Craftsman Press, 1985)

Buchanan, John, *The Road to Guilford Courthouse* (New York: John Wiley & Sons, Inc.: 1997)

Buell, Augustus C., *History of Andrew Jackson* (2 vols.; London: Bickers & Son, 1904)

Buick, George R. and David Buick, "On a Small Collection of Presbyterian Communion Tokens," *Ulster Journal of Archaelogy*, n.s., IX (1903), 17–29

Bullock, Steven C., *Revolutionary Brotherhood: Freemasonry and the Transformation of the American Social Order, 1730–1840* (Chapel Hill: The University of North Carolina Press, 1996)

Bushman, Richard L., *The Refinement of America: Persons, Houses, Cities* (New York: Vintage Books, 1993)

Butler, Jon, *Awash in a Sea of Faith* (Cambridge, Mass.: Harvard University Press, 1990)

Butler, Lindley S., *Rockingham County: A Brief History* (Raleigh: North Carolina Department of Cultural Resources, 1982)

Caldwell, Mary French, *Tennessee: The Dangerous Example* (Nashville: Aurora Publishers, Inc., 1974)

Calhoun, Daniel H., *Professional Lives in America: Structure and Aspiration, 1750–1850* (Cambridge, Mass.: Harvard University Press, 1965)

Calvert, Karin, "The Function of Fashion in Eighteenth-Century America," pp. 252–283, in Cary Carson, Ronald Hoffman, and Peter J. Albert, eds., *Of Consuming Interests: The Style of Life in the Eighteenth Century* (Charlottesville: University Press of Virginia, 1994)

Caruthers, E. W., *The Old North State in 1776* (Greensboro, N. C.: The Guilford County Genealogical Society, 1985; first published 1854–1856)

Cash, W. J., *The Mind of the South* (New York: Alfred A. Knopf, 1941)

Chalkley, Lyman, *Chronicles of the Scotch-Irish Settlement in Virginia* (3 vols.; Baltimore: Genealogical Publishing Company, 1966; first published 1912)

Chamberlain, Hope Summerall, *This Was Home* (Chapel Hill: The University of North Carolina Press, 1938)

Chambers, William Nisbet, *Old Bullion Benton: Senator from the West* (Boston: Little, Brown and Company, 1956)

. . . .
Bibliography

Chroust, Anton-Hermann, *The Rise of the Legal Profession in America* (2 vols.; Norman: University of Oklahoma Press, 1985)

Clark, Wallace, *Linen on the Green* (2nd edition; Belfast: The Universities Press, 1983)

Collins, Brenda, "Proto-Industrialization and Pre-Famine Emigration," *Social History* [GB], VII, 2, 127–146

Connell, K. H., *Irish Peasant Society* (Oxford: Clarendon Press, 1968)

Corbitt, D. L., comp., "Judicial Districts of North Carolina," NCHR, 12 (June 1935): 45–61

Cousar, James English, *Down the Waxhaw Road* (Florence, S. C.: Privately printed, 1953)

Cox, Millard, *Derby: The Life & Times of the 12th Earl of Darby* (London: J. A. Allen, 1974)

Craighead, James G., *The Craighead Family* (Philadelphia: Privately printed, 1876)

Craighead, James G., *Scotch and Irish Seeds in American Soil* (Philadelphia: Presbyterian Board of Publication, 1878)

Crass, David Colin, et al., eds., *The Southern Colonial Backcountry: Interdisciplinary Perspectives on Frontier Communities* (Knoxville: The University of Tennessee Press, 1998)

Crawford, W. H., "Change in Ulster in the Late Eighteenth Century," in Bartlett and Hayton, 186–203

Crawford, W. H., *Domestic Industry in Ireland: The Experience of the Linen Industry* (Dublin: Gill and Macmillan, 1972)

Crawford, W. H., "The Evolution of Ulster Towns, 1750–1850, in Roebuck, 140–156

Crawford, W. H., *The Irish Linen Industry* (Belfast[?]: Ulster Folk and Transport Museum, 1987)

Crawford, W. H., "Ulster Landowners and the Linen Industry," in J. T. Ward and R. Wilson, eds., *Land and Industry* (Newton Abbot: David & Charles, 1971)

Crawford, W. H., and B. Trainor, eds., *Aspects of Irish Social History, 1750–1800* (Belfast: H. M. Stationery Office, 1973)

Crittenden, Charles C.,"Means of Communication in North Carolina, 1763–1789," NCHR 8 (October 1931), 373–383

Crittenden, Charles C.,"Overland Travel and Transportation in North Carolina, 1763–1789," NCHR 8 (July 1931), 239–257

Crozier, Alan, "The Scotch-Irish Influence on American English," *American Speech*, 59 (Winter 1984), No. 4, 310–331

Curtis, James C., *Andrew Jackson and the Search for Vindication* (Boston: Little, Brown and Company, 1976)

Davidson, Chalmers G., "Independent Mecklenburg," NCHR 46 (Spring 1969), 122–127

Davidson, Chalmers G., *Gaston of Chester* (Davidson, N. C.: Privately printed, 1956)

Davidson, Chalmers G., *The Colonial Scotch-Irish of the Carolina Piedmont* (Richburg, S. C.: Chester County Geneological [sic] Society, 1979)

Davidson, Donald, *The Tennessee*, vol. I, "The Old River: Frontier to Secession" ("Rivers of America"; New York: Rinehart & Company, Inc., 1946)

Davis, Robert Scott Jr., "Thomas Pinckney and the Last Campaign of Horatio Gates," SCHM 86 (April 1985), 75–99.

Denslow, Ray V., *Freemasonry and the Presidency, U.S.A.* (n.p.: The Missouri Lodge of Research, 1952)

Dickson, Robert J., *Ulster Emigration to Colonial America, 1718–1775* (London: Routledge and Kegan Paul, 1966)

Dictionary of American Biography, ed. Allen Johnson (10 vols.; New York: Charles Scribner's Sons, 1927–1936)

Doyle, David Noel, "The Irish and the Christian Churches of America," in Doyle and Owen Dudley Edwards, eds., *America and Ireland, 1776–1976* (Westport, 1980), 117–191

Doyle, David Noel, *Ireland, Irishmen, and Revolutionary America, 1760–1820* (Dublin: The Mercier Press, 1981)

Dunbar, Gary S., "Colonial Carolina Cowpens," *Agricultural History*, 35 no. 3 (July 1961), 125–130

Dunlap, Lily Doyle, "Old Waxhaw," *N. C. Booklet*, 19, no. 4 (April 1920), 139–144

Dunlevy, Mairead, *Dress in Ireland* (New York: Holmes & Meier, 1989)

Eid, Leroy V., "Irish, Scotch, and Scotch-Irish, A Reconsideration," *American Presbyterians*, 64 (1986), No. 4, 211–225

Eliason, Norman E., *Tarheel Talk: A Historical Study of the English Language in North Carolina to 1860* (Chapel Hill: The University of North Carolina Press, 1956)

Ely, James W. Jr., "The Legal Practice of Andrew Jackson," *Tennessee Historical Quarterly*, 38 (1979), 421–435

Ernst, Joseph A., and H. Roy Merrens, "'Camden's Turrets Pierce the Skies!': The Urban Process in the Southern Colonies during the Eighteenth Century," W&MQ, 3s, 30 (1973), 562–565

Evans, E. Estyn, "Cultural Relics of the Ulster-Scots in the Old West of North America," *Ulster Folklife*, 11 (1966):33–38

Evans, E. Estyn, *Irish Folk Ways* (London: Routledge and Kegan Paul, 1957)

Evans, E. Estyn, *Mourne Country: Landscape and Life in South Down* (Dundalk: Dundalgan P., 1967)

Evans, E. Estyn, "The Scotch-Irish in the New World: An Atlantic Heritage," *Journal of the Royal Antiquaries of Ireland*, XCV (1965), 39–49

Evans, E. Estyn, "The Scotch-Irish: Their Cultural Adaptation and Heritage in the American Old West," in Green, 69–86

Fabel, R. F. A., "Montfort Browne's Corps: The Prince of Wales American Volunteers," *Journal of the Society for Army Historical Research* (GB) 1992, 70 (Autumn 1992): 157–173

Faragher, John Mack, *Daniel Boone* (New York: Henry Holt and Company, 1992)

Farmer, Fannie M., "Bar Examination and Beginning Years of Legal Practice in North Carolina, 1820–1860," NCHR 29 (1952):159–170

Faulkner, Charles H., "'Here are Frame Houses and Brick Chimneys': Knoxville, Tennessee, in the Late Eighteenth Century," in Crass et al., eds., 137–161

Ferguson, Terry A., and Thomas A. Cowan, "Iron Plantations and the Eighteenth- and Nineteenth-Century Landscape of the Northwestern South Carolina Piedmont," in

Bibliography

Linda F. Stine, Martha Zierden, Lesley F. Drucker, and Christopher Judge, eds., *Carolina's Historical Landscapes: Historical Perspectives* (Knoxville: The University of Tennessee Press, 1996), 113–144

Fischer, David H., *Albion's Seed* (New York: Oxford University Press, 1989)

Fleming, Rev. John Kerr, *History of the Third Creek Presbyterian Church, Cleveland, North Carolina* (Raleigh: Offset Compositors, 1967)

Floyd, Viola Caston, *Descendants of William Harper, Irish Immigrant to Lancaster County, South Carolina* (Lancaster, S.C.: Lancaster Center Press, 1965)

Foote, William Henry, *Sketches of North Carolina* (New York: Robert Carter, 1846)

Ford, Henry J., *The Scotch-Irish in America* (Princeton, N. J.: Princeton University Press, 1915)

Foster, R. F., *Foster's Complete Hoyle* (Philadelphia: J. B. Lippincott Company, 1946)

Foster, William Omer, "The Career of Montfort Stokes in North Carolina," NCHR 16 (July 1939): 237–272.

Fraser, Walter J. Jr., *Charleston! Charleston!* (Columbia: University of South Carolina Press, 1989)

Fraser, Walter J. Jr., *Patriots, Pistols, and Petticoats* (2nd ed.; Columbia: University of South Carolina Press, 1993)

Frey, Sylvia R., *Water from the Rock: Black Resistance in a Revolutionary Age* (Princeton, N. J.: Princeton University Press, 1991)

Friedman, Lawrence M., *A History of American Law* (New York: Simon and Schuster, 1973)

Friedman, Reuben, *Scabies—Civil and Military: Its Prevalence, Prevention and Treatment* (New York: Froben Press, 1941)

Gailey, Alan, "The Scotch-Irish in Northern Ireland: Aspects of Their Culture," Jack W. Weaver, ed., *Selected Proceedings of the Scotch-Irish Heritage Festival at Winthrop College* (n.p., 1981), 33–53

Gailey, Alan, *Scotland, Ireland, and America: Migrant Culture in the 17th and 18th Centuries* ("Irish Studies Committee, Northeastern University, Working Papers"; Boston: Northeastern University, 1984)

Gallup, Andrew, *A Sketch of the Virginia Soldier in the Revolution* (Bowie, MD: Heritage Books, Inc., 1999)

Gardner, Frances Tomlinson, "The Gentleman from Tennessee," *Surgery, Gynecology, and Obstetrics*, 88 (March 1949): 404–411

Garrett, Mary Winder, "Pedigree of the Pollok or Polk Family . . . ," *American Historical Magazine* (Nashville), 3 (1898):42–73, 155–189, 230–239

Garrett, William, *Reminiscences of Public Men of Alabama* (Atlanta: Piedmont Publishing Company's Press, 1872)

Gault, Pressley B., and Elizabeth Pinkerton Leighty, *William Gault Family History, 1735 to 1948* (Sparta, Ill.: Privately printed, 1948)

Gehrke, William H., "The Transition from the German to the English Language in North Carolina," NCHR, 12 (January 1935):1–19

Gerlach, Russel L., "The Ozark Scotch-Irish: The Subconscious Persistence of an Ethnic Culture," *Pioneer American Society Transactions,* 7 (1984):47–57

Gill, Conrad, *The Rise of the Irish Linen Industry* (Oxford: Oxford University Press, 1925)

Gillis, John, *For Better, For Worse* (New York: Oxford University Press, 1985)

Glassie, Henry, *Passing the Time in Ballymenone* (Philadelphia: University of Pennsylvania Press, 1962)

Glassie, Henry, "The Types of the Southern Mountain Cabin," in Jan Harold Brunvand, ed., *The Study of American Folklore: An Introduction* (New York: W.W. Norton & Company, 1974)

Goff, Rheda C., "A Physical Profile of Andrew Jackson," *Tennessee Historical Quarterly,* 28 (Fall, 1969):297–309

Goodrich, Frances Louisa, *Mountain Homespun* (Knoxville: The University of Tennessee Press, 1989; first published 1931)

Goodwin, Ellis Munson, "The Other Andrew Jackson," *National Genealogical Society Quarterly,* 59 (1971):89–90.

Goodwin, Ellis Munson, "Crafford of New River, North Carolina," *National Genealogical Society Quarterly,* 53 (1965):251–262; 55 (1967):21–28, 253– 257; 57 (1969):298–303

Gordon, William, *The History of the Rise, Progress, and Establishment of the Independence of the United States of America . . .* (3 vols.; New York: Hodge, Allen, and Campbell, 1789)

Green, E. R. R., ed., *Essays in Scotch-Irish History* (London: Routledge and Kegan Paul, 1969)

Gregorie, Anne King, *Thomas Sumter* (Columbia, S. C.: The R. L. Bryan Company, 1931)

Gunby, A. A., *Colonel John Gunby of the Maryland Line* (Cincinnati: The Robert Clarke Company, 1902)

Haines, Francis, *Horses in America* (New York: Thomas Y. Crowell Company, 1971)

Hamilton, Milton W., "Augustus C. Buell, Fraudulent Historian," PMHB 80 (October 1956):478–492

Hammer, William C., remarks, *Congressional Record,* June 18, 1926, pp. 11534ff.

Haywood, Marshall De Lancey, *The Beginnings of Freemasonry in North Carolina and Tennessee* (Raleigh, N. C.: Weaver & Lynch, 1906)

Harris, Max, *The Andrew Jackson Birthplace Problem* (Raleigh: North Carolina State Department of Archives and History, 1963)

Harrison, Richard A., *Princetonians, 1769–1775: A Biographical Dictionary* (Princeton, N. J.: Princeton University Press, 1980)

Harrison, Richard A., *Princetonians, 1776–1783: A Biographical Dictionary* (Princeton, N. J.: Princeton University Press, 1981)

Harrison, Fairfax, *Early American Turf Stock, 1730–1830* (2 vols.; Richmond: The Old Dominion Press, 1934–1935)

Hatley, Tom, *The Dividing Paths: Cherokees and South Carolinians Through the Era of Revolution* (New York: Oxford University Press, 1993)

Heiskell, S. G., *Andrew Jackson and Early Tennessee History* (Nashville: Ambrose Printing Company, 1918)

. . . .
Bibliography

Henderson, Archibald, "Andrew Jackson," *Raleigh News and Observer,* October 10, 17, 24, 31; November 7, 1926

Henderson, Archibald, "The Career of Colonel Samuel Henderson," in *The Callaway and Henderson Families* (Louisville: The Standard Printing Co., 1941), 25–38

Henderson, Archibald, *The Conquest of the Old Southwest* (New York: The Century Co., 1920)

Henderson, Archibald, *Washington's Southern Tour* (Boston: Houghton Mifflin Company, 1923)

Herd, E. Don, Jr., *Andrew Jackson, South Carolinian* (Columbia, S. C.: Lancaster County Historical Commission, 1963)

Herman, Judith Lewis, M. D., *Trauma and Recovery* (New York: Basic Books, 1992)

Heslinga, M.W., *The Irish Border as a Cultural Divide* (Assen: Van Gorcum, 1979)

Hilborn, Nat and Sam, *Battleground of Freedom: South Carolina in the Revolution* (Columbia, S. C.: Sandlapper Press, 1970)

History of Franklin County, Pennsylvania (Chicago: Warner, Beers & Co., 1887)

Holcom, Brent, comp. *Fairfield County, South Carolina: Minutes of the County Court, 1785–1799* (Easley, S. C.: Southern Historical Press, 1981)

Hood, David Foard, *The Architecture of Rowan County, North Carolina* (Raleigh, N. C.: Rowan County Historic Properties Commission, 1983)

Hopkins, Donald R., *Princes and Peasants: Smallpox in History* (Chicago: The University of Chicago Press, 1983)

Horton, C. G., "The Records of the Freemasons in Ireland," *Familia,* 2, no. 2 (1986), 65–69

Hoskins, J. A., "Andrew Jackson A Member of the Guilford, North Carolina Bar," *North Carolina Booklet,* 19 (January 1920), 116–118.

Howe, George, *History of the Presbyterian Church in South Carolina* (2 vols.; Columbia, S. C.: Duffie & Chapman, 1870)

Huey, V. H., comp., *Huey Family History* (Birmingham, Ala.: Author, 1963)

Hughes, Fred, *Guilford County: A Map Supplement* (Jamestown, N. C.: The Custom House, 1988)

Huneycutt, James E. and Ida C., *A History of Richmond County* (Rockingham, N. C.: Privately printed, 1976)

Ingersoll, Louise, *Lanier: A Geneology [sic] of the family . . .* (Springfield, Va.: Goetz Printing Company, 1981)

Irving, John B., *The South Carolina Jockey Club* (Charleston, S. C.: Russell & Jones, 1857)

Isaac, Rhys, *The Transformation of Virginia, 1740–1790* (Chapel Hill: The University of North Carolina Press, 1982)

James, Marquis, *Andrew Jackson: The Border Captain* (Indianapolis: The Bobbs-Merrill Company, 1933)

James, William D., *A Sketch of the Life of Brig. Gen. Francis Marion* (Marietta, Ga.: Continental Book Company, 1948; first published 1821)

Johnsen, David C., "Oral Cavity," in Richard E. Behrman, ed., *Nelson Textbook of Pediatrics* (14th ed.; Philadelphia: W.B. Saunders Co., 1992), 932–935

Jones, Maldwyn A., "The Scotch-Irish and Colonial America," in Blake, 10–18

Jordan, Terry G., and Matti Kaups, *The American Backwoods Frontier* (Baltimore: The Johns Hopkins University Press, 1989)

Kane, Harnett T., *The Southern Christmas Book* (New York: David McKay Company, Inc., 1958)

Karpeles, Maud, *Cecil Sharp: His Life and Work* (Chicago: The University of Chicago Press, 1967)

Kegley, Tracy M., "James White Stephenson: Teacher of Andrew Jackson," *Tennessee Historical Quarterly,* 7 (March 1948):38–51

Keller, Kenneth W., "What Is Distinctive about the Scotch-Irish?" in Mitchell, 69–86

Kendall, Amos, *The Life of General Andrew Jackson* (New York: Harper & Brothers, 1844)

Kennedy, David, "Thurot's Landing at Carrickfergus," *The Irish Sword,* 6 (1963–64):149–153.

Kirkland, Thomas J., and Kennedy, Robert M., *Historic Camden: Part One, Colonial and Revolutionary* (Columbia, S. C.: The State Company, 1905).

Klein, Rachel N., *Unification of a Slave State: The Rise of the Planter Class in the South Carolina Backcountry, 1760–1808* (Chapel Hill, N. C.: The University of North Carolina Press, 1990)

Lambert, Robert Stansbury, *South Carolina Loyalists in the American Revolution* (Columbia: University of South Carolina Press, 1987)

Lane, Mills, *Architecture of the Old South: North Carolina* (New York: Abbeville Press, 1985)

Lasseray, Andre, *Les francais sous les treize etoiles* (Macon: Imprimerie Protat freres, 1935)

Lassiter, Mable S., "Pattern of Timeless Moments," *A History of Montgomery County* (n.p.: Montgomery County Board of Commissioners, 1976)

Lathan, ——— "A Hero of the Revolution," CCGSB, 4 (March 1981):3–5.

Landrum, J. B. O., *Colonial and Revolutionary History of Upper South Carolina* (Spartanburg, S. C.: The Reprint Company, 1977; first published 1897)

Lee, Henry, *A Biography of Andrew Jackson,* ed. Mark A. Mastromarino ("Occasional Pamphlet No. 3"; Knoxville, Tenn.: Tennessee Presidents Trust, 1992)

Lefler, Hugh T., and A. R. Newsome, *The History of a Southern State: North Carolina* (Chapel Hill: The University of North Carolina Press, 1954)

Leighton, Samuel, *History of Freemasonry in the Province of Antrim* (Belfast: Wm. Brown & Sons, Limited, 1938)

Leslie, William James, *Leslies of the Waxhaws* (Sacramento, Cal.: Privately printed, 1981)

Lessley, Samuel B., *Lessley Family Records* (Claremore, Okla.: Privately printed, 1983)

Lewis, Johanna Miller, "Women Artisans in Backcountry North Carolina, 1753–1790," NCHR 68 (July 1991): 214–236

Lewis, Kenneth E., *Camden: A Frontier Town* ("Anthropological Studies," #2; Columbia, S. C.: Institute of Archaeology and Anthropology, 1976)

Lewis, Kenneth E., "The Camden Jail and Market Site: A Report on Preliminary Investigations," *South Carolina Institute of Archaeology and Anthropology Notebook,* 16 (October–December, 1984)

Bibliography

Lewis, Kenneth E., "Economic Development in the South Carolina Backcountry: A View from Camden," in Crass et al., eds., 87–107.

Leyburn, James G., *The Scotch-Irish: A Social History* (Chapel Hill: The University of North Carolina Press, 1962)

Linn, Jo White, "Hugh Montgomery of Rowan County: One Man with a Fast Horse," *Rowan County Register,* 7, no. 3 (August 1992), 1591–1606

"Local Historic Scraps," *Ulster Journal of Archaeology,* 14 (1908): 133–135

Lossing, Benson J., *Pictorial Field-Book of the Revolution,* 2 (New York: Harper & Brothers, 1860)

Lucas, A. T., "Irish Food before the Potato," *Gwerin,* 3 (1960–1962), pt. 2, 8–43

Lumpkin, H. Henry, *From Savannah to Yorktown* (Columbia: University of South Carolina Press, 1981)

Lunney, Linde Connolly, "Attitudes to Life and Death in the Poetry of James Orr, an Eighteenth-Century Ulster Weaver," *Ulster Folklife,* 31 (1985): 1–12

McAllister, J. T., ed., *Virginia Militia in the Revolutionary War* (Hot Springs, Va.: McAllister Publishing Co., 1913)

McCartney, D. J., *The Ulster Jacksons* (Carrickfergus: Carrickfergus Borough Council, 1997)

McClelland, Aiken, "Folklife Miscellanea from Eighteenth- and Nineteenth-Century Newspapers," *Ulster Folklife,* 19 (1973): 68–71

McClelland, Aiken, "The Ulster Press in the Eighteenth and Nineteenth Centuries," *Ulster Folklife,* 20 (1974): 89–99

McCrady, Edward, *The History of South Carolina in the Revolution, 1775–1780* (New York: Paladin Press, 1969; first published 1901)

McDonnell, Pat, *They Wrought Among the Tow* (Belfast: Ulster Historical Foundation Publications, 1990)

McGeachy, Neill R., *A History of the Sugar Creek Presbyterian Church* (Rock Hill, S. C.: Record Printing Co., 1954)

McKelway, A. J., "The Scotch-Irish of North Carolina," *North Carolina Booklet,* 4, no. 11 (March 1905), 3–24

McLachlan, James, *Princetonians, 1748–1768* (Princeton, N. J.: Princeton University Press, 1976)

McMaster, Fitz Hugh, *History of Fairfield County, South Carolina* (Columbia, S. C.: The State Commercial Printing Company, 1946)

McNeely, Robert Ney, "Union County and the Old Waxhaw Settlement," *North Carolina Booklet,* 12 (July 1912): 6–20

M'Skimin, Samuel, *The History and Antiquities of the County of the Town of Carrickfergus* (Belfast: privately printed, 1829)

Malone, Michael T., "Sketches of the Anglican Clergy Who Served in North Carolina during the Period, 1765–1776," *Historical Magazine of the Protestant Episcopal Church,* 39 (December 1970): 399–438

Martin, Cheryl Lynn, ed., *The Heritage of Randolph County, North Carolina* (Asheboro, N. C.: Randolph Heritage Book Committee, 1993)

Maurer, David W., *Kentucky Moonshine* (Lexington: The University Press of Kentucky, 1974)

Medley, Mary L., *History of Anson County, North Carolina, 1750–1976* (Wadesboro, N. C.: Anson County Historical Society, 1976)

Meehan, Thomas R., "Courts, Cases, and Counselors in Revolutionary and Post-Revolutionary Pennsylvania," PMHB 91 (January 1967): 3–34.

Meriwether, Robert L., *The Expansion of South Carolina, 1729–1765* (Kingsport, Tenn.: Southern Publishers, 1940)

Merrell, James H., *The Indians' New World* (Chapel Hill: The University of North Carolina Press, 1989)

Metzger, Charles H., *The Prisoner in the American Revolution* (Chicago: Loyola University Press, 1971)

Miller, David W., "Presbyterianism and 'Modernization' in Ulster," *Past and Present,* 80 (1978): 66–90

Mitchell, Robert D., ed., *Appalachian Frontiers: Settlement, Society, & Development in the Preindustrial Era* (Lexington: University Press of Kentucky, 1991)

Mogey, John M., *Rural Life in Northern Ireland* (London: Oxford University Press, 1947)

Monahan, Amy, "An Eighteenth Century Family Linen Business," *Ulster Folklife,* 9 (1963): 30–43

Montell, William Lynwood, *Killings: Folk Justice in the Upper South* (Lexington: University Press of Kentucky, 1986)

Moody, T. W., "The Ulster Scots in Colonial and Revolutionary America," Studies, an *Irish Quarterly Review,* 34 (1945)

Morison, Samuel Eliot, *John Paul Jones* (New York: Time Incorporated, 1964; first published 1959)

Mosher, Merrill Hill, "Origin of the John, Mathew & Robert Kirk Families of Lancaster County, South Carolina," *South Carolina Magazine of Ancestral Research,* 23 (Spring 1995): 75–79

Moss, Bobby G., "Reverend William Martin—A Scotch-Irish Patriot of the American Revolution," Jack K. Weaver, ed., *Selected Proceedings of the Scotch-Irish Heritage Festival at Winthrop College* (n.p., 1981), 67–75

Moss, Bobby G., *Roster of South Carolina Patriots in the American Revolution* (Baltimore: Genealogical Publishing Co., Inc., 1983)

Mount, Allen Wade Sr., *Our Stephenson Family and Allied Lines* (Lee's Summit, Mo.: Author, 1981)

Nadelhaft, Jerome J., *The Disorders of War: The Revolution in South Carolina* (Orono, Me.: The University of Maine at Orono Press, 1981)

Nevin, Alfred, *Churches of the Valley* (Philadelphia: Joseph M. Wilson, 1852)

Nisbet, Newton A., *Nisbet Narrations* (Charlotte: Crayton Printing Co., 1961)

O'Neall, J. Belton, *Biographical Sketches of the Bench and Bar of South Carolina* (2 vols.; Charleston: S. G. Courtenay & Co., 1859)

Ownby, Ted, *Subduing Satan: Religion, Recreation, and Manhood in the Rural South, 1865–1920* (Chapel Hill: University of North Carolina Press, 1990)

Bibliography

Palmer, Gregory, *Biographical Sketches of Loyalists of the American Revolution* (Westport, Ct.: Meckler Publishing, 1984)

Parker, Elmer O., "Samuel Morrow of Chester County Fought the Redcoats in Overalls at Fishing Creek," CCGSB, 3 (December 1980): 70–71

Parlett, David, *A History of Card Games* (Oxford: Oxford University Press, 1991)

Parramore, Thomas C., *Launching the Craft* (Raleigh, N. C.: Grand Lodge of North Carolina, 1975)

Parton, James, *Life of Andrew Jackson* (3 vols.; New York: Mercer Brothers, 1860)

Patrick, Millar, *Four Centuries of Scottish Psalmody* (London: Oxford University Press, 1949)

Paterson, T. G. F., "Bullet Throwing in County Armagh," *Ulster Folklife,* 10 (1964): 95

Petrucelli, Katherine Sanford, ed., *The Heritage of Rowan County, North Carolina* (Salisbury, N. C.: The Genealogical Society of Rowan County, 1991)

Pettus, Louise, *The Waxhaws* (Rock Hill, S. C.: Privately printed, 1993)

Polk, William M., *Leonidas Polk, Bishop and General* (2 vols.; New York: Longmans, Green, and Co., 1915)

Powell, William S., ed., *Dictionary of North Carolina Biography* (6 vols.; Chapel Hill: The University of North Carolina Press, 1979–1995)

Power, J. Tracy, "'The Virtue of Humanity Was Totally Forgot': Buford's Massacre, May 29, 1780," SCHM 93 (January 1992): 5–14.

Preyer, Norris W., *Hezekiah Alexander and the Revolution in the Back Country* (Charlotte: Preyer, 1987)

Ramsay, David, *The History of the Revolution of South-Carolina . . .* (Trenton, N. J.: Isaac Collins, 1785)

Ramsay, David, *The History of South Carolina* (2 vols.; Charleston: David Longworth, 1809)

Rankin, S. M., *History of Buffalo Presbyterian Church and Her People: Greensboro, N. C.* (Greensboro, Joseph J. Stone & Co., n.d.)

Raynor, George, *Germans and Politicians in Rowan County* ("Piedmont Passages: III"; Salisbury, N. C.: privately printed, 1990)

Reed, Alfred Z., *Training for the Public Profession of the Law* (Washington D.C.: Carnegie Institution, 1921)

Reid, James Seaton, *History of the Presbyterian Church in Ireland* (3 vols.; Belfast: William Mullan, 1867)

Reid, John, and John Henry Eaton, *The Life of Andrew Jackson* (Philadelphia: Samuel F. Bradford, 1824)

Reitz, Elizabeth J., Martha Zierden, and Jeanne Calhoun, "The Eighteenth Century Charleston Beef Market," *Current Research in the Historical Archaeology of the Carolinas, Research Series* 4 (Columbia, S. C.: Chicora Foundation, Inc., 1985), 1–13

Remini, Robert V., *Andrew Jackson* (New York: Twayne Publishers, Inc., 1966)

Remini, Robert V., *Andrew Jackson and the Course of American Empire, 1767–1821* (New York: Harper & Row, Publishers, 1977)

Rhyne, Martha McJunkin, *McJunkin: A Family of Memories* (Greenville, S. C.: A Press, 1989)

Ribes, F., "Salive," *Dictionnaire des sciences medicales* (Paris: C. L. F. Pancoucke, 1820), 49:457–467

Rice, Lee M., and Glenn R. Vernam, *They Saddled the West* (Cambridge, Md.: Cornell Maritime Press, 1975)

Roberts, Allen E., *Freemasonry in American History* (Richmond: Macoy Publishing & Masonic Supply Co., Inc., 1985)

Roberts, B. W. C., "Cockfighting: An Early Entertainment in North Carolina," NCHR 42 (Summer 1965), 306–313

Roberts, Russ, *Moonshine, Murder, Mercy, and More: West Tennessee-North Mississippi, 1889–1989* (Pickwick Dam, Tenn.: privately printed, 1989)

Robinson, Blackwell P., "Guilford County's First 150 Years," Vol. I of *The History of Guilford County, North Carolina, U. S. A.* (2 vols. in 1; Greensboro, N. C.: Guilford County Bicentennial Commission, 1980 [?])

Robinson, Blackwell P., *William R. Davie* (Chapel Hill: The University of North Carolina Press, 1957)

Robinson, Philip, "Hanging Ropes and Buried Secrets," *Ulster Folklife,* 32 (1986): 3–15

Roebuck, Peter, ed., *Plantation to Partition: Essays in Honor of J. L. McCracken* (Belfast: Blackstaff, 1981)

Rouse, Parke Jr., *The Great Wagon Road* (Richmond: The Dietz Press,1992)

[Revill, Janie], *President Andrew Jackson's Birthplace As Found by Janie Revill* (Columbia, S. C.: State Printing Company, 1960)

Roeber, A.G., "Authority, Law, and Custom: The Rituals of Court Day in Tidewater Virginia, 1720–1750," W&MQ, 3, 37 (1980): 29–53.

Rogers, George C. Jr., *Charleston in the Age of the Pinckneys* (Norman, Okla.: University of Oklahoma Press, 1969)

Rogin, Michael Paul, *Fathers and Children: Andrew Jackson and the Subjugation of the American Indian* (New York: Alfred A. Knopf, 1973)

Rorabaugh, W. J., *The Craft Apprentice: From Franklin to the Machine Age in America* (New York: Oxford University Press, 1986)

Royster, Charles, *A Revolutionary People at War* (Chapel Hill, N. C.: The University of North Carolina Press, 1979)

Rumple, Jethro, *History of Rowan County, North Carolina* (Salisbury, N. C.: J. J. Bruner, 1881)

Sabine, Lorenzo, *The American Loyalists* (Boston: Charles C. Little and James Brown, 1847)

Sajna, Mike, *Buck Fever: The Deer Hunting Tradition in Pennsylvania* (Pittsburgh: University of Pittsburgh Press, 1990)

Salomon, R. A., *Dictionary of Leather-Working Tools, c. 1750–1950* (New York: Macmillan Publishing Company, 1986)

Sanchez-Saavedra, E. M., comp., *A Guide to Virginia Military Organizations in the American Revolution, 1774–1787* (Richmond: Virginia State Library, 1978)

Saunders, James Edmonds, *Early Settlers of Alabama* (Baltimore: Genealogical Publishing Company, 1969; first published 1899)

Saye, James H., "Cedar Shoal Church and Congregation, Chester County, South Carolina," CCGSB 4 (December 1981):87

Saye, James Hodge, *Memoir of Major Joseph McJunkin* (Greenwood, S. C.: n.p., 1925)

Bibliography

Schulz, Judith J., "The Hinterland of Revolutionary Camden, South Carolina," *Southeastern Geographer*, 16 (2):91–97

Sellers, Charles G. Jr., *James K. Polk, Jacksonian, 1795–1843* (Princeton, N. J.: Princeton University Press, 1957)

Shurkin, Joel N., *The Invisible Fire* (New York: G. P. Putnam's Sons, 1979)

Shute, J. Ray, "Washington Lodge, No. 15," *Nocalore*, 6 (1936):48–63

Shute, J. Ray, "Old Cone Lodge," *Nocalore*, 6 (1936): 11–24

Shute, J. Ray, "The McCauley Apron," *Nocalore*, 2 (1932):237–243

Shy, John, "American Society and Its War for Independence," in Don Higginbottom, ed., *Reconsiderations on the Revolutionary War* ("Contributions in Military History," No. 14; Westport, Ct.: Greenwood Press, 1978)

Silver, Timothy, *A New Face on the Countryside: Indians, Colonists, and Slaves in the South Atlantic Forests, 1500–1800* (New York: Cambridge University Press, 1990)

Simpson, Archibald N., "Rev. John Simpson," *Southern Presbyterian Review* (April 1853), 546–558

Simpson, W. G., *The History and Antiquities of Freemasonry in Saintfield, Co. Down* (Downpatrick, Northern Ireland: Down Recorder office, 1924)

Skaggs, Marvin L., *North Carolina Boundary Disputes Involving Her Southern Line* (Chapel Hill: University of North Carolina Press, 1941)

Smith, Brian, *The Horse in Ireland* (Dublin: Wolfhound Press, 1991)

Smith, Paul H., *Loyalists and Redcoats: A Study in British Revolutionary Policy* (Chapel Hill: University of North Carolina Press, 1964)

Sprague, William B., *Annals of the American Pulpit, III* (New York: Robert Carter & Brothers, 1859)

Spruill, Julia Cherry, *Women's Life and Work in the Southern Colonies* (Chapel Hill: The University of North Carolina Press, 1932)

Steen, Andrea D.V., *Stoneboro: An Historical Sketch of a South Carolina Community* (Spartanburg, S.C.: The Reprint Company, 1993)

Stenhouse, James A., *Journeys into History*, 1951, mimeographed copy, Charlotte-Mecklenburg Public Library

Stephenson, Jean, *Scotch-Irish Migration to South Carolina, 1772: Rev. William Martin and His Five Shiploads of Settlers* (Strasburg, Va.: Shenandoah Pub. House, 1972)

Stevenson, John, *Two Centuries of Life in Down, 1600–1800* (Belfast: M'Caw, Stevenson & Orr, 1920)

Stevenson, W. F., *Wounds in War* (New York: William Wood and Company, 1898)

Stockard, Sallie W., *The History of Guilford County, North Carolina* (Knoxville, Tenn.: Gant-Ogden Co., 1902)

Struna, Nancy L., *People of Prowess: Sport, Leisure, and Labor in Early Anglo-America* (Urbana: University of Illinois Press, 1996)

Tallmadge, William H., "The Scotch Irish and the British Traditional Ballad in America," *New York Folklore Quarterly*, 24 (December 1968):261–274

Thomas, Earle, *Greener Pastures: The Loyalist Experience of Benjamin Ingraham* (Belleville, Ont.: Mika Publishing Company, 1983)

Thompson, Ernest T., *Presbyterians in the South, Vol. 1: 1607–1861* (Richmond: John Knox Press, 1963)

Thorp, Daniel B., "Doing Business in the Backcountry: Retail Trade in Colonial Rowan County, North Carolina," W&MQ (3), 48 (July 1991): 387–408

Thorp, Daniel B., "Taverns and Communities: The Case of Rowan County, North Carolina," in Crass et al., 76–86

Thorp, Daniel B., "Taverns and Tavern Culture on the Southern Colonial Frontier: Rowan County, North Carolina, 1753–1776," *Journal of Southern History,* 62 (November 1996):661–688

Tompkins, Daniel A., *History of Mecklenburg County* (2 vols.; Charlotte, 1903)

Turner, Herbert S., *Bethel and Her Ministers, 1745–1946* (Verona, Va.: McClure Printing Company, 1974)

Tylden, Geoffrey, *Horses and Saddlery* (London: J. A. Allen & Company, 1965)

Ulmer, S. Sidney, "Some Eighteenth Century South Carolinians and the Duel," SCHM, 60 (January 1959): 1–9

van der Kolk, Bessel A., *Psychological Trauma* (Washington: American Psychiatric Press, Inc., 1987)

Veach, Mary Frances Thomas, *Sorting the Waxhaw Crawfords* (Elverta, Cal.: privately printed, 1993)

Wade, Mary Kell, "Robert Gaston of Little Lynches Creek," CCGSB 5 (December 1982):95–98

Wardlaw, Joseph G., *Genealogy of the Witherspoon Family* (Yorkville, S. C.: Printed at the Enquirer Office, 1910)

Waring, Joseph I., *A History of Medicine in South Carolina, 1670–1825* (Columbia, S. C.: The South Carolina Medical Association, 1964)

Warwick, Edward, Henry C. Pitz, and Alexander Wyckoff, *Early American Dress* (New York: Benjamin Blom, Inc., 1965)

Watson, Harry L., *An Independent People: The Way We Lived in North Carolina, 1770–1820* (Chapel Hill: The University of North Carolina Press, 1983)

Weatherly, A. Earle, *The Saga of the McNairy House* (Greensboro, N. C.: Greensboro Historical Museum, 1969)

Webb, R. A., *History of the Presbyterian Church of Bethel . . .* (Gastonia, N. C.: Gazette Print, 1887)

Weeks, Stephen B., *Libraries and Literature in North Carolina in the Eighteenth Century* (Washington: Government Printing Office, 1896)

Weigley, Russell F., *The Partisan War: The South Carolina Campaign of 1780–1782* ("Tricentennial Booklet Number 2"; Columbia: University of South Carolina Press, 1970)

Weir, Robert M., *Colonial South Carolina: A History* (New York: KTO Press,1983)

Weller, Jac, "Irregular But Effective: Partizan Weapons Tactics in the American Revolution, Southern Theatre," *Military Affairs,* 21 (1957):118–131

. . . .

Bibliography

Wettach, Robert H., ed., *A Century of Legal Education* (Chapel Hill: The University of North Carolina Press, 1947)

Wheeler, John H., *Reminiscences and Memoirs of North Carolina* (Baltimore: Genealogical Publishing Company, 1966; first published 1884)

Wheeler, John H., *Historical Sketches of North Carolina* (2 vols.; Philadelphia: Lippincott, Grambo and Co., 1851)

White, Newman I., ed., *The Frank C. Brown Collection of North Carolina Folklore*, 6 (Durham, N. C.: Duke University Press, 1961)

Whitley, Olga R., *The Howe Line: Pennsylvania—South Carolina—Kentucky* (Commerce, Tex.: n.p., 1967)

Wickwire, Franklin E., *Cornwallis: The American Adventure* (Boston: Houghton Mifflin, 1970)

Wilkins, Joseph C., Howell C. Hunter Jr., and Richard F. Carrillo, *Historical, Architectural, and Archaeological Research at Brattonsville (38YK21), York County, South Carolina* ("Research Manuscript Series, No. 76"; Columbia: Institute of Archaeology and Anthropology, University of South Carolina, 1975)

Williams, Cratis, "Moonshining in the Mountains," *North Carolina Folklore Review* (1968), 11–18

Williams, Michael Ann, *Homeplace: The Social Use and Meaning of the Folk Dwelling in Southwestern North Carolina* (Athens: University of Georgia Press, 1991)

Williams, Samuel C., "William Tatham, Wataugan," *Tennessee Historical Magazine*, 7 (October, 1921:154–173.

Wilson, Eddie W., "The Gourd in Southern History," NCHR 26 (July 1949), 300–305

Wilson, H. McC., *The Tinkling Spring: Headwater of Freedom* (Fishersville, Va.: Tinkling Spring and Hermitage Presbyterian Churches, 1954)

Wing, Conway P., *A History of the First Presbyterian Church of Carlisle, Pa.* (Carlisle: "Valley Sentinel Office," 1877)

Wright, Joseph, ed., *The English Dialect Dictionary* (6 vols.; Oxford: Oxford University Press, 1981; first published 1905)

Wright, Richardson, *American Wags and Eccentrics from Colonial Times to the Civil War* (New York: Frederick Ungar Publishing Co., 1965; first published 1939)

Wyatt-Brown, Bertram, *Southern Honor* (New York: Oxford University Press, 1982)

Zinsser, Hans, *Rats, Lice and History* (Boston: Little, Brown & Company, Inc., 1935)

MAPS

Anonymous, Virginia–North Carolina map, 1779, route from Burke Co., North Carolina, to the Potomac, Alderman Library, University of Virginia

Hughes, Fred, *Guilford County: Historical Documentation*, map (Jamestown, N. C.: The Custom House, 1980)

Sauthier, C. J., Plan of the Town of Salisbury in Rowan County, North Carolina, 1770, Rowan Public Library

NEWSPAPERS AND PERIODICALS

Chester County Genealogical Society Bulletin
Daughters of the American Revolution Magazine, 1920
Maryland Gazette, July 18, 1780
North Carolina Mercury
Salisbury (North Carolina) *Post*
South Carolina Gazette, 1765–1770;1783–1784.
Virginia Almanack for 1780
Western Carolinian (Salisbury, North Carolina), February 17, 1824

THESES AND DISSERTATIONS

Batt, Richard John, "The Maryland Continentals, 1780–1781," Ph. D. diss., Tulane University, 1974

Coker, Kathy R., "The Punishment of Revolutionary War Loyalists in South Carolina," Ph.D. diss., University of South Carolina, 1987.

Huss, Wayne A., "Pennsylvania Freemasonry: An Intellectual and Social Analysis, 1727–1826," Ph.D. diss., Temple University, 1984

Lawrence, Stephen S., "The Life and Times of John McNairy," M.A. thesis, Middle Tennessee State University, 1971

Schulz, Judith J., "The Rise and Decline of Camden as South Carolina's Major Inland Trading Center, 1751–1829," M.A. thesis, University of South Carolina, 1972

Smith, Raymond Augustus III, "A Traveller's View of Revolutionary America," Ph. D. diss., University of Texas, 1981

Waldrup, John Charles, "James Iredell and the Practice of Law in Revolutionary Era North Carolina," Ph. D. diss., University of North Carolina, 1985

MISCELLANEOUS

American Art Association catalog, April 8, 1926 (microfilm copy in AJ Papers, LC)

Index

. . . .

Index

Index

316

Young Hickory

Patterson, Joseph, 173–74
Pearce, Winger, 198
Philadelphia Convention, 185
Picket, William, 188, 277n. 1
Poindexter, David, 196
Polk, Charley, 184–85, 188, 277n. 1
Polk, Thomas, 50, 192
Polk, Will, 59–60, 92, 184–85, 192
Presbyterian church
    British attack on ministers of, 54–55
    catechism of, 20–21
    education through, 27–28, 32–33
    in Guilford community, 81
    images of, in American history, 226–27n.
        25
    in Waxhaws, 4–5
Providence Church, 9
Purdy, Joseph, 98

Quakers, 81–82
Queen, William, 197

Ramsey, Alexander, 121
Ramsey, John, 121, 122
Randolph County, North Carolina, 196–98
Rawdon, Francis Lord, 51, 88, 103
Remini, Robert V., xiii, 213
Richardson, Nancy, 20, 21
Richardson, William, 7, 19–20, 21
Richmond County, North Carolina, 183
Roberts, B. W. C., 43
Rockingham County, North Carolina, 187,
    195
Rocky Mount, Battle of, 60–61, 240n. 18
Roman Catholic church, 216n. 3
Rowan County, North Carolina, 188
    See also Salisbury, North Carolina
Rowan County Court, 172–73
Rowan House, 157, 158–59
Rutherford, Griffith, 204

Saddlery, 115–16, 257n. 21
Salisbury, North Carolina, 79
    county courts in district surrounding,
        180–81, 275n. 6, n. 7
    court week in, 154, 156

inhabitants, 156
Jackson's trip to, 136, 138
Masonry in, 176
physical description, 152–54
religious life in, 154
social life in, 154
Scabies, 29
Scotch–Irish, 25–26, 216–17n. 3
    See also Irish, the
Searcy, Bennett
Jackson living with, 141
    in Masonic Order, 175
    trip to Tennessee, 190, 193, 204, 278n. 4
Searcy, Tom, 141–42, 145, 204
Sharpe, Billy, 173
Simpson, John, 54, 130
Slaves
    debate on, 185–86
    in Guilford community, 82
    housing for, 8
    Jackson lacking, in Charleston, 127–28
    Jackson on, 41, 186
    owned by Crawford family, 16
    owned by Stokes brothers, 180
    selling of, 136, 138
    in Waxhaws, 232–33n. 31
Smallpox, 105, 106–8, 251n. 14
Smart, Susan, 74, 206–7, 208, 209
Smith, Billy, 28, 134
Smith, Jack, 104
Smoking, 149–50
Sorting the Waxhaw Crawfords (Veach), 214
South Carolina
    border with North Carolina, 9, 13–14
    establishment of, 13
    as Jackson's birthplace, 10–12
    See also Waxhaws
South Carolina Gazette, 45
Spratt, Susan, 92, 249n. 13
Stapleton, Roger, 186
Steele, John, 198
Stephenson, Elizabeth, 22–24, 225n. 21
Stephenson, James White, 28, 33, 61, 134
Stephenson, John, 23, 225n. 21
Stephenson, Moses, 70
Stephenson, Nat, 33